U0118541

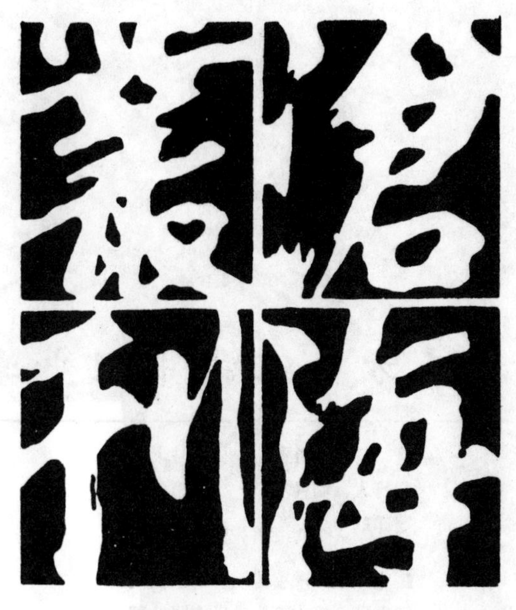

與西方史家論中國史學

杜維運 著

東大圖書公司 印行

©與西方史家論中國史學

著　者　杜維運

發行人　劉仲文

著作財產權人　東大圖書股份有限公司

總經銷　三民書局股份有限公司

印刷所　東大圖書股份有限公司

復興店／臺北市復興北

重慶店／臺北市重慶南

郵　撥／〇一〇七一七

初　版　中華民國 七 十 年八月

三　版　中華民國八十二年十月

編　號　E 60003

基本定價　肆元肆角肆

行政院新聞局登記證局版臺業

著作權執照臺內著字第一七三

ISBN 957-19-0483-X（平裝）

新寫本自序

民國六十七年春天，三民書局主持人劉振強先生過港相訪，言及拙著「與西方史家論中國史學」為書商翻印，紙張印刷皆極粗劣，慨然欲為重排問世。因感其盛意，允為再蒐集資料，慎重改寫，以期不負士林期望。惟當時未立即著手，待翌年二月長久撰寫的「史學方法論」一書付梓，始傾力進行，迄於今年三月，凡歷時二年，改寫工作完成，字數由十萬言增至三十萬言，持論亦有不盡同於舊著者，因名曰「新寫本與西方史家論中國史學」。

新寫本在蒐集西方正統史家及非正統史家論及中國史學的言論，較舊著有顯著的增加。舊著僅收有湯普森 (J. W. Thompson)、白特費爾德 (Herbert Butterfield)、奈芬司 (Allan Nevins)、巴拉克勞甫 (Geoffrey Barraclough)、魏吉瑞 (A. G. Widgery)、卡耳 (E. H. Carr)、等六家的言論，新寫本則增加瑞查森 (Alan Richardson)、艾爾頓 (G. R. Elton)、盧克斯 (John Lukacs)、浦朗穆 (J. H. Plumb)、葛蘭特 (Michael Grant)、馬爾威克 (Arthur Marwick)、瓦爾班德 (T. W. Wallband)、巴容 (Jacques Barzun)、麥尼耳 (W. H. McNeill)、傅爾 (N. E. Fehl)、但斯 (E. H. Dance) 等十一家的言論。西方漢學家的言論，增加有限，是極為遺憾的。維運長時期醉心閱讀西方史家（包括正統史家及非正統史家）討論史學之書，其點滴涉及中國史學者，即箚記別紙，積久遂多。西方漢學家的作品，則涉獵不勤，倉猝蒐讀，難及萬一。這是最為汗顏無地的。去歲八月出席在臺北舉行的國際漢學會議，維運曾以「西方史家心目中的中國史學」為題，在大會宣讀，李恩涵兄即席建言，謂西方史家所知中國史學，悉由西方漢學家而來，不妨寫一西方漢學家論中國史學的專書。其言甚具卓識，謹記於此，以待來者。

西方史家對中國史學的認識，仍未至精深。成見的存在，文字的隔閡，是雙重障礙。破除成見，非一朝一夕之功；浩如煙海的中國史籍，讓西方史家寢饋其中，而藉見其精蘊，無異是一種苛求。以致西方史家論中國史學之作，最佳者多為論某家的史學，或專論某一史學上的問題，以材料有限容易控制之故；通論中國史學者，則每浮泛粗略，偏頗之論，叢出不已。拙著之作，蓋激於此。惟為之分析，與之衡論，是消極的。應積極的重建詳贍的中國史學史。中國長久發展的科學史，已由西方學者所重建，英人李約瑟（Joseph Needham）的「中國之科學與文明」(*Science and Civilization in China*) 一書，近期內難為國人之作所代替。但是重建中國史學史，主要應是中國史家的責任。中國史學的博大精深，非任何西方史家所能完全瞭解。沉浮在浩瀚廣大的中國史學史資料中，築起壯觀的史學樓閣，對中國史家而言，現在應是其時了！

維運初寫與改寫此著，前後相差十五年之久。初寫在民國五十三年至五十四年之間，以不及一年時間，匆匆寫成十萬言，於五十五年獲得中國學術著作獎助委員會資助，梓行問世。學林以其書有發前人所未發者，遂不棄之，而師友的啓發、鼓勵與批評，所賜者尤多。今謹不憚繁言，縷述於後：

在師長輩中，首先須感謝的，是英國劍橋大學漢學教授浦立本（E. G. Pulleyblank）師。民國五十一年初秋至五十三年仲夏，維運讀書劍大，浦師為指導教授，在英國劍橋或牛津大學的指導教授，是有無上威權的，每週面對面的一次指導，勢在必行，學子視之為畏途。浦師規定我每週一下午四至五時到他研究室見面，一小時的時間，長如永晝，所討論者多為中西史學的異同問題，浦師就問題發問，且步步緊迫，至我瞠目無以應為止。談至興高采烈時，則被延至其家，邊飲邊談，浦師酒量甚佳，師母亦善飲，我則力敵之而立於不敗之地。浦師每說我喝酒後活潑多了，英文也流暢多了！喝酒之益有如此。我之得知西方正統史家對中國史學的成見，以及中西史學異同方面的一些問題，鮮非浦師之賜。

劍大鄭德坤師於看到拙著後，對我的鼓勵最多，多次通信中，皆提及其內容，尤許其「態度誠懇，詞氣謙和，與諸氣浮心粗，妄自尊大者，實有天淵之別。」實則此為維運所應努力的目標，曷敢云已臻於此？

臺灣大學的師長對我的教誨，是罄竹難書的。姚從吾、沈剛伯、張致遠、劉壽民諸師，開啓我西方史學的知識，李玄伯、方杰人、夏卓如、勞貞一諸師，奠立我中國史學的基礎。拙著問世後，他們微笑嘉勉，只取其長而置其短。為弟子護短，似是中外的通病。為弟子者，應逆知其意，百尺竿頭，更進一步。不然，施施以驕於人，祇取敗辱！

旅法三十年的左景權先生，對拙著是最為偏愛的。六、七年的書信往返，他對拙著提出最有價值的修正意見，如認為拙著過分側重英文論著，而未能兼顧其他；過分注重形式（章節過分分明），而未能神明變化，皆是卓越之見。惟維運以語文程度限制，以及疏懶成性，兩者皆未能遵示修正（拙文「西方史家心目中的中國史學」，稍打破形式，謹附於後），慚愧萬千！景權先生於一九七八年出版「司馬遷與中國史學（*Sseu-ma T'sien et L'historiographie Chinoise*）一書，用法文寫成，議論精闢，能道時人所不能道（維運不通法文，曾請人將其中數節，譯成英文，讀之歎服不已。惟拙著中未曾稱引，恐失其原意故。），西人視之，則不啻洪水猛獸，先生來信感慨言之。先生刻正用法文寫「希羅多德與司馬遷」（*H'erodote et Sseu-ma Ts'ien*）一書，書成後，則擬以餘力用中文寫作，謹拭目以待之。

在朋友群中，須感謝者，更僕難終。臺大歷史系同班同學周廣美女士，最能細心閱讀拙著，所提意見，極為珍貴。她認為拙著所涉及的每一個問題，幾乎都可寫成一本書，或一篇長文。維運記取其言，而改寫後的情況，未見大有改善。細密詳贍，是拙著所未及的。

李方中、傅秀實、易君博、閻沁恆、張存武、文崇一、林伯羽、呂士朋、何佑森、陳捷先、孫同勛、張朋園、王爾敏、王樹槐、王璽、劉鳳翰、顧立三、張奕善、毛漢光、郎德渝諸兄，都是二三十年的老朋友，談天雕龍，益我最多，羽觴交錯之際，亦莊亦諧亦頌亦諷之論出，能消清愁，能滌神智。沁恆、朋園、爾敏、立三、漢光諸兄論及拙著的長信，以語多溢美，謹珍存之，自我欣賞，發表則所不敢，其建議已逐一採納，在此不復贅述。

學生中，許逖朝夕為拙著鼓吹，不但寫專文評介（東方雜誌復刊第二卷第六期載其「一本為外國人寫的而中國人必須讀的書」一文，卽評介拙著），且廣為口頭宣傳，岌岌不可終日；陳錦忠在未相識時，寫成「比較史學初探」一文（載於民國五十七年八月十八日的中央日報副刊），以與拙著相商榷；邢義田始終表現出最大的興趣，通信中時相討論；黃俊傑不時提醒我注意西方史家的文化背景及其成見的由來；黃進興在資料的供應上，使我省了很多蒐集的辛勞；君蜜小姐一字一句的細讀，改正了不少的錯誤。其他熱心者紛紛，皆銘記於心，不敢忘。

在初寫與改寫的過程中，內子孫雅明的功勞，不能隱沒。猶憶初寫時，適值新婚，住臺北市溫州街，竹籬茅舍，情調幽雅，寫至艱澀處，則良久不產一字，而客人適來，內子卽於院中生火，煮酒烹茗，賓主盡歡而散。待客人去，難以捉摸的文思又來。有時寫至深夜，燈火熒熒，內子特備「宵夜」，案頭食之，味美無窮，眞極寫作的雅事。改寫的兩年，講學香港，人地生疏，處囂塵之世，有若蟄居，家中情況則與十五年前大異，老大宗騏十四歲巳身高六呎，老二宗蘭喜問故事，老三宗驥精力無盡無窮，家中寫作，已不可能。猶幸香港大學的研究室在半山，極清淨，每天早晨習慣七時至，十二時離去，其間甚少人事干擾，回家後則將改寫情形告內子，內子傾聽，唯唯諾諾，蓋日久而形成習慣如此。今改寫旣竣，不能不長揖一謝。

拙著未能寫成英文本，誠為憾事。師友的期望，辜負至多。惟所考慮者，傾數年之力，頗懷疑自己能否寫出水平以上的英文作品，反不如致力於中國史學史的研究為愈。且國人對中國史學的藐視，有甚於西人者；西人之論，國人亦有諗知的必要。區區一再用中文寫作，蓋有不得已的苦衷，惟幸大雅亮察。

民國七十年五月

杜 維 運

序於香港大學中文系研究室

原 序

學術不能孤立，交流會通，乃能昌大。在廣濶的世界上，不同源流的學術，紛然並存。當其分途發展，不過自成經緯，各顯休光於一隅。及其不期相遇，則互相激盪，互相發明，由互異而至於互通，由相隔而至於默契，於是較富世界性的新學術誕生，其光輝亦自能燦爛於寰宇。

史學為一綜合性的科學，居世界學術的樞紐，史學發達之域，往往是人類文明的重心，智慧的淵藪。不同源流的史學，會而合之，比而觀之，更是學術上的盛事。缺乏史學思想的互通，人類將難有完全互相瞭解之一日。所以比較史學是一門值得提倡的新學問，將世界不同源流的史學，彙於一室，作比較研究，擷精取華，汰其糟粕，博大的新史學，將自此產生。

有歷史發生成長的地區，不一定有史學，埃及、巴比倫都是文明古國，而無史學可言。由悠久的歷史，蔚為綿延不絕的史學，不是一種普通的發展。中國自春秋以來，史學醞釀發展，兩千餘年，蔚為一博大精深的學問。而西方世界，繼承希臘傳統，迄於二十世紀的今日，史學絢麗輝煌，傲視瀛寰。舉世史學，值得稱道謳歌者，不出此兩大系統。此兩大系統，相去絕遠，各自獨立發展數千年，不通聲息。以致其史學淵源、史學思想、史學方法以及史學與其他學問的關係，史學對社會與人群所發生的影響，皆絕相殊異。其同者，不過冥冥中的暗合而已。比較兩者，以求會通，是一種學術上的偉大工作，中西史學界偏執固陋之習，將藉此而澄清，富世界性的新史學，將指日而可待。

一九六二年初秋，至一九六四年仲夏，維運負笈英倫，側身劍大，從事於比較史學的研究，凡西人論史學之書，皆儘量蒐購而閱讀之。其西方史家論及中國史學之處，尤深致注意，見之卽箚記別紙，日久盈積遂多，覺其言有極精當足發國人深省者，有荒誕不經不能不據實以辯者，於是草成「與西方史家論中國史學」一書，期以藉西哲之言，發國史之蘊，以通於比較史學之路而已。

學術乃天下公器，西方史家以另一背景論中國史學，不惟中國史學之幸，亦世界史學之幸。國人論中國史學，必有所蔽，國人所蔽者，西人開啓之；西人又新有所蔽，故願與之討論商榷之。拙著不憚繁言，或不徒供世人之覆瓿歟？

維運初學，所知不博，所見不廣，惟護惜學術之心，可與天下共白。斯作中有關與西方史家討論之處，語氣務求謙和，態度出之誠懇，以期略贖主觀之過。尚希海內外博雅君子，不吝教正。

民國五十四年四月

杜　維　運

序於臺北市溫州街維雅齋

與西方史家論中國史學 目次

第三章　與西方正統史家論中國史學

第四章　西方非正統史家論中國史學

第五章　與西方非正統史家論中國史學

第六章　西方漢學家論中國史學

第七章 與西方漢學家論中國史學

參考書目

附　錄

第一章　中西史學的交流

第一節　中國史學的獨立發展

歷史是人類智慧的淵藪，自有文字，人類便可能有歷史。歷史經過演變發展，記錄盈積，異同互見，於是有批評，有研討，而史學出現。世界的遼濶，人類的龐雜，是歷史發生成長的優良背景，而世界眞正歷史悠久的地區，不可多覯；史學是歷史的神髓，由悠久的歷史，蔚爲綿延不絕的史學，擧世求之，尤覺寥寥。中國自春秋以來，史學綿延發展，未嘗一日中絕，其餘力復開闢鄰近國家的史學，如日本、韓國、越南等國，其史學無一不深受中國史學的影響。而西方世界，自希臘時代起，經過羅馬、中世紀、文藝復興而至近代，史學發展成一門燦爛的學問，英、法、美、德等國的史學，都是屬於此一史學系統。擧世史學，値得稱道謳歌者，不出此兩大系統。所以雖說中國史學與西方史學是世界史學的總遺產，亦未嘗不可。❶

世界兩大系統的中西史學，相去絕遠，各自獨立發展兩千餘年，不通聲息。以中國方面言之，十九世紀末葉以前，中國史學自闢蹊徑，不受西方史學任何激盪。雖然明清之際，西方學術一度急驟輸入中國，而當時中國朝野人士所欣賞的西學，乃天文、地理、水利、曆法等應用科學，西方史學不曾於此時影響中國。兩種文化接觸，到史學能够互相影響，發生交流作用，是極爲後期的。中國文化與西方文化，千餘年來，有過不少的接觸與相互影響，從中國科學技術的西傳，中國儒家思想的影響及於西方的啓蒙運動，到西方耶穌會敎士的東來，以及晚近西方學術、政治、軍事、經濟勢力的如怒潮湧至，無一不是中西文化交流史上的大事。但是在晚近以前，中國史學不曾流傳到西方去，西方史學也未曾輸入中土。作爲文化中樞的史學，極不易爲人類發現其價值。

第二節　西方史學的輸入中國

西方史學輸入中國的確定時間，是一個頗難有明確答案的問題。十九世紀中葉以後，中國朝野人士，由於受西力的壓迫，紛言變法圖强，清廷也屢屢派遣留學生赴海外留學，然當時留學生在海外所攻習的科目，爲軍事、敎育、經濟、政治等等，朝野人士所談的變法，也不出軍事、敎育、經濟、政治等範圍以外，當時從未有談變史學以及在海外專門攻習西方史學者。所以在李鴻章等如火如荼推行洋務運動之際，西方史學似未曾輸入中國。

西方史學的輸入，大致在清政權卽將結束的十餘年間，此與晚清思想界有極密切的關係。

晚淸是中國新舊思想互相激盪的一個時代，保守的人士，對於日漸向中國輸入的西學，持極力反抗的態度。如曾廉云：

「中人之學西學，不過爲通西人語言、文字諸藝術，借以刺取外國之國情，奪其利權而制之。」

「無學之人學之，但知順夷意而變我民，使人相率入于夷狄；然苟其人爲學問通達，不一定能學外國語言文字，故西學實無提倡之必要。」❷

此種觀念，普及於一般讀書人的腦海中，對於接受西方史學，實爲莫大的障礙。於是稍有世界性眼光者，倡出西學源出中國之說。如皮錫瑞云：

「西學出於中國，本周秦諸子之遺，莊列關尹諸書所載，是其明證。史記漢書皆云七國之亂，疇人子弟，分散海外。大約此時中國失傳，而外國得之。今仍傳入中國。仲尼問官於剡子曰，天子失官，學在四夷。據聖人之言，西學苟可采用，不必過分畛域。」❸

江標則云：

「凡諸西學之急需，皆我中邦之素習。蓋格致之學，本大學之所兆基，特機械之心，爲我儒所不尙耳。至於合中西爲一學，則異柯同本，異派同源，並非舍己而從人，背師而他學也。」❹

西學與中學，本爲兩個世界的文化產物，絕不相同，其間雖有類似，祇是在「東海西海有聖人焉，此心同，此理同」的情況下，所自然形成的。一定說西學源出中國，實極盡牽強附會之能事。不過晚淸流行的西學源出中國說，另有其積極的意義，卽爲西學的輸入作護符。「西學苟可采用，不必過分畛域。」「合中西爲一學，則異柯同本，異派同源，並非舍己而從人，背師而他學。」此適可破保守派「西學實無提倡之必要」的主張。所以到眞正通西學的嚴復，便進一步說：

「夫西學之最爲切實，而執其例可以御審變者，名、數、質、力四者之學是已。而吾易則名數爲經，質力以爲緯，而合而名之曰易。大宇之內，質力相推，非質無以見力，非力無以呈質。凡力皆乾也，凡質皆坤也。奈端 (Sir Isaac Newton) 動之例三：其一曰：靜者不自動，動者不自止。動路必直，速率必均。此所謂曠古之慮。自其例出，而後天學明人事利者也。而易則曰：乾其靜也專，其動也直。後二百年有斯賓塞爾 (Herbert Spencer)者，以天演自然言化，著書造論，貫天地人而一理之，此亦晚近之絕作也。其爲天演界說曰：翕以合質，闢以出力，始簡易而終雜糅。而易則曰：坤其靜也翕，其動也闢。至於全力不增減之說，則有自彊不息爲之先。凡動必復之說，則有消息之義居其始。而易不可見，乾坤或幾乎息之旨，尤與熱力平均天地乃毀之言相發明也。此豈可悉謂之偶合也耶？雖然，由斯之說，必謂彼之所明，皆吾中土所前有，甚者或謂其學皆得於東來，則又不關事實，適用自蔽之說也。夫古人發其端，而後人莫能竟其緒，古人擬其大，而後人未能議其精，則猶之不學無術未化之民而已。祖父雖聖，何救子孫之童昏也哉?!」❺

承認中西之學相通，而不認爲西方之所明，皆吾中土所前有，尤其否認其學皆得於東來，這已較西學源出中國之說，更進一步了。

晚清思想界旣開放，西方史學遂有輸入的可能。當時有反中國傳統史學的理論出現。如梁啓超卽攻擊中國史學「知有朝廷而不知有國家」,「知有個人而不知有群體」,「知有陳迹而不知有今務」,「知有事實而不知有理想」❻；攻擊中國正史爲帝王家譜的論調，尤響徹雲霄,「西人之史，皆記國政及民間事，故讀者可考其世焉。中國正史，僅記一姓所以經營天下保守疆土之術，及其臣僕翼載褒榮之陳迹，而民間之事，悉置不記載。然則不過十七姓家譜耳，安得謂之史哉？故觀君史民史之異，而立國之公私判焉矣。」❼中國正史是否爲帝王家譜，中國史學是否祇知有朝廷而不知有國家，祇知有個人而不知有群體，祇知有陳迹而不知有今務，祇知有事實而不知有理想，殊待商榷。但是在當時此乃一開放的論調，更足以反應西方史學的浪潮，已衝入了中國。

西方史學首先輸入中國的，應是歷史進化論，這是在光緒二十四年（一八九八）嚴復翻譯赫胥黎（T. H. Huxley, 1825-1895）的天演論（Evolution and Ethics）以後。輸入西方史學的第一功臣，應是晚清民初言論界驕子梁啓超，他在光緒二十八年（一九〇二）發表的一篇題名叫做「新史學」的文章，係在西方史學的影響下而寫成，尤其深受歷史進化論的影響。自此以後，班漢穆（E. Bernheim, 1854-1937）、朗格諾瓦（Ch. V. Langlois, 1863-1929）、瑟諾博司（Ch. Seignobos, 1854-1942）的史學❽，輸入到中國來了；魯賓孫（J. H. Robinson, 1863-1936）的新史學❾，輸入到中國來了，蘭克（Leopold von Ranke, 1795-1886）的科學治史方法❿，輸入到中國來了，湯恩比（Arnold Toynbee, 1889-1975）的史學⓫，也輸入到中國來了⓬。兩千年以來中國史學所奠定的權威地位，大爲動搖。模倣西方史學體例，採用西方史學方法，以撰寫新的國史，變爲近代中國史學界的風氣。史家勇於拋棄紀傳、編年二體，而以西方的新紀事本末體作秉筆的極則，選題詳述，溯其淵源，明其發展，而窮其究極；歷史的背景、潮流、影響，皆不憚縷述；人物的傳記，由簡言直敍，而長篇鉅製，曲折舖陳；考訂史料，也不奢言乾嘉傳統，而以德國史家蘭克的語文考證爲準則。發展兩千餘年一向缺乏外來刺激的中國史學，滲入了新成分，新血輪；中國史學由獨立發展，開始與世界史學合流。這是中國史學界的可喜現象，也將大有裨益於世界史學。

今日的中國史學界，已很少有人否認西方史學的重要性，懷疑中國史學的價值與成就者，則大有人在。縱然國人所瞭解的西方史學，仍很嫌不够，縱然用新方法寫出來的史籍，不能令人完全滿意，但是國人兼容並包的恢濶胸襟，取人之長以補己之短的開明態度，可以自豪於全世界而無愧。

史學交流，是雙方的事，中國史學西學，西方史學是否肯東學於中國，其史學界對中國史學的認識及批評如何，是中國史學界所應當注視的問題。

第三節 中國史學的西傳

中國的絲茶，中國的科學技術，中國的儒家思想，西傳於歐洲，而發生重大的影響，是世界史上的大事。中國博大精深的史學，其西傳則是極爲晚近的。一九四二年美國史家湯普森（J. W. Thompson）出版其大著史籍史（A History of Historical Writing）時，似乎不甚清楚中國有史學著作⑬；一九六一年英國史家白特費爾德（Herbert Butterfield, 1900- ）在倫敦大學亞非研究院（School of Oriental and African Studies）講「歷史與人類對過去之態度」（History and Man's Attitude to the Past）則云：「我相信沒有任何文化比西歐一四五〇年到一八五〇年間的文化，更富歷史觀念。爲窺尋此一期間西歐文化的淵源，我們必須注意到亞洲去；但是知道什麼因素促使我們文化的發展如此特殊，也同樣的有用。」「如果東方學者能從西方史學獲得啓示，那麼西方學者非到他瞭解了東方，將永不能領悟到重要問題的神奥處。一旦我們試着超越我們自己的思想界，等量齊觀地看中西兩大史學系統，主要的分歧，便暴露無遺。此兩文化對歷史與傳統皆有其可怕的成見；兩者歷史精神太不相同，兩者思想系統（太不相同的系統）太複雜。」⑭一直到一九六九年浦朗穆（J. H. Plumb, 1911- ）仍然說：

「自文藝復興以來，史家逐漸決定致力於瞭解曾經發生的往事，爲瞭解而瞭解，不是爲宗教，不是爲國運，不是爲道德，也不是爲神聖化的制度；……史家日趨於窺探往事的眞相，而希望自此建立有歷史根據的社會轉變的軌跡。這是一西方的發展，本人認爲如此。部分我所尊敬的史家，將持異議，他們會感覺我過份誇大了中國與西方史學的區別。竭盡能力閱讀翻譯作品，我已知曉中國史學的精細，知曉中國史學的重視文獻，知曉中國史學的發展其制度變遷的觀念，已大致能排除借歷史以衍出的天命觀念。中國唐代史家顯然遠優於恩哈德（Einhard），或奧圖（Otto of Freising），或任何中世紀早期編年家，就像中國聖人在技藝或行政方面的優越一樣。但是中國史學的發展，永遠沒有突破通往眞歷史的最後障礙——希望窺探往事的眞相，不顧由此引發與利用過去的時賢衝突。中國人追逐博學，然永遠沒有發展批判史學（the critical historiography）。批判史學是過去兩百年西方史學的重要成就。至於中國人永遠沒有意思視歷史爲客觀的瞭解（objective understanding），則更不待細說了。」⑮西方史家在西方逐漸失去軍事、政治、經濟方面的優勢時，仍然不肯輕易承認中國史學曾到達西方史學所到達的最高境界。虛心的接受中國史學，對目前西方史學界而言，尙沒有這種意識型態出現。

學術是天下的公器，綜合中西史學，以開創今後更進步更豐富的具世界性的新史學，應是人類學術史上的新猷。這種中西史學的綜合工作，是中西史家的共同責任。中國史家盡力吸收西方史學之長，西方史家亦應摒除成見，竭誠採納中國史學的精華。一旦世界性的新史學出，蒙其利者，又豈有畛域之分?!

第一章 註釋:

❶中國史學與西方史學之外，世界上自有其他的史學，如阿拉伯史學卽爲其一，但皆難與中西史學分庭抗禮。

❷籌辦夷務始末，同治朝，卷四七，頁二四。

❸湘報類纂乙案卷下頁三。

❹江標變學論。

❺嚴幾道詩文鈔卷四頁二一三。

❻見梁啓超「新史學」一文，飲冰室文集第四册頁一。

❼徐仁鑄之語，見湘學新報第三十册。

❽有西方史學方法論鼻祖之稱的 Ernst Bernheim 於一八八九年出版「史學方法論」(*Lehrbuch der historichn methode*)；法國史家 Charles Victor Langlois 及 Charles Seignobos 合著「史學原論」(*Introduction aux E'tudes Historiques*)，於一八九八年出版。

❾J. H. Robinson 的 *The New History* 出版於一九一二年，中國史家何炳松於一九二一年將其譯成中文。

❿Lespold von Ranke 的科學治史方法，甚風行中土。

⓫Arnold Toynbee 的「歷史研究」(*A Study of History*) 極受國人注意，爲文介紹及節譯之者甚多。

⓬有關西方史學輸入中國的詳情，參見拙文「西方史學輸入中國考」，台灣大學歷史學系學報第三期，民國六十五年五月。

⓭J. W. Thompson, *A History of Historical Writing*, 1942, p.354

⓮白氏演講後，復將講詞簡化，於同年九月二十一日在英國廣播公司廣播，Listener 雜誌刊其全文，今係自其中節引。

⓯J. H. Plumb, *The Death of the Past*, 1969, pp. 12–13

第二章　西方正統史家論中國史學

在歐洲，治歐洲史以及歐洲國別史的史家，往往被視爲正統史家（academic orthodox historians）[1]。這一類史家，不容諱言的，爲精華之所薈萃，他們文字表達能力高超，接受的西方史學訓練徹底，其史學著作往往光耀歐洲史學界，故其地位若泰山北斗，極爲崇高。但是他們的觀念偏狹，歷史的視線不够廣濶，歐洲以外的世界及其歷史，在他們的心目中不佔重要地位。他們認爲歐洲得天獨厚，爲人類歷史的重心，一部歐洲史，卽象徵一部世界史，亞洲史及非洲史皆其附庸，談歐洲擴張（the expansion of Europe）史時涉及之卽可。直至科學將世界距離縮短到幾乎無以復加的今天，這些西方正統史家們，不輕易修正他們的傳統偏見。[2]

西方正統史家治史的態度如此，其論及中國史學，自極盡蔑視嘲弄之能事，偶有稱頌，也鮮能觸及中國史學的精華。今謹就湯普森（J. W. Thompson）、瑞查森（Alan Richardson）、艾爾頓（G. R. Elton）、盧克斯（John Lukacs）、浦朗穆（J. H. Plumb）、葛蘭特（Michael Grant）、馬爾威克（Arthur Marwick）、白特費爾德（Herbert Butterfield) 諸家所論及者，縷述於后:

第一節 湯普森 (J. W. Thompson, 1869-1941)

湯普森治西洋中古史，著有「中世紀後期歐洲經濟社會史」(Economic and Social History of Europe in the Later Middle Ages, 1300-1350, 1931)、「中世紀歐洲導論」(An Introduction to Medieval Europe, 300-1500, 1937) 等書。其身後出版的「史籍史」(A History of Historical Writing, 1942)，裡面談到中國史，使人感覺他似乎極不清楚中國史書出版的情況:

> 「惟一用蒙古文寫成的蒙古史，而存於今日者，係出於 Sanang Setsen 之手，其人爲蒙古人，皈依佛教。該書原稿於一八二〇年在西藏發現，其寫成有賴於蒐輯中國編年史 (Chinese annals) 中的資料。在遠東方面，尤其在中國方面，蒙古史的知識，盡於此而已。」❸

湯氏如不憚煩，略一翻檢所謂中國編年史及蒙古史，當知其誤謬的嚴重。誤謬的形成，由於湯氏不曾看過有關中國史的書，也不知中國史書的浩如煙海，所以便如此草率言之了。

第二節 瑞查森 (Alan Richardson, 1905-)

瑞查森爲當代西方宗教史家，曾出版「聖經研究序論」(Preface to Bille-study, 1950)、「宗教史與世俗史」(History Sacred and Profane, 1964) 等書。在「宗教史與世俗史」一書中，他曾論及亞洲文化的缺乏歷史意味:

「西人在十九世紀，已富有歷史觀念，適如其在十七世紀已富有科學觀念一樣。」❹

「事實上，亞洲與非洲正迅速歐化；其億萬人開始參與『歷史』。這種參與，不僅爲接受近代的科學與技術，也意味着近代歷史觀念（modern historical-mindedness）的獲得，雖然後者較不顯著。在過去，亞洲文化很少歷史的意識（sense of history），就像巴拉克勞甫教授（Professor Barraclough）所提醒我們的一樣」。❺

這無異是說中國文化的缺乏歷史意味了。

第三節　艾爾頓（G. R. Elton, 1921-　）

任教英國劍橋大學的艾爾頓，治英國史，以「一二〇〇年至一六四〇年的英國」（England, 1200-1640, 1969)、「都德王朝下的英國」（England under the Tudors, 1974)、「改政與宗教改革：一五〇九年至一五五八年的英國」（Reform and Reformation: England, 1509-1558, 1977）諸書馳名。一九六七年出版的「歷史的訓練」（The Practice of History）一書，尤膾炙人口。他在「歷史的訓練」一書中，認爲中國的古典思潮裡，隱藏著顯著漠視歷史的態度：

「在印度與中國的古典思潮裡，隱藏著顯著漠視歷史的態度。任何史學史有待注視希臘與猶太，一個主要學術大樹（intellectual tree）的根柢所在。沒有其他原始宗教作品，像舊約（Old Testament）那樣嚴格的編年，那樣富歷史性，明白記錄上帝爲後代的命運作安排，基督教的後裔在所有宗教中，爲惟一自歷史事件引出其典據（authority）者。在另一方面，有系統的研究人類過去與現在的事件，始自希臘。某類的歷史，已在各地研究、撰寫，從埃及與秘魯的編年史，至愛斯基摩人 (Eskimos) 與波里尼西亞人 (Polynosians) 的神話，皆是，但是祇有源自猶太與希臘的文化，歷史受到重視，歷史成爲將來的導師，歷史變作宗教的根據，歷史協助說明人類的生存與目的。」❻

第四節 盧克斯 (John Lukacs, 1923-)

盧克斯治歐洲近代史，一九七七年出版了「最後的歐洲戰爭」(The Last European War: September 1939-December 1941) 一書。一九六八年出版的「歷史意識」(Historical Consciousness)，代表了他很多史學觀念:

「歷史思想 (historical thinking) 仍然是屬於『歐洲的』或『西方的』。」❼

「我相信在過去三、四世紀，我們的文化最重要的發展，不僅爲科學方法的應用，同時爲歷史意識的增長。」❽

「僅僅一百五十年以前，歷史研究 (historical approach) 纔變成一種思想的型態 (a form of thought)，一些人纔承認研究任何事物 (包括歷史)，就其歷史的發展 (historical development) 以研究有其可行性。此一進展的主要德國史家邁乃克 (Meinecke) 稱之爲近代『西方思想最大的精神革命』(the greatest spiritual revolution)。」❾

「西方以外，過去的追憶，顯然是缺乏歷史性 (historical insufficiency) 的。重建相當近的過去，甚至於需要考古學或人種學；即使有文字的記錄存在，像一些亞洲國家，其記錄的性質是有缺陷的: 此類記錄均爲編年史，充塞了傳奇，點綴着連篇累牘的軼聞遺事。(William Haas 說:『即使是被認爲最偉大的中國史家司馬遷，也沒有超越這種模式。』又見 The Modern Researcher:『西方文化可以說是卓越的歷史文化，而與存在於印度或中國的古代歷史，幾盡不同。』) 用東方學者海思 (William Haas) 的話來說，『東方在歷史知識 (historical knowledge) 方面的成就，遠不能與西方相比……惟有在西方文化中，眞歷史 (genuine history) 始興起成長。印度、中國、波斯、日本等其他民族的信史 (the reliable histories)，均已由西人撰寫了。』」[10]

「西方以外，史家學術 (historianship) 的不足，頗爲明顯，不僅由於方法的缺乏，也由於智力 (mentality) 的歧異：不僅由於『記錄』的殘闕，也由於文化的不同，其所追憶其過去者亦殊異。這是西方歷史所以在世界歷史中比較重要的原因之一。縱使在今天，西方的某人，可以忽視大部分的東方歷史，而對於歷史進展的瞭解，所失者甚少。相反則不然：沒有東方智者 (intelligent oriental)，可不知西方歷史，尤其是歐洲歷史。這不是由於西方統治東方時間較東方統治西方時間較長，而是由於歷史思想屬於西方的成就，縱然是相當晚期的成就；也由於西方歷史特別是『範例的』(paradigmatic) ——充滿了有效的訓誨例子。」[11]

第五節　浦朗穆 (J. H. Plumb, 1911-　　)

浦朗穆爲英國劍橋史家，主治英國史，著有「十八世紀的英國」(England in the Eighteenth Century, 1950)、「華爾波爾爵士」(Sir Robert Walpole, 1956)、「一六七五至一七二五年間英國政治安定之發展」(The Growth of Political Stability in England, 1675-1725,

1967)、「過去的死亡」(The Death of the Past, 1969) 諸書。在「過去的死亡」一書中，他對中國史學，有很多的評論：

「自文藝復興以來，史家逐漸決定致力於瞭解曾經發生的往事，爲瞭解而瞭解，不是爲宗教，不是爲國運，不是爲道德，也不是爲神聖化的制度；……史家日趨於窺探往事的眞相，而希望自此建立有歷史根據的社會轉變的軌跡。這是一西方的發展，本人認爲如此。部分我所尊敬的史家，將持異議，他們會感覺我過份誇大了中國與西方史學的區別。竭盡能力閱讀翻譯作品，我已知曉中國史學的精細，知曉中國史學的重視文獻，知曉中國史學的發展其制度變遷的觀念，已大致能排除借歷史以衍出的天命觀念。中國唐代史家顯然遠優於恩哈德 (Einhard) 或奧圖 (Otto of Freising)，或任何中世紀早期編年家，就像中國聖人在技藝或行政方面的優越一樣。但是中國史學的發展，永遠沒有突破通往眞歷史的最後障礙——希望窺探往事的眞相，不顧由此引發與利用過去的時賢衝突。中國人追逐博學，然永遠沒有發展批判史學 (the critical historiography)。批判史學是過去兩百年西方史學的重要成就。至於中國人永遠沒有意思視歷史爲客觀的瞭解 (objective understanding)，則更不待細說了。」⑫

「古代中國最偉大的史家司馬遷……其史記一書，誠一傑作，然亦爲令人百思不解之作，其大部分爲編纂，司馬遷自其所能發現之古典資料中，逐一鈔錄，略作文字上的潤色，大部分則無條件接受。傳奇與眞理混而爲一，特別是佔史記大半的列傳部分。有時司馬遷覺悟到獲致歷史眞理的困難。然彼於甚不可信的詳細對話記錄，却不稍置疑。……此一傑作……，殊非我們所謂歷史。在很多方面，它爲官吏的手册，將過去告訴這些官吏。……

無我們所謂歷史考據（historical criticism）——無企圖瞭解不同於我們的過去。……對他而言，過去為一道德性的指導（a moral guide），更高眞理的例證，原理的說明，而非為可分析之物。……他的書，雖如彼其浩瀚不可測，如彼其有珍貴價値，究其實，其為一道德的敍事，勝過為一歷史的敍事（a narrative of morality than a narrative of history）。」⑬

「歷史在中國所扮演的角色，與在西方所扮演的角色，其差別是顯而易見的。中國以朝代與朝代相接，而積有大量歷史檔案，其「繁與西歐的歷史資料相埒，且所涉及時間之長過之。惟中國運用此類資料的方法，與綜合此類資料的方法，代代相因，無基本上的變化，二十世紀早期的中國學者運用歷史資料，其實際目的，無殊於唐朝或漢朝。在其傳統綜合的基本原則範圍內，他們偶而能瞥及超乎朝代更替的制度的發展，但是中國歷史永遠沒有發展自我批評與發現（self-criticism and discovery）的方法，無情的考驗通則（the relentless testing of generalization），有目的的蒐求文獻以證明假設，而此為西方歷史的特徵。因此，當傳統中國史學在十九世紀末葉開始崩潰之時，其結果是混亂的。中國史家在西方學生的協助下，攫取西方的通則，以應用於中國材料，特別是馬克斯主義者的。但是這頗像高等化學的細密概念（the detailed concepts of advanced chemistry），被應用到大量新發現的生物資料上去一樣。西方歷史的通則，是經過窮年累月耐心的辨難而得出的精確產品，在其間通則與新資料不斷切磋。有意的應用此類通則到相關的中國資料上，殆不切實際。一旦舊的通則被取代了，中國歷史就碎屍萬斷了。自然朝代的敍事仍在，然其解釋則煙消霧失。」⑭

「歐洲知識份子，即使在第四、五世紀，亦有兩個過去在競爭。在啓蒙運動時代，他有三個。兩個其他的過去經常在隱祕接觸，或公開衝突，各深深自我陶醉，但在解釋方面不同，在應用資料方面也不同——猶太人的過去與回教人的過去。因此歐洲人的過去，永未擁有一致（coherence）或統一（unity），若中國人的一切確定者然。這就是歐洲為什麼能發展批判歷史（critical history）的關鍵所在了。歐洲眞的是應當發展出批判歷史的。」⑮

第六節 葛蘭特（Michael Grant, 1914- ）

葛蘭特治歐洲上古史及歐洲文化史，著有「羅馬世界」(The World of Rome, 1960)、「歐洲文化」(The Civilization of Europe, 1965)、「古代史家」(The Ancient Historians, 1970)、「羅馬史」(History of Rome, 1973)、「羅馬帝國的衰落；一個新的審察」(The Fall of Roman Empire; a Reappraisal, 1976) 等書。其在「古代史家」一書中云：

「波力比阿斯（Polybius）的作品，與其他尚存的古代作品相比較，很顯然的是政治家的示例書（a case-book），頗像稍後一兩世紀出現而意在訓練文官的中國史一樣。」（創自司馬遷，約公元前一世紀。）⑯

第七節 馬爾威克（Arthur Marwick, 1936- ）

馬爾威克治英國史，並喜討論歷史的性質與寫作，著有「全面戰爭世紀的不列顛：一九〇〇年至一九六七年間的戰爭，和平與社會變遷」(Britain in the Century of Total War: War, Peace, and Social

Change, 1900-1967, 1968)、「歷史的性質」(The Nature of History, 1970)、「寫歷史的基本問題」(Basic Problems of Writing History, 1971)、「一九一四年至一九七〇年英國社會的爆炸」(The Explosion of British Society, 1914-1970, 1971) 諸書。其於「歷史的性質」一書中云:

「我們的西方文化, 從猶太基督教 (Judaeo-Christianity) 繼承了一種特別强烈的歷史意識 (a particularly strong sense of history), 但是醉心歷史與依賴歷史, 非僅西方爲然。回教的歷史學派, 與偉大的中國歷史學派 (the great Chinese school of history), 皆爲其文化中的主要成分。」⑰

「我們能欣賞遍佈於人類學術活動的整個洪流中的歷史作品, 也能從其中獲益, 像修西蒂笛斯 (Thucydides)、司馬遷、比得 (Bede)、馬克維利 (Machiavelli) 等人的作品皆是。但是我們必須注意, 系統的研究歷史 (the systematic study of history), 視歷史爲一種學術 (history as a discipline), 是最近的事, 爲歐洲與北美洲大學在十九世紀所創立。」⑱

第八節　白特費爾德 (Herbert Butterfield, 1900-)

白特費爾德是英國當代大史家, 曾任劍橋大學國家講座教授 (Regius professor), 一九三一年其「輝格黨的歷史解釋」(The Whig Interpretation of History) 一書問世後, 卽享譽史學界, 厥後相繼出版「英國人及其歷史」(The Englishman and His History, 1944)、「近代科學的起源」(The Origins of Modern Science, 1949)、「基督教與歷史」(Christianity and History, 1949)、「歷史與人類的關係」(History and Human Relations, 1951)、「人類論過去」(Man on His Past, 1955)、「喬治三世與史家」(George Ⅲ and the Historians, 1957) 諸書，大半是談史學之作。白氏談西方史學，犀利明辨，見解獨到，每能糾謬發覆，爲英國史學界開蠶叢。惟白氏近二十年來，喜談中國史學，一九六〇年二月他第一次公開評論中國史學云:

「雖然我們常常自我提醒，西方文化獨能發展自然科學，可是我們每每忽略西方文化同樣地以富有歷史觀念 (historical-mindedness)，而卓然與世不同。古代的中國，科學工藝甚發達，歷史著作極豐富，但是未臻於相當於西方十七世紀科學革命與十八世紀末十九世紀初史學運動 (The Historical Movement of the late eighteenth and early nineteenth centuries) 的境界 (亦未有若何跡象將能臻此境界)。」⑲

一九六一年白氏在倫敦大學亞非研究院 (School of Oriental and African Studies) 講「歷史與人類對過去的態度」(History and Man's Attitude to the Past)，又對中國史學大肆批評。同年九月二十一日將講詞簡化，復在英國廣播公司廣播，期以擴大影響，聽衆 (Listener) 雜誌刊其全文，今擇要引之如下:

「我相信沒有任何文化比西歐一四五〇年到一八五〇年間的文化更富歷史觀念。爲窺尋此一期間西歐文化的淵源，我們必須注意到亞洲去；但是知道什麼因素促使我們文化的發展如此特殊，也同樣的有用。」⑳

「很多早期的編年史 (annals)，並非源於恢復既往的動機，僅欲爲君王留不朽於將來而已。在美索不達米亞蔚成一趨勢，凡闡釋百事，皆追尋其淵源，此實變爲歷史寫作的强有力的原動力，所以在巴比倫引導出宇宙創造的故事、洪水的故事及巴比倫塔的故事出來了。在西方世界以及東方，歷史多歸功於掌管曆法的官吏，此類官吏，皆記錄意義重大事件的日期。在東方，歷史特別有賴於一類秘書，他們掌管純爲商業性質的記錄，最初一點也不是爲了綿延歷史。」㉑

「如果東方學者能從西方史學獲得啓示，那麼西方學者非到他瞭解了東方將永不能領悟到重要問題的神奧處。一旦我們試着超越我們自己的思想界，等量齊觀地看中西兩大史學系統，主要的分歧，便暴露無遺。此兩文化對歷史與傳統皆有其可怕的成見；兩者歷史精神太不相同，兩者思想系統（太不相同的系統）太複雜。」㉒

「從公元前第二世紀起，中國即有考據學（textual criticism）的產生。……惟此一考據學的發展，未能達到一較高境界，不配我們稱之爲批評。換言之，即爲未能對證據作科學的評價與分析。其中原因之一，爲中國的特殊修史制度，這是中國史學與世不同的主要原因之一，已曾有人作過重要的研究。決定性的因素，在於中國的修史太爲一種官方事業了，太爲官僚化的組織了。歷史被視爲統治者的有效輔導，大體上歷史亦由官吏而寫，爲官吏而寫。中國歷史太有特徵被稱之爲資治歷史（civil service history）了。在中國史學後面，有一假想，即凡屬歷史記載（historical record），皆完全客觀。客觀被認爲僅僅將事實登錄上（registering the facts）即可獲得。避免涉及史實互相銜接（the interconnectedness of events）的問題，甚至避免描述背景或追問原因；避免談論歷史發展的整個觀念，甚至連世界的漸變也不去敍述了。客觀事實（the objective facts）一旦被他們列入記載，即有其獨

立性，所有未來史家所必須做的，是重複既已確定的敍述，或者或許是從既已確定的敍述中去自己選取。」㉓

「具有如此堅實的非有機的史料觀（hard and inorganic view of historical data），中國人能做龐大的分類工作，能編纂驚人的百科全書，並且能出產他們數不盡的瑣碎餖飣的地方史（local histories），但是他們不能到達我們所謂的『綜合』（synthesis）的境界，他們沒有發展歷史解釋的藝術（the art of historical explanation）。不斷的襲用舊史原文，任憑私意的選用文獻而卽目之爲可信（取此而捨彼的原因不予以討論），顯示出一牢不可破的歷史標準（a firm historical canon）已經確立，考據限於自我證明的工作上，而不科學地窺尋史學的眞相與看看史料與實際發生的事實符合的程度。所謂官方歷史(official history)，實際上衹含着一些歷史的意味，是由委員會產生的，這够令人驚訝的了！中國豐富的史籍，像是備官僚偶然的參考，而不是較廣大群衆的普通讀物。我時常懷疑，當西方史學脫離蘭克（Ranke）的一些健全的指導時，是否不走此同一的路線？這裡或許是一個更進一步的原因，爲什麼西方學者應該審查東方。研究東方學問的人可能不原諒我，但是如果我說西方學者必須注意中國僅爲了習知歷史學如何可能走錯路就好了，他們將會瞭解我。」㉔

如此評論中國史學，凡稍通中國史學者，聞之自無不譁然。當時首先起來反對的是任敎劍橋大學的漢學敎授浦立本（E. G. Pulleyblank）先生，一九六一年九月二十八日他致聽衆雜誌編者的信云：

「作爲一個作者，保持緘默，無疑的是有益而謙虛的，但是也難免有怏怏之感。我有此感覺，是由於我爲『亞洲民族史籍』（Historical Writing on the Peoples of Asia）叢書中『中日史家』(Historians of China and Japan) 一書的投稿者與聯合編輯之一，而白特費爾德教授即用此書作出發點來演講（九月二十一日的聽衆雜誌)。當然當他談到中國官方史學的缺點時，他是對的，世界其他地區的官方史學，也有如此缺點。中國自己的批評家劉知幾（約第七世紀)、章學誠（十八世紀）已對之作猛烈的抨擊。但是說到『任憑私意的選用文獻而即目之爲可信（取此而捨彼的原因不予以討論)』，眞是天哉枉也！這是他基於司馬光與其同修史諸公之寫史態度而發出者乎？說中國對證據不作科學的評價與分析，無較高境界的批評，可是我們可曾曉得中國懷疑理性主義（sceptical rationalism）的悠久傳統，燦然蔚成第七世紀與十八世紀的批評著作乎？由於中國經學的權威力量，關於經書的眞實、組成及遞變等重要問題，中國學者都一一予以探究。後期的史學，接受此傳統，同樣的能重徹底的審察（thorough scrutiny)。

雖然中國史家永沒有十分發展西方史家職在『創造的綜合』(creative synthesis) 的概念——中國史家或視此爲小說家的領域——，可是當歐洲編年史家（European chroniclers）仍虔誠地認爲人類歷史操縱於上帝不可思議的手中的時候，中國人很早已放棄他們天人神秘合一的信仰，而尋求人類事變的合理的人爲原因。

還有，一個人不要太使人不愉快，終於被『歷史的祭司長』(the high priests of History) ㉕注意到，這對治中國史的學人講，是不無意義，所以如果我不能瞭解白特費爾德教授，我最低限度能原諒他。如果他和他的同道開始考慮，他們有些方面要向中國史家學習，縱然是爲了想知其錯誤，談論可以開始。我們

這方面可以學習着更適當的表達我們。」㉖

同年十月五日白特費爾德教授在致聽衆雜誌編者的信中答覆浦立本教授說:

「我必須勉力答覆九月二十八日聽衆雜誌上浦立本教授的信，因爲他爲我久所設想的提供了實證。我絲毫沒有意思觸怒他，但是我無法使他確信有一概念的壁壘 (conceptual barrier) 存在，除非說他的那篇文章使我更堅信我原來在演講中的評論是絲毫不爽。在他的信中，他僅擧出司馬光來駁斥我，可是在書中（一五八頁。㉗）他批評此人不審訂史料！他那篇文章標題中的另一人是劉知幾，「我不知西方史學界人士將覺得此人如何？(特別是從一四八至一四九頁去看。)」㉘

白氏在信中又說他在倫敦大學亞非研究院與英國廣播公司播講「歷史與人類對過去的態度」以前，從沒有看到「中日史家」一書，有關中國史學的知識，是由英國漢學家李約瑟博士 (Dr. Needham) 所轉告。待浦立本教授的信在聽衆雜誌上出現了，他才開始看此書，且在一九六二年六月，又寫了一篇「東方的歷史」(The History of the East)，大大修正了他的偏見:

「如果在比較文化研究(the comparative study of civilizations)上作更驚人的進展，我們將獲益極大，這是我們正面臨到的千載良機。」㉙

「我們文化有些方面，我們自己將永遠不能瞭解，除非我們知道其他大陸的一些文化，最低限度是以比較法去研究一些專題。誠然西方思想有些方面，今天需要研究，那不僅是歐洲史的一部分，也是世界現象的流露。在其中歷史思想的興起，我們對過去意識的發展便是問題之一。」㉚

「對研究史學史的人來講，在西方之外，另一偉大的中國文化，在歷史方面蔚爲一可觀的發展，且精神與作品與西方迥然不同，這是極富意義的。其洋洋巨觀的作品，頗多（雖然只佔極小部分）由於譯成歐洲語文，已有助於一般西方學者。我們通東方學的學者們，無論如何正集絕大部分注意力於中國史學的特性。最近他們大體上對中國史學瞭解已多，且知道那些爲西方學者所需要。所以這是西方學者爲什麼要與東方學者會合的關鍵所在。」[31]

「不移入亞洲，我們甚至不能討論我們歷史著作與歷史思想的淵源。」[32]

「此一新著（指 Historical Writing on the Peoples of Asia, 1961，中日史家爲其中一種）對很多西方有興趣於一般史學史的學者，是重要的。部分興趣源於欲移向一較高處的慾望，不僅僅被禁錮在東方世界裡，而且卓然立於東西方之上，調合二者，介紹其一的知識，以增大我們對另一方面的瞭解。」[33]

「近年來令人興奮的發現與推想（discoveries and speculation），促使凡事新奇，我們能窺知世界任何角落歷史寫作的起始，或看出世界各地第一次對過去流露興趣的徵象。記錄與追念（records and commemorations）的原始，是歷史與人類學的重大問題之一；在此一論題上，是否能有比來自亞洲的見解更重要的，頗可置疑。整個問題令人增加興趣的是刺激歷史記錄的在最初不是對過去發生興趣，不是我們所謂歷史的興趣。研究歷史寫作的前身，充滿着驚人之事（surprises）；我們所稱的史家，其職責在最初像是一點也不是導源於歷史的。」[34]

「更進一步的意義，是此書對想擴展眼界，最低限度想一窺世界史某些論題的人們，具有特殊意義。與世界其他地區相比，中國與西歐都發展了富有科學特性與歷史觀念的文化。中國像是永未臻於相當於十七世紀的科學革命，亦永未現出向此一方向移動的跡象。直到直接受到西方影響之前，難以避免的結論，爲中國亦永未臻於相當於十八世紀末十九世紀初的史學革命——蘭克及其前哲的治史技術在此革命中確立。有兩事爲西方世界的特產，當西方與其遭遇的問題及經驗奮鬥時，不僅自過去吸取知識，而且根據過去，肆力研究。但是中國史學在另外方向的發展，如此其壯觀，比較此兩大系統，說明兩者太不相同的歷史精神類型，爲一相當有趣之事。」㉟

「有證據可以證明中國史家雖欲批評其前代史家的敍事，甚或具有了懷疑所有過去作者的態度。考據學發展到一崇高境界，似昭然若揭，中國史家無疑問已臻於所謂智力的洗練（intellectual refinement)。」㊱

「我們今天很難對一種未能深入史家所用的原始資料且用複雜的設備以批評此類資料的史學，視之爲一種眞正的批判史學。……但是中國史家是否發現了以新原始證據考核其史學傳統的方式，或者追尋一種比傳統自我符合更進一步的方法，不够淸楚。中國史學與歐洲一四五〇年至一七五〇年間史學，蓋在伯仲之間。近代西方用於原始資料的批判性的設備，一定會使中國的歷史寫作與硏究發生很大的變化。」㊲

一九七一年白氏到香港中文大學參加中國歷史與世界歷史的討論會，他以「世界歷史與文化的比較研究」(Universal History and the Comparative Study of Civilization) 爲題，對中國史學，發表了更進一步的意見：

「有些民族與文化，永無意於知其過去，他們或爲視發生於過去的事件若泡沫的哲學或宗教所支配——一切像在風中飛舞的枯葉，了無意義。有些民族，像是離說神話故事的階段不遠——不渴望更好，沒悟及可以幾於更好。兩個大的例外，一是巨大的中國文化，產生了可觀的歷史文獻，對世界有其永恆價值，一是我們所謂西方文化，溯源至古典的希臘，遠一點可追至古代的美索不達米亞與埃及。但是在自然科學的發展上，中國文化與西方文化是同樣重要的，同樣在各個時代爲世界的領導者。卽使在古希臘時代，歷史的研究，與起於科學觀念及物質宇宙的研究開始出現之時。歷史與科學往往在其無數世紀的發展中，不尋常的連在一起。」㊳

「我們面對兩個極端重要的產物，我們所有的人皆須鄭重考慮。西方文化，有其活力，有其創造力，發展出特殊的科學方法……但是也有一巨大的古代中國文化，西方人正開始傾力去瞭解它，雖然我們淸楚所知者實在太少了。」㊴

「業餘如我，僅讀翻譯成西方文字的古代中國的歷史作品，卽已發現在歷史思想上，在寫歷史的方式上，東西的歧異，彰明較著；企圖闡釋與瞭解其歧異，寄望得其起源，使人相當深入於此兩文化的歧異的整個問題上去。我的老朋友李約瑟，傾其大半生研究中國較古代的科學，希望窺見爲何西方科學完全爲一另外發展。僅僅這類簡單問題，就使他深入到中國文化與中國智力（Chinese mentality）的整個問題上去。」㊵

他的眼光，也似乎開始世界化了：

「我們不要忘記，在十九世紀後半期，更淸楚的在二十世紀，整個寰宇，已凝成一個了。一個地區的事件，影響及於世界的相反的一端，凡事皆連在一起，此不僅限於文化觀念（cultural ideas）的擴展——也意味着政治、外交、國際關係及大部分文化生活變成了全球性。凡此皆待以全球性的規模，自全人類的觀點去研究，即使說我們將以西方觀點或中國觀點去研究全球歷史，也是錯的——我想必須儘量採用全球性的觀點，在心目中僅存一個世界文化。……我們需要一個歷史態度（historical attitude），對待當代事件——在今天的日子裡，是提升至一個全球性的觀點。」㊶

另外在題名「史學發展的停滯與畸論」(Delays and Paradoxes in the Development of Historiography）一文中，白氏對中國的史學原理，也表示了極大的興趣:

「凡有關某一時代的兩種權威資料存在，而其說不同，每宜協調兩者，作一綜合敍述。如失敗，不得已而有選擇其一的必要。在中國史學傳統中，也出現此一原理，這是尤令人感興趣者。」㊷

第二章　註釋:

❶E. G. Pulleyblank, *Chinese History and World History*, 1955

❷E. H. Carr, *What is History?* 1961, p. 146; Geoffrey Barraclough, *History in a Changing World*, 1955, p.61

❸J. W. Thompson, *A History of Historical Writing*, Volume I, 1942, p. 354:

"The sole history of the Mongols written in the Mongol language which has survived is that of Sanang Setsen, who was a Mongol convert to Buddhism. The original was discovered in Tibet in 1820. This book, supplemented by some information gleaned from Chinese annals, is the sum total of our knowledge of the history of the Mongols in Far Asia, especially in China."

❹Alan Richardson, *History Sacred and Profane*, 1964, p. 103:

"Western man became historically-minded in the nineteenth century, as in the seventeenth century he had become scientifically-minded."

❺Ibid., p. 268:

"Asia and Africa are, in fact, being Europeanized with increasing rapidity; their millions are beginning to participate in 'history'. Such participation involves not only the acceptance of modern science and technology, but also the acquisition of modern historical-mindedness, though the need for this latter quality is less obviously apparent. In the past the Asian civilizations had little sense of history, as Professor Barraclough himself reminds us."

❻G. R. Elton, *The Practice of History*, 1967, pp. 11–12:

"There is something markedly a-historical about the attitudes embedded for instance, in the classic minds of India and China, and any history of historiography must needs concentrate on the Hellenic and Judaic roots of one major intellectual tree. No other primitive sacred writings are so grimly chronological and historical as is the Old Testament, with its express record of God at Work in the fates of generations succeeding each other in time; and the Christian descendant stands alone among the religions in deriving its authority from an historical event. On the other hand, the systematic study of human affairs, past and present, began with the Greeks. Some sort of history has been studied and written everywhere, from the chronicles of Egypt and Peru to the myths of Eskimos and Polynesians, but only in the civilization which looks back to the Jews and Greeks was history ever a main concern, a teacher for the future, a basis of religion, an aid in explaining the existence and purpose of man."

❼John Lukacs, *Historical Consciousness*, 1968, p. 2:

"Historical thinking is still something particularly 'European' or 'Western'"

❽Ibid., p. 5:

"I believe that the most important developments in our civilization during the last three or four centuries include not only the applications of the scientific method but also the growth of a historical consciousness."

❾Ibid., p. 18:

"If in only about 150 years ago that the historical approach became a form of thought, that some people recognized that it is possible to study everything (including history) through its historical development. Meinecke, the principal German historian of this process, called it 'the greatest spiritual revolution which Western thought has undergone' in modern times."

❿Ibid., p. 23:

"Outside the West the memory of the past in marked by a kind of historical insufficiency. Archaeology or ethnography is needed for the reconstruction of even relatively recent developments; and even when written records exists, as in certain Asian countries, their quality is defective: they are Chronicles stuffed with legends and interspersed by long anecdotes. (William Haas: 'Not even Szu Ma Chien, who is considered the greatest Chinese historiographer, transcends this general model.' Also see The Modern Researcher: 'Western culture may be said to be the historical culture par excellence, and that almost nothing like ancient histories exist in Indian or Chinese literature.) In the words of the Orientalist William Haas, the East, in historical knowledge, 'has produced little comparable to the achievements of the West ...... Only in Western civilization could genuine history have arisen and grown as it did' The reliable histories of otherwise highly articulate peoples of India, China, Persia, Japan have been written by Westerners."

⑪Ibid., p. 24:

"It is rather evident that this inadequacy of historianship outside the West has involved not merely a deficiency of a method but differences of mentality: not only insufficiencies of 'records' but distinct differences in which different cultures have remembered their past. And this is one of the reasons of the relative importance of Western history even on the scale of world history. Even now a person in the West way disregard most of Oriental history with little consequent loss to his proper understanding of the processes of history, while the converse is not so: no intelligent Oriental can afford to remain ignorant of western, and specifically of European, history. And this is true not because the West has ruled the East longer than the East ruled the West; it is true because historical thinking has been a Western, though relatively recent, achievement."

⑫J. H. Plumh, *The Death of the past*, 1969, pp. 12–13:

"From the Renaissance onwards there has been a growing determination for historians to try and understand what happened, purely in its own terms and not in the service of religion or national destiny, or morality, or the sanctity of institutions; ......The historian's growing purpose has been to see things as they really were, and from this study to attempt to formulate processes of social changs which are acceptable on historical grounds and none other. This to my mind is a Western development. Some scholars whom I admire will disagree, for they feel that I exaggerate the difference between Chinese and Western historiography. I am aware, as far as reading of translations of secondary authorities permits, of the subtlety of Chinese historiography, of its preoccupation with documentation and its development of concepts of institutional change which, to some extent, broke through the basic historical generalizations of the Mandate of Heaven concept. Obvionsly, Chinese historians of the T'ang dynasty were infinitely superior to Einhard or Otto of Freising or any other early medieval chronicler, as superior as Chinese sages were in technology or in administration. Be that as it may, their development never broke the final barriers that lead to true history—the attempt to see things as they were, irrespective of what conflict this might create with what the wise ones of one's own society wake of the past. The Chinese pursued erudition, but they never developed the critical historiography which is the signal achievement of Western historians over the last two hundred years. They never attempted, let alone succeeded, in treating history as objective understanding."

⑬Ibid. pp. 18–19:

"The greatest historian of Classical China, Ssu-ma Chién......The Memoirs of an Historian is a remarkable, but odd, achievement.

Most of it is compilatory. Ssu-ma Chién copied out those archaic texts which he could discover, modernizing the language somewhat but largely accepting what he was told. Legends and truth are intermingled, particularly in the biographies of dukes, officials, sages and bandits which form so large a part of his work. Nevertheless, at times Ssu-ma Chién demonstrates a sophisticated awareness of the difficulty of arriving at historic truth. On the other hand he accepts the records of the most improbable and detailed conversations without the slightest expression of doubt. ...... This remarkable book ...... is quite unlike what we regard as history. In many ways it is a handbook for bureancrats. telling them of the past. ......There is no historical criticism as we know it — no attempt to understand the past as a time different from our own. ......The past for him was a moral guide, the example of the higher truths, an illustration of principles, not a matter for analysis. ...... His book, vast and valuable as it is. is more a narrative of morality than a narrative of history."

⑭Ibid., pp. 87–88:

"The contrast between the role of history in China and in the West is illuminating. China, as dynasty followed dynasty, acquired a large historical archive, as diverse and as mountainous as the historical material of Western Europe, and stretching over a longer period of time. Yet Chinese methods of using this material and generalizing about it did not fundamentally change from dynasty to dynasty and Chinese scholars were using historical materials for the same pragmatic purposes in the early twentieth century as in the T'ang or Han dynasties. Within the tenets of their traditional generalizations they could be subtle and on occasion glimpse the problem of the growth of institutions outside the dynastic context, but Chinese history never developed the process of self-criticism and discovery, the relentless testing of generalization, the purposefull search for documentation to prove hypotheses which marks Western history. In consequence, when traditional Chinese historiography began to collapse in the late nineteenth century, the result was chaos and confusion. Chinese historians, aided and abetted by Western students of their country, snatched at Western generalizations, particularly Marxist ones, and applied them to Chinese data. But this was rather as if the detailed concepts of advanced chemistry were used on a large quantity of freshly discovered biological facts. The generalizations of Western history were the refined end-product of years of patient argument in which generalization and fresh facts had created an ever more sophisticated dialogue. To apply these in any meaningful way to China on the data available was well-nigh impracticable. Once the traditional generalizations were removed, Chinese history collapsed into fragments. The narrative of dynasties remained, of course, but explanation vanished."

⑮Ibid., pp. 89–90:

"The European intellectual, even in the fourth and fifth centuries of our era had two pasts to contend with. By the time of the Enlightenment he had three. Always in subterranean contrast, or overt conflict, there were two others, deeply involved in his own, yet different in interpretation and different too, in usage of materials — the past of the Jews and the past of Islam. Hence the European's past nerver possessed the coherence or the unity, the all-embracing certainty of the Chinese. And here lies the key to why Europe could, indeed was bound to, develop critical history."

⑯Michael Grant, *The Ancient Historians*, 1970, p. 156:

"Polybius' work, more than any other ancient writing that has survived, is deliberately and openly a case-book for politicians, rather as

Chinese history which came into being a generation or two later was intended to train civil servants." (Created by Ssu-ma Chién, c. 100 B. C.)

⑰Arthur Marwick, *The Nature of History*, 1970, p. 13:

"Our own Western civilization has inherited from Judaeo-Christianity a particularly strong sense of history. But interest in, and dependence upon, history is no occidental monopoly: both the Muslim school and the great Chinese school of history have been central elements in their own civilizations."

⑱Ibid., p. 15:

"We can enjoy and profit from historical works spread across the entire timespan of human literary activity, such as those of Thucydedes, Ssŭ-ma Chién, Bede or Machiavelli: but We must note that the systematic study of history, history as a discipline, is a very recent phenomenon, becoming established in West European and North American universities only in the nineteenth century."

⑲Herbert Butterfield's Preface to the Beacon Edition of Man on His Past, 1960:

"Though we often tell ourselves that Western civilization is unique in the development it has given to the natural sciences, we do not always remember that it is similarly distinguished for its 'historical-mindedness'. Ancient China was remarkably productive in science and technology as well as in the writing of history: but it did not achieve (or show signs of ever being able to achieve) anything that corresponded to the Scientific Revolution of the seventeenth century or the Historical Movement of the late eighteenth and early nineteenth centuries."

⑳Herbert Butterfield, *History and Man's Attitude to the Past*, in Listener, 21 September, 1961:

"I believe that no other civilization became historically minded in the way that western Europe did between 1450 and 1850. For the origin of this we must look at Asia; but it is also useful to know what factors helped to make our development a peculiar one."

㉑Ibid.:

"Many of the early annals did not spring from any urge to recover the past—they were really attempts on the part of monarchs to perpetuate their memory in the future. In Mesopotamia there developed a tendency to explain things by inguiring into their origins. This was to become a powerful motor behind historical writing, and in Babylon it led to the stories of the Creation, the Flood, and the Tower of Babel. In both the Western world and in the Orient, history owed much to the officer who had charge of the Calendar and who entered on its pages the dates of significant events. Particularly in the East it owed much to a kind of secretary who kept records for business purposes and not at all, at first, for historical reasons."

㉒Ibid.:

"But if the oriental student may gain hints from Western historiography, the Western student can never learn the profundity of the problems that he has to face until he acquaints himself with the East. It is when we try to transcend our own circle of ideas, and see, standing side by side, the two great systems of historical scholarship—the Western and the Chinese—that the basic issues become apparent. These two civilizations are remarkable for their tremendous preoccupation with history and tradition; yet two vastly different historical mentalities are involved, and two complicated systems (vastly different systems) of ideas."

㉓Ibid.:

"Considerable studies have been made of the extraordinary development of textual criticism in China from the second century B. C. ...... The development of textual criticism did not bring with it any great advance in the higher forms of what we should call criticism —namely, the scientific assessment of the value of evidence. and there has been a considerable study of one of the reasons for this —one of the main reasons for the peculiar character of Chinese historiography—namely, the remarkable organization that lay behind the historical writing.

The decisive element was the fact that historical writing was so much an official affair, and was bureaucratically organized. History came to be regarded as a useful guide for governors of states, and it was written on the whole by officials, for officials. It had the peculiar characteristics of what I should call civil service history.

Behind it there was the assumption that the historical record, once achieved is completely objective, and indeed is achieved once and for all. The objectivity was supposed to be secured by simply registering the facts, as found in official papers, and avoiding the question of the interconnectedness of events, avoiding even the description of the background or the examination of causes, avoiding the whole notion of process in history or even the description of the gradual changes that take place in the world. The objective facts, once they had been put on record, had their own independent existence; all that the future historian had to do was to repeat the established version, or perhaps make his own selection from it."

④Ibid.:

"Possessing this hard and inorganic view of historical data, the Chinese could perform a prodigious work of classification, could compile amazing encyclopaedias, and could produce their countless local histories, with further ramification of detail; but they could not reach what we should call a synthesis and they did not develop the art of historical explanation. The constant copying of ancient texts, the arbitrary choice of the documents that should be authoritative (without discussion of the reasons for choosing one rather than another) meant that a firm historical canon or traditional corpus was established, and the criticism was confined to the task of making this consistent with itself—not setting out scientifically to get behind the historiography and see how far it corresponded with the things that had actually happened. It was to an astonishing degree official history, bearing something of the character of the kind of history which is produced by commissions and committees. In all its copiousness, it seemed intended more for a bureaucrat to refer to on special occasions than as general reading for a wider public. I sometimes wonder whether Western historiography, as it breaks away from some of the healthy teaching of Ranke, is not moving in the same direction. Here is perhaps a further reason why the Western student should examine the East. Orientalists may not forgive me, but they will understand me, if I say that the Western student ought to look to China if only in order to learn how historical scholarship may go wrong."

㉕白特費爾德爲宗教史家，故浦立本如此諷言之。

㉖*The Listener*, 28 Sept. 1961

Letter to the Editor:

"Sir,—It is no doubt instructive and humbling, but also frustrating, for an author to find that he has failed to communicate. I feel this as one of the contributors and the joint editor of the volume Historians of China and Japan in th series 'Historical writing on the peopoles of Asia', which Professor Herbert Butterfield used as starting off point for his lecture (The Listener September 21). Of course he is right when he talks about the faults of official historiography in China as elsewhere. They were vigorously expressed and castigated by China's own critics, Liu Chih-chi (c. A. D. 700) and Chang Hsüeh chéng in the eighteenth century. But to talk about the 'arbitrary choice of the documents that should be authoritative (without discussion of the reasons for choosing one rather than another)'! Dear me. Is this what he gets out of the description of how Ssu-ma Kuang and his collaborators went about their work? 'No scientific assessment of the value of evidence', no higher criticism—have we failed to convey anything at all of the long tradition of sceptical rationalism, coming to its fine flowering in the critical works of the seventeenth and eighteenth centuries? For all the great weight of authority that resided in the Chinese classics, the major problems concerning thier authenticity, composition and transmission were all explored by Chinese scholars and the received tradition about the history of later times was subjected to the same thorough scrutiny.

Though the Chinese historians never quite developed the Western conception of the historian's task as aiming at a creative synthesis—this they would probably have regarded as the province of the writer of fiction—it may be said in their favour that while European chroniclers were still piously seeing human history as manipulated by the inscrutable hand of providence, the Chinese had long since given up their belief in a mysterious sympathy between Heaven and man and looked for rational human couses for human events.

Yet one must not be too ungrateful. It is something for a student of Chinese history to be taken notice of at all by the high priests of History. So if I cannot understand professor Butterfield. I can at least forgive him. If he and his fellows begin to think they have something to learn from the Chinese historians, even in a negative sense. the dialogue can begin. We for our part may learn to express ourselves more adequately.

Cambridge E. G. Pulleyblank"

㉗指「中日史家」一書

㉘*The Listener*, 5 Oct. 1961

Letters to the Editor:

"Sir,—

I must try to answer Professor Pulleyblank's letter in The Listener of September 28 because he provides an example of what I had in mind. I do not in the least wish to provoke him, but I do not see how I can convince him that there is a conceptual barrier, except by saying that his chapter strengthened my belief that I had been right in the judgment I had originally made in my lecture. In his letter he adduces against me, by name, only Ssu-ma Kuang; but in the book (page 158) he criticizes this man for 'the failure to study sources as such'. The other name in the tittle of his chapter in Liu chih-chi, I wonder what student of Western historiography will feel about this man (especially page 148–9).

....

Cambridge H. Butterfield"

㉙Herbert Butterfield, *The History of East, in History.* vol. XLVII No. 160, June 1962, p. 157:

"We are reaching, the moment at which it would have been very profitable to us if we had made more imposing advances in the comparative study of civilizations."

㉚Ibid., p. 158:

"There are some aspects of our own civilization which we shall never understand until we know something of other continents, pursuing the comparative method at least in respect of limited topics. There are, indeed, some aspects of Western thought that now require to be studied not merely as part of the history of Europe but also as manifestations of a universal phenomenon. Amongst these is the question of the rise of historical thinking, the development of our sense of the past."

㉛Ibid., p. 158:

"For the student of the history of historiography, it is of the greatest significance that, besides the West, another great culture—that of China—made a remarkable development on the historical side, all of which issued, however, in a mentality and a literature vastly different from our own. A considerable amount (though only a very small proportion) of this massive literature is available to the ordinary Western student through translation into European languages. Our orientalists themselves are in any case directing their attention much more to the peculiar characteristics of Chineses historiography. Also, nowadays, they work with a much better knowledge of historiography in general, and of the things that the Western scholar needs. Here, therefore, is a point at which the student of the West ought to be meeting the student of the East."

㉜Ibid., p. 158:

"We cannot discuss the origins of even our own historical writing and thinking without moving into Asia."

㉝Ibid., p. 160:

"The new work is important to many students in the West—important for those who are interested in the general history of historiography. Part of its interest springs from the desire to move to a higher altitude—not merely to be locked in the world of the orientalist, but to stand above both East and West, mediating the one to the other, and bringing the knowledge of the one to enlarge our understanding of the other."

㉞Ibid., pp. 160–161:

"The exciting discoveries and speculations of recent years give importance to everything new that we can learn about the beginnings of historical writing, or the first signs of an emerging interest in the past, in any part of the world. The origins of records and commemorations is one of the grand questions of history and anthropology; and on such topics it is doubtful whether anything can ever be so important as the light that comes from Asia. The whole problem gains added interest from the fact that the stimulus behind historical records is at first not an interest in the past as such—not an interest that we should call historical. The study of the antecedents of historical writing is full of surprises; and the office of what we call the historian seems to spring out of functions which were not primarily historical at all."

㉟Ibid., p. 162:

"There is a further sense in which the present volumes should have a peculiar interest for those who wish to extend their horizon and to see at least certain topics in the framework of world history. Compared with the rest of the world, both China and Western Europe developed civilizations that were remarkable not only for their scientific character but also for their preoccupation with history. It would seem that China never achieved anything that would correspond with our scientific revolution of the seventeenth century, and never showed signs of really moving in the same direction. It is difficult to avoid the conclusion that, until she had been directly influenced by the West, China also never attained anything corresponding to our historical revolution of the late eighteenth and early nineteenth centuries—the establishment of the techniques that we associate with Ranke and his predecessors. Here were two things which were the peculiar products of the Western world, not merely drawn from the past but hammered out as the West wrestled with its own problems and experience. Yet Chinese historiography was so imposing in the developments made in other directions that the comparison of these two great systems—the explanation of the two vastly different types of historical mentality—is a matter of unusual interest."

㊱Ibid., p. 165:

"There is evidence that Chinese historians were ready to criticize the narratives of their predecessors and even perhaps to reach an attitude of scepticism towards all the writers of the past. It seems clear that textual criticism reached a high degree of development and there can be no doubt concerning what might be called the intellectual refinement that the Chinese historians could achieve."

㊲Ibid., p. 165:

"We today could hardly regard as truly critical a form of historiography which failed to get behind the historian to his original sources and to apply a complicated apparatus to those documents themselves.......But it is not clear that the Chinese historians found ways of checking their historiographical tradition against new primary evidence or pursued a method that would do more than make the tradition consistent with itself. Their parallels in Europe belong to the period 1450–1750. Modern Western critical apparatus, directed upon the primary materials, must have made a great change in historical writing and research in China."

㊳Herbert Butterfield, *Universal History and the Comparative Study of Civilization*, in Sir Herbert Butterfield Cho Yun Hsu & William H. Mcneill on Chinese and World History, 1971, p. 20:

"Some peoples and civilizations never acquired the longing to know about the past, and perhaps they were governed by philosophies or religions which regarded the events that happen in time as nothing more than froth or foam—all as pointless as dead leaves drifting in the wind. Some peoples seen not to have gone further than telling legends and mythical stories about the past—not longing for anything better, not realizing that anything better could be achieved. The two great exceptions are, on the one hand, the tremendous civilization of China, which produced a colossal historical literature that is of permanent value to the world, and on the other hand, what we call Western civilization, which goes back to classical Greece, and then further than that to ancient Mesopotamia and Egypt. But the Chinese civilization and that of the West were equally important, equally the leaders of the world at various times, in the development of the natural sciences. And even in ancient Greece, the study of history emerged at a time when the scientific outlook and the study of the physical universe had begun to appear. History and science are sometimes curiously connected in their development through the centuries."

㊴Ibid., p. 24:

"We are faced with two vastly important things which all of us ought to consider seriously. There is Western civilization, which has been a dynamic affair and a tremendously creative thing, evoluing peculiarly scientific methods.......But there is also the tremendous civilization of ancient China, and the West is beginning to wake great efforts to understand it, though we are conscious of knowing far too little about it."

㊵Ibid., p. 25:

"Even as an amatear I have found that by merely reading the

historical writings of ancient China, as I find them translated into Western languages, The differences between West and East just in historical ideas, and in the way of writing about history, are a revelation, and the attempt to explain and to understand the differences, to get at the genesis of them, carries one fairly deeply into the whole question of the differences between the two cultures. An old friend of mine, Joseph Needham, has spent a great part of his life studying the Chinese science of older times, and trying to see why Western science ultimately developed so differently. And just these simple problems have caused him to cut very deeply into the whole problem of Chinese culture and the Chinese mentality."

㊶Ibid., p. 26:

"We ought not to forget that somewhere in the latter half of the nineteenth century, and still more clearly in the twentieth century, the whole globe became one. Events in one region had effects at the opposite end of the world, and everything came to be interconnected. This involved not merely the spread of cultural ideas—it meant that politics, diplomacy, international relations and a large section of cultural life became global. They ought to be studied on a global scale, and from the point of view of mankind as a whole. It would be wrong even to say what we will study global history from the Western point of view or the Chinese point of view—I think it is necessary that we should strive as much as we can for a global point of view, having in mind the overall development of one single world civilization. ......We need a historical attitude to contemporary events—and in these days it means trying to rise to a global point of view."

㊷Herbert Butterfield, *Delays and Paradoxes in the Development of Historiography*, in Studies in International History, edited by K.

Bourne & D. C. Watt, 1967, pp. 4–5:

"Where there were two available authorities for a period, and these had giveen different stories, it was sometimes explicitly recommended that the object should be to produce a narrative which would comprise both and achieve a reconciliation. Only when this process failed would it be necessary to choose between the two sources. This point is the more interesting because it appears also in the Chinese historical tradition."

第三章　與西方正統史家論中國史學

人類的成見，有其形成的背景。雄據東亞數千年的中國，在歐風美雨尚未來襲之前，絕難承認有優於中國文化的文化存在，也極難想像中國史學之外復有所謂史學。一旦歐風美雨驟至，初則驚愕，繼者迷惘，終至接受或與固有者調和。所以在「全盤西化論」及「中西合璧論」出現以前，「西學源出中國論」的風靡一時，是必然的。「西學出於中國，本周秦諸子之遺。」[1]「凡諸西學之急需，皆我中邦之素習。」[2]此類學說，與「西學無提倡之必要」[3]，「何必師事夷人」[4]一類反抗西學的論調，在維護中國學術的立場上，是沒有二致的。心目中的偶像，不易破除；知識的限制，形成胸襟的狹隘。

在中國如此，在西方亦然。發源於希臘的西方文化，有其宗敎的傳統，有其科學的大原，西方人視之，浩浩乎，蕩蕩乎，擧世未有其比。其史學在其宗敎的與科學的文化背景下，發展成一門燦爛輝煌的學問，西方人尤時時以其驕傲於世人。所以中國史學在他們心目中，本來是很難佔到什麼重要地位的。他們口頭上藉快己意的輕蔑批評，想像中難以縷數；能形之於翰墨，不憚其煩的討論，雖毀多於譽，對於中國史學，已是相當尊敬與珍視了。以劍橋史學派（The Cambridge History School）爲例，白特費爾德與浦朗穆爲此派中肯用文字批評中國史學的史家，其同道則多在口頭上冷諷熱嘲⑮。所以中國史的課，不是在劍橋大學歷史系裡面開，中國史與西洋史，自劍橋史家看來，爲風馬牛不相及，開中國史的人，不屬於歷史系的一員，也不被視作史家，歷史系所開「歐洲擴張」一類的課，雖涉及中國史，但不是爲中國史講中國史，而是炫耀歐洲影響力的巨大。無怪一九五五年浦立本教授於就職演講（inaugural lecture）「中國史與世界史」（Chinese History and World History）中，要大聲疾呼，「中國不能被摒諸人類歷史的主流以外」⑯了！一九六一年英國治俄國史的史家卡耳（E. H. Carr, 1892-　）也曾感慨的說：

「在最近四百年，英語世界的歷史，不容置疑的爲一歷史的大時代，但是將它視之爲世界史的重心，而其他則皆居於附庸地位，那是對人類遠景的不幸的曲解。大學有責任矯正此類流行的曲解，本校近代史學派（the school of modern history）在我看來像是未能履行此一責任。一所主要大學裡，歷史榮譽學位候選人，除英語外，不精通任何近代語言，而仍獲准參與學位考試，且視爲當然，其爲錯誤，是不容置疑。……擁有亞洲、非洲或拉丁美洲知識的候選人，在今天已很少有機會在所謂『歐洲擴張』的論文上，一舒展其所學。所謂歐洲擴張，不幸地其名稱與其內容適相符；候選人沒有被邀請知道甚至具有重要而富史料性歷史的國家如中國或波斯的任何知識，除非歐洲人企圖將它們接管的時候。有人告訴我，本校俄國史、波斯史及中國史不是由歷史系的先生講授。五年前中文教授在就職演講中所表明的信念『中國不能摒諸人類歷史的主流以外』，劍橋史家已當作耳旁風了。」

❼

劍橋史學派的史家，對中國歷史的態度如此，其睥睨中國史學的狂態，自然可以想像。劍橋史學派如此，他可類推。所以文字上所能看到西方正統史家對中國史學的種種批評，是極為後期的。筆者勉力蒐集到的，多在一九六〇年以後，而且時間愈後，稱譽中國史學的論調愈增。人類的互相瞭解，有待經歷悠長的時間，中國史學，也極耐舉世的考驗。

就湯普森等所論，西方正統史家對中國史學所下的評論，約略如下：

1. 認為產生史學最基本的重視歷史的態度與觀念為西方文化所獨有，而中國則極度缺乏，差不多是一致的論調。「在過去，亞洲文化很少歷史的意識」，「在印度與中國的古典思潮裡，隱藏着顯著漠視歷史的態度」，「西方以外，過去的追憶，顯然是缺乏歷史性的」，「沒有任何文化，比西歐一四五〇年到一八五〇年間的文化更富歷史觀念」，「西方文化可以說是卓越的歷史文化，而與存在於印度或中國的古代歷史，幾盡不同」，「祇有源自猶太與希臘的文化，歷史受到重視，歷史成為將來的導師，歷史變作宗教的根據，歷史協助說明人類的生存與目的。」幾乎異口同聲地否定了西方或西歐以外曾有重視歷史的文化誕生。其持論如此，自然認為「惟有在西方文化中真歷史始興起成長」，「有系統的研究人類過去與現在的事件，始自希臘」，「歷史思想屬於西方的成就」，「系統的研究歷史，視歷史為一種學術，是最近的事，為歐洲與北美洲大學在十九世紀所創立。」

2. 中國史學的發展，永遠沒有突破通往真歷史的最後障礙——希望窺探往事的真相，永遠沒有發展批判史學，永遠沒有意思視歷史為客觀的瞭解。他們認為「史家日趨於窺探往事的真相，而希望自此建立有歷史根據的社會轉變的軌跡，這是一西方的發展。」「批判史學是過去兩百年西方史學的重要成就。」他們也認爲「今天很難對一種未能深入史家所用的原始資料且用複雜的設備以批評此類資料的史學，視之爲一種眞正的批判史學。」「近代西方用於原始資料的批判性的設備，一定會使中國的歷史寫作與研究，發生很大的變化。」

3. 中國的考據學沒有到達西方的境界，未能對證據作科學的評價與分析；中國歷史永遠沒有發展自我批評與發現的方法，無情的考驗通則，有目的的蒐求文獻以證明假設。在這種肯定下，他們甚至認爲中國沒有他們所謂「歷史考據」，經過窮年累月耐心的辨難，以求歷史的通則，也是屬於西方的研究歷史的方式。

4. 中國史學未能到達西方「綜合」的境界，也沒有發展歷史解釋的藝術。這是他們在看到「中國人能做龐大的分類工作，能編纂驚人的百科全書，並且能出產數不盡的瑣碎餖飣的地方史」以後所下的結論。

5. 中國有「一切確定」的觀念，相信凡屬歷史記載，皆完全客觀。「客觀事實一旦被它們列入記載，即有其獨立性，所有未來史家所必須做的，是重複既已確定的敍述，或者或許是從既已確定的敍述中去自己選取。」「任憑私意的選用文獻而即目之爲可信（取此而捨彼的原因不予以討論）。」論及史記一書，認爲是「令人百思不解之作，其大部分爲編纂，司馬遷自其所能發現之古典資料中，逐一鈔錄，略作文字上的潤色，大部分則無條件接受，傳奇與眞理混而爲一，特別是佔史記大半的列傳部分。」「此一傑作……殊非我們所謂歷史。」

6. 中國的修史制度，太官方化；中國歷史太有特徵被稱爲「資治歷史」。「歷史被視爲統治者的有效輔導，大體上歷史亦由官吏而寫，爲官吏而寫。」於是史記變成了「官吏的手册」，「爲一道德的敍事，勝過爲一歷史的敍事。」「中國豐富的史籍，像是備官僚偶然的參考，而不是較廣大群衆的普通讀物。」

7. 中國史學精細，中國史學重視文獻，中國歷史資料浩繁。「中國以朝代與朝代相接，而積有大量歷史檔案，其浩繁與西歐的歷史資料相埒，且所涉及時間之長過之。」「巨大的中國文化，產生了可觀的歷史文獻，對世界有其永恒價值。」「古代的中國，科學工藝甚發達，歷史著作極豐富。」像湯普森那樣，不清楚中國有所謂史書與史料者，在今天已少有其人。

8. 中國史學與歐洲一四五〇年至一七五〇年間史學，蓋在伯仲之間。 這是西方史家最大的一個結論，他們承認中國史學超過了西方的中世紀，但並不承認能與十八世紀末期以後的西方史學並駕齊驅。屢談中國史學的白特費爾德持論如此，竭力想窺中國史學之秘的浦朗穆，也以此作其最大的信念。

從上面看起來，西方正統史家對中國史學雖有稱譽的地方，基本上則是毀多於譽的。很明顯的他們不承認中國史學能與西方史學分庭抗禮，超過了中世紀，徘徊於歐洲一四五〇年至一七五〇年之間，但是西方史學的偉大時代——近兩百年，則未能企及。他們所肯定的中國史學的缺陷，促使中國史學落於西方史學之後。相信凡屬歷史記載，皆完全客觀，不希望窺探往事的眞相，不採取批判的態度，復缺乏重視歷史的觀念，中國史學怎能比美西方史學？綜合的境界不高，歷史解釋的藝術沒有發展，修史又是官方事業，中國雖歷史資料浩繁，歷史著作豐富，其史學又豈能望及西方史學的項背？他們肯說「中國史學與歐洲一四五〇年至一七五〇年間史學，蓋在伯仲之間」，已是一種過分的恭維了！

西方正統史家對中國史學的批評，不是沒有中肯處，但是厚誣、誤解過多，有不能已於言者，今願與西方正統史家一討論之：

第一節　中國文化中富有產生史學最基本的重視歷史的態度與觀念

歷史觀念 (historical-mindedness) 的興起，也就是人類對過去發生興趣，而開始記錄往事，是史學出現的最重要的條件之一。西方正統史家肯定了西方文化最富歷史觀念，而其他文化則否，是特殊化了西方文化。早在十八世紀，德國哲學家赫德 (Herder, 1744-1803) 卽曾云：

> 「只有歐洲，人類的生活是眞正歷史的。中國、印度或美國土著，都沒有眞正的歷史進化，僅是一些靜的無變化的文化，或是一連串由舊生活方式到新生活方式的新陳代謝，裡面沒有規律的累積的發展，而規律的累積的發展，正是歷史進化的特性。因此歐洲是人類生活得天獨厚的地區。」❽

赫德的進化觀念，將歐洲特殊化了，歐洲的大變動，裡面有規律的累積的發展，是眞正的歷史進化，因之歐洲人類的生活，是眞正歷史的生活。中國、印度等地區是靜態的，沒有規律的累積的發展，因之沒有眞正的歷史進化，其人類的生活，自非眞正歷史的生活。赫德以後的西方學者，說到中國爲非歷史的 (unhistorical)，卽以中國數千年無變化爲理論根據。赫格爾 (Hegel, 1770-1831) 認爲中國是一個「沒有歷史的國家」(state with no history)，卽基於中國的靜止不變。❾迄今「不變的中國」(unchanging China)、「不變的亞洲」(unchanging Asia) 之說，在西方仍然極普遍流行。

中國旣數千年不變，中國自缺乏歷史觀念。所以西方正統史家很肯定地認爲西方文化以富有歷史觀念而卓然與世不同。在西方這幾乎成了不爭之論。「西方人永遠富有歷史觀念，此一特徵，在過去兩世紀更格外顯著。」⑩「不像其他文化，我們的文化經常極端注視其過去。……我們的初祖希臘人與羅馬人，是屬於寫歷史的民族(history-writing peoples)。基督敎是一史家的宗敎。」⑪「我們『正進入世界史的時代』。西方文化現已擴及整個世界；科學的方法或歷史的專業研究（the professional study of history)，已非復歐洲與美洲的學術專科（intellectual monopolies)。惟歷史意識（historical conscionsness）仍顯然是『西方的』。」⑫「西方社會經常富有歷史觀念，擁有可觀的以往文獻，其性質與數量與任何其他已知文化所存留者不同。所以如此的原始力量，來自希臘的天才。其次的因素，是基督敎的影響，基督敎始終是寓有歷史意識的，不同於佛敎與婆羅門敎，或任何其他東方的宗敎，不管是古代的或近代的。最後，在過去兩個世紀中，近代科學的進步與物質的發展，深深影響了西方世界的思想。」⑬種種類似的論調，不勝枚擧。配合「西人在十九世紀，已富有歷史觀念，適如其在十七世紀已富有科學觀念一樣；」「在過去三、四世紀，我們的文化最重要的發展，不僅為科學方法的應用，同時為歷史意識的增長」；「祇有源自猶太與希臘的文化，歷史受到重視」；「西方文化從猶太基督敎繼承了一種特別强烈的歷史意識」；「沒有任何文化比西歐一四五〇年到一八五〇年間的文化更富歷史觀念」等已引述的論調，我們可以歸納出西方正統史家從西方的科學、基督敎及其初祖希臘人羅馬人三方面，推衍出西方文化在世界文化中最富歷史觀念，尤其是近幾世紀。中國文化以及其他任何文化，缺乏上述三者，自然無法產生所謂歷史觀念。西方正統史家的武斷結論，蓋有其似是而非的根據。(白特費爾德論調的前後不同，容於後文討論。)

西方文化富有歷史觀念，固然不待爭辨，但是說它是世界唯一最富歷史觀念的文化，却非公允之說。中國文化數千年來歷史觀念之深，較之西方，有過之而無不及，西方正統史家認爲中國文化不富歷史觀念，是一種誤解，是囿於先入爲主的成見。

誤解自認爲中國數千年不變始。以中國與西方比較，中國不曾發生過類似英國的工業革命，法國式的大革命，中國歷史不曾有過幾個希臘羅馬、中世紀、近代等明顯段落，所以西方史家認爲中國歷史是靜止的，數千年來不曾變化。看慣波瀾狀濶的西方歷史，自易有此錯覺與誤解。殊不知數千年來，中國歷史無時無刻不在變，由三代的封建制度到秦漢以後的郡縣制度是變；由魏晉南北朝的門第政治到隋唐以後的文人政治是變；由外族的屢次入侵而形成民族的大融合締造簇新的大帝國更是變。中國富「中庸」思想，中國歷史上的變是漸變，比較柔和，不若西方之變，暴烈急驟，這正是眞正的歷史之變，祇是西方正統史家不能瞭解罷了。世界第二次大戰以後，歐洲進入靜止狀態，而不變的中國，不變的亞洲，正遭逢多事之秋，這又該作何解釋？

中國歷史上的變，凡知中國歷史者，皆能言之；中國文化富有歷史觀念，凡稍通中國史學者，亦能剖析而明辨之：

宋元之際，中國史學上有一個極重要的「國可滅，史不可滅」的觀念出現，這是極濃厚的歷史觀念。在宋德祐二年（一二七六）宋都臨安陷落的時候，元將董文炳在臨安主留事曾說：「國可滅，史不可沒。宋十六主，有天下三百餘年，其太史所記，具在史館，宜悉收以備典禮。」於是得宋史及諸注記五千餘册，歸之國史院。⑭首先建議修金史的劉秉忠則云：「國滅史存，古之常道。宜撰金史，令一代君臣事業，不墜於後世。」⑮這是在元中統元年（一二六〇）以前數年提出。元至元元年（一二六四），王鶚請修遼金二史，其言曰：「自古有可亡之國，無可亡之史。蓋前代史册，必代興者與修，是非與奪，待後人而後公故也。」其後至正四年（一三四四）阿魯圖進金史表云：「竊惟漢高帝入關，任蕭何而收秦籍，唐太宗卽祚，命魏徵以作隋書。蓋歷數歸眞主之朝，而簡編載前代之事，國可滅，史不可滅，善吾師，惡亦吾師。矧夫典故之源流，章程之沿革，弗披往牒，曷蓄前聞！」⑯ 自宋末至元修宋遼金三史，所能見到有關「國可滅，史不可滅」觀念的文字記錄，大致如此。值得注意的是元的一位將軍竟有這種觀念而保存了宋史及諸注記五千餘册，足證這已是宋末極普遍的一種觀念，爲存往事而打破了國界！首先建議修金史的劉秉忠是元世祖時代博學多識的一位諫臣；王鶚則爲元世祖所禮遇的金遺民，其所謂「自古有可亡之國，無可亡之史」，已有了存故國歷史的意味。執筆起草進金史表的歐陽玄（阿魯圖是名義上的），幼年曾從宋故老習爲詞章，經史百家，靡不研究⑰，他强調「歷數歸眞主之朝，而簡編載前代之事，國可滅，史不可滅」，也多少代表了一些宋遺民的意見。如以另外一位金史家元好問來看，國亡後矢志存故國之史，當時已頗不乏人，金史元好問傳云：「金亡不仕……晚年以著作自任，以金源氏有天下，典章法度幾及漢唐，國亡史作，己所當任。時金國實錄在順天張萬戶家，乃言於張，願爲撰述，旣而爲樂夔所沮而止。好問曰：『不可令一代之跡，泯而不傳。』乃構亭於家，著述其上，因名曰野史，凡金源君臣遺言往行，采摭所聞，有所得輒以寸紙細字爲記錄，至百餘萬言。」自此大致可以看出當時爲故國而存史的觀念，已漸流行。

元亡明興，明太祖於洪武二年（一三六九）謂廷臣曰：「近克元都，得元十三朝實錄，元雖亡國，事當記載。況史紀成敗，示勸懲，不可廢也。」於是詔修元史，以李善長爲監修，以宋濂、王禕爲總裁，並徵山林遺逸之士汪克寬、胡翰、宋禧、陶凱、陳基、趙壎、曾魯、高啓、趙汸、張文海、徐尊生、黃箎、傅恕、王錡、傅著、謝徵十六人同爲纂修，開局於天界寺，取元經世大典諸書，以資參考。諸儒至時，明太祖諭之曰:「自古有天下國家者, 行事見於當時, 是非公於後世, 故一代之興衰, 必有一代之史以載之。元主中國, 殆將百年, 其初君臣朴厚, 政事簡略, 與民休息, 時號小康。然昧於先王之道, 酣溺胡虜之俗, 制度疏闊, 禮樂無聞。至其季世, 嗣君荒淫, 權臣跋扈, 兵戈四起, 民命顚危, 雖間有賢智之臣, 言不見用, 用不見信, 天下遂至土崩。然其間君臣行事, 有善有否, 賢人君子, 或隱或顯, 其言行亦多可稱者。今命爾等修纂, 以備一代之史, 務直述其事, 毋溢美, 毋隱惡, 庶合公論, 以垂鑒戒。」⑱這是中國史學上極值得注意的一件大事, 存勝國之史, 而又大量徵勝國遺民參與修史, 且自在上者發動。從此延聘前朝遺民修前朝史的新傳統形成, 這是極富歷史觀念的新傳統。

清以異族入主中國, 繼承了延聘前朝遺民修前朝史的傳統。康熙十八年 (一六七九), 詔修明史, 當時最熟悉明史的明遺民萬斯同被請至京師, 萬氏爲盡遺民之節, 係以布衣參史局, 從康熙十八年到康熙四十一年, 二十餘年的悠長時間, 不署銜, 不受俸, 與人往來, 其自署惟曰布衣萬斯同, 這是純爲故國而存史的,「塗山二百九十三年之得失, 竟無成書, 其君相之經營創建, 與有司之所奉行, 學士大夫之風尙源流, 今日失考, 後來者何所據乎? 昔吾先世, 四代死王事, 今此非王事乎? 祖不難以身殉, 爲其曾玄, 乃不能盡心網羅, 以備殘略, 死尙可以見吾先人地下乎? 故自己未以來, 迄今二十年間, 隱忍史局, 棄妻子兄弟不顧, 誠欲有所冀也。」㉙萬氏自己將隱忍史局的隱情, 完全吐露出來了。不肯赴明史館的明遺民黃宗羲, 更屢屢强調「國可滅, 史不可滅」的觀念㉚, 他與明史館總裁葉方藹、徐元文屢通款曲, 不能解釋爲向淸廷獻媚, 而實是他想藉着這種關係, 保存有明三百年的歷史, 所以史局大案, 往往咨正於他, 歷志出吳任臣之手, 總裁千里遺書, 迄黃氏審正而後定; 嘗論宋史別立道學傳, 爲元儒之陋, 明史不當仿其例, 於是明史不立道學傳；明史的儒林傳，也多本於其明儒學案。清廷也下詔浙中督撫，凡黃氏素所論著及所見聞，有資明史者，鈔錄來京，宣付史館。黃氏以亡國之民，感嘆潮息湮沉之不暇，而其記述得登於明史，這不但是黃氏之幸，也是歷史之幸了。

自清初以後，「國可滅，史不可滅」的觀念，由於民族思想的配合，甚爲流行。迄於晚近，世界大通，滅人之國先滅其史的觀念又起，這是極不幸的發展，但這已超出中國史學的傳統了。㉑

從上面看起來，中國史學上「國可滅，史不可滅」的觀念，是極濃厚的歷史觀念。爲存往事，消滅了敵國，却不消滅敵國的歷史，元修宋遼金史，明修元史，清修明史，皆不因異族國家而兼滅其史。勝國遺民的矢志爲故國存史，新朝的延聘舊朝遺民修史，尤其富有歷史的意味。而且在修史原則上，是務求「直述其事，毋溢美，毋隱惡」，一種永遠不能變的修史原則，被奉爲圭臬，這豈不是歷史觀念的最高表現？

宋以前，雖然由於國家民族意識的淡薄，「國可滅，史不可滅」的觀念，沒有形成，但是存史的觀念，却早已發達。如唐設史館，修前代史，即主要出於存史的觀念。首先建議唐高祖修前代史的令狐德棻，其所持的理由是：「竊見近代已來，多無正史，梁陳及齊，猶有文籍，至周隋遭大業離亂，多有遺闕。當今耳目猶接，尚有可憑，如更十數年後，恐事跡湮沒。陛下旣受禪於隋，復承周氏歷數，國家二祖功業，並在周時，如文史不存，何以貽鑑今古？如臣愚見，並請修之。」㉒爲了存即將湮沒的往事，爲了繼承前朝的正統，爲了垂鑑當代及將來，所以議修前代史。唐高祖所下的修書詔，理由也極類似：「司典序言，史官記事，考論得失，究盡變通，所以裁成義類，懲惡勸善，多識前古，貽鑑將來，伏犧以降，周秦斯及，兩漢傳緒，三國受命，迄于晉宋，載籍備焉。自有魏南徙，乘機撫運，周隋禪代，歷世相仿，梁氏稱邦，跨據淮海，齊遷龜鼎，陳建皇宗，莫不自命正朔，綿歷歲祀，各殊徽號，刪定禮儀。至於發跡開基，受終告代，嘉謀善政，名臣奇士，立言著績，無乏於時。然而簡牘未編，紀傳咸闕，炎涼已積，謠俗遷訛，餘烈遺風，倏焉將墜！朕握圖馭宇，長世字人，方立典謨，永垂憲則，顧彼湮落，用深軫悼，有懷撰次，實資良直。中書令蕭瑀給事中王敬業著作郎殷聞禮可修魏史，侍中陳叔達秘書丞令狐德棻太史令庾儉可修周史，兼中書令封德彝中書舍人顏師古可修隋史，大理卿崔善爲中書舍人孔紹安太子洗馬蕭德言可修梁史，太子詹事裴矩兼吏部郎中祖孝孫前秘書丞魏徵可修齊史，秘書監竇璡給事中歐陽詢秦王文學姚思廉可修陳史，務加詳覈，博採舊聞，義在不刊，書法無隱。」㉓很清楚的表示了爲存往事，爲繼正統，爲垂鑑戒而修前代史，而且務要詳覈博採，書法無隱。唐太宗貞觀二十六年（六四六）的修晉書詔，更强調了存往事的重要：「自沮誦攝官之後，伯陽載筆之前，代列史臣，皆有刪著。仲尼修而採檮杌，倚相誦而闡丘墳；降自西京，班馬騰其茂實；逮於東漢，范謝振其芳聲；蕞爾當塗，陳壽覈其國志；眇哉劉宋，沈約裁其帝籍；至梁陳高氏，朕命勒成；惟周及隋，亦同甄錄。莫不彰善癉惡，激一代之清芬，褒古懲凶，備百王之令典。」㉔以往各代，莫不有史，所以唐於修成梁、陳、北齊、北周、隋五代之史以後，進一步要修不令人滿意的晉代歷史。前人所修的晉史，「雖存記注，而才非良史，事虧實錄」㉕，致使「典午清高，韜遺芳於簡册，金行曩志，闕繼美於驪騵」㉖。於是唐再加修撰，這是爲存往事而修史，史學上的一個極高境界。從此後朝修前朝史的史學制度，也姍姍出現了。

唐以前分崩離析近四百年的魏晉南北朝時代，寫史的風氣極盛。隋書經籍志著錄這一時期的史學著作在萬卷以上，自然這些著作絕大部分已經不見了，存下來而被列入正史的，如陳壽的三國志，范曄的後漢書，沈約的宋書，都有其代表性。陳壽寫三國志，「辭多勸誡，明乎得失」㉗，其目的固在垂鑑戒。范曄刪衆家後漢書爲一家之作，已多少有了綿延往史的意味，「詳觀古今著述及評論，殆少可意者」㉘，於是他便慨然操筆削之任了，而且「諸細意甚多」㉙，其所謂諸細意，大體不外所謂「貴德義，抑勢利，進處士，黜姦雄，論儒學則深美康成，褒黨錮則推崇李杜，宰相無多述，而特表逸民，公卿不見采，而特尊獨行」㉚，這又是史家垂鑑戒的微意了。沈約於齊永明五年奉敕撰宋書，次年二月告成，不及一年，一百卷的大著完成，其成書之快，由於大半根據徐爰舊作而成，議者每病其草率，但是他在上宋書表中，已大致說明前人撰述宋書的經過，他不過踵其成㉛，這是繼前人而存往事。他又「常以晉氏一代竟無全書，年二十許便有撰述之意」㉜，所撰晉書一百二十卷，雖已亡失，但足以說明他富有極濃厚的存往事的觀念。爲存往事而遭慘誅的，崔浩則是最顯著的例子，他以史官而撰國書（崔浩時代的當代史），直書不諱，又立石銘，載國書，以彰直筆，石銘顯在衢路，往來行人，咸以爲言，史禍遂起㉝，爲存眞往事而不顧一切，這是何等崇高的歷史觀念！

秦漢以上，存往事、垂鑑戒的觀念，也已出現了。中國自上古以來設立的史官，其主要的職務爲記事，其記事遵守共同必守之法，「君擧必書」，「書法不隱」㉞。幾部代表性的史學著作，如春秋、史記、漢書，爲存往事，兼爲垂鑑戒。「春秋之稱，微而顯，志而晦，婉而成章，志而不汙，懲惡而勸善」㉟，春秋所以垂鑑戒，是極爲明顯的。但是「周室既微，載籍殘缺，仲尼思存前聖之業，乃稱曰：『夏禮吾能言之，杞不足徵也。殷禮吾能言之，宋不足徵也。文獻不足故也。足則吾能徵之矣。』以魯周公之國，禮文備物，史官有法，故與左丘明觀其史記，據行事，仍人道，因興以立功，敗以成罰，假日月以定歷數，藉朝聘以正禮樂。」㊱孔子爲存往事而作春秋，也昭昭然不可誣。司馬遷作史記，爲垂鑑戒，更爲存往事。其父司馬談臨終時所言：「自獲麟以來四百有餘歲，而諸侯相兼，史記放絕。今漢興，海內一統，明主賢君忠臣死義之士，余爲太史而弗論載，廢天下之史文，余甚懼焉！」㊲很清楚的寓有濃厚的存往事的意味。司馬遷繼其父志，網羅天下放失舊聞，寫成了一部一百三十卷的史記，主要是爲存往事。班固著漢書，同樣存往事的意味甚濃，「漢紹堯運，以建帝業，至於六世，史臣乃追述功德，私作本紀，編於百王之末，厠於秦項之列。太初以後，闕而不錄。故探纂前記，綴輯所聞，以述漢書。」班氏在敍傳裡面，說的十分清楚。存往事的觀念極早出現，是中國史學最可以向全世界驕傲的地方。爲存往事，中國的古史官有時棄國出奔，「夏太史令終古出其圖法，執而泣之，夏桀迷惑，暴亂愈甚，太史令終古乃出奔如商」㊳；「殷內史向摯見紂之愈亂迷惑也，於是載其圖法，出亡之周」㊴；「晉太史屠黍見晉之亂也，見晉公之驕而無德義也，以其圖法歸周」㊵。這似乎又是後世「國可滅，史不可滅」的遠源了。

中國從遠古時代起，最晚從春秋時代起，既已有了極濃厚的存往事的觀念，這種觀念，不容置疑的卽西方史家所盛稱的歷史觀念，史學所以產生的本原。若細察西方古代的歷史觀念，似遠落於中國之後。根據西方史家的解釋，西方歷史之父希臘大史家希羅多德（Herodotus, c. 484–c. 425 B. C.）實際上沒有繼承人，雖然修西蒂笛斯（Thucydides, 471?–400 B. C.）繼其統，但是修西蒂笛斯之後便成絕響了。希臘古典學者很少關心將來與過去，修西蒂笛斯認爲歷史事件以前與以後發生些什麼都無意義。當時希臘思想界且有一反歷史的趨勢（anti-historical tendency），天才的希羅多德戰勝了那一趨勢，但他死之後，不變與永恆知識的尋求，逐漸窒息了歷史意識（the historical consciousness）。

㊶如此言之，西方的古希臘時代，是遠不如中國古代富有歷史觀念了。所以西方所持以驕傲的西方史學搖籃的希臘，實際上沒有多少歷史觀念，以中國人與希臘人（包括上羅馬人）比較，希臘人也算不上是屬於寫歷史的民族，因此西方正統史家主要認爲近兩世紀或近五、六世紀（一四五〇年以後）是西方最富歷史觀念的世紀，同時認爲西方「很多早期的編年史，並非源於恢復既往的動機」，「刺激歷史記錄的在最初不是對過去發生興趣，不是所謂歷史的興趣」，西方「最早留下的大量歷史文獻，不是對過去有興趣的人們的作品——他們僅渴望其事業功勳永垂後世，這種情勢最低限度維持了千年之久」㊷。如果他們清楚中國古代的史官與史家爲存往事而表現的興趣與精神，當知研究「歷史思想的興起」，研究人類「對過去意識的發展」，應從中國古代的史官與史家身上去尋求了。

如此看起來，中國不一定比近兩百年的西方更富歷史觀念，而整個言之，中國歷史觀念之深，及其發源之早，綿延之久，西方世界，似不能望其項背。

中國文化中既富有重視歷史的觀念，其重視歷史的態度，自然極爲明顯。今僅從中國史官地位的尊貴及中國極端重視歷史教育兩方面說起：

中國史官設立的時代極早，黃帝時代，倉頡沮誦，實居史官之職。㊷三代以降，史官設置益多，迄於清末，中國沒有一代不設史官。這是世界其他國家其他民族所沒有的。史官職務，愈古愈繁，近乎卜祝之間，掌理天人之間各種事務。繼則職權縮小，以記事爲主。史官地位，極爲尊貴。古代主天官者皆上公，漢武帝時置太史公，位在丞相上，天下計書，先上太史公，副上丞相。直至清代，國史館的纂修官，一定由翰林院的編修兼任，翰林院是極清貴的地方，人才也極精華之選，平常人稱翰林爲太史，則清代史官地位的尊重亦可知㊸。史官地位旣如此尊貴，則中國重視歷史的態度，可見一斑。所以當史官爲直書而表現出大無畏的精神時，誠如梁啓超所說:「不怕你奸臣炙手可熱，他單要捋虎鬚！」㊹史官從尊貴的地位，表現出高貴的精神。這「自然是國家法律尊重史官獨立，或社會意識維持史官尊嚴，所以好的政治家不願侵犯，壞的政治家不敢侵犯，侵犯也侵犯不了！」㊺「這種好制度不知從何時起，但從春秋以後，一般人暗中都很尊重這無形的法律」㊻，這又怎能說在中國文化中，隱藏顯著漠視歷史的態度呢？尊史官卽所以尊歷史，這是不待辨而可知的。

中國的重視歷史敎育，是世界任何其他國家所難以比擬的。西方一直到近代，才將歷史當成一門嚴肅的敎育科目。中國則自上古以來，歷史始終居於敎育科目的中心，「古之儒者，博學乎六藝之文。六藝者，王敎之典籍。」㊼中國古代的敎本，是所謂詩書易禮樂春秋的六藝。孔子開放平民敎育，卽以六藝敎人。晚年，刪詩書，定禮樂，演周易，據魯史作春秋，後世因尊孔子所刪定的六藝爲「經」，六藝於是亦稱六經。孔子刪定六經，目的在敎萬世，六經直可視爲孔子所寫的萬世敎科書。自漢以後，經學地位崇高，經學敎育是敎育的主流，士子入學，無不自讀經開始（民國以後例外）。但是揆以「六經皆史」之說，讀經無異讀史。六經中的尙書、春秋，是標準的史書，易、詩、禮、樂都有史料的意味在其中。數千年來，士子寖饋於六經，無異寖饋於歷史。那麼中國的經學敎育，實際上就是歷史敎育。

自然，自漢以後，經以外的史籍，紛紛出現，其納入歷史課程而定爲敎本者，自極有限。劉宋文帝元嘉中（西元四二四至四五〇年間），儒玄史文四學並建，明帝泰始六年（四七〇），又分爲玄儒文史四科，科置學士各十人，南齊沿之，此類史實，則說明了南北朝時代重視歷史敎育的概況。唐以後，中國盛行考試制度（卽科擧制度），考試科目，經與詩文以外，歷史佔很重要的份量。按新唐書選擧志，唐代鄉貢科目，有一史，有三史，而盛行的明經之中有史科；凡史科，每史問大義百條，策三道，能通一史者，自身視五經三傳，有出身及前資官，視學究一經，三史皆通者，獎擢之。按唐代的一史，係指史記，三史係指史記、前後漢書及三國志。到了宋代，仍設三史科，紹興二年（一一三二），詔擧賢良方正能直言極諫科，凡應詔者，先具所著策論五十篇，繳進兩省侍從參考之，分爲三等，次優以上，召赴祕閣，試論六首，於九經、十七史、七書國語荀揚管子文中子內出題。㊽是宋代政府除獎勵讀史記、前後漢書及三國志以外，復擴大範圍至十七史。宋以後，科擧考試，必考策論，考策論是考應試者的歷史程度，於是寫史論文章的風氣盛行，寒窗十年，差不多都可以寫「留侯論」「賈誼論」「項籍論」一類的文章，十七史以及通鑑自然變成閱讀的對象了，明以後鋼鑑、通鑑輯覽一類簡單的歷史敎本出現，也就不足爲奇了。

總之，中國數千年來極端重視歷史敎育，不容置疑。既重視歷史敎育，則在中國文化中，又豈會有漠視歷史的態度存在？

中國自上古時代起，史官地位尊貴，歷史敎育受到重視，存往事的觀念，「國可滅，史不可滅」的觀念，又綿延發展，那麼中國文化從上古時代起，卽富有重視歷史的態度與觀念，昭昭然不可誣。時間愈演進，態度愈嚴肅，觀念愈深刻。擧目世界，未有其他任何文化，能幾於此！

第二節　中國官修正史是一極優良的史學傳統

中國文化中既富有重視歷史的態度與觀念，種種保存歷史的史學制度，自應運而興，官修正史制度，即其中之一。

中西史學最大的不同，在於中國有歷久不衰的官修正史制度，這是中國史學的最大特色，也是極優良的史學傳統。史學工作，艱鉅浩大，舉一代數十年或數百年之史，以一人之力而任之，難期周密詳審。集全國精英，通力合作，國家且以全力獎勵之，資助之，自易產生比較理想的歷史。中國自唐迄清，代設史館，修前代史，唐修晉、梁、陳、北齊、北周、隋六代之史，宋修唐史，元修宋、遼、金三史，明修元史，清修明史，修史演變爲國營企業，蔚爲制度化，環顧世界各國，未有有國家如此重視史學者。這是中國可向全世界驕傲之處。

西方世界從無類此的史學傳統，所以西方正統史家不瞭解中國官修正史的優點所在，他們祇認爲那是一種官方事業，組織太官僚化，太官僚化的東西，一定有其副作用，於是歷史在中國，被視爲統治階級的有效輔導（所謂資治），歷史由官吏而寫，亦爲官吏而寫。實際上這是一種誤解，這是一種推理的錯誤。細究中國官修正史的眞相，即可知其大謬不然。

中國史館所蒐集的材料，極爲廣泛，不僅限於政治性的材料，也不僅限於官方材料，前代由官方修撰的日曆、起居注、時政記、實錄、國史，自在蒐集之列，即諸家傳記小說以至私人文集，皆普遍網羅之；中央方面的材料，政治方面的材料蒐集之，地方方面的材料，社會、經濟方面的材料，也儘量冥搜博羅。由清修明史，可以證明。清順治五年（一六四八），諭將天啓、崇禎年間有關檔案抄送史館；順治八年（一六五一），又懸賞徵求天啓、崇禎實錄抄本及邸報；順治十二年（一八五五），康熙四年（一六六五），皆曾下諭徵求邸報及野史。湯斌等亦屢有請徵求遺書的建議㊾。徵求遺書，徵求野史，足可見史館對材料積極蒐集的程度了。

史館修史所根據的材料，自然主要是實錄及國史。實錄、國史是由另一類的史館所修撰。唐代以後，史館分爲兩種，一種修前代史，屬於臨時性質，其書修成，其職卽罷，太宗、高宗年間，所修晉、梁、陳、齊、周、隋各朝史的史館，卽屬此類，也就是我們所稱官修正史的史館。另一種爲國史館，所修爲實錄及國史，其性質較前一類爲永久，有史官專任執筆撰寫，有時史官外任，仍以修史自隨。國史館修實錄、國史，不但根據日曆、起居注、時政記，也廣泛應用各方面的材料。由唐史館所收材料，可以作最好說明。唐會要卷六十三載諸司應送史館事例：

「祥瑞：禮部每季錄送；天文祥異：太史每季並所占候祥驗回報；蕃國朝貢：每使至，鴻臚勘問土地風俗，衣服貢獻，道里遠近，並其主名字報；蕃夷入寇來降：表狀，中書錄狀報，露布，兵部錄報，軍還日，軍將具錄陷破城堡，傷殺吏人，掠擄蓄產，並報；變改音律及新造曲調：太常寺具所由及樂詞報；州縣廢置及孝義旌表：戶部有卽報；法令變改，斷獄新議：刑部有卽報；有年及饑，並水旱蟲霜風雹，及地震流水泛濫：戶部及州縣，每有卽勘其年月日，及賑貸存恤同報；諸色封建：司府勘報，襲封者不在報限；京諸司長官，及刺史都督護，行軍大總管、副總管除授：並錄制詞，文官吏部送，武官兵部送；刺史縣令善政異跡：有灼然者，本州錄附考使送；碩學異能，高人逸士，義夫節婦：州縣有此色，不限官品，勘知的實，每年錄附考使送；京都司長官薨卒：本司責由歷狀跡送；刺史都督都護，及行軍副大總管以下薨：本州本軍責由歷狀，附便使送；公主百官定諡：考績錄行狀諡議同送；諸王來朝：宗正寺勘報。以上事，並依本條所由，有卽勘報史官，修入國史。」

據此則唐代史館所蒐集的材料，極爲普遍，連變改音律、新造曲調以及地方上碩學異能、高人逸士、義夫節婦的言行都一一網羅了。此蓋仿漢代天下計書先上太史的傳統，將四方所有的史料，皆集中於史館，史館據之以修屬於當代史的實錄國史。如此修成的實錄國史，自是一國的全史，無遺錙銖之細。後一代據之以修正史，自易博大，而不僅限於朝廷史及政治史了。

實錄國史主要根據的材料，是日曆、起居注、時政記。日曆的撰寫，明人徐一夔言之極詳：

「近世論史者，莫過於日曆。日曆者，史之根柢也。自唐長壽中，史官姚璹請撰時政記，元和中韋執誼又奏撰日曆。日曆以事繫日，以日繫月，以月繫時，以時繫年，猶有春秋遺意。至於起居注之說，亦專以甲子起例，蓋記事之法無踰此也。往宋極重史事，日曆之修，諸司必關日，如詔誥則三省必書，兵機邊務則樞司必報，百官之進退，刑賞之予奪，臺諫之論列，給舍之繳駁，經筵之論答，臣僚之轉對，侍從之直前啓事，中外之囊封匭奏，下至錢穀甲兵，獄訟造作，凡有關政體者，無不隨日以錄。猶患其出於吏牘，或有訛失，故歐陽修奏請宰相監修者，於歲終檢點修撰官日所錄事，有失職者罰之。如此則日曆不至訛失，他時會要之修取於此，實錄之修取於此，百年之後紀志列傳取於此，此宋氏之史所以爲精確也。」(50)

起居注當濫觴於漢代，漢書藝文志著錄漢著記百九十卷，顏師古注曰，若今之起居注。現著錄於隋書經籍志者，以漢獻帝起居注五卷爲最早，其後晉、宋、齊、梁、陳、魏、周、隋各代起居注，共五十三種。起居注與實錄不同，起居注撰於當時，而實錄則修於稍後，史通言起居注記載之法極詳：

「起居注者，論次甲子之書，至於策命、章奏、封拜、薨免，莫不隨事記錄，言惟詳審。凡欲撰帝紀者，皆因之以成功，即今爲載筆之別曹，立言之貳職。」㊶

唐有起居郞及起居舍人專司其事：

「每天子臨軒，侍立於玉階之下，郞居其左，舍人居其右；人主有命，則逼階延首而聽之，退而編錄，以爲起居注。」㊷

武后長壽之後，更有時政記，專由宰相撰錄，以記載退朝後所論國事，按月彙送史館。此頗類近代政界要人的回憶錄，而即時回憶，即時記載，自然較能存眞。

隋志以下所著錄的起居注，唐宋宰相所寫的時政記，宋著作郞所撰的日曆，皆有中國古代史官記注的遺意。中國史官設置之早及其職責，已如前述，中國史官所保持的優美傳統，則非西方史家所能想像與瞭解。中國的史官，不是爲政治而歷史的，而是爲歷史而歷史的。爲存信史，往往冒生命的危險，政治勢力不能左右他，他超然於政治之上，而負有神聖的使命。如果說他頗像西方歷史的女神克麗歐（Clio），倒不是完全荒誕不經的。左傳上有兩段記載：

宣公二年，趙穿攻靈公於桃園，太史書曰：「趙盾弑其君。」以示於朝。宣子曰：「不然。」對曰：「子爲正卿，亡不越竟，反不討賊，非子而誰？」宣子曰：「嗚呼！我之懷矣，自詒伊慼，其我之謂矣！」孔子曰：「董狐古之良史也，書法不隱。」

襄公二十五年，太史書曰：「崔杼弑其君」。崔子殺之，其弟嗣書，而死者二人。其弟又書，乃舍之。南史氏聞太史盡死，執簡以往，聞旣書矣，乃還。

這是何等直書的精神！中國歷代史官，在原則上都能保持直書的傳統。唐代天子不觀起居注的不成文規定，便是爲了保障史官的直書而無形中制定的。天子如欲觀起居注，史官每嚴辭拒絕，不假以顏色。新唐書上有幾段記載：

> 唐太宗嘗欲觀起居注，朱子奢曰：「以此開後世史官之禍，可懼也。史官全身畏死，則悠悠千載，尙有聞乎？」[53]
>
> 唐文宗嘗與宰相議事，適見鄭朗執筆螭頭[54]下，謂曰：「向所論事，亦記之乎？朕將觀之。」朗曰：「臣執筆所書者，史也。故事天子不觀史。昔太宗欲觀之，朱子奢曰：史不隱善，不諱惡。自中主而下，或飾非護失，見之則史官無以自免，且不敢直筆。褚遂良亦稱史記天子言動，雖非法必書，庶幾自飾。」文宗曰：「朗……可謂善守職者。……朕恐平日之言不協治體，爲將來之羞，庶一見得以自改。」朗遂上之。[55]
>
> 後文宗又欲觀魏謩起居注，謩曰：「古置左右史，書得失，以存鑒戒。陛下所爲善，無畏不書。不善，天下之人亦有以記之。」文宗曰：「不然，我旣嘗觀之。」謩曰：「向者取觀，史氏爲失職。陛下一見，則後來所書，必有諱屈，善惡不實，不可以爲史，且後代何信哉？」乃止。[56]

鄭朗將起居注上之天子，是一位失職的史官，但是他也知道史不隱善諱惡以及天子不觀起居注的傳統；一再想看起居注的唐文宗，也推許最初不想上呈起居注的鄭朗能善守其職，這可以充分表現出中國史官的神聖任務及中國史官設置的眞正精神了。

一直到明淸之際，中國史官能維持直書的傳統於不墜。如聲名狼籍的錢謙益，其人自不足取，其阿附閹黨與淸兵下江南親自迎降，皆爲略具羞恥之心者所不忍爲。但是中國史官的直書精神，最能從他身上反映出來。他一生以史官自居，「謙益史官也，有紀志之責。」[57]於所作王圖行狀云：「謙益舊待罪太史氏，竊取書法不隱之義，作爲行狀，其或敢阿私所好，文致出入，曲筆以欺天下後世，不有人禍，必有天刑。」[58]於所作路振飛神道碑云：「謙益以石渠舊老，衰殘載筆，其何敢辟時畏禍，媕婀噥胡，以貽羞於信史？」[59]於所作劉一爆墓誌銘云：「謙益萬曆舊史官也，定陵復土，奔喪入朝，移宮甫定，國論廷辨，歷歷在聽覩中。洊歷坊局，與聞國故，與群小水火薄射，不相容貫，皆深知其所以然，其忍不抵死奮筆，別白涇渭？庸以媕婀黨論，偭錯青史？」[60]於所作孫承宗行狀云：「謙益壯而登公之門，今老矣，其忍畏勢焰，避黨讎，自愛一死，以欺天下萬世？謹件繫排纘，作爲行狀，以備獻於君父，下之史館，牒讀編錄，垂之無窮。」[61]於所作楊漣墓誌銘云：「嗚呼！公之死慘毒萬狀，暴屍六晝夜，蛆蟲穿穴，畢命之夕，白氣貫北斗，災害疊見，天地震動。其爲寃天猶知之，而況於人乎？當其舁櫬就徵，自邳抵汴，哭送者數萬人，壯士劍客，聚而謀篡奪者幾千人；所過市集，攀檻車，看忠臣，及炷香設祭，祝生還者，自豫冀達荆吳，綿延萬餘里；追贓令極，賣菜洗削者，爭持數錢投縣令匭中，三年而後止；昭雪之後，街談巷議，動色相告，芸夫牧豎，有歎有泣，公之忠義，激烈波蕩海內，夫豈待誌而後著？擊奸之疏，愍忠之綸，大書特書，載在國史，雖徵誌誰不知之？若夫光宗皇帝之知公，與公之受知於先帝，君臣特達，前史無比，公之致命遂志，之死不悔者，在此；而群小之定計殺公者，亦在此。謙益苟畏禍懼死，沒而不書，則擧世無有知之者矣。」[62]中國史官不畏勢焰，秉筆直書的精神，皆從錢氏的身上影射出來了。

中國史官爲直書而表現的不畏强禦的精神，是史家最偉大的精神。英國大史家艾克唐（Lord Acton, 1834–1902）認爲十九世紀檔案的開放（the opening of the archives），爲史家對有强烈慾望掩蓋眞理的權勢人物而作的戰鬭（fight against "men in authority" who had a "strong desire to hide the truth") 63，那麼中國作類此戰鬪的史官，眞是所謂更僕難終了。爭取檔案開放，是想擴大史料領域；記載史實眞情，是想傳信史於千古。檔案裡面有隱秘，權勢人物亟欲掩蓋，去爭取，是一種冒險的戰鬥；史實眞情時有難以公之於天下之處，權勢人物日思隱之，去記載，也是一種冒險的戰鬥。後者且更能暴白歷史眞相，而得禍亦愈速。論中西史學，於此等處看，庶乎可以得之。

中國史官直書以存信史的精神如此，由史官所寫的日曆、起居注，自有其高度的眞實價值。實錄、國史主要根據日曆、起居注以成書，歷代官修正史又主要以實錄、國史爲材料淵藪，那麼中國官修正史根據的材料似極爲可信，不應視之爲太官僚化的東西，而貶之爲統治階級的輔導教材。何況中國史館在蒐集材料方面，又富有兼容並蓄的精神！

中國史館裡面撰寫正史的人，也不全是政府裡面的官吏，宰相等政府官所兼的監修、總裁，是名義上的，主要秉筆者是眞知歷史的史家，宋元以後，往往是前朝遺民，如明修元史，徵山林遺逸之士三十二人，清修明史，延聘明末遺民尤殷，明史的完成，主要出於明末遺民萬斯同之力。這些遺民，含亡國之痛，往往慨然以保存勝國的歷史爲己任。政治上的壓力，監修、總裁對他們的影響，不是決定性的，一代成敗得失，很自然的能定於其手。以萬斯同爲例，他於赴史館前，其師黃宗羲贈以詩云：

史局新開上苑中，　　一時名士走空同；
是非難下神宗後，　　底本誰搜烈廟終。
此世文章推婺女，　　定知忠義及韓通；
憑君寄語書成日，　　糾謬須防在下風。64

又云：

管村彩筆掛晴霓，　　季野觀書決海堤；

卅載繩牀穿皁帽，　　一篷長水泊藍溪。

猗蘭幽谷真難閉，　　人物京師誰與齊；

不放河汾聲價倒，　　太平有策莫輕題。⑥⑤

以一代賢奸相託付，並寄語莫題太平之策，師生期許之殷，故國之思，以及為前代存信史的精神，數百年後猶令人肅然起敬意。清代新例，史局中徵士，待以七品，稱翰林院纂修官。萬氏則請以布衣參史局，不署銜，不受俸，期以表白其完全為保存有明三百年歷史的誠意。他於清康熙十八年（一六七九）到康熙四十一年（一七〇二），二十餘年間，隱忍史局，棄妻子兄弟不顧，是完全為歷史的，而清廷能優禮他，則清設史館修明史，又豈完全出於政治的目的？

總之，中國的官修正史，不是一種太官僚化的東西，秉筆者常是反現實政治的史家；史館所蒐集的材料，不盡為官方的實錄國史；實錄國史的記注者，亦富有獨立的精神，而超然於政治之上。說中國官修正史由官吏而寫，為官吏而寫，其作用在資治，是一種誤解，是一種推理的錯誤。徒徇其名而不求其實，古今中外，往往如此，令人一嘆！

中國的官修正史，不是沒有缺點，中國的史家劉知幾、萬斯同皆對之作猛烈的攻擊，但是他們的攻擊，並不能否定中國官修正史的真正價值。「古之國史，皆出自一家，如魯、漢之丘明、子長，晉、齊之董狐、南史，咸能立言不朽，藏諸名山。未聞藉以衆功，方云絕筆。唯後漢東觀，大集群儒，著述無主，條章靡立。由是伯度譏其不實，公理以為可焚，張、蔡二子糾之於當代，傅、范兩家嗤之於後葉。今者史司取士，有倍東京。人自以為荀、袁，家自稱為政、駿，每欲記一事，載一言，皆閣筆相視，含毫不斷，故頭白可期，而汗青無日。」⑥⑥「昔遷固才既傑出，又承父學，故事信而言文。其後專家之書，才雖不逮，猶未至如官修者之雜亂也。譬如入人之室，始而周其堂寢匽湢，繼而知其蓄產禮俗，久之其男女少長性質剛柔輕重賢愚，無不習察，然後可制其家之事。若官修之史，倉卒而成於衆人，不暇擇其材之宜與事之習，是猶招市人而與謀室中之事也。」[67]站在成一家之言的立場，官修正史，自極難符合理想。但是浩繁的史料，由國家之力來蒐集，由衆人之力來處理，且互相切磋，反復討論，必有事半功倍之效。所以整個說起來，中國的官修正史，是一個極優良的史學傳統。修史變成了國家的制度，寫前代史變成了後一代的義務，其統綿綿延延，傳之千餘年而不絕。擧目寰宇，有類此的史學傳統否？

第三節　中國史學的發展已突破通往真歷史的最後障礙——紀實與求真

西方正統史家浦朗穆認爲希望窺探往事的眞相（致力於瞭解曾經發生的往事），是西方近代史學的發展，此一發展，「突破了通往眞歷史的最後障礙，以致極重要的批判史學出。中國史學雖精細，中國史學雖重視文獻，中國人雖追逐博雅，但永未突破通往眞歷史的最後障礙——希望窺探往事的眞相，致未發展批判史學，中國人亦無意視歷史爲客觀的瞭解。

這是西方正統史家很自傲很肯定的一番議論，也定出了中西史學的高低。但是實際上是否如此呢？則有待同情的洞察與心平氣和的討論。

所謂希望窺探往事的眞相，一方面表現在紀實上，一方面表現在求眞上。兩者凝合，而批判史學出。中國數千年來，史學上的紀實與求眞，蔚爲一可觀的發展，此或出西方正統史家的意外，今願一論述之：

先從紀實方面談起：

西方十九世紀大史家蘭克（Leopold von Ranke, 1795-1886）序其

大著「一四九四年至一五三五年羅馬民族與日爾曼民族史」(Geschichte der Romanischen und Germanischen Völker von 1494 bis 1535) 云:「世人咸認歷史的職務，爲鑑既往，明當代，以測未來。本書則無此奢望，所欲暴陳者，僅爲往事的眞相而已 (wie es eigentlich gewesen, 英文譯爲 what actually happened 或 how things actually were)。」❻❽自此「暴陳往事的眞相」，成爲西方史學中最有名與最有影響力的格言。所謂「暴陳往事的眞相」，與浦氏所謂「希望窺探往事的眞相」，大致相同，衹是前者較爲肯定、樂觀而已。立於其先者，則爲紀實，完成之者，則爲求眞。其轟動西方史學界，則足以說明西方史學中的紀實與求眞，是相當晚期的發展。

中國在上古時代，史學上的紀實卽已出現了。史官所表現的直書，「君擧必書」,「書法不隱」,「寧爲蘭摧玉折，不作瓦礫長存」❻❾，像「南董之仗氣直書，不避强禦，韋崔之肆情奮筆，無所阿容」❼⓪，是偉大的紀實精神。史家所發表的有關言論，尤屢見不鮮:

> 「史之敍事也，當辯而不華，質而不俚，其文直，其事核，若斯而已矣。」❼❶

> 「夫爲史之要有三，一曰事實，二曰褒貶，三曰文采。有是事而如是書，斯謂事實。因事實而寓懲勸，斯謂褒貶。事實褒貶既得矣，必資文采以行之，夫然後成史。至於事得其實矣，而褒貶文采則闕焉，雖未能成書，猶不失爲史之意。若乃事實未明，而徒以褒貶文采爲事，則是既不成書，而又失爲史之意矣。」❼❷

> 「史者，紀實之書也。」❼❸

> 「史家紀事，唯在不虛美，不隱惡，據事直書，是非自見。」❼❹

> 「大抵作史者宜直敍其事，不必弄文法，寓予奪；讀史者宜詳考其實，不必憑意見，發議論。」❼❺

「大抵史家所記，典制有得有失，讀史者不必橫生意見，馳騁議論，以明法戒也，但當考其典制之實，俾數千百年建置沿革，瞭如指掌，而或宜法，或宜戒，待人之自擇焉可矣。其事蹟則有美有惡，讀史者亦不必强立文法，擅加與奪，以爲褒貶也，但當考其事蹟之實，俾年經事緯，部居州次，紀載之異同，見聞之離合，一一條析無疑，而若者可褒，若者可貶，聽之天下之公論焉可矣。書生胸臆，每患迂愚，卽使考之已詳，而議論褒貶，猶恐未當，況其考之未確者哉！蓋學問之道，求於虛不如求於實，議論褒貶，皆虛文耳。作史者之所記錄，讀史者之所考核，總期於能得其實焉而已矣，外此又何多求耶？」[76]

「其文直，其事核」，「有是事而如是書」，「據事直書」，「作史者之所記錄，讀史者之所考核，總期於能得其實」，種種言論，足以說明紀實是中國史學的一大傳統。所以「實錄」一詞在中國極爲流行，「其文直，其事核，不虛美，不隱惡」，謂之「實錄」[77]。南朝以後，修實錄變成了一種史學制度，而「纂修實錄之法，惟在據事直書」[78]，不徒徇其名而務其實，中國史學上的紀實，卽此可以想見了。

紀實不可缺少的一個條件是闕疑，而中國自上古時代起，史學上的闕疑卽出現。孔子寫春秋，能闕所疑。顧炎武於日知錄卷四「王入于王城不書」條云：「襄王之復，左氏書夏四月丁巳，王入于王城，而經不書。其文則史也，史之所無，夫子不得而益也。」同卷「所見異辭」條云：「孔子生於昭、定、哀之世，文、宣、成、襄則所聞也，隱、桓、莊、閔、僖則所傳聞也。國史所載，策書之文，或有不備，孔子得據其所見以補之。至於所聞，則遠矣。所傳聞，則又遠矣。雖得之於聞，必將參互以求其信。信則書之，疑則闕之，此其所以爲異辭也。」信則書之，疑則闕之，此爲史學上的闕疑。孔子固屢言：「多聞闕疑，愼言其餘。」⑲「吾猶及史之闕文也。」⑳「君子於其所不知，蓋闕如也。」㉑「夏禮吾能言之，杞不足徵也。殷禮吾能言之，宋不足徵也。文獻不足固也。足則吾能徵之矣。」㉒多聞闕疑，凡所不知，凡文獻所不足徵者，則闕之，穿鑿之習，附會之說，自然從此而廓清了。孔子的闕疑，蓋有所沿襲。孔子以後，中國的史家，大致恪守孔子之敎不渝，「信古而闕疑」㉓，「凡無從考證者，輒以不知置之，寧缺所疑，不敢妄言以惑世。」㉔必如是，歷史上的眞，才隱約出現。

中國史家能闕疑，故凡所撰述，皆有根據，左傳根據百國寶書，史記根據尙書、國語、左傳、世本、國策、秦紀、楚漢春秋諸記載㉕，自己所撰寫者不過十之一，刪述所存者十之九；早於左傳、史記的百國寶書以及尙書、國語諸記載，又各有其根據，而史官記錄，爲根據的大原。史官記錄，史家撰述，不外記言與記事，「古人記言與記事之文，莫不有本。本於口耳之受授者，筆主於創，創則期於適如其事與言而已；本於竹帛之成文者，筆主於因，因則期於適如其文之指。」㉖而「記事之法，有損無增，一字之增，是造僞也。往往有極意敷張，其事弗顯，刊落濃辭，微文旁綴，而情狀躍然，是貴得其意也。記言之法，增損無常，惟作者之所欲，然必推言者當日意中之所有，雖增千百言而不爲多，苟言雖成文，而推言者當日意中所本無，雖一字之增，亦造僞也。或有原文繁富，而意未昭明，減省文字，而意轉刻露者，是又以損爲增，變化多端，不可筆墨罄也。」㉗中國史官與史家秉筆之際，其態度的愼重，可以想像。所以撰述時嚮壁虛造，在中國是極爲不道德的一件事，「造爲典故以欺人」，「信口臆說」，「不考古而妄言」，「改古書以就已」㉘，皆爲士林所不恥。於是因襲成文，變成了「史家運用之功」㉙，如漢書武帝紀前，紀傳多用史記文，而卽以爲己作，這就無怪西方正統史家大爲驚訝中國史家的「不斷的襲用舊史原文」，無止境的「重複旣已確定的敍述」了！他們也就由此斷定中國有「一切確定」的觀念，相信「凡屬歷史記載，皆完全客觀」了！

反觀西方，史學上的紀實，實遠落於中國之後。希臘羅馬史家寫史，大用修詞學的方法，一位將軍在戰幕揭開前向軍隊的激昂演說，一位政客在議會上的慷慨陳詞，實際上沒有文獻的根據，而多係出於史家的想像。英國當代女史家司茂麗（Beryl Smalley）於「中世紀史家」（Historians in the Middle Ages）一書中云：

> 「羅馬史家的文章風格與治史方法，顯示出歷史與修詞學之間的密切關連。有文學上的慣例，史家將演辭託諸其人物之口：一位將軍在戰爭揭幕前對其軍隊演說，一位政客在議會中提出其案件，諸如此類，讀者不必寄望其爲眞實錄音，甚或曾經說過的正確報告：它們可能僅其大要，其眞正作用爲潤飾文章的風格。中世紀的學者，欣羨塞勒（Sallust）的演辭，汲汲鈔撮。習俗准許不必斤斤計較於正確，時日可以不用，文獻不被蒐求。」[90]

修西蒂笛斯（Thucydides）在其所著「伯羅邦內辛戰史」（History of the Peloponnesian War）一書中，卽寫入自己很多的想像，如伯里克里斯的葬禮演詞（the Funeral Oration of Pericles），實際上沒有文獻根據，而是由他自己想像當時伯里克里斯可能那樣講而寫的。史家自出抒機，想像史事當時可能發生的情況而予以創造，在中國，這是極端不可思議的。英國十九世紀史家麥考萊（Lord Macaulay, 1800-1859）曾激烈的批評「希羅多德（Herodotus）是一位可愛的傳奇小說家，修西蒂笛斯（Thucydides）是最偉大的描繪全景的名家，但不是一位有深度的思想家，浦魯達克（Plutarch）幼稚，波力比阿斯（Polybius）陰沈，從無史家若李維（Livy）全然蔑視眞理，泰希塔斯（Tacitus）是最傑出的人物素描家與最卓越的古代劇作家，但是他不可相信」[91]，希臘羅馬最傑出的幾位史家，幾皆與小說家、劇作家接近，而非紀實的史家。直到文藝復興時代寫義大利史（History of Italy）的大史家基察第泥（Guicciardini）仍然虛構演說，竄改條約㉜。文藝復興以後，西方史家在眞理的概念上，趨於嚴格，所謂「逐漸決定致力於瞭解曾經發生的往事」，十九世紀以後，「窺探往事的眞相」，變成了西方史家最大的希望，於是他們興奮的認爲西方史學突破了通往眞歷史的最後障礙，而到達史學的最高峰，世界其他史學，皆俯首其下，這未免過分睥睨天下史學了！如果西方正統史家知道中國史學在紀實方面，兩千年以前，即已有長足的發展，他們似應當修正他們武斷的結論了！

紀實而未必實，於是史學上的求眞，爲史學到達高峰的必要條件。中國史學在求眞方面的發展，於下節詳述。

第四節　中國考據學居於世界領先的地位

西方史學，在紀實方面，落於中國之後，在求眞方面，也不如中國發展之早。英國史家顧屈（G. P. Gooch, 1873-1968）於「十九世紀的史學與史家」（History and Historians in the Nineteenth Century）一書中云:

「中世紀……不知印刷爲何物，書籍缺略，對文獻的批評，尚未開始，也沒有感覺有批評的必要。沈醉於僧院圖書館的珍藏之中，虔誠的編年家不停的搜索，而鈔錄較早編纂物的錯誤於其作品之中。雖然僞造證狀爲一正常的商業行爲，辨僞的方法，尚未發明。文字記錄的事件，無條件接受，對傳統的認同，保證了每日發生的事件的眞實。最後，中世紀的氣氛，浸淫於神學之中。……歷史是說教，而非科學，是基督證據（Christian evidences）

中的運用，而非無偏私的嘗試追尋與闡釋文明的發展方向。」[93]

西方的中世紀，尙未開始批評文獻，也沒有感覺有批評的必要，辨僞方法，茫無所知，歷史又受神學的影響，停留在說教的階段，那麼此時西方的史學，似尙未出現求眞。文藝復興以後，西方史家始「逐漸決定致力於瞭解曾經發生的往事」，於是求眞的考據學，日漸發展，十七、十八世紀的博學者奠其基，而十九世紀以後極其盛，迄於今日，擧世爲之披靡，西方史家乃持以傲於世人。

不知就考據學的發展史而言，中國的考據學實居於世界領先的地位。

誠如浦立本教授所言，中國有一懷疑理性主義（sceptical rationalism）的悠久傳統，考據學的出現，它是最重要的一個條件。支配中國學術思想界達兩千餘年之久的儒家，始終是反對怪力亂神，而具有懷疑理性的，先秦儒家不必論，漢以後較醇的儒家，皆理智清明，力反迷信，范縝的神滅論，石介的石徂徠集，謝應芳的辯惑編，皆是懷疑理性主義方面的大作品。以謝應芳的辯惑編而言，係反迷信資料的薈編，其中有徵引儒家學者攻擊求長生者，攻擊爲死者燒紙錢者，攻擊釋家不朽與地獄觀念者，攻擊輪廻或轉生者，攻擊易經之占卜者，攻擊星命學者，攻擊吉凶日者，攻擊風水學者，攻擊相術者。從此已可見儒家返迷信的積極以及懷疑理性主義在中國流行的程度了。

懷疑理性主義及於史學，爲促使史家不輕信旣有的文字記載，這是史學上極重要的懷疑精神，訂譌正謬的考據學，自此萌芽。春秋時代，孔子寫春秋，能闕所疑，至戰國時代，一生以繼孔子之業爲矢志的孟子，則倡言「盡信書則不如無書，吾於武成，取二三策而已。仁人無敵於天下，以至仁伐至不仁，而何其血之流杵也？」[94]這是史學上的懷疑精神。自此中國史家，能闕疑復能懷疑。司馬遷網羅天下遺文古事，著史記，於洪荒難稽之史，時時致其懷疑，觀其於五帝本紀贊云：「學者多稱五帝，尙矣。然尙書獨載堯以來，而百家言黃帝，其文不雅馴，薦紳先生難言之。孔子所傳宰予問五帝德及帝繫姓，儒者或不傳。余嘗西至空峒，北至涿鹿，東漸於海，南浮江淮矣。至長老皆各往往稱黃帝堯舜之處，風敎固殊焉。總之不離古文者近是，予觀春秋國語，其發明五帝德帝繫姓章矣，顧弟弗深考，其所表見皆不虛。書缺有間矣，其軼乃時時見於他說。非好學深思，心知其意，固難為淺見寡聞道也。余並論次，擇其言尤雅者，故著為本紀書首。」⑨⑤不輕信百家不雅馴之言，而必以親所訪問及孔子所傳五帝德、帝繫姓兩篇有關黃帝堯舜的正式記錄作依據，旁及春秋國語所載，司馬遷已由懷疑而創出他的一套考據學了。而且他已建立了考據的標準，「載籍極博，猶考信於六藝」⑨⑥，在浩如煙海的資料中，以言雅而較為原始的六藝，作為考信的標準，這已是一種極為進步的考據學了。所以說史記「大部分為編纂，司馬遷自其所能發現之古典資料中，逐一鈔錄，略作文字上的潤色，大部分則無條件接受，傳奇與眞理混而為一」，無異以管窺天，殊失事實的眞相。

降至魏晉南北朝，盛行談辯，治經者重辯，其重辯在於辯名理以求其義；治史者亦重辯，其重辯在於辯事實以求眞。談辯影響及於史學者為考據，這是史學上的考據。如蜀人譙周，陳壽之師，著古史考，辯史記與群籍相異者，這是以考據治史第一部書見于著錄者。晉司馬彪繼之，據新出的史料竹書紀年（汲冢紀年）補考譙周之所未及（條古史考中凡一百二十二條事為不當）。二書雖皆已佚，其方法顯為聚群籍而互作比較，與司馬遷的「載籍極博，猶考信於六藝」大異。司馬彪以後，從事於考史者，有孫盛，著魏氏春秋，別著魏氏春秋異同評，蓋以考史料的異同。隋書經籍志不著錄其書，裴松之注三國志引之。如魏志袁紹傳云：「簡精卒十萬，騎萬四，將攻許。」世語云：「紹步卒五萬，騎八千。」孫盛評曰:「案魏武謂崔琰曰: 昨案貴州戶籍，可得三十萬衆。由此推之，但冀州勝兵已如此，況兼幽并及青州乎？紹之大舉，必悉師而起，十萬近之矣。」⑰像這樣的考據，豈非十分精當？惜其書已佚，僅存裴注所引十條。孫盛以後，又有裴松之。裴松之鳩集衆書，補陳壽的闕漏，引書至二百種之多，其中發明史法，考據史事者殊多。其考據史事者，如魏志武帝紀載操與袁紹相拒於官渡云:「時公兵不滿萬，傷者十二三。」裴注云:「魏武初起兵已有衆五千，自後百戰百勝，敗者十二三而已矣。但一破黃巾，受降卒三十餘萬衆，所吞併不可悉記，雖征戰損傷，未應如此之少也。夫結營相守，異於摧鋒決戰。本紀云，紹衆十餘萬，屯營東西數十里。魏太祖雖機變無方，略不世出，安有以數千之兵，而得逾時相抗者哉？以理而言，竊謂不然。紹爲屯營數十里，公能分營與相當，此兵不得甚少，一也。紹若有十倍之衆，理應悉力圍守，使出入斷絕，而公使徐晃等擊其運車，公又自出擊淳于瓊等，揚旌往還，曾無抵閡，明紹力不能制，是不得甚少，二也。諸書皆云公坑紹衆八萬，或云七萬。夫八萬人非八千人所能縛，而紹之大衆皆拱手就戮，何緣力能制之？是不得甚少，三也。將欲記述者欲以少見奇，非其實錄也。」⑱綜合記載，而覈諸事理，非徒斤斤求之於記載的異同，這應是極高明的考據學了。⑲

劉知幾生値魏晉南北朝之後，直接受魏晉南北朝考據史學的影響，他在史通中，極注重史料的考據，認爲史家不單靠蒐集史料而已，史料貴在靠得住，所以主張精密的考據史料，前人所不敢懷疑的他敢懷疑，從論語、春秋、孟子以至諸子，都舉出不可信的證據出來。其惑經一篇，說春秋有五虛美十二未喩。自此史家更淸楚史事不可輕信，史料不可輕用。唐代的考據學，於是也現出了曙光。

宋代的考據學，已極精密。專門考據史事異同的書，有吳縝的新唐書糾謬，五代史纂誤，以比較方法，證明新唐書、新五代史本身的矛盾與錯誤。自著成一書，而加以考據，以說明史料去取的原因，則有司馬光的通鑑考異。自著書而自考據，中外史家之所難，而第十一世紀中國的一位第一流歷史創作家又同時是第一流歷史考據學家，以一身而兼二者之長，則不能不算中國史學界的盛事。

司馬光有一套極客觀的處理史料考據史料的方法，他不是隨得史料隨寫通鑑的，而是有他由蒐集史料到處理史料的程序；他也不是「任憑私意的選用文獻而即目之為可信」的，而是有他去取的客觀標準。

由叢目而長編，由長編而通鑑，是司馬光處理史料的程序。觀其與范內翰論修書帖云：

「夢得今來所作叢目，方是將實錄事目標出，其實錄中事應移在前後者，必已注於逐事下訖。自舊唐書以下，俱未曾附注，如何遽可作長編也。請且將新舊唐書紀志傳及統紀補錄并諸家傳記小說以至諸人文集稍干時事者，皆須依年月日添附。無日者，附於其月之下，稱是月；無月者，附於其年之下，稱是歲；無年者，附於其事之首尾；有無事可附者，則約其時之早晚，附於一年之下。但稍與其事相涉者，即注之過多不害。嘗見道原云，只此已是千餘卷書，日看一兩卷，亦須二三年功夫也。俟如此附注俱畢，然後請從高祖初起兵修長編，至哀帝禪位而止。……

其修長編時，請據事目下所記新舊紀志傳及雜史小說文集，盡檢出一閱，其中事同文異者，則請擇一明白詳備者錄之；彼此互有詳略，則請左右采獲，錯綜銓次，自用文辭修正之，一如左傳敍事之體也。此並作大字寫。若彼此年月事迹，有相違戾不同者，則請選一證據分明情理近於得實者，修入正文，餘者注於其下，仍為敍述所以取此捨彼之意。(先注所捨者，云某書云云，今按某書證驗云云，或無證驗，則以事理推之云云，今從某書爲定。若無以考其虛實是非者，則云今兩存之。其實錄正史未必皆可據，雜史小說未必皆無憑，在高鑒擇之。)」[100]

其叢目頗類似近代的資料目錄，長編則是經過選擇而極爲豐富的資料彙編，所謂寧失於繁無失於略，是當時修長編的原則。無疑問的如此蒐集史料，是極科學的方法。所以自戰國以至五代所能蒐集的史料，皆彙於一編，而無遺漏之患。一旦由繁富的長編，再擷精取華，自易寫成體大思精的通鑑。此與漫無計劃，隨得史料隨動筆寫，不能窺其全而見其大，相去實不可以道里計。舉目世界，能遵守如此程序以蒐集史料處理史料者，蓋不可多覯。

司馬光由繁富的長編，寫成體大思精的通鑑，更有其去取史料的客觀標準。修長編之初，已將史料經過一番選擇，所謂事同文異者，擇明白詳備者錄之，彼此年月事迹有相違戾不同者，選證據分明情理近於得實者用之，是極客觀的選擇。取此捨彼的原因，亦一一加以敍述，由其敍述，知其普遍的應用了比較研究法，以兩種或兩種以上的書互相比較，得到證據，便取此捨彼。如無證驗，則以事理推之。所謂「實錄正史未必皆可據，雜史小說未必皆無憑，在高鑒擇之」，是司馬光用史料，胸中無成見，而着重於自己的鑒擇，明白詳備證據分明而又近於情理，是其鑒擇的標準。至於他與范內翰論修書帖所云：

「詩賦等若止爲文章，詔誥等若止爲除官，及妖異止於怪誕，詼諧止於取笑之類，便請直刪不妨。若詩賦有所譏諷，詔誥有所戒諭，妖異有所儆戒，詼諧有所補益，並告存之。」

不但充分表現出他以史資治的標準，也足以說明其採用史料的廣度。

修長編時，去取史料的標準如此，由長編寫成通鑑，其愼於去取，可推想而知。三十卷的通鑑考異，是司馬光寫通鑑時去取史料的最佳說明。裡面不但反映出他用比較研究法，將各種不同的史料放在一起比較，同時反映出他有時以當時的情理作爲論斷的標準，在遇到迹近荒誕的史實而又無確切的證據以證其非實時，這是極上乘的考據方法。如後人引爲美談的漢初四皓故事，他則非之：

「按：高祖剛猛伉厲，非畏搢紳譏議者也，但以大臣皆不肯從，恐身後趙王不能獨立，故不爲耳。若決意欲廢太子，立如意，不顧義理，以留侯之久故親信，猶云非口舌所能爭，豈山林四叟片言遽能柅其事哉？借使四叟實能柅其事，不過汚高祖數寸之刄耳！何至悲歌云：羽翮已成，矰繳安施乎？若四叟實能制高祖，使不敢廢太子，是留侯爲子立黨以制其父也，留侯豈爲此哉？此特辯士欲夸大四叟之事故云然；亦猶蘇秦約六國從，秦兵不敢闚函谷關十五年，魯仲連折新垣衍，秦將聞之，却軍五十里耳。凡此之類，皆非事實，司馬遷好奇，多愛而采之，今皆不取。」⑩

又如晉莊宗三矢事，新五代史極稱之，他亦不以爲然：

「五代史闕文：『世傳武皇臨薨，以三矢付莊宗曰：一矢討劉仁恭，汝不先下幽州，河南未可圖也。一矢擊契丹，且曰，阿保機與吾把臂而盟，結爲兄弟，誓復唐家社稷，今背約附梁，汝必伐之。一矢滅朱溫，汝能成善志，死無恨矣。莊宗藏三矢于武皇廟庭。及討劉仁恭，命幕吏以少牢告廟，請一矢，盛以錦囊，使親將負之，以爲前驅。凱旋之日，隨俘馘納矢于太廟。伐契丹，滅朱氏，亦如之。』按薛使契丹傳，莊宗初嗣位，亦遣使告哀，賂以金繒，求騎軍以救潞州，契丹答其使曰：我與先王爲兄弟，兒即吾兒也，寧有父不助子邪？許出師，會潞平而止。廣本〔按廣本，劉恕所編，考異中亦時稱劉恕廣本，或即五代長編之別稱〕，劉守光爲守文所攻，屢求救於晉，晉王遣部兵五千救之，然則於時莊宗未與契丹及守光爲仇也。此蓋後人因莊宗成功，撰此事以誇其英武耳。」⑩²

由上可知司馬光不但是一位第一流的歷史創作家，同時也是一位第一流的歷史考據家，他有一套極富科學精神的歷史考據學，取材時有其標準，有其客觀考據方法，不以史事的新奇可喜而予以輕信。白特費爾德教授說中國史學後面，有一假想，卽凡屬歷史記載，皆完全客觀，說中國史家任憑私意的選用文獻而卽目之爲可信，取此而捨彼的原因，不予以討論，說中國的考據限於自我證明的工作上，而不科學地窺尋史學的眞相與看看史料與實際發生的事實符合的程度；說中國的考據學未能對證據作科學的評價與分析，無較高境界的批評。我們祇要舉出司馬光的歷史考據學來，就可以知道白氏的厚誣中國了。浦立本教授的反駁很扼要，祇是白氏不能瞭解罷了。⑩³

時至清代，中國的考據學，發展至最高峯。清代三百年學術，一言以蔽之，是考據學。其學倡自淸初顧炎武，極盛於乾嘉時代，晚淸學風轉變，而考據學之統不絕。淸代的考據學，自顧氏起，最重證據，顧氏寫日知錄，寫音學五書，皆普遍歸納證據，反復批評證據，確切提出證據，審愼組合證據⑩⁴。如於音學五書唐韻正卷四「牙」字下，註云「古音吾」，共列舉三十九條證據，「家」字下，註云「古音姑」，共列舉六十二條證據，唐韻正卷五「行」字下，註云「古音杭」，共列舉三百七十六條證據，爲證明文字的古音，無不遍蒐證據。而且對證據的原始性，極爲重視，不取「廢銅」，而重「采山之銅」⑩⁴；又能大致做到引原文，注出處；「每一事必詳其始末，參其證佐，而後筆之於書」⑩⁵，「有一疑義，反覆參考，必歸於至當；有一獨見，援古證今，必暢其說而後止」⑩⁶。這是何等對證據作科學評價與分析的考據學！與顧氏同時的學者閻若璩，沈潛三十餘年，寫成尙書古文疏證一書，證明了千餘年來中國舉國上下視爲神聖不可侵犯的古文尙書爲僞書，更是專門的大考據學。閻氏嘗謂讀書不尋源頭，雖得之殊可危。手一書，至檢數十書相證，侍側者頭目皆眩，而精神涌溢，眼爛如電。一義未析，反覆窮思，饑不食，渴不飲，寒不衣，熱不扇，必得其解而後止[107]。他寫尙書古文疏證，就篇數的不合，篇名的不合，文字的不合，證明古文尙書之僞；以古論對證，以孟子對證，以史記對證，以說文對證，證明古文尙書之僞；復就書法的錯誤，史例的矛盾，證明古文尙書之僞。綜觀疏證全書，凡其所言，皆有證據，絕少鑿空懸揣之辭，自此古文尙書之僞，遂成定讞。有人問閻氏的考據學方法的旨要，他回答道：不越乎「以虛證實，以實證虛」而已。他舉孔子適周之年作例，舊說孔子適周共有四種不同的說法，一爲昭公七年（水經注），二爲昭公二十年（史記孔子世家），三爲昭公二十四年（史記索隱），四爲定公九年（莊子）。閻氏根據曾子問禮說，孔子從老聃助葬恰遇日食一條，用算法推得昭公二十四年夏五月乙未朔日食，故斷定孔子適周在此年。[108]這是何等精密的科學考據方法……以這等考據方法，復殫畢生精力考據學術史上的一個問題，誰說「中國歷史永遠沒有發展自我批評與發現的方法，無情的考驗通則，有目的蒐求文獻以證明假設」呢？

清初以文才史才名而非考據學家的戴名世，於一篇文章中，也談到歷史考據的方法：「夫史之所籍以作者有二，曰國史也，曰野史也。國史者，出於載筆之臣，或鋪張之太過，或隱諱而不詳，其於群臣之功罪賢否，始終本末，頗多有不盡，勢不得不博徵之於野史。而野史者，或多狥其好惡，逞其私見，卽或其中無他，而往往有傷於辭之不達，聽之不聰，傳之不審，一事而紀載不同，一人而褒貶各別。嗚呼！所見異辭，所聞異辭，吾將安所取正哉？書曰，三人占，則從二人之言。吾以爲二人而正也，則吾從二人之言；二人而不正也，則吾仍從一人之言；卽其人皆正也，而其言亦未可盡從，夫亦惟論其世而已矣。一事也，必有一事之終始；一人也，必有一人之本末。綜其始終，核其本末，旁參互證，而固可以得其十八九矣。子曰，衆好之，必察焉，衆惡之，必察焉。察之而有可好，亦未必遂無可惡者，察之而有可惡，亦未必遂無可好者。衆不可矯也，亦不可狥也。設其身以處其地，揣其情以度其變，此論世之說也。吾旣論其人之世，又諳作野史者之世，彼其人何人乎？賢乎否乎？其論是乎非乎？其爲局中者乎？其爲局外者乎？其爲得之親見者乎？其爲得之逖聽者乎？其爲有所爲而爲之者乎？其爲無所爲而爲之者乎？觀其所論列之意，察其所予奪之故，證之他書，參之國史，虛其心以求之，平其情而論之，而其中有可從有不可從，又已得其十八九矣。」⑩⑨這實是極精湛的歷史考據方法，而且大體上已到達西方十八世紀末十九世紀初史學運動（或史學革命）的境界。西方十八世紀末十九世紀初史學運動的代表人物爲德國大史家尼博爾（Barthold George Niebuhr, 1776-1831）與蘭克（Leopold von Ranke, 1795-1886），他們開創了一種語言文字的批評方法，從語言文字方面着手，追尋史料形成的來源，批評史料可信的程度，這自然是極富科學精神的歷史考據方法。以尼博爾而論，他對於史料，不但不雜有宗教、種族與文學的偏見，並且常持有尋源、懷疑與批評的態度。第一，要問史料的來源如何？卽史料本身是不是原手的史料（是否原作者的親筆著作）？第二，要問所用史料是否雜有後人的意見？曾否被人修改？第三，原手史料不存，方許用最早的副料（轉手的史料），但副料不能代替原料。第四，原料與副料價值的判斷，依時間、地域、親見或傳聞爲主，不偏重文辭的是否優美與形式的是否完備。第五，要注意記載人記載事實的動機與態度。以此原則，尼博爾批評李維（Livy, 59 B. C. -17 A. D.）的羅馬史，具體的指出，那些與實際情實不符合，那些全部的鈔襲他書，那些局部的鈔襲他書。於是學者對於李維的書信心動搖，從此研究羅馬史的人，有興趣從古文書、古遺物中尋求實證，因而有孟蓀（Theodor von Mommsen, 1817-1903）優美可信的羅馬史。羅馬史因尼博爾的方法論而重建了⑩。以蘭克而論，一八二四年他出版的名著「一四九四年到一五三五年間羅馬民族與日爾曼民族的歷史」(Geschichte der Romanischen und Germanischen Völker von 1494 bis 1535）後面，附一長文，名爲「近代歷史作者評議」(Zur Kritik neuer Geschichtschreiber)，在其中他將尼博爾的原則，進一步發揮，他認爲最接近事件的目擊者爲最佳證據提供人；當事人的信件較編年家所錄的逸聞爲有價値；案牘、報告、古物與親見親聞的史料，要去搜羅；作者的個性，要去瞭解；作者從何處獲得其見聞，要去探究。而且他最有名與最有影響力的格言「暴陳往事的眞相」，也在此名著的序言中出現⑪。自此西方史學進入一新世紀。以尼博爾、蘭克二人所開創的新史學亦即所開創的新歷史考據方法，與十七世紀末十八世紀初中國的戴名世（1653-1713）隨意在一篇文章裡所談的相比較，其間相去並不甚遠。戴氏在追問史料的來源方面，在判斷史料的價値方面，在注意記載人記載事實的動機與態度方面，在瞭解記載人（即蘭克所謂作者）的個性，探究記載人從何處獲得其見聞方面，皆與尼、蘭二氏所談，若合符節。祇是戴氏未能將其形成一股潮流罷了。至於從語言文字方面，追尋史料形成的來源，批評史料可信的程度，以及從古文書、古遺物中尋求實證，清初顧、閻等考據學家，皆優爲之⑫。所以十八世紀末十九世紀初西方史學運動所到達的境界，中國在十七世紀末十八世紀初已悠然的到達了。

清代的考據學，發展到乾嘉時代，形成兩大潮流，一爲經學上的考據學，一爲史學上的考據學，兩者皆有極高的成就。經學上的考據學以戴震所領導的皖派，最爲出色。皖派治學，不主一家，惟求其是，最富求眞精神。戴氏曾云：

「凡僕所以尋求於遺經……尋求而獲，有十分之見，有未至十分之見。所謂十分之見，必徵之古而靡不條貫，合諸道而不留餘議，鉅細畢究，本末兼察。若夫依於傳聞以擬其是，擇於衆說以裁其優，出於空言以定其論，據於孤證以信其通，雖溯流可以知源，不目覩淵泉所導，循根可以達杪，不手披枝肄所歧，皆未至十分之見也。」⑬

此最足代表皖派治學的精神與方法，凡所研究經學上的問題，必追根窮源，以明其眞相，廣徵博據，以斷其是非，以至於十分之見。戴氏弟子段玉裁著說文解字注，先就說文融會貫通，以求義例（類似歸納），然後以義例律之本書（類似演繹），致創見疊出，被推爲「千七百年無此作」⑭。高郵王氏父子王念孫、王引之的治學，尤令人心折，凡立一說，必廣求參驗，引申觸類，務求其安，故其著書，極爲審愼，窮年累月，然後泐定一說，其精審遂在各家之上。［如經義述聞「孰爲」條云：

「趙盾曰：『天乎？天乎？予無罪，孰爲盾而忍弒其君者乎？』范注曰：『廻己易他，誰作盾而當忍弒君者乎？』釋文曰：『孰爲盾絕句。』家大人曰：『范訓爲爲作，謂誰作盾而當忍弒君，義甚迂曲。陸又讀孰爲盾絕句，皆非也。爲猶謂也，言誰謂盾而忍弒其君也。』（禮器，誰謂由也而不知禮乎？家語公西赤問篇作孰爲。）公羊傳曰：『趙盾曰：「吾不弒君，誰謂吾弒君者乎？」』是其證矣。古書爲字，或與謂同義。楚策『賁諸懷錐刃而天下爲勇，西施衣褐而天下稱美。』爲勇，即謂勇也。孟子公孫丑篇，『管仲曾西之所不爲也，而子爲我願之乎？』言子謂我願之也。

告子篇,『爲是其智弗若與?曰,非然也。』言謂是其智弗若也。爲與謂同義,故二字可以互用。文王世子曰:『父在斯爲子,君在斯謂之臣。』莊子天地篇曰:『四海之內共利之之謂悅,共給之之爲安。』盜跖篇曰:『今謂臧聚曰,女行如桀紂,則有作色,有不服之心。今爲宰相曰(秦策、秦令周取爲楚王曰,齊策,淳于髡爲齊王曰,墨子魯問篇,墨子爲魯陽君曰,韓子內儲說篇,嗣公爲關吏曰,商臣爲其傅潘崇曰。爲字並與謂同義。),子行如仲尼、墨翟,則變容易色,稱不足。』楚策曰:『今爲馬多力則有矣,若曰勝千鈞則不然者,何也?夫千鈞非馬之任也。今謂楚強大則有矣,若越趙魏而鬥兵於燕,則豈楚之任也?』爲亦謂也。故大戴禮文王官人篇,『此之爲考志也。』逸周書官人篇,爲作謂。莊二十二年左傳,『是謂觀國之光。』史記陳杞世家,謂作爲。墨子公輸篇,『宋所爲無雉兎鮒魚者也。』宋策,爲作謂。莊子讓王篇,『今某抱仁義之道,以遭亂世之患,其何窮之爲?』呂氏春秋愼人篇,爲作謂。」

爲證明「孰爲」作「孰謂」解,可謂極盡廣求參驗,引申觸類的能事了。經義述聞上的各條,皆類似,其精當「實足令鄭朱俛首」[115],這是高郵王氏父子積兩代的心血結晶,窮年累月,愼思博證,致每一說出,皆令人渙若冰釋。然則又如何能說中國學者不能「無情的考驗通則,有目的的蒐求文獻以證明假設」呢?

乾嘉時代史學上的考據學,以錢大昕、王鳴盛、崔述等爲代表人物。他們治史,最能求眞,實事求是,不涉虛誕,反對馳騁議論,反對書法褒貶,主張史家應不虛美,不隱惡,據事直書,以期不失史實眞相。錢大昕云:

「史家以不虛美不隱惡爲良,美惡不揜,各從其實。」[116]

王鳴盛云:

「大抵史家所記，典制有得有失，讀史者不必橫生意見，馳騁議論，以明法戒也，但當考其典制之實，俾數千百年建置沿革，瞭如指掌，而或宜法，或宜戒，待人之自擇焉可矣。其事蹟則有美有惡，讀史者亦不必强立文法，擅加與奪，以爲褒貶也，但當考其事蹟之實，俾年經事緯，部居州次，記載之異同，見聞之離合，一一條析無疑，而若者可褒，若者可貶，聽之天下之公論焉可矣。書生匈臆，每患迂愚，卽使考之已詳，而議論褒貶，猶恐未當，況其考之未確者哉？蓋學問之道，求於虛不如求於實，議論褒貶，皆虛文耳。作史者之所記錄，讀史者之所考核，總期於能得其實焉而已矣，此外又何多求耶？」117

崔述云:

「今考信錄中，凡其說出於戰國以後者，必詳爲之考其所本，而不敢以見於漢人之書者，遂眞以爲三代之事。」118

「余爲考信錄，於漢晉諸儒之說，必爲考其原本，辨其是非，非敢詆諆先儒，正欲平心以求其一是。」119

「今爲考信錄，不敢以載於戰國秦漢之書者，悉信以爲實事，不敢以東漢魏晉諸儒之所注釋者，悉信以爲實言，務皆究其本末，辨其同異，分別其事之虛實而去取之。雖不爲古人之書諱其誤，亦不至爲古人之書增其誤。」120

「今爲考信錄，凡無從考證者，輒以不知置之，寧缺所疑，不敢妄言以惑世。」121

「大抵文人學士，多好議論古人得失，而不考其事之虛實。余獨謂虛實明而後得失或可不爽。故今爲考信錄，專以辨其虛實爲先務，而論得失者次之。」122

乾嘉史家如此銳意求眞，所以他們發展了極富科學精神的歷史考據學。崔氏治史，務在窮源，他引用諺語「打破沙鍋紋到底」，即可表明其窮源的精神。崔氏之源，在六經，而認爲「大抵戰國秦漢之書皆難徵信，而其所記上古之事尤多荒謬」[123]，戰國秦漢之書是否皆如此可疑，六經是否完全可靠，是有待商榷的問題，但是儘量追求歷史最後的來源，是治史最重要的原則，也是歷史考據學的極高境界。十八世紀中國的史家崔述知窮源，而又奉之爲圭臬，凡說必爲「考其原本」，「辨其虛實」，這足可證明十八世紀中國的歷史考據學所到達的境界了。

錢大昕、王鳴盛所代表的歷史考據學，尤值得稱道：

乾嘉時代絕大多數的史家，將考據學變爲史學的最終目的，爲考據而考據，史家如不以考據治歷史，即不足齒諸史家之林。以章學誠的卓才宏識，大聲疾呼，謂考據不足以盡史學，而絲毫不能有所動。風氣所趨，如狂風，如怒濤，不可遏禦。於是浩浩蕩蕩的歷史考據學派形成，錢大昕、王鳴盛便是此一學派的代表人物。他們治史，充分利用歸納方法，讀史皆作劄記，心有所得，則條記於紙，每每積至數千百條，由此儲蓄的大量資料，再歸納而得其史學上的新說。像錢大昕的十駕齋養新錄，即應用此法的結晶。凡立一說，必憑證據，由證據而產生其說，非由其說而找尋證據；證據的選擇，以最原始爲尚，如漢書與史記牴牾，則寧信史記而不信漢書；孤證不定其說，其無反證者姑存之，得有續證則漸信之，遇有力之反證則棄之；隱匿證據或曲解證據，則認爲大不德。於是形成一種爲學問而學問的學術研究風氣，治史不先有任何觀點，不滲有其他因素，由史而治史，由屢次發生的史蹟，以說明歷史的現象，故往往能訂古人之僞，發千載之覆。

錢王等歷史考據學派的史家，治史亦廣泛利用輔助科學，以作史實考據的工具，如經學、小學、輿地、金石、板本、音韻、天算諸專門學問，都用之以助考史；史家亦往往兼爲經學家、小學家、輿地學家、金石學家、板本學家、音韻學家、天算學家，此與近代歐美史家利用語言學、文字學、古文書學、印章學、泉幣學、族譜學、年代學、地理學以及社會學、政治學、經濟學等社會科學以治史，科目雖不盡同，而其欲以輔助科學，使歷史研究幾於科學的研究者則一。如錢大昕學問之博，一時無兩，求之中國古今史家，亦殆罕其匹。凡與歷史有關的輔助學問，他皆無不通，亦皆無不精，故其所著廿二史考異、十駕齋養新錄等書，考據的精審縝密，往往卓絕千古，錢氏亦因此變爲中國歷史上最優越的歷史考據學家。

從以上看起來，清乾嘉時代經學上的考據學與史學上的考據學，皆已發展到極高的境界，皆已形成極科學的考據方法，我們豈能說中國的考據學限於自我證明的工作上，而不科學地窺尋史料與實際發生的事實符合的程度？我們豈能說中國永遠沒有發展自我批評與發現的方法，無情的考驗通則，有目的的蒐求文獻以證明假設？我們又豈能說中國史學的發展，永遠沒有突破通往眞歷史的最後障礙——希望窺探往事的眞相，永遠沒有發展批判史學，中國人永遠沒有意思視歷史爲客觀的瞭解？

第五節　中國史家長於敍事藝術

敍事、解釋與綜合是史學的三大要素，史家同時具有敍事、解釋與綜合的藝術，是世界最優越的史家。中國史家未曾發展西方史家那一套解釋與綜合的藝術，而數千年來，他們却發展了一套敍事藝術，其精湛且似可獨步寰宇。

孔子作春秋，已頗盡史家敍事的能事。所謂春秋書法，或許不是先有意用一二字以行褒貶，祇不過爲了敍述史實的眞相，所以於所用的字，特別審愼。史實須用字以來表現，用字的正確與否，與史實的眞相關係至大。用字不正確，史實便走樣。孔子作春秋，注重書法，似乎是在愼重地選用正確的字以敍事。如春秋云：

「僖公十有六年，春王正月，戊申朔，隕石於宋五。是月，六鷁退飛，過宋都。」

便是最簡單最正確的敍事，石自天而降，速度甚快，先聽到隕聲，一看，是石，落於宋地，細數起來，五塊。隕石於宋五，是最簡單不過的敍事了，且極合邏輯，每一個字的位置都不能移動，移動了便不能敍明史實實際發生時的情況。六鷁退飛過宋都，情況就不同，鷁在高空飛，速度顯着很慢，且不易看淸楚是什麼東西在飛，所以最先能看到的只是天空有六個東西，細看，是鷁，再細看，是退飛，經過宋都。由此看起來，孔子寫春秋，每一個字都費盡心思斟酌，不多用一個字，不亂用一個字，由字所組成的句子，極合邏輯，能完全符合史實發生時的情況。在史學求眞的最高原則下，這是史家最基本也是最重要的藝術。史記孔子世家，稱孔子作春秋，「筆則筆，削則削，游夏之徒，不能贊一詞」，可知其筆削的藝術，非一般人所能幾及的了。

左丘明作左傳，敍事的藝術，進入另一境界，史實比春秋敍述得詳盡曲折了，文辭比春秋優美委婉了，且其敍事有系統，有別裁，對重大問題，往往溯原竟委，前後照應，使讀者相悅以解。以編年史而能如此敍事，是極高的藝術。善乎杜預序春秋云：

「左丘明……身爲國史，躬覽載籍，必廣記而備言之，其文緩，其旨遠，將令學者原始要終，尋其枝葉，究其所窮，優而柔之，使自求之，饜而飫之，使自趣之，若江海之浸，膏澤之潤，渙然冰釋，怡然順理，然後爲得也。」

司馬遷作史記，達到史家敍事藝術的極高峰，天下遺文古事，畢陳於前，而化裁調劑，使其歸於粹然精一，艱澀如尙書之文，予以明暢的譯述，不雅馴如百家之言，加以適當的修飾。千載而下，讀其文者，但覺昌茂爾雅，斐然自成一體，而不知其已經過史家一番點竄陶鑄的甘苦。其點竄陶鑄，在於使史文一致，使史事明暢，而又一一基之於文獻，故又足以徵信千古。自史記之體一開，後之史家，敍事遂咸以之爲準則，雖神奇不逮，而風範猶存。

班固、范曄皆工敍事，洎乎劉知幾，歸納出史家敍事的原則：

一曰敍事尙簡　儘量省字，儘量省句，如句盡餘贉，字皆重複，史之煩蕪，便無法避免。「餌巨魚者，垂其千鈞而得之在於一筌。捕高鳥者，張其萬罝而獲之由於一目。夫敍事者，或虛益散辭，廣加閑說，必取其所要，不過一言一句耳。苟能同夫獵者漁者，旣執而罝鈞必收，其所留者，唯一筌一目而已。則庶幾駢枝盡去，而塵垢都捐，華逝而實存，滓去瀋在矣。」⑫④

二曰敍事用晦　省字約文，事溢於句外，期以由晦而顯，意義流露於無窮。「夫能略小存大，舉重明輕，一言而巨細咸該，片語而洪纖靡漏，此皆用晦之道也。昔古文義，務却浮詞，虞書云：帝乃殂落，百姓如喪考妣。夏書云：启呱呱而泣，予不子。周書稱前徒倒戈，血流漂杵。虞書云：四罪而天下咸服。此皆文如闊略，而語實周贍，故覽之者初疑其易，而爲之者方覺其難，固非雕虫小技所能斥苦其說也。旣而丘明受經，師範尼父。夫經以數字包義，而傳以一句成言，雖繁約有殊，而隱晦無異。故其綱紀而言邦俗也，則有士會爲政，晉國之盜奔秦；邢遷如歸，衞國忘亡。其款曲而言人事也，則有犀革裹之，比及宋，手足皆見；三軍之士，皆如挾纊。斯皆言近而旨遠，辭淺而義深，雖發語已殫，而含義未盡，使夫讀者望表而知裏，捫毛而辯骨，覩一事於句中，反三隅於字外，晦之時義，不亦大哉？」⑫⑤

三曰敍事存眞　史異於文，文可虛飾，而史必存眞。因此史的語言，不宜倣古，倣古便易失眞。應以當代語言，記當代史事。「戰國以前，其言皆可諷詠，非但筆削所致，良由體質素美，何以覈諸？至如鶉賁鸜鵒，童豎之謠也；山木輔車，時俗之諺也；皤腹棄甲，城者之謳也；原田是謀，輿人之誦也，斯皆芻詞鄙句，猶能溫潤若此，況乎束帶立朝之士，加以多聞博古之識者哉？則知時人出言，史官入記，雖有討論潤色，終不失其梗槩者也。夫三傳之說，旣不習於尙書，兩漢之詞，又多違於戰策，足以驗甿俗之遞改，知歲時之不同，而後來作者，通無遠識，記其當世口語，罕能從實而書，方復追效昔人，示其稽古，是以好丘明者，則偏模左傳，愛子長者，則全學史公，用使周秦言辭，見於魏晉之代，楚漢應對，行乎宋齊之日，而僞修混沌，失彼天然，今古以之不純，眞僞由其相亂。」「夫天地長久，風俗無恆，後之視今，亦猶今之視昔，而作者皆怯書今語，勇效昔言，不其惑乎？」「工爲史者，不選事而書，故言無美惡，盡傳於後。若事皆不謬，言必近眞，庶幾可與古人同居，何止得其糟粕而已。」[126]

劉氏提出的史家敍事原則如此，所以在他的理想中，文約而事豐，是述作的尤美者。虛加練飾，輕事雕彩，體兼賦頌，詞類俳優，文非文，史非史，他極力反對。他雖然以駢文寫史學批評，却不主張以駢文寫史。「史之敍事也，當辯而不華，質而不俚，其文直，其事核，若斯而已矣。」[127]是劉氏論史家敍事藝術的最高境界。

劉知幾的理論，在中國史學界發生頗大的影響，唐以後的史家，大致能遵守不以駢文寫史的原則，「文直事核」，每爲史家所懸的最高鵠的。清代史家章學誠論史家敍事藝術，尤爲精闢。他認爲一切史文必有所本，記言要適如其言，記事要適如其事，不能憑虛別構。記事的原則，是有損無增，一字之增，視爲造僞；記言的原則，是增損無常，不過一定要能符合言者當時的意旨，如爲言者當時意中所本無，雖一字之增，也是造僞。其言曰：

「古人記言與記事之文，莫不有本。本於口耳之受授者，筆主於創，創則期於適如其事與言而已；本於竹帛之成文者，筆主於因，因則期於適如其文之指。」⑫⑧

「記事之法，有損無增，一字之增，是造僞也。往往有極意敷張，其事弗顯，刊落濃辭，微文旁綴，而情狀躍然，是貴得其意也。記言之法，增損無常，惟作者之所欲，然必推言者當日意中之所有，雖增千百言而不爲多，苟言雖成文，而推言者當日意中所本無，雖一字之增，亦造僞也。或有原文繁富，而意未昭明，減省文字，而意轉刻露者，是又以損爲增，變化多端，不可筆墨罄也。」⑫⑨

於是因襲成文，被視爲「史家運用之功」⑬⓪，爲史家應有的權利，與文士的勦竊，迥然不同。惟史筆點竄塗改，是一通常的法則，因襲成文之際，並非一味的鈔撮，而是貴能有所陶鑄化裁。能陶鑄化裁，然後龐雜紛亂的史料，才能起昇華作用，歸於粹然精一，成爲完美整潔的一家之言。所以史家對於紛然雜陳的史料，要有抉擇去取，文劣而事庸者，刊而去之，既經採取，便要加以消化，古語加以疏通，俚言加以潤色，猥鄙繁冗之處，加以刪削淨化，以期變成一致的語言。司馬遷所曾經實踐者，到章學誠而理論化原則化了。觀章氏之言曰：

「工師之爲巨室度材，比於燮理陰陽，名醫之製方劑炮灸，通乎鬼神造化。史家詮次群言，亦若是焉已爾。是故文獻未集，則搜羅咨訪不易爲功，觀鄭樵所謂八例求書，則非尋常之輩所可能也。觀史遷之東漸南浮，則非心知其意不能迹也。此則未及著文之先事也。及其紛然雜陳，則貴抉擇去取。人徒見著於書者之粹然善也，而不知刊而去者，中有苦心而不能顯也。旣經裁取，則貴陶鎔變化，人第見誦其辭者之渾然一也，而不知化而裁者，中有調劑，而人不知也。卽以刊去而論，文劣而事庸者，無足道矣。其間有介兩端之可，而不能不出於一途；有嫌兩美之傷，而不能不忍於割愛；佳篇而或乖於例；事足而恐徇於文，此皆中有苦心，而不能顯也。如以化裁而論，則古語不可入今，則當疏以達之；俚言不可雜言，則當溫以潤之；辭則必稱其體；語則必肖其人；質野不可用文語，而猥鄙須删；急遽不可以爲宛辭，而曲折仍見；文移須從公式，而案牘又不宜徇；駢麗不入史裁，而詔表亦豈可廢，此皆中有調劑，而人不知也。」⑬

章氏推崇司馬遷可謂到達極點，而中國史家的敍事藝術，亦可概見。

綜合上面所言，中國史家的敍事藝術，實已到達一極高的境界，審愼的遣詞用字，不以文字而失去史實之眞；委婉的窮原竟委，不以旣往的陳迹而失去詞章之美；文求其約，在省筆墨；事求其豐，在垂往事；而華質適中，是史筆點竄之奇；文直事核，乃鑒擇去取之功。司馬遷司馬光皆備此藝術之全，劉知幾章學誠神而明之，遂歸納出一套完整的理論。有理論，有實踐，中國史家的敍事藝術，是可以向舉世驕傲了。

尤富有意義者，爲中國史家敍事，最能將歷史萬象，鉅細托出，無遺無漏。初視之，像是「瑣碎餖飣」，細稽之，却盡是往史的剪影。舉目世界，未有如中國史家敍事如此詳盡者。此無他，與中國博大的史學體例有關。中國的史學體例，編年之外，有紀傳，紀傳之外，有紀事本末。編年一體，有僅揭大事爲綱者，如魯春秋及魏竹書紀年；有敍事詳密，詳目略綱者，如左傳、通鑑。紀事本末體，揭事爲題，詳備原委，有統貫全史爲一書者，如通鑑紀事本末；有僅記一代之事者，如宋史紀事本末；有僅記一國之事者，如西夏紀事本末。至於紀傳體，範圍尤廣，紀以記大事，傳以傳人物，表以通紀傳之窮，志以述風俗制度。司馬遷以紀、表、書、世家、列傳，創爲全史，實兼有編年本末之長，所以紀傳一體，歷兩千餘年爲中國史學的正宗。中國的正史，皆紀傳體，其優點卽在於博大，能兼容並包，天下鉅細，靡不可收而載之。以大海之可滙百川來比喻，不爲過分。趙翼曾極譽之云：

「古者左史記言，右史記事，言爲尙書，事爲春秋，其後沿爲編年、記事二種。記事者，以一篇記一事，而不能統貫一代之全。編年者，又不能卽一人而各見其本末。司馬遷參酌古今，發凡起例，創爲全史，本紀以序帝王，世家以記侯國，十表以繫時事，八書以詳制度，列傳以誌人物，然後一代君臣政事，賢否得失，總彙於一編之中。自此例一定，歷代作史者，遂不能出其範圍，信史家之極則也。」⑬²

西洋史上的史書，其體例大多類似中國的紀事本末體，而再加上作者的一些解釋與綜合，一事的起訖演變，原因影響，皆細細分析，娓娓道來。章學誠所謂「體圓用神」⑬³，誠可當之而無愧。中國史上的紀事本末體，雖貌似而精神全異，相去殆不可以道里計。然謂之爲史學上精深的體例則可，謂之爲博大的體例則不可。在西方的史學體例下，史家能深入的討論問題，而以注意史實間的關聯與和諧，注意整個事件的分析與討論，每每不能容納衆多史實。史實在西方史學中被犧牲被埋沒者，正不知凡幾。歷史現象，林林總總，錯綜龐雜，從某一面敍述之，從某一觀點研究之，合我的材料則取之，不合者則去之，究不能窺歷史的全貌。所以中西史學，以體例上比較，中國史學，自是正宗。中國有兼容並包的紀傳體，西方的史學體例，則狹隘多了。

史爲敍事之書。無敍事卽無史學。曾經如何如何的往事，翔實而生動的敍述了，史家的責任，便已盡到大半，解釋、綜合是敍事以後的事。有敍事而無解釋、綜合，仍不失其爲史；有解釋、綜合而無敍事，則將流於玄學家之言，難儕於歷史之林。中國史家拙於解釋、綜合，而長於敍事，是中國史家，已得史學之大者。且中國史家，並非僅堆積史料，並非無別識心裁，想通古今之變，成一家之言的史家，比比皆是。不過，中國的史家，樂於隱藏在史實背後，不輕易出面，而將見解史實化，隱約其見解於史實敍述之中，使讀者讀其所述即知其所欲言。不得已時，在論贊中發揮，論贊在正文之後，與歷史敍述，嚴劃此疆彼界。比較之西方史家的邊敍事邊解釋，作者的臆見，作者的當代觀點，往往滲入其中者，更易得歷史之眞。史家太露鋒芒，動輒解釋綜合，發表意見，每易混淆歷史，而近代西方史家則但視此類歷史作品爲歷史，是偏激之論。

中國班馬之書，陳范之史，如日月麗天，歷萬古而常新。後有作者，踵事增華則可，而不能將其完全代替，以其包括史事豐富，史家不能旦夕離此材料淵藪。西方的史學著作則不然，一部光芒萬丈的大著，往往風行數年而被代替焉，往往流傳數十年而銷聲歛跡焉。古希臘史家的作品，固已僅有古典文學的價值，十九世紀英國大史家麥考萊（Lord Macaulay, 1800-1859）的英國史（History of England）及卡萊爾（Thomas Carlyle, 1795-1881）的法國革命史（The French Revolution），也早爲以後的英國史與法國革命史所代替，二十世紀初英國已少有人閱讀其書[84]，其論點甚多被推翻或修正。像十八世紀吉朋（Edward Gibbon, 1737-1794）的羅馬帝國衰亡史（The History of the Decline and Fall of the Roman Empire），迄今仍不可廢，算是享壽最久的了。西方的史學著作，敍事少，解釋多，綜合多，其敍事是爲了支持其解釋，其解釋又須配合其綜合，一部大著，究能寫上多少史蹟，大是問題。一旦有人深入研究，另有新解釋，新綜合，那麼舊著便全部崩潰瓦解，自無繼續存在的價值了。西方史學著作，永遠在新陳代謝，新著推舊著，西方人士也都承認這一點。中國史書敍事多，故能長存，西方史書解釋多綜合多，故常更易。其間孰優孰劣，不待辨而可知。白特費爾德說西方學者必須注意中國僅是爲了習知史學如何可能會走錯路，那麼中國學者必須注意西方更會有同樣的理由了。

西方史學重解釋、綜合的結果，產生了許多看似精奧而實際不能成立的歷史定律，[從赫格爾、馬克斯到斯彭格勒（Oswald Spengler, 1880-1936）、湯恩比（Arnold Toynbee, 1889-1975）、都是想以歷史定律來決定以往、現在及未來的演變及發展，而其定律，是由部分歷史材料而獲得，以部分來概括全體，而又推之於現在與未來，其荒謬固不待言，最嚴重者爲有時足以貽患人類於無窮。第二次世界大戰以後，西方史家逐漸覺悟了，他們不再認爲從歷史上可以得到什麼定律，一九五四年伯麟（Isaiah Berlin, 1909-）⑬⑤出版他的名著「歷史必然論」（Historical Inevitability），提出嶄新的看法，他的看法是由反動當代科學史家（scientific historians）與歷史哲學家（philosophers of history）而出發的，科學史家與歷史哲學家認爲歷史有其必然性，不能加以人爲的判斷與解釋。伯麟則認爲歷史不遵守科學的規律，將決定論（determinism）應用到歷史上是不可能的；將史實中性化，使其脫離人的影響，尤其是脫離人的褒與貶（praise and blame），是離奇而荒謬的；以爲過去有一簡單型態（a single patterned structure），人類錯綜龐雜的萬象，皆可用之解釋而包容其中，是不折不扣的神話（myth），曲解了歷史。

一九五七年頗柏（K. R. Popper, 1902- ）⑬⑥的「歷史主義的貧乏」（The Poverty of Historicism）一書問世⑬⑦，更是革命性的著

作。他所謂歷史主義，是指所有相信歷史決定論（historical determinism）的理論，認爲歷史主要的目的是預測（historical prediction），欲預測，則必須去發現韻律（rhythms）、模型（patterns）、定律（laws）、趨勢（trends），以劃定歷史的演化（the evolution of history）⑱。頗氏則不認爲有所謂歷史定律，因爲歷史不像物體，有一定規律的運動。歷史上的趨勢，雖可以尋找，但趨勢不是定律，趨勢是現存事實的一種說明（a historical statement），而不是一個用之四海而皆準的定律（a universal law），它有時間性與地點性。所以頗氏堅持歷史上沒有最後的解釋（final interpretations），沒有歷史是完全符合史實發生時的眞相的，史家不能作詳盡的預測（a prediction of details），歷史的特徵是表現在實際的單一的或特殊的事件上，而不是表現在定律上或通則上，去解釋一件事的原因，即是去說明它如何與爲什麼發生的，換句話說，是將它的故事說出來（to tell its "story"）！這是對柏拉圖、維科（Giambattista Vico）、斯彭格勒迄於湯恩比以來循環論（cyclical determinism）的攻擊，也是對赫格爾、馬克斯理論的大革命。

允尼爾（G. J. Renier）在其「歷史之目的與方法」（History: Its Purpose and Method）一書中⑲，更强調敍事的重要，反對解釋的歷史，他一再的向史家呼籲：「講出歷史的故事來！」即使是白特費爾德也大聲的說：「歷史誠然是屬於描述一類的作品，就像遊記書一樣。」「歷史研究（historical study）的整個過程，是一種移向歷史探尋（historical research）的運動，帶我們從一般到特殊，從抽象到具體。」⑭更早一點的先覺者崔衞林（G. M. Trevelyan, 1876-1962）自二十世紀初葉便已頻頻疾呼了，「歷史不是純粹材料的蒐集與解釋」⑭，「因爲當代史家受德國化科學分類法（Germanizing hierarchy）的訓練，致不視歷史爲『故事』，而視之爲『科學』，史家最主要的敍事藝術（the art of narrative），被大大地遺忘了。敍事在近代著作中是最弱的一環，我想那是太嚴重的弱點了。有些作者像是永遠沒有研究如何敍述一個故事的藝術。……而歷史乃一『故事』，是歷史不變的本質。」⑫

這種由解釋、綜合返向敍事的趨勢，說明西方史學界已覺悟到着重解釋、綜合的危險性，而思有以矯正之，以挽救歷史的危機。當代歷史決定論的代表史家湯恩比，其大著「歷史研究」（A Study of History）受盡西方後起史家的攻擊。荷蘭史家吉爾（Pieter Geyl）在「與史家辯」（Debates with Historians, 1955）一書中不留情的駁斥他。許多英國史家認爲他的努力完全失敗，卡爾（E. H. Carr, 1892- ）在「何謂歷史？」（What is History? 1961）一書中說:

> 「世界第一次大戰以後，湯恩比決心以歷史循環論代替歷史直線發展論，這是一種社會沒落的代表論。自湯恩比失敗以後，英國史家已多滿足地縮回他們的手，同時宣佈說：在歷史上根本沒有什麼通則。」⑬

西方史學界此一轉變，可以作中國史學沒有走錯路的最佳解釋。數千年來中國史學所走的路是康莊大道，所操的步伐很穩健，近兩百年來西方波瀾壯濶的史學，仍不得不轉向，重走中國所久已走熟的路。其源遠者其流長，中國史學是有其不可及之處了。如中國史家在所敍故事的周圍，兼敍述時代潮流，社會背景，以及可能的原因與影響，那麼中國史家的敍事藝術，將是「百尺竿頭，更進一步」。

第六節　從白特費爾德觀念的轉變看中國史學的卓越性——兼論中國史學的世界地位

自一九六一年年底，白特費爾德對中國史學的看法，驟起轉變。他所發表的「東方的歷史」、「世界歷史與文化的比較研究」等文，修正了以前不少的偏見：

他不再認爲西方文化獨富歷史觀念，而說：「與世界其他地區相比，中國與西歐都發展了富有科學特性與歷史觀念的文化。」「巨大的中國文化，產生了可觀的歷史文獻，對世界有其永恒的價值。」

他不再認爲中國的考據學未達到一較高的境界，而說：「有證據可以證明中國史家雅欲批評其前代史家的敍事，甚或具有了懷疑所有過去作者的態度，考據學發展到一崇高境界，似昭然若揭，中國史家無疑問已臻於所謂智力的洗練。」

他承認了中國史學的特殊性與重要性：「對研究史學史的人來講，在西方之外，另一偉大的中國文化，在歷史方面蔚爲一可觀的發展，且精神與作品與西方迥然不同。這是極富意義的。」「業餘如我，僅讀翻譯成西方文字的古代中國的歷史作品，即已發現在歷史思想上，在寫歷史的方式上，東西的歧異，彰明較著。」「不移入亞洲，我們甚至不能討論我們歷史著作與歷史思想的淵源。」「中國史學在另外方向的發展，如此其壯觀，比較此兩大系統（另指西方史學系統），說明兩者太不相同的歷史精神類型，爲一相當有趣之事。」這與他以前狃於東方學者能輕易地自西方史學獲得啓示，西方學者則不易窺得東方史學的精奧以及如不爲想知道中國史學如何走錯了路，則似無研究中國史學必要的成見，不啻有霄壤之別。

他也承認了比較文化研究的重要性以及研究時應採用全球性的觀點:「我們文化有些方面，我們自己將永遠不能瞭解，除非我們知道其他大陸的一些文化，最低限度是以比較法去研究一些專題。」「我們不要忘記，在十九世紀後半期，更清楚的在二十世紀，整個寰宇，已凝成一個了。一個地區的事件，影響及於世界的相反的一端，凡事皆連在一起，此不僅限於文化觀念的擴展——也意味着政治、外交、國際關係及大部分文化生活變成了全球性。凡此皆待以全球性的規模，自全人類的觀點去研究，即使說我們將以西方觀點或中國觀點去研究全球歷史，也是錯的——我們必須儘量採用全球性的觀點，在心目中僅有一個世界文化……我們需要一個歷史態度，對待當代事件——在今天的日子裡，是提升至一個全球性的觀點。」

從上面看來，白氏觀念的轉變，是極為鉅大的，也是極富意義的。其轉變的關鍵，在於白氏的知識問題上。以前他對中國史學無所知，故所在「設想」，恣意批評。一旦詳讀了西方漢學家所寫的「中日史家」一書，以及聽漢學家李約瑟的口頭轉告後，遂恍然於中國史學的悠久博大，於是重著於筆墨，以正西方史學界的視聽，學術之公，未泯於白氏，這是白氏令人敬佩之處，也更可證明中國史學的卓越性了。人不分中西，凡稍知中國史學者，卽知尊之貴之，如白氏所知更多，將不知如何評論與推崇中國史學了。

自然白氏所知中國史學，仍極有限。他肯定的認為「中國史學與歐洲一四五〇年至一七五〇年間史學，蓋在伯仲之間」，無疑是說中國史學未到達西方史學的最高境界（十八世紀末葉以後西方史學才到達最高境界），不足與西方史學分庭抗禮，這是極令人不能心服而氣平的。中西史學，整個比較起來，實難分軒輊，各有其特殊成就，各有其世界的地位。如論史學起源之早，成熟之速，綿延之久，範圍之濶，西方實遜於中國；若就晚近數世紀西方新興史學而言，其治史方法的爭奇鬪艷，其史學體例的五光十彩，其蒐集史料、批評史料的富有科學精神，其分析史實、解釋史實的獨擅精密系統，也非中國所能望及。中西史學在世界史學潮流裡，所代表的是兩股主流，將兩者互作比較，進而會通，則世界性的新史學，可期其姍姍其現。

第三章 註釋:

❶皮錫瑞語，見湘報類纂乙集卷下頁三

❷江標變學論

❸曾廉語，見籌辦夷務始末，同治朝，卷四七，頁二四

❹倭仁語，見同上。

❺浦立本在致聽衆雜誌編者的信中（一九六一年九月二十八日），曾指出白氏的同道，則對中國史學有議論，不是白氏一人。

❻E. G. Pulleyblank, *Chinese History and World History,* 1955, p. 36

❼E. H. Carr, *What is History?* 1961, pp. 145–146:

"The history of the English-speaking world in the last 400 years has beyond question been a great period of history. But to treat it as the centre-piece of universal history, and everything else as peripheral to it, is an unhappy distortion of perspective. It is the duty of a university to correct such popular distortions. The school of modern history in this university seems to me to fall short in the discharge of this duty. It is surely wrong that a candidate should be allowed to sit for an honours degree in history in a major university without an adequate knowledge of any modern language other than English.......a candidate possessing some knowledge of the affairs of Asia, Africa or Latin America has at present a very limited opportunity of displaying it in a paper called with magnificent nineteenth-century panache 'The Expansion of Europe'. The title unfortunately fits the contents: the candidate is not invited to know anything even of countries with an important and well-documented history like China or Persia except what happened when the Europeans attempted to take them over. Lectures are, I am told, delivered in this university on the history of Russia and Persia and China—but not by members of the faculty of history. The conviction expressed by the professor of Chinese in his inaugural lecture five years ago that 'China cannot be regarded as outside the mainstream of human history' has fallen on deaf ears among Cambridge historians."

❽R. G. Collingwood, *The Idea of History,* 1946, p. 90:

"In Europe alone human life is genuinely historical, whereas in China or India or among the natives of America there is no true historical progress but only a static unchanging civilization or a series of changes in which old forms of life are replaced by new forms without that steady cumulative development which is the peculiarity of historical progress. Europe is thus a privileged region of human life."

❾參見 D. C. Twitchett, *Chinese politics and society from the Bronge Age to the Manchus,* in Half the World, the History and Culture of China & Japan, ed. by Arnold Toynbee, 1973, p. 53; W. H. Dray, *Philosophy of History,* 1964, p. 71

❿J. R. Strayer 寫 Marc Bloch (1886–1944)「史家技術」(*The Historian's Craft*) 一書的導論(Introduction)時所强調者:

"Western man has always been historically minded, and this trait has been accentuated during the last two centuries." (Marc Bloch, The Historian's Craft, 1954, p. vii)

⓫Marc Bloch, *The Historian's Craft,* 1954, p. 4:

"Unlike others, our civilization has always been extremely attentive to its past.......Our first masters, the Greeks and the Romans, were history-writing peoples. Christianity is a religion of historians".

⓬John Lukacs, *Historical Consciousness,* 1968, p. 23:

"We 'are entering the age of universal history'. Western civilization has now spread all over the world; neither the scientific method nor the professional study of history are any longer European and American intellectual monopolies. Yet historical consciousness is still something specifically 'Western'."

⑬J. W. Thompson, *Preface to a History of Historical Writing*, 1942, p. vii:

"Western society has always been historically minded, and possesses a mass of literary evidence on its past which differs in quality and quantity from that of any other culture known. The primary force in this direction came from the Greek genius. The next factor has been the influence of Christianity, which has always been history-conscious, unlike Buddhism and Brahmanism, or any other oriental religion, ancient or modern. Finally, the advance of modern science and the material progress achieved in the last two centuries have profoundly affected the thinking of the Western world."

⑭見元史董文炳傳及新元史董文炳傳。按元史董文炳傳五千餘册作五十餘册，恐誤，今從新元史。

⑮見元史劉秉忠傳。

⑯進金史表實際的作者是歐陽玄，見歐陽玄圭齋文集卷十三。

⑰見元史歐陽玄傳

⑱見明實錄太祖實錄卷三十九

⑲劉坊「萬季野行狀」

⑳如南雷文約卷一戶部貴州清吏司主事兼經筵日講官次公董公墓誌銘；南雷文案卷三旌表節孝馮母鄭太安人墓誌銘

㉑討論「國可滅，史不可滅」此一史學觀念的文章，中文方面有毛一波的「由『史不可滅』引起的話（中央日報文史第七十二期，民國六十八年九月十八日）及拙文「國可滅，史不可滅」（時報雜誌第四期，民國六十八年十二月三十日至六十九年一月五日）；英文方面有楊聯陞的 *The Organization of Chinese Official Historiography: Principles and Methods of the Standard Histories from the Tang Through the Ming Dynasty*, in *Historians of China and Japan*, ed. by W. G. Beasley & E. G. Pulleyblank, 1961, pp. 46-47

㉒見舊唐書令狐德棻傳

㉓同上

㉔修晉書詔載於晉書前

㉕見修晉書詔

㉖同上

㉗見晉書陳壽傳

㉘范曄獄中與諸甥姪書，載於宋書范曄傳。

㉙同上

㉚見王鳴盛十七史商榷卷六十一

㉛見宋書自序，趙翼於廿二史劄記卷九「宋書多徐爰舊本」條曾論及之。

㉜見宋書自序

㉝參見魏書崔浩傳及北史崔浩傳

㉞語出左傳莊公二十三年、宣公二年。討論中國史官記事遵守共同必守之法，說詳見柳詒徵國史要義「史權」篇。

㉟左丘明稱美春秋之語，見左傳成公十四年。

㊱見漢書藝文志

㊲見史記太史公自序

㊳見呂氏春秋卷十六先識覽

㊴同上

㊵同上

㊶R. G. Collingwood, *The Idea of History,* 1946, pp. 25–29; E. H. Carr, *What is History?* 1961, pp. 103–104

㊷H. Butterfield, *Universal History and the Comparative Study of Civilization,* in Sir Herbert Butterfield Cho Yun Hsu & William H. Mcneill on Chinese and World History, 1971, p. 19:

"In my quarter of the globe the first people who developed historical literature were the leaders of great military empires who wrote about their own present times, wrote about themselves—they were monarchs who wanted their victories in war to be remembers by furture generations. It was like Winston Churchill writing about the events in which he had taken part. The first big body of historical literature in my region of the globe was the work of people not interested in the past at all—they were just anxious that their own deeds, their own successes, should be remembered by future generations. And that was the situation for at least a thousand years."

㊷黃帝時中國設史官，雖不必深信，然至遲到殷代必已有史官，因地下材料殷墟甲骨文中時時出現史官的名字。

㊸梁啓超於中國歷史研究法補編頁一五五云：

「一直到清代， 國史館的纂修官一定由翰林院的編修兼任。翰林院是極清貴的地方，人才也極精華之選，平常人稱翰林爲太史，一面尊敬，一面也就表示這種關係（按梁氏所謂這種關係，係指史官地位的高貴而言）。一個國家，以如此地位，妙選人才以充其選，其尊貴爲外國所無，科擧爲人才唯一出身之途，科擧中最清貴的是太史，可以說以全國第一等人才做史官了。」

㊹見梁啓超中國歷史研究法補編頁一五四

㊺同上

㊻同上

㊼見漢書儒林傳

㊽見宋史選擧志

㊾見清實錄及楊椿上明鑑綱目館總裁書

㊿見明史文苑傳，朱彝尊曝書亭集徐一夔傳文字有小異。

51見史通史官篇

52同上

53見新唐書朱子奢傳

54唐文宗始詔左右史立螭頭下，記宰相奏對。見新唐書張次宗傳。

55見新唐書鄭朗傳

56見新唐書魏謩傳（附於魏徵傳）

57見錢謙益初學集卷三十五汪母節壽序

58 同上卷四十八故禮部尚書兼翰林院學士協理參事贈太子太保諡文肅王公行狀

59 見錢謙益有學集卷三十四光祿大夫柱國太子太師吏兵二部尚書武英殿大學士贈特進光祿大夫左柱國太傅諡文貞路公神道碑

60 同上卷二十八特進光祿大夫柱國少傅兼太子太傅吏部尚書中極殿大學士諡文端劉公墓誌銘

61 見初學集卷四十七特進光祿大夫柱國少師兼太子太師兵部尚書中極殿大學士孫公行狀

62 同上卷五十都察左副都御史贈右都御史加贈太子太保諡忠烈楊公墓誌銘

63 Lord Acton, *Lectures on Modern History*, 1906; Also see Herbert Butterfield, *Man on His Past*, 1955

64 見南雷詩歷卷二

65 同上

66 見史通忤時篇

67 見錢大昕潛研堂文集萬季野先生傳

68 *Preface: Histories of the Latin and Germanic Nations from 1494-1514*, in Fritz Stern's the Varieties of History, 1956, p. 57

69 見史通直書篇

70 同上

71 見史通鑒識篇

72 見吳縝新唐書糾謬序

73 見錢大昕潛研堂文集春秋論二

74 見錢大昕十駕齋養新錄唐書直筆新例條

75 見王鳴盛十七史商榷唐史論斷條

76 見王鳴盛十七史商榷序

77 漢書司馬遷傳贊云:「自劉向、揚雄博極群書, 皆稱遷有良史之才, 服其善序事理, 辨而不華, 質而不俚, 其文直, 其事核, 不虛美, 不隱惡, 故謂之實錄。」

78 顧炎武日知錄卷十八「三朝要典」條云:「崇禎帝批講官李明睿疏曰:『纂修實錄之法, 惟在據事直書, 則是非互見。』大哉王言, 其萬世作史之準繩乎!」

79 見論語爲政篇

(80)見同書衞靈公篇

(81)見同書子路篇

(82)見同書同篇

(83)見顧炎武日知錄卷二豐熙僞尙書條

(84)見崔述考信錄提要卷上

(85)司馬遷寫史記時，天下遺文古事，靡不畢集於前，其所依據的資料，固不僅上述數種，近人已作了不少這方面的詳細研究。

(86)見章學誠文史通義「答邵二雲書」

(87)見章學誠章氏遺書卷十四「與陳觀民工部論史學」

(88)見全祖望鮚埼亭集外編卷十二「蕭山毛檢討別傳」

(89)同註八七

(90)Beryl Smalley, *Historians in the Middle Ages*, 1974, p. 19:

"Both the style and the method of Roman historians show the close links between history and rhetoric. There were literary conventions, the historian puts speeches into his characters' mouths: a general addresses his troops before battle, a statesman puts his case in assembly, and so on. Readers are not supposed to take these as tape-recordings or even as an accurate report of what was said: they may represent the gist of it, but their real function is to adorn the style. Medieval students delighted in Sallust's speeches and copied them eagerly. Convention allowed a certain freedom from accuracy. Dates could be dispensed with. Documentation was not called for."

(91)G. P. Gooch, *History and Historians in the Nineteenth Century*, 1913, p. 227:

"Macaulay explained his conception of the task of the historian in an essay entitled 'History'. To be a really great historian, he declared, was perhaps the rarest of intellectual distinctions. There were many perfect works of science, poems and speeches; there was no perfect history. Herodotus was a delightful romancer. Thucydides was the greatest master of perspective but not a deep thinker. Plutarch was childish, Polybius dull. No historian ever showed such complete indifference to truth as Livy. Tacitus was the greatest portrait-painter and the greatest dramatist of antiquity."

(92)Ibid., p. 75

(93)Ibid., p. 1:

"The Middle Ages......Printing was unknown and books were rare. The critical treatment of documents had not begun, nor was it realised that there was any need to treat them critically. Happy in the treasures of his monastic library, the pious chronicler did not stop to investigate their value, and copied the errors of earlier compilations into his pages. Though the forging of charters was a regular trade, the means of discovering deception had not been invented. Recorded events were accepted without challenge, and the sanction of tradition guaranteed the reality of the occurence. Finally, the atmosphere of the Middle Ages was saturated with theology.......History was a sermon, not a science, an exercise in Christian evidences, not a disinterested attempt to trace and explain the course of civilization."

(94)見孟子盡心篇

(95)見史記五帝本紀

(96)見史記伯夷列傳

(97)見三國志魏志卷六袁紹傳注引

(98)見三國志魏武帝紀建安五年

(99)論魏晉以來談辯影響於考據學，請參見牟潤孫就職香港中文大學講座教授講演「論魏晉以來之崇尚談辯及其影響」，該講詞於一九六六年由香港中文大學出版。

(100)司馬光「與范內翰論修書帖」，附見於明萬曆刊本通鑑。

(101)見資治通鑑考異，太子客使呂釋之夜見呂后條

(102)見同上晉王命克寧等立存勗條

⑩③白特費爾德給「聽衆」編者的一封信，說浦立本談司馬光的一段文章「中日史家一書的一五五至一五六頁」難讀，而浦氏那一段文章正是談司馬光的編叢目及長編；白氏說：「他那篇文章（指浦氏「中國史學批評：劉知幾與司馬光」一文）標題中的另一人是劉知幾，我不知西方史學界人士將覺得此人如何？」可見白氏是太不清楚中國史學的行情了！

⑩④參見拙文「顧炎武與清代歷史考據學派之形成」，故宮文獻第三卷第四期及第四卷第一期，民國六十一年九月、十二月

⑩⑤見四庫全書日知錄提要

⑩⑥見潘耒日知錄序

⑩⑦見閻詠先府君行述

⑩⑧參見尚書古文疏證卷八第一百二十條及胡適「治學的方法與材料」一文（胡適文存第三集）

⑩⑨戴南山集「史論」

⑪⓪參見費特兒（Ed. Fueter, 1876–1928）所著「現代史學史」（*Geschichte der neven Historiographie*, 1911）及姚從吾師所寫「近代歐洲歷史方法論的起源」一文（載於中國歷史學會所編史學集刊第二期，後收入姚從吾先生全集（一）歷史方法論）。

⑪①G. P. Gooch, *History and Historians in the Nineteenth Century*, 1913, p. 75

⑪②閻若璩寫尚書古文疏證，已用了語言文字方面的知識（如上文所言及），顧炎武在蒐集與應用古文書、古遺物的資料方面，尤爲積極，他常「懷毫舐墨，躑躅於山林猿鳥之間」，並用金石文字資料，與史書互相發明。詳見拙文「顧炎武與清代歷史考據學派之形成」。

⑪③見戴震文集卷九「與姚孝廉姬傳書」

⑪④見王念孫「說文解字注序」

⑪⑤見方東樹漢學商兌

⑪⑥見潛研堂文集「史記志疑序」

⑪⑦見十七史商榷序

⑪⑧見考信錄提要卷上，頁九

⑲同上，頁一七

⑳同上，頁一八

㉑同上，頁二三

㉒同上，頁三四

㉓同上，頁一〇

㉔見史通敍事篇

㉕同上

㉖皆見史通言語篇，類此見解，亦見於敍事篇及摹擬篇

㉗見史通鑒識篇

㉘見文史通義「答邵二雲」

㉙見章氏遺書「與陳觀民工部論史學」

㉚參見文史通義「黠陋」篇及章氏遺書「與陳觀民工部論史學」

㉛同㉙

㉜見廿二史劄記卷一「各史例目異同」條

㉝參見文史通義「書教下」篇

㉞G. M. Trevelyan 於*Clio, A Muse* (1913) 一文中慨乎言之。

㉟伯麟現爲英國牛津大學社會政治理論教授 (Professor of Social and Political Theory)，並且是 Fellow of All Souls College，刻在英國史學界極有名。

㊱頗柏是倫敦大學邏輯與科學方法教授 (Professor of Logic and Scientific Method)，他另一名著是 *The Open Society and its Enemies*。

㊲其中收有頗柏一九四四、一九四五年的論文。

㊳按 Hans Meyerhoff 之説(見其一九五九年所編 *The Philosophy of History in our Time* 一書頁二九九至三〇〇)，頗柏將 historicism 一詞用錯，他沒有深究 historicism 一詞的發展及演變，恰又將此名詞用反。historicism 謂世界上所有的觀念都是有歷史條件的，由此，是有限制而相對的。經驗事實 (empirical facts) 以及歷史上的邏輯方法 (the logical techniques in history)，是不同於抽象的普通科學的。這正與頗柏所謂 historicism 相反，而頗柏本人卽屬於其中的一員。

⑬⑨允尼爾是英國倫敦大學教授，荷蘭籍，一九五〇年出版其「歷史之目的與方法」一書

⑭⓪H. Butterfield, *The Whig Interpretation of History*, 1931, p. 67 and p. 69

⑭①G. M. Trevelyan, *Clio, A Muse*, 1913, p. 162

⑭②Ibid., pp. 148–149

⑭③E. H. Carr, *What is History?* 1961, p. 37

第四章　西方非正統史家論中國史學

治亞洲史、美洲史或非洲史的西方史家，可以稱之爲非正統史家。他們傾注於歐洲以外地區的歷史，離開歷史的中心，而作側面的研究，所以不被視之爲正統。但是他們所接觸的面廣，歷史的視線比較遼濶，所以觀念較西方正統史家開明，歐洲爲得天獨厚的歷史地區，在他們的心目中，大致已煙消霧釋了。平等的看人類，一視同仁的研究世界各個角落的歷史，是他們治史的態度，以致胸中無成見，而對胸中有成見的西方正統史家，往往施以猛烈的攻擊。中國史學，他們所知者仍然很少，中國史在世界史中所佔的重要地位，則大致能爲他們所承認。富有歷史的同情與諒解，使他們能超越了西方正統史家的藩籬。

第一節　奈芬司（Allan Nevins, 1890–1971）

奈芬司是美國史家，一九三一年到一九五八年間任哥倫比亞大學美國史教授，治美國史及人物傳記，著作甚多，如「美國的殘酷考驗」（Ordeal of the Union, 1947)、「羅斯福在歷史上的地位」（The Place of Franklin D. Roosevelt in History, 1965)、「美國簡史」(A Short History of the United States, 1966)、「阿當穆斯: 美國夢想的史家」(James Truslow Adams: Historians of the American Dream, 1968) 及「歷史入門」(The Gateway to History, 1938, revised, 1962) 等, 皆頗著稱。其於「歷史入門」一書中論及東西史學的異同云:

「歷史像一盞燈, 由人類提着, 一步一步的走向前去, 此一觀念較之認爲歷史僅爲說有趣的掌故, 描寫栩栩如生的情景, 或敍述一組活龍活現的人物, 自然是廣濶多了。這本質上是西方的與現代的。至於東方, 甚至於連上古希臘, 歷史是偶發事件的混合體, 不可理解, 或是壁紙型式 (a wallpaper pattern), 一再重複。」❶

又論歷史要求普遍性云:

「歷史要求普遍性, 視所有人類的活動, 爲其領域。……西方作家, 包括美國作家在內, 很久以來, 太少注意到斯拉夫歷史, 更少注意到東方背景。」❷

第二節　瓦爾班德 (T. W. Wallband, 1901-　)

瓦爾班德與泰勒 (A. M. Taylor, 1915-　) 於一九四九年合著「文化的過去與現在」(Civilization Past and Present) 一書, 其中有很值注意的一段:

「中國是史家的樂園。在那裡, 史家偃受尊敬, 其作品備受珍視。以此之故, 中國留下了近乎齊全的歷史記錄 (the most nearly complete historical records)。但是當我們遠溯至邃古時代, 則所見的記錄, 僅爲神話, 而非歷史。在這方面, 中國與所有其他民族一樣，因爲神秘的而非逼眞的解釋隱秘的過去，是人類的天性。但是當希臘民族與印歐民族（the Indo-Aryans）寫史詩以頌揚其祖先之際，中國人已創始用散文作歷史敍事了。其敍事如果不是實在的（factual），却是迷人的（fascinating）。」❸

瓦爾班德曾編輯「印度的瓜分：原因與責任」（The Partition of India: Causes and Responsibility, ed., 1966）一書，泰勒則另著「印尼獨立與聯合國」（Indonesian Independence and the United Nations, 1960），二人的歷史視野，皆頗遼濶。

第三節　巴容（Jacques Barzun, 1907-　）

巴容與葛勒福（H. F. Graff, 1921-　）於一九五七年合著「現代研究者」（The Modern Researcher, 1957, revised, 1970）一書，其中有云：

「在中國語文中，我們發現『史』（historian）字的原形爲手執盛簡册的容器，在狩獵時史所以記錄。從記錄此類激動的事件，不同文化的人們，開始記錄皇室典禮、宗教犧牲以及轟動的事件。最後逐日的記錄（a day-to-day record）保存下來了——在中國，是衆所周知的春秋，縱然春秋非逐日記錄而係編年。在此頗爲乏味的編年史（西元前八世紀）之前，中國尙有記言的尙書，滙集了鍼砭官吏的名言。此較早的尙書，比春秋枯燥的記事，更富詩意與吸引力，可與奇幻的政府檔案（fanciful archive of state papers）相比擬。春秋則屬於公家日記一類。兩者對我們而言，都是眞歷史（true history）的資料。

在西方文化中，發現同類情況，而大不同者有二，如以荷馬敍述初殘戰爭（Trojan War）與中國的尙書相比，我們發現希臘作品爲內容遠爲豐富，組織遠爲精密的傳說歷史（legendary history）——一較富藝術性的作品。當我們拿希臘公元前五世紀的希羅多德（Herodotus）的作品與春秋相比時，我們不僅發現文學藝術方面的超越，也發現作者對其他民族及其歷史的深度好奇心——如埃及人、米底亞人（Medes）、波斯人等等。」❹

巴容另著「美國大學」（The American University, 1968）、「克麗歐與其醫生：心理歷史、量化歷史與歷史」（Clio and the Doctors: Psycho-history, quanto-history and History, 1974）等書，葛勒福則曾主編「美國帝國主義與菲律賓叛亂」（American Imperialism and the Philippines Insurrection, ed., 1969）一書。

第四節　卡耳（E. H. Carr, 1892-　）

卡耳是英國史家，以治俄國史而享名。一九六一年出版「何謂歷史」（What is History?）一書❺，風行西方史學界。他呼籲史家擴大範圍，跳出英國去，跳出西歐去，一窺世界之大。因此他對中國史有親切感，而盛推李約瑟博士（Dr. Needham）所著「中國之科學與文明」（Science and Civilization in China）極可能爲二十世紀六十年代劍橋大學出版的最偉大的歷史著作：

「在過去十年中，極可能被將來視爲劍橋出版最偉大的歷史著作，而又完全在劍橋歷史系以外所寫，未得其絲毫協助，我推荐李約瑟博士的中國之科學與文明。」❻

他認爲中國爲

「具有重要而富史料性歷史（well-documented history）的國

家」❼,

但是他似乎不認爲中國古代的文化是歷史的:

「就像亞洲古代文化一樣, 古典的希臘羅馬文化, 基本上是非歷史的 (unhistorical)。」❽

第五節　魏吉瑞 (A. G. Widgery, 1887-　)

魏吉瑞曾任美國公爵大學 (Duke University) 哲學教授, 其精力瘁於史義的研究, 所以可以將他視作史家。一九六一年印行「歷史解釋」(Interpretations of History) 一書, 從中國的孔子談到英國的湯恩比, 其中論中國的史學云:

「從古代起, 在中國就有數量相當可觀的歷史著作, 就現存的來看, 它們主要的是『編年史』(annals), 大都是關於統治階級的描素, 他們的生平, 內部的紛爭, 以及新朝的興起與昌隆, 很少論及歷史的性質與意義。不曾爲任何遠景, 繼續不斷的努力, 以發現歷史過程及歷史事件的深意。注意力注於現在與過去。西方有學養的人, 已被中國的藝術、繪畫、象牙雕刻、碧玉雕刻、木刻等作品以及北平的宮殿所迷惑, 而且深受影響。但是這些藝術品的數量, 不管單獨看是如何可觀, 與中國悠久的歷史及衆多的人口比起來, 是嫌區區不足數的。在中國整個歷史上, 中國人始終從事於農業及手工業, 他們的生活本質上是單簡的。從他們單簡的生活, 我們可以瞭解他們對歷史的態度。」❾

又云:

「中國的思想家, 往往將歷史視作道德的教材, 罪惡永遠被懲罰, 美德永遠得到佳報。其結果不經常或立刻顯現, 帝位可能被惡人攫取，但是說者謂惡人不能保有它。縱然表面上惡人能現佳運，內心方面他們是悲哀的。戰爭爲衞護正義必獲勝利的信念而毅然掀起。

考慮到中國人對歷史的態度，必須顧及他們普遍的平靜性格。他們的平靜性格，甚至比印度人更普遍而明顯。在他們的歷史上，個人不怎麼常受到邪惡勢力的騷擾；他們也少深受他們社會史上所發生的慘禍的激動。……

中國人對歷史的態度，可以稱之爲靜寂主義者。」⑩

一九六七年魏氏又出版「歷史中的意義」(The Meaning in History) 一書。

第六節　巴拉克勞甫 (Geoffrey Barraclough, 1908–)

巴拉克勞甫是英國史家，以治中古史及現代史而馳名。著有「中世紀德國」(Mediaeval Germany, 1938)、「近代德國的起源」(The Origins of Modern Germany, 1946)、「變動世界中的歷史」(History in a Changing World, 1955)、「歐洲在思想與行動上的統一」(European Unity in Thought and Action, 1963)、「現代史導論」(An Introduction to Contemporary History, 1964)、「中古時代的東歐與西歐」(Eastern and Western Europe in the Middle Ages, 1970)、以及「世界毀滅」(The World Crash, 1977) 等書。

巴氏曾任國際史學委員會 (The International Committee of the Historical Association) 主席，第二次世界大戰期間，又曾在中東服役於皇家空軍，以致他眼界遼濶，觀念開明，反對「歐洲爲歷史重心的成見」(Europacentri view of the past) ⑪，在其著作中，不斷大聲疾

呼:

「主要從西歐觀點解釋事件，已經不够了，我們必須嘗試採用較廣濶的世界史觀點。」⑫

「跳出歐洲去，跳出西方去，將視線投射到所有的地區與所有的時代。」⑬

「我們必須擺脫太狹隘的歐洲觀念；譬如列中國史於中世紀，是既無益而又使人誤解，因爲中國人民一點也不是中世紀的。」⑭

「責備希臘人與埃及人，中國人與印度人，沒有到達我們所到達的境界，既不公平，又無利益，因爲沒有理由推想他們計劃到達像是合我們意的。」⑮

「遲至十九世紀中葉，大部分非洲內部，未經開發，甚爲神秘，所知東方，爲神話與傳說的混合，難語於歷史。……十九世紀發展的歷史思想（historical thinking），敎我們考慮與珍重過去的每一方面，如此始能解脫自己環境的枷鎖，進入外國人的標準與立場之中，以欣賞其文化。然而此一對世界史的緩慢探索，在基本上是歐洲民族的成就……醉心歷史，篤信歷史的價值，甚至自歷史內涵（historical context）及歷史遠景（historical perspective）以看事件的趨勢，是一西方態度，對我們西方人而言，這是極爲自然的，很少能覺察到做到什麼程度。在中國或印度，沒有恰似的態度。在中國，誠然保存了極好的編年史與年表，最低限度提供了歷史的骨幹（the bare bones of history）；但是印度在歐洲人侵入以前，少有現代標準下的所謂歷史，兩個國家皆極少關心保存歷史記錄。」⑯

第七節　麥尼耳（W. H. McNeill, 1917-　　）

麥尼耳是加拿大史家，任敎於美國芝加哥大學，以「西方的興起」（The Rise of the West, 1963）一書而馳名。其後曾主編「古典中國」（Classical China, ed., by W. H. McNeill and J. W. Sedlar, 1970）與「回教世界」（The Islamic World, ed., by W. H. McNeill and M. B. Waldman, 1973）兩書。其一卷本的「世界史」（A World History, 1967, revised edition, 1971），則能擺脫歐洲人的觀點，相當客觀的描述亞洲社會的發展⑰。一九七〇年他在「學校中的世界史」（World History in the Schools）一文中說:

「所有或者幾乎所有的人類社會，都有其闡釋世界開創的神話。猶太人、中國人與希臘人三者，持續發展不間斷的敍事，於是產生一種癖好與一類文獻，我們稱之爲歷史。這三種民族任何其一的歷史視野（historical vision），都是『世界性的』（universal），凡事皆重要，凡所知曉，皆納入於其史家的敍述中。舊約中歷史的與預言的部分，闡釋上帝的目的，係爲人類，其目的就定義上看，是世界性的。希羅多德（Herodotus）縱覽他所知的整個世界，以作爲縷述其大波斯戰爭（the Great Persian Wars）的背景。中國學術性的史學傳統（Chinese scholarly historical tradition）奠基者司馬遷，較之希羅多德更進一步，他將所有出現於眼簾者，作遠爲系統化的縱覽。」⑱

「人類所追尋者，爲一簡單的原理，能由他們加入任何資料與所有新資料於其旣定的類例中，不着痕跡，不費力氣。就此觀點而言，司馬遷是極度成功的，他的朝代史的體例（dynastic structure for history)，延至今日，卽使硏究中國過去的西方學者，亦沿用之；直至一九〇五年，中國學校學生如此接受歷史教育，或直接讀公元前二世紀時司馬遷所寫的書。」⑲

一九七一年麥氏到香港中文大學參加中國史與世界史的討論時，也曾經說：

「我諷刺歐洲史觀（the view of European history），而我自己則是歐洲史觀培養出來的；不過，我想我不是毫無所覺的向其投降。」⑳

「忘記中國的過去，或憎惡中國的過去，就像本世紀初傳統中國顯著衰微之時有些人所做的，對我來講，與盲目固守陳腐的信仰，似是同樣可悲的。儒學就像英國的輝格傳統（Whig tradition）及許多其他退色的信仰一樣，需要我們現代的環境與我們所採納的最好邏輯標準去再考慮、再估價。一味拒絕與盲目信仰是同樣沒有答案的。」㉑

第八節　傅爾（N. E. Fehl, 1917-　）

傅爾於一九五九年自美國芝加哥大學來香港任敎，一九六四年任香港中文大學世界史講座敎授，著有「世界史之硏究」（The Study of World History, 1966）、「禮；文獻與生活中的儀節；古代中國文化史的回顧」（Li（禮）；Rites and Propriety in Literature and Life; a Perspective for Cultural History of Ancient China, 1971）、「歷史中的人物與模型」（Personality and Pattern in History, 1975）諸書。一九七一年香港中文大學召開的中國史與世界史的討論會，他是主持人，他在所提論文「疆界」（The Frontier）一文中云：

「在十八世紀，中國是世界最大的帝國——人口方面，比西班牙、法國、俄國諸國的人口還多，較之鄂圖曼帝國、蒙古帝國，或大英帝國的人口，也有過之。其刻印之書，卷帙之富，比起所有其他民族出版品的總數，還要超出。」㉒

「在整個中國史學中，有一特殊的道德論調（moral tone），完全爲唯物論者的解釋所掩，將是不適當的。」㉓

在「導言」(Introduction) 中他又說:

「中國歷史可以視之爲一特殊歷史（a special history)，本質上與其他歷史相去絕遠，局促於其特殊的見識之中，僅能用其自有的方法研究。其自有的方法，殊異於西方發展出來用以解釋歐洲經歷的史學標準。」㉔

「眞正有意義的事實之一，有關於中國歷史與世界歷史的相關問題者，是中國學者受西方歷史的特殊訓練者，絕無僅有。負笈海外攻讀歷史的大批中國研究生，選讀西洋歷史課程者，寥寥無幾，數以千百計讀歷史的中國研究生，僅攻讀中國歷史。很少有可能世界歷史的教本或大學水準的西洋歷史教本由中國人用中文寫成。由歐洲人、美國人、澳洲人、日本人、甚至非洲人寫成的中國歷史書，則爲數甚夥。由中國人所寫的權威性西洋歷史的研究，可幾於大學或研究水準者，眞如鳳毛麟角。沒有佔世界人口四分之一的大民族能堪以如此漠視世界另四分之三人口的歷史的——尤其是西方歷史。」㉕

第九節 但斯 (E. H. Dance)

但斯是英國史家，著有「馬來亞與世界歷史」(Malayan and World

History, 1959-60)、「歷史出賣者」(History the Betrayer, 1960) 及「大同世界史」(History for a Unitid World, 1971) 諸書。他在「歷史出賣者」一書中云:

「在中國……直到最近，他們未曾有接近於西方的精確史學 (accurate historiography)，縱然在近代，他們也未貯蓄公文一類的歷史原始資料，像我們西方所做的。」㉖

「不像印度人那樣，中國人寫歷史，包括當代史在內，其當代史像我們安格魯撒克遜編年史 (Anglo-Saxon Chronicle) 一樣，已歷經無數世紀——據說其年表最低限度像西方大多數現代年表一樣可靠。唐代的作者也編纂了地方地形的記錄，可與英格蘭土地勘查記錄書 (Domesday Book) 相比。陸賈作品中論及國家的興衰，甚至在西元前二世紀，有一個中國湯恩比 (Chinese Toynbee) 問世了。第九世紀時，他們於紙及印刷以外，有一種速寫。參攷書方面，中國的百科全書，使大英百科全書 (Encyclopaedia Britannica) 看起來像袖珍型的書。此類書自第九世紀開始出產，在十八、十九世紀，最新出者擴至一千七百卷，但比起十五世紀一萬一千卷本，已不足道。其內容有很多對歐洲批評家而言，全無意義，但是沒有疑問的，十五世紀歐洲文學的大部分，對現代中國人而言，也像是毫無意義。」㉗

在「大同世界史」中他說:

「在中國，縱是音樂或藝術，慣例不止於爲音樂而音樂，爲藝術而藝術。文學亦然，直到近世紀，才開始產生抒情詩。一切皆用於提高社會水準。卽使歷史的寫作亦然。在中國，歷史永遠不純是一種消遣，就像西歐直到吉朋 (Gibbon) 和麥考萊 (Macaulay) 時代那樣。它是知識的倉庫，對政府有用，因其有用，故有待系

統彙存。」㉘

「遠在漢以前，中國政府已致力保存記錄，並將其撰寫成書，藉供閱讀與參攷。每一朝皆命一史家，蒐集前朝記錄，修成一部敍事性的歷史，頗類不列顛年鑑（the British Annual Register)。這是一個有力而健全的傳統。沒有朝代爲其本朝寫史，而讓與較爲客觀的下一代去寫。到了西元前二世紀的末葉，漢武帝任用了一位史官，他是所有時代最偉大的史家之一。其人名司馬遷，希羅多德（Herodotus）與修西蒂笛斯（Thucydides）的化身——同時更多一些。像希羅多德那樣，他不辭辛勞，遍遊其帝國，盡力網羅過去傳說與當代瞪言；像修西蒂笛斯那樣，他提醒其同時代的人，正視其現在；尊知識爲學術，宛如修西蒂笛斯精確，而遠超過希羅多德。不像希羅多德及修西蒂笛斯那樣，他沒有在文學領域內，贏得不朽。他的職務是出產……第一部古今歷史，小心翼翼的編纂，有憑有據（with full reference to the available authorities)。健全史學（sound historiography）所需要者不過如此。

誠然，他幸運手中握有資料，希羅多德與修西蒂笛斯自口中所講者獲其所有的證據，司馬遷則兼有文獻（documents)。」㉙

「在英國史的全部檔案中，最珍貴的收藏之一，是英格蘭土地勘查記錄書（Domesday Book)。這是僅一見的，常被形容成『無與倫比』(unique)。實際上並不如此。英國人與整個歐洲人理直氣壯的以此而驕傲，因爲在歐洲誠然是『無與倫比』的。……英格蘭土地勘查記錄書如此完整，如此詳盡，如此有效，洵爲歐洲史家最有價值的參攷文獻之一。」㉚

「歐洲以外，在亞洲，遠在十一世紀以前，已有了方志（local

surveys)，比英格蘭土地勘查記錄書詳盡數千倍。……亞洲的方志，大多數編纂於中國，已知中國約有六千種至七千種方志，可能未發現者尚多。其中最早者始於第四世紀，與後出者相比較，區區不足道（僅十七卷而已）。然而在如此早的時代，其中已普遍涉及該地區的動植物，農工業資源，主要貿易品（其中包括了飾貌之粉！），以及最重要的名勝古跡；它也包括了名人的傳記。事實上，這是從司馬遷時代以來爲前四、五世紀編纂的一類史書的延伸，祇不過方志的基礎係奠立在地方上，而不是建立在國家上，且脫離國史而單獨發行。在第八世紀的時候，其包括的資料，已擴及到灌溉、郵置、附設學校的寺院、『稀世珍玩』、甚至流行曲調。」㉛

「英格蘭土地勘查記錄書爲僅有的一種記錄。較後的時代，既未繼之續作，亦未將其修訂。相反的，中國此類記錄，則經常由官方任命的人士司其事，不曾間斷。」㉜

「事實上，在中國，所有的歷史與史學，不管是全國性的或地方的，包括爲地方史基礎的方志，都是爲了實用。中國既不知爲歷史而歷史，也不知爲眞理而眞理。歷史在中國每被視爲記錄的經驗(recorded experience)，在國家或地方陷於困境時，取爲殷鑑。」㉝

「爲一般所接受的西方原理，史家必不可預測，中國史家如接受，將被視爲荒謬不經。對中國人而言，預測是史家職務的一部分——史家不預測，誰又能掌握過去如此廣大的經驗以形成其預測的基礎呢？」㉞

第四章 註釋:

❶Allan Nevins, *The Gateway to History*, 1962, p. 14:

"This conception of history as a lantern carried by the side of man, moving forward with every step taken, is of course far ampler than the concept of a mere interesting tale to be told, a vivid scene to be described, or a group of picturesque characters to be delineated. It is essentially western and modern. To the Oriental, and even to the ancient Greek, history was an incomprehensible chaos of happenings, or a repetitive wallpaper pattern."

❷Ibid., p. 35:

"History makes a claim to universality, taking all human activity for its province.......Western writers, including Americans, long paid little attention to Slavonic history, and still less to Oriental backgrounds."

❸T. W. Wallband and A. M. Taylor, *Civilization Past and Present*, Volume 1, 1949, p. 110:

"China is the historian's paradise, for there the historian has always been honored and his works prized. For this reason China has the most nearly complete historical records left by any civilization. When, however, we push back the centuries far enough, we come to accounts which are no longer history but mythology. The Chinese are like all other people in this respect, for it is human nature to explain the mysterious past supernaturally rather than naturally. But whereas the Greeks and the Indo-Aryans wrote epic poetry in their attempts to glorify their ancestors, the Chinese created historical romances in prose. Their accounts are fascinating if not factual."

❹Jacques Barzun & Henry F. Graff, *The Modern Researcher*, revised edition, 1970, p. 47:

"In the Chinese language we find that the original form of the character for 'historian' represented a hand holding a receptacle used to contain tallies at archery contests. From recording this or similar matters of passionate interest, men in various civilizations came to record other things—court ceremonies, religious sacrifices, and striking events. Ultimately a day-to-day record was kept—in China it was known as the Spring and Autumn Annals though it covered the entire year. But this rather dull chronicle (eighth century B. C.) had been preceded by a collection of notable sayings and moral injunction to officials that is called The Book of Documents or Book of History. This earlier record was a more poetic and attractive work than the dry calendar of facts and can be likened to a fanciful archive of state papers. The Annals were a sort of public diary. Both together would be, to us, materials for a true history.

In Western culture the same sequence of interests and expression is found, with two important differences. If we take Homer's account of the Trojan War as paralleling the Chinese Book of Documents, we find in the Greek work a much richer, more highly organized piece of legendary history—a better work of art. And when we look for a Greek parallel to the Annals in Herodotus, who lived in the fifth century B. C., we find not only superb literary art once again, but also a deep curiosity about other peoples and their history—the Egyptians, Medes, Persians, and so on."

❺卡耳「何謂歷史」一書是六次「崔衛林演講」(The George Macaulay Trevelyan Lectures) 的講稿，一九六一年一月至三月講於劍橋大學。

❻E. H. Carr, *What is History?* 1961, pp. 146–147:

"What may well be regarded in the future as the greatest historical work produced in Cambridge during the past decade has been written entirely outside the history department, and without any assistance from it: I refer to Dr. Needham's Science and Civilization in China."

❼Ibid., p. 146

❽Ibid., p. 103:

"Like the ancient civilizations of Asia, the classical civilization of Greece and Rome was basically unhistorical."

❾A. G. Widgery, *Interpretations of History, From Confucious to Toynbee*, 1961, p. 15:

"From early times there was a considerable amount of written history in China. From what remains, it appears to have been mainly 'annals' with reference mostly to individuals of the ruling classes, the events of their lives, civil conflicts, and the rise and fortunes of successive dynasties. There was little reflection on the nature and meaning of history. There was no continued effort to find significance in historical processes and events in any remote goal. Attention was on the present and the past. The cultured of the occident have been fascinated and tremendously impressed by Chinese works of art, paintings, carvings of ivory, jade, and wood, and by the palaces of Peiping. But the amount of such art, however large it may seem independently considered, is comparatively little when thought of with reference to the long history and the teeming millions of the people of China. Throughout their history the masses of Chinese have been occupied with agriculture and handicrafts. Their lives have been essentially simple and it is from this standpoint that we may understand their attitudes to history."

❿Ibid., p. 18:

"Chinese thinkers often regarded history as teaching moral lessons, showing vice to be always punished and virtue always rewarded. Such results of conduct were not always or immediately apparent.

Imperial power might be attained by the wicked; but it was urged that they could not keep it. Even though the wicked might appear fortunate in externals, inwardly they were miserable. War should be undertaken for defence with the conviction that the righteous will eventually win.

Consideration of the Chinese attitude to history must take into account a trait of character almost universal amongst them: their temperament of equanimity. Their imperturbability has been more general and conspicuous even than of peoples of India. Individuals are not often very greatly disturbed by evils in their own histories; and they are rarely deeply moved by calamities in their social history as a people.......

The Chinese attitude to history may be called Ouietist."

⑪Geoffrey Barraclough, "*Universal History*", in H. P. R. Finberg, ed., *Approaches to History*, 1962, p. 98

⑫Geoffrey Barraclough, *History in a Changing World*, 1955, p. 133:

"An interpretation which surveys the events essentially from the point of view of western Europe is no longer adequate. We have to try to take the wider view of world history."

⑬Ibid., p. 27:

"A history that looks beyond Europe and the west to humanity in all lands and ages".

⑭Ibid., p. 61:

"We have to rid ourselves of our too exclusively European point of view; it is (for example) useless and misleading from the point of view of Chinese history to classify as 'mediaeval' centuries which, for the Chinese people, were not mediaeval at all.

⑮Ibid., p. 231:

"It is unfair and unprofitable to blame the Greeks and Egyptians, the Chinese and the Indians, for having failed to achieve what we have achieved, for there is no reason to suppose that they set out to achieve what seems to us desirable."

⑯Geoffrey Barraclough, "*Universal History*", in H. P. R. Finberg. ed., *Approaches to History*, pp. 95–97:

"As late as the mid-nineteenth century most of the interior of Africa was unexplored and mysterious and what was known of the Orient was less history than a compound of myth and legend.......No less important was the influence of historical thinking, as developed in the nineteenth century, which taught us to consider and value every aspect of the past for its own sake, and so made it possible to escape the fetters of our own environment and appreciate alien civilization by their own standards and in their own right. The fact remains, however, that this gradual and stumbling approach to world-history—or, more accurately, to the preconditions which make world-history possible—has been in all essential ways an achievement of the European peoples.......Interest in history, belief in the value of history, even the tendency to view events in historical context and historical perspective, which is so natural to us that we are rarely conscious of the extent to which we do it, is a western attitude which has no exact counterpart in China or India. China, indeed, has preserved excellent annals and chronological lists, which provide at least the bare bones of history; but India before the European invasions has little that, by modern standards, can be called history at all, and both countries have shown very little concern for the perservation of historical records.

⑰Wes Lawrence, *Review of W. H. McNeill's A World History,* in Cleveland Plain Dealer:

"Professor McNeill has covered something like 10,000 years in 446 pages and made it a most readable and instructive outline of man's progress......He has managed to pack an enormous amount of information in few words......But what is really remarkable about McNeill's work is his ability to relieve himself of a point of view as a European and describe the development of society in Asia quite objectively."

⑱W. H. McNeill, "*World History in the Schools*, in Martin Ballard, ed., New Movements in the Study and Teaching of History, 1970, p. 16:

"All, or almost all, human societies have myths to explain how the world came to be. Three—the Jews, the Chinese and the Greeks—went on to develop a running account of events, thus generating a habit of mind and a genre of literature we recognise as historical. The historical vision of each of these peoples was 'universal' in the sense that everything important, known to them, had to find a place in their historians' account. Thus the historical and prophetic books of the Old Testament explain God's purposes for men, which are, by defination, universal. Herodotus surveyed the entire circuit of the world as known to him to provide a setting for his account of the Great Persian Wars. And Ssu-ma Ch'ien, the formulator of the Chinese scholarly historical tradition, improved upon Herodotus' practice with a far more systematic survey of all that lay within his purview."

⑲Ibid:

"What men seek is a simple principle that will allow them to fit any and all new dada into a pre-existing scheme of classification, smoothly and without undue effort. From this point of view, Ssu-ma Ch'ien was supremely successful. His dynastic structure for history endures to this day, even among western scholars who deal with the Chinese past; and until 1905 Chinese schoolboys were taught history in the mode, and even from the book, Ssu-ma Ch'ien wrote in the second Century B. C."

⑳W. H. McNeill, "*The Relevance of World History*", in Sir Herbert Butterfield Cho Yun Hsu & William H. McNeill on Chinese and World History, 1971, p. 51:

"I caricature the view of European history to which I was myself brought up; but not, I think, so harshly as to render it unrecognizable."

㉑Ibid.:

"To forget the Chinese past or despise it, as some did when the weakness of traditional China become obvious early in this century, seems to me no less deplorable than to adhere blindly to old and outworn assumptions and beliefs. Confucianism, like the English Whig tradition and many other fading faiths, requires re-consideration and re-evaluation in the light of our modern circumstances and the best standards of logic we can apply. Simple repudiation is no answer any more than blind faith."

㉒N. E. Fehl, "*The Frontier*", in Sir Herbert Butterfield Cho Yun Hsu & William H. McNeill on Chinese and World History, 1971, p. 64:

"In the 18th century. China was the world's largest empire—larger in population than the realms of Spain, France, Russia or the empires of the Ottoman, the Mongal or the British. She had produced a larger volume of printed books than the combined total of the publications of all other peoples."

㉓Ibid., p. 65:

"There is throughout Chinese historiography a distinctively moral tone which it would be wrong to bury completely under a materialist explanation."

㉔N. E. Fehl, "*Introduction: Some Problems in the Relation of Chinese History and World History*", in Sir Herbert Butterfield Cho Yun Hsu

& William H. McNeill on Chinese and World History, pp. 1-2:

"Chinese history might be regarded as a special history, essentially isolated from other histories, yielding its own unique insights only as studied by its own methods, quite distinct from the canon of historiography developed in the West for the interpretation of European experience."

㉕Ibid., p. 8:

"One of the really significant facts central to the problem of the relation between Chinese history and world history is that of the almost complete absence of Chinese scholars specially trained in Western history. Of the thousands of Chinese graduate students who study history abroad, only a few take any courses in Western history at all. Chinese graduate students in history by the hundreds study Chinese history exclusively. There is little choice of world history text or of university level text, in Western history written by Chinese in Chinese. There are hundreds of books on Chinese history written by Europeans, Americans, Australians, Japanese and even Africans. There are very few indeed authoritative studies in Western history by Chinese on the university or research level. No great people, one quarter of the world's population, can afford such neglect of interest in the history of the other three quarters of the world's population—especially of the West."

㉖E. H. Dance. *History the Betrayer*, 1960, p. 87:

"In China......they had not, until recent years, anything approaching the accurate historiography of the West, and even in modern times they have not stored their documents, the raw material of history, as we in the West have done."

㉗Ibid., pp. 104-105:

"Unlike the Indians, the Chinese wrote histories, including a current contemporary history which ran, like our Anglo-Saxon Chronicle, for centuries—and whose chronology is said to be at least as reliable as most contemporary chronologies in the West. Writers of the T'ang also compiled records of local topography comparable with Domesday Book. In Lu Chia and his work on the rise and fall of states there was even a Chinese Toynbee in the second century B. C. By the ninth century A. D., besides paper and printing they had a sort of shorthand. As for works of reference, Chinese encyclopaedias make the Encyclopaedia Britannica look like a pocket-book. They were being produced from the ninth century onwards. In the eighteenth and nineteenth centuries the most up-to-date of them was extended to 1700 volumes, and that was nothing to an encyclopaedia of the fifteenth century which reached 11,000 volumes. A good deal of their contents have appeared nonsense to European critics; but then no doubt most of the literature of fifteenth century Europe would seem nonsense to a modern Chinese."

㉘E. H. Dance, *History for a United World*, 1971, p. 49:

"In China, not even music or art were, as a rule, ends in themselves; nor was literature, until later dynasties began to produce lyric poetry. All were used for raising the tone of society. This was true even of the writing of history. In China, history was never, as in Western Europe until the days of Gibbon and even Macaulay, merely a pastime. It was a repository of knowledge useful to the Government, and, since it was to be used, it had to be systematized and filed."

㉙Ibid., pp. 49–50:

"Long before the Han, Chinese Governments had made a practice of preserving records and writing them up for reading and reference. Each dynasty appointed an historian to collect the records of its predecessor, and edit them into a continuous historical narrative rather in the manner of the British Annal Register. This was a powerful and healthy tradition. No dynasty wrote its own history: that was left to the more impartial minds of the next age. Towards the end of the second century B. C. the Emperor Wu appointed as Government historiographer a man who proved to be one of the greatest historians of all time. His name was Ssu-ma Chien. He was Herodotus and Thucydides rolled into one—and then more. Like Herodotus, he took the trouble to wander around the empire, learning what he could from the folklore of the past and the gossip of the present; like Thucydides, he sounded his contemporaries about their own times; and he treated both kinds of knowledge with a scholarship as meticulous as that of Thucydides, and far superior to that of Herodotus. Unlike Herodotus and Thucydides, he did not earn immortality in the realm of literature: his job was to produce......the first history of ancient and modern times, compiled as carefully and conscientiously, with full reference to the available authorities, as sound historiography demands.

He was, certainly, fortunate in the materials he had at hand. Herodotus and Thucydides obtained all their evidence by word of mouth: Ssu-ma Chien had documents as well."

㉚Ibid., p. 85:

"One of the most precious possessions in the entire archives of English history is Domesday Book. It is an isolated phenomenon, so isolated that it is usually described as 'unique', which it is not. The English, and all Europe, are justifiably proud of it, for in Europe it is indeed unique. ......Domesday Book is so full, so detailed, so efficient, that it ranks deservedly as one of the most valuable documents available to European historians."

㉛Ibid., pp. 85–86:

"Beyond Europe, in Asia, and long before the eleventh century, there were local surveys, far more thorough than Domesday Book—thousands of them. ......most of them were compiled in China, where between six and seven thousand of them are known, and where presumably there are many more as yet undiscovered. The earliest of them dates from the fourth century A. D. and, compared with later examples, it is a very small affair—twelve Chinese 'chapters'. Even so early, however, it surveys the fauna and flora of the district, its resources in agriculture and industry, the chief commodities of trade (they include face-powder!), and the most important monuments; it also contains biographies of the most famous local people. It was, in fact, an extension of the sort of 'histories' which had been compiled for the previous four or five centuries, since the time of Ssu-ma Chien, but they were on a local instead of a national basis, and they were issued separately and independently of the national histories. In the eighth century A. D. the information contained was extended to things like irrigation, posts, temples with their schools, 'marvels', and even popular songs."

㉜Ibid., p. 87:

"Domesday Book was a once-for-all record. It was neither repeated nor revised in later times. The Chinese records, on the contrary, were constantly kept up to date by officials specially appointed to that task."

㉝Ibid., pp. 87–88:

"In fact, in China at any rate, all history and historiography, national and local, including these local surveys, which are the basis of local history, was for practical use. China knows neither history for history's sake nor truth for truth's sake. History in China has always been regarded as recorded experience, to be drawn upon in times of national or local dilemma, precisely as individuals draw upon their experience for guidance in their private dilemma."

㉞Ibid., p. 88:

"A Chinese historian would regard as absurd the commonly accepted Western principle that historians must not prophesy. Prophecy, to a Chinese, is part of the historian's business—who else commands so wide an experience of the past to form the basis of prophecy?"

第五章　與西方非正統史家論中國史學

自奈芬司等九家之說，清楚的可以看出西方非正統史家遠較西方正統史家富有世界心胸。「主要從西歐觀點解釋事件，已經不够了，我們必須嘗試採用較廣濶的世界史觀點。」「跳出歐洲去，跳出西方去，將視線投射到所有的地區與所有的時代。」「歷史要求普遍性，視所有人類的活動，爲其領域。」這是何等心胸！既有此等心胸，所以他們論中國史學，字裡行間，不再盡是充滿輕蔑之意，論點有時甚爲可取，其荒謬不經處，亦見出誠意。以下是其論點之大者：

1. 中國自上古時代起保存了近乎齊全的歷史記錄

「中國留下了近乎齊全的歷史記錄」；「當希臘民族與印歐民族寫史詩以頌揚其祖先之際，中國人已創始用散文作歷史敍事了」；「遠在漢以前，中國政府已致力保存記錄，並將其撰寫成書，藉供閱讀與參攷。每一朝皆命一史家，蒐集前朝記錄，修成一部敍事性的歷史，頗類不列顚年鑑；」「從古代起，在中國就有數量相當可觀的歷史著作。」認爲中國自上古時代起，即致力保存歷史記錄，而且近乎齊全，是他們在西方所發出的大論調之一。自然認爲中國「極少關心保存歷史記錄」，「縱然在近代，也未貯蓄公文一類的歷史原始資料」等相反論調，也競出其間。

2. 中國盛產富有史料性與敍事性的歷史

「不像印度人那樣，中國人寫歷史，包括當代史在內。其當代史像我們安格魯撒克遜編年史一樣，已歷經無數世紀。」承認了中國人寫歷史，但是並不承認中國人所寫的歷史與西方相同，中國的尙書與春秋，對他們而言，都是「眞歷史的資料」，尙書「可與奇幻的政府檔案相比擬」，春秋則「屬於公家日記一類」，以致中國在他們的心目中，是「具有重要而富史料性歷史的國家」，中國所保存的「極好的編年史」，「提供了歷史的骨幹」，而且「大都是關於統治階級的描素，他們的生平，內部的紛爭，以及新朝的興起與昌隆」，中國盛產史料性與敍事性的歷史，是他們很肯定的論斷。

3. 中國纂修了驚人的類書與方志

「中國的百科全書，使大英百科全書，看起來像袖珍型的書」；「中國約有六千種至七千種方志」，比「英格蘭土地勘查記錄書詳盡數千倍」，而英格蘭土地勘查記錄書在英國史的全部檔案中，是最珍貴的收藏之一，「常被形容成『無與倫比』」，同時它是「僅有的一種記錄，較後的時代，旣未繼之續作，亦未將其修訂」。中國的方志，則「經常由官方任命的人士司其事，不曾間斷。」他們對中國纂修的類書與方志，驚訝與欽佩，兼而有之。

4. 中國歷史作品仍遜於西方甚遠

中國歷史，是「偶發事件的混合體，不可理解，或是壁紙型式，一再重複」(其所言東方，自包括中國在內)，「很少論及歷史的性質與意義，不曾爲任何遠景，繼續不斷的努力，以發現歷史過程及歷史事件的深意」；「以荷馬敍述初殘戰爭與中國的尙書相比，我們發現希臘作品爲內容遠爲豐富，組織遠爲精密的傳說歷史」，「拿希臘西元前五世紀的希羅多德的作品與春秋相比時，我們不僅發現文學藝術方面的超越，也發現作者對其他民族及其歷史的深度好奇心」。司馬遷的作品，則是他們最爲欣賞的，以爲其人是「希羅多德與修西蒂笛斯的化身——同時更多一些」，其作品係「小心翼翼的編纂，有憑有據，健全史學所需要者不過如此」，「希羅多德與修西蒂笛斯自口中所講者獲其所有的證據，司馬遷則兼有文獻」。

5. 中國史學仍難與西方史學比美

「醉心歷史，篤信歷史的價值，甚至自歷史內涵及歷史遠景以看事件的趨勢，是一西方態度。」「在中國或印度，沒有恰似的態度」。「中國人對歷史的態度，可以稱之爲靜寂主義者。」中國對歷史的態度如此，於是他們認爲「中國歷史可以視之爲一特殊歷史，本質上與其他歷史相去絕遠，侷促於其特殊的見識之中，僅能用其自有的方法研究，其自有的方法，殊異於西方發展出來用以解釋歐洲經歷的史學標準」；直到最近，中國「未曾有接近於西方的精確史學」，「在中國，所有的歷史與史學，不管是全國性的或地方性的，包括爲地方史基礎的方志，都是爲了實用，中國既不知爲歷史而歷史，也不知爲眞理而眞理。歷史在中國每被視爲記錄的經驗，在國家或地方陷於困境時，取爲殷鑑。」

6. 認清了中國歷史不能列入於中世紀，但是却認爲中國古代文化基本上是非歷史的（其言亞洲，自包括中國在內）。中國史學中的道德論調，也被指出。

以下與其平情以論之：

第一節 概 論

西方正統史家認爲產生史學最基本的重視歷史的態度與觀念爲西方文化所獨有，而中國則極度缺乏，在這方面，西方非正統史家的論調，大致是與其一致的。「就像亞洲古代文化一樣，古典的希臘羅馬文化，基本上是非歷史的」，斷定古典的希臘羅馬文化，基本上是非歷史的，而以亞洲古代文化相比擬，可見在他們心目中久已毫無疑問的將以中國爲中心的亞洲古代文化，當成非歷史的了。極有世界觀的巴拉克勞甫敎授也很鄭重的說：「醉心歷史，篤信歷史的價值，甚至自歷史內涵及歷史遠景以看事件的趨勢，是一西方態度，對我們西方人而言，這是極爲自然的，很少能覺察到做到什麼程度。在中國或印度，沒有恰似的態度。」

西方正統史家認爲中國永遠沒有發展批判史學，永遠沒有意思視歷史爲客觀的瞭解，西方非正統史家則肯定中國未曾有接近於西方的精確史學，中國所有的歷史與史學，都是爲了實用，中國旣不知爲歷史而歷史，也不知爲眞理而眞理。兩者相較，語氣容有不同，而論點則無差別。

西方正統史家認識了中國史學重視文獻，認識了中國歷史資料浩繁，在這方面，西方非正統史家的認識，更爲淸楚，更爲具體。他們認爲遠在漢以前，中國政府已致力保存記錄，而且以欣羨的眼光，力言中國留下的歷史記錄，近乎齊全，這是西方正統史家所未見及的。驚佩中國的類書與方志，認爲遠駕西方之上，也是西方正統史家所不忍言與絕難承認的。西方非正統史家心胸寬濶，能虛心閱讀西方漢學家的作品，以瞭解中國，致所見遂較西方正統史家眞切。

認爲中國歷史不能列入於中世紀，是西方非正統史家的眞知灼見。西方史家列中國歷史於中世紀，是有意的低視與壓抑。在西方世界，中世紀是黑暗、退化的象徵，宗教腐敗，社會封建，特權充斥，迷信色彩濃厚。十九世紀以來，西方雖較十八世紀對中世紀有諒解，認爲中世紀有其文明，有其對歷史的貢獻，但是成見深入於人心，牢不可破，中世紀總不是西方世界的光彩。列中國歷史於中世紀，是想將中國歷史納於黑暗的一角，否定其重要價值。巴拉克勞甫教授起而反對，是有其遠見與勇氣。誠如巴氏所說，「這是旣無益而又使人誤解的，因爲中國人民一點也不是中世紀的。」中國不是宗教的國家，中國是世界上最不迷信的民族，中國沒有類似西方中世紀型的特權，中國的封建社會，也與西方中世紀的封建社會，有顯著的不同。兩者相去絕遠，遽相比擬，豈是學術性的公評？卽以中國的編年史與西方中世紀的編年史比較，亦貌似而神異，一則已達極高的境界（如通鑑），一則仍類村店所用的流水賬簿；一則秉筆者思想超向開明，一則含毫者觀念始終怪誕。浦立本教授所說「當歐洲編年史家仍虔誠地認爲人類歷史操縱於上帝不可思議的手中的時候，中國人很早已放棄他們天人神秘合一的信仰，而尋求人類事變的合理的人爲原因，」⑪是公平之論。

以荷馬的作品，與中國的尙書相比，是不倫不類的；認爲中國的歷史著作，主要是編年史，是大錯而特錯的；堅信中國歷史僅能用其自有的方法研究，是拘於方隅之見，而不知天地之大的。凡此，皆不待喋喋深辨。至於將西元前二世紀的陸賈，看成中國的湯恩比，是過份的附會；認爲司馬遷不像希羅多德及修西蒂笛斯那樣，在文學領域內，贏得不朽，是常識的不足。外邦人士對中國學問的一知半解，往往如此。

說中國歷史是偶發事件的混合體，不可理解；是壁紙型式，一再重複；很少論及歷史的性質與意義，不曾爲任何遠景，繼續不斷的努力，以發現歷史過程及歷史事件的深意，仍極同於西方正統史家的論調。西方史家遽看中國歷史，持論每如此，似是而大謬不然。下面擬詳論之。兼與西方非正統史家論中國的歷史精神及中國人對歷史的態度。

第二節　中國史學著述有史義立於事文之外

氣浮心粗，妄自尊大的西方史家，動輒說中國無史學；透過翻譯作品，乍一涉獵中國史學著述的西方史家幾異口同聲說，盈天地間的中國史學著述，無一不是史料，不可與語歷史。衆口鑠金，在西方史學界，此殆成一定論，不僅卡耳認爲中國是「具有富史料性歷史的國家」而已。此種輿論的形成，一則由於西方史家不知中國史學，一則由於西方史家對歷史的基本觀念與中國殊異，遂駭然於中國的歷史，非西方所謂歷史。中國的二十五史、兩通鑑、九通、五紀事本末乃至其他別史雜史，於是都淪於史料地位，不得躋於史學著述之林。史籍浩如煙海之國，乃一變而僅爲史料的淵藪，眞不能不令人有愴涼之感了！

對歷史的基本觀念，中西自古即有不同。西方語文內，初無史字，到希臘時代希羅多德周遊列國，始作書名 historiai，後人即以此字爲史字的起源，希羅多德在西方，也因此有了「歷史之父」之稱。考希臘文 historiai 一詞，實爲研究調查之意，西人沿用此字（拉丁文與西班牙文爲 historia，法文爲 histoire，意大利文爲 storia，英文爲 history），亦沿襲其意，視歷史爲一種富研究性的學問。此與中國說文所謂「史，記事者也」，視歷史爲一種記載，似有天壤之別。中國沿襲史爲記事的傳統，數千年綿延發展，不離其宗。西方到演進的史學出現，歷史的研究，也完全變成了一種科學的研究，以純粹的材料研究爲範圍，期以明瞭事實的因果及其相互關係。十九世紀以來，演進的史學，尤盛極一時。整個十九世紀，社會科學的觀念在逐漸發展；科學研究自然界的方法，被應用到人事的研究上去。這一時期的早期，牛頓傳統（Newtonian tradition）流行，社會與自然界一樣，被認爲是機械（mechanism）。稍後達爾文倡另一科學革命，社會科學家開始認爲社會等於一有機體（organism）。但是達爾文革命的眞正貢獻，是將歷史帶進了科學裡面去。科學不再是靜止的及無時間性的，而是有其變化與發展的過程。研究科學的方法，也同樣可以作爲研究歷史的方法。❷二十世紀初葉，英國史家布瑞（J. B. Bury, 1861-1927）於是倡言：「歷史是科學，不多也不少。」❸一時目歷史爲科學，蔚爲一種風氣。科學上有定律，史家於是也忙着在歷史上找定律；科學上有眞理，史家於是也忙着在歷史上找眞理。科學是將歷史徹首徹尾的征服了。一九三〇年史家柯林吾（R. G. Collingwood, 1889-1943）雖起而在自然世界（the world of nature）與歷史世界（the world of history）之間，劃出一顯明的界限，但是他仍然提倡科學的歷史（scientific history），認爲惟有科學的歷史，才是眞歷史，外此者皆不得稱之爲歷史。❹第二次世界大戰以後，西方史學界，驟起新轉變，而科學史學的傳統，仍深入於人心，一般史家仍以科學家的見解論歷史。中國的史學著述主記事，不是分析事實的因果及其相互關係的研究，所以他們目之爲史料性的歷史，目之爲偶發事件的混合體，不可理解。換言之，中國的史學著述，不是歷史，祇是史料，雜然相陳，殊無史家的深意。

「責備希臘人與埃及人，中國人與印度人，沒有到達我們所到達的境界，旣不公平，又無利益，因爲沒有理由推想他們計劃到達像是合我們意的。」巴拉克勞甫教授之言，極有眞理。中西史學，各自獨立發展，雖造詣不同，而其爲歷史的發展則一。同歸而殊途，一致而百慮，豈能以方隅之見，抹殺其一的價值？如果說中國史學著述是史料，不是歷史，那麼西洋史學著述應是玄學之言了。且中國史學著述，並非僅流於事文之末，事文之外，有極深的史義，史實之間，亦有相當的默契與和諧。此點頗非西方史家所能知，願略言之。

孔子作春秋，最重史義，不徒求事文之末。孟子屢屢發之，太史公自序亦云:

「余聞董生曰：周道衰廢，孔子爲司寇，諸侯言之，大夫壅之，孔子知言之不用，道之不行也，是非二百四十二年，以爲天下儀表，貶天子，退諸侯，討大夫，以達王事而已矣。子曰，我欲載之空言，不如見之行事之深切著明也。夫春秋上明三王之道，下辨人事之紀，別嫌疑，明是非，定猶豫，善善惡惡，賢賢賤不肖，存亡國，繼絕世，補敝起廢，王道之大者也。……撥亂世，反之正，莫近於春秋。春秋文成數萬，其旨數千，萬物之散聚，皆在春秋。」❺

春秋是中國史學的大原，後之史家，受其影響，每能知重史義。司馬遷著史記，實欲以究天人之際，通古今之變，而成一家之言。班固之書，究西都之首末，窮劉氏之廢興，事甚該密，言有深意，所謂準天地，統陰陽，闡元極，步三光，窮人理，該萬方，緯六經，綴道綱，總百氏，贊篇章，函雅故，通古今❻，是班書的史義。司馬光通鑑，不是徒堆材料，人人而知。鄭樵生千載而後，慨然有見於古人著述之源，而知作者之旨，不徒以詞采爲文，考據爲學，獨取三千年來遺文故册，運以別識心裁，而自爲經緯❼。中國第一流史家，於事文之外，固鮮有不重視史義者。

中國正史的志，是同類的材料，經過史家的細心選擇，能說明一些歷史問題。中國正史的列傳，每以類相從，循史、酷吏、儒林、文苑、獨行、方術等專傳不論，一般列傳，也有時不拘時代，而各就其人的生平，以類相從，如史記中老子與韓非同傳，屈原與賈誼同傳，便是其例。此外又有類敍法的發明，因爲人各一傳，則不勝傳，而不爲立傳，則其人又有事可傳，於是其人不必立傳，而其事以類敍於某人傳內。漢書、後漢書、三國志、宋書、齊書、梁書、明史皆普遍應用此法❽。列傳之間，以類相從，一傳之內，以類帶敍，是中國史籍中的列傳，也不是孤立而互不相關。至於紀事本末體的因事命篇，不拘常格，更是體圓用神，與西方的史籍體例相呼應。所以中國的史學著述，史實之間，有相當的默契與和諧，不是偶發事件的混合體，而難以理解。中國史家並非不曾爲任何遠景，繼續不斷的努力，以發現歷史過程及歷史事件的深意，他們仍然經過一番慘澹經營的工夫，將史實系統化、見解化，使讀者讀其書而知其所欲言。

中國的史學著述，事文之外，有史義；史實之間，有默契與和諧，旣援西人論史的準則，亦不得不謂之爲歷史。西人治史，先廣蒐史料，再加以解釋，史料所蒐者無窮（亦有略蒐史料卽加解釋者），而所採用者無幾，史料之於史家，居於附庸地位，受史家的氣指頤使。所以近代西方史家高倡一切歷史都是現代史之說❾，歷史是透過史家的當代思想而反映出來的，眞實性不大，於是有人提出史家應重視基本史實（basic facts）的主張，以挽救歷史的厄運。如一七八九年在法國發生大革命，卽基本史實，大革命發生的時間是一七八九年，地點是在法國，史家不能使其錯誤。外此者則多是史家的解釋，未必是歷史眞相。中國史家治史則不然，史家不輕易出面，別識心裁立於事文之外，史料有去取，而非侷於某一觀點，亦不若西方史家的大量割捨，所以保存的眞歷史較多，最低限度歷史的基本事實，蘊藏豐富，此點眞非西方史家所能瞭然。班馬之書，如日月麗天，後人雖有新作，而不減其光輝。劍橋近代史（Cambridge Modern History）素享盛譽，且以詳贍稱，自近年新劍橋近代史（New Cambridge Modern History）出，已近半爲土苴矣。論中西史學者，於此等處看，似乎可分出其優劣了。

第三節 中國史學充滿和平精神

以中國歷史的發展，與西方歷史的發展相比較，大致是一爲靜態，一爲動態；一在風平浪靜中悠游蕩漾，一在驚濤駭浪中猛力衝激；西方歷史上慣見劇烈的變動，大規模的殘酷戰爭，中國歷史上則大致一片祥和，在和平中進展，在和諧節奏中轉移到新階段⑩。此爲中西歷史發展的最大不同處。有人比中國歷史像一首詩，西洋歷史像一本劇⑪，甚是佳喩。詩代表中國文學的最美部分，西方則以作劇爲文學家的聖境，此可爲佐證。卽以人物而言，蘇格拉底死於一杯毒藥，耶穌死於十字架，孔子則夢奠於兩楹之間，晨起扶杖逍遙，詠歌自輓。三位民族聖人的死去，其景象不同如此，正足反映歷史精神的全部。

中西歷史發展的不同如此，史學最是關鍵。

西方史學謳歌戰爭，謳歌歷史英雄，亞歷山大、拿破崙都是史家筆下的偶像人物；西方史學有國家觀念，有民族意識，普魯士學派（The Prussian School）所倡國家主義及民族優越論，都是德國統一及强大的主要因素。然而普魯士史家引起了兩次全人類的最大悲劇，世界生靈爲之塗炭；亞歷山大、拿破崙型的人物，也未嘗不是西方歷史的亂源！西方史學如此，所以西方歷史上便多事了。

反觀中國史學，則另是一番景象。

中國史學有經世思想，章學誠云：

「天人性命之學，不可以空言講也。故司馬遷本董氏天人性命之說，而爲經世之書。儒者欲尊德性，而空言義理以爲功，此宋學之所以見譏於大雅也。夫子曰:『我欲託之空言，不如見諸行事之深切著明也。』此春秋之所以經世也。聖如孔子，言爲天鐸，猶且不以空言制勝，況他人乎？故善言天人性命，未有不切於人事者。三代學術，知有史而不知有經，切人事也。後人貴經術，以其即三代之史耳。」⑫

中國史學中的經世思想⑬，富和平精神，「撥亂世，反之正」，是和平精神;「寓褒貶，別善惡」，亦在假歷史的懲勸力量，以維持人間的和平;春秋大一統之義，更是崇高的和平境界，中華民族在一天然的地理環境中，數千年生活在一起，過一致的文化生活，是由於受史學中大一統觀念的影響。中國史家幾無不尊奉大一統之義，秦漢以後的統一局面，賴以絕而復續者屢，戰禍以之而減少，生靈藉之以復蘇。如春秋戰國的形勢不變，中國數千年歷史，豈不完全演另一歐洲列强紛爭之局？中國的和平，賴於中國的統一。中國的統一，由於中國史學中大一統之義的涵育。西方史學無此涵育，致歐洲由統一而分裂，而戰禍無窮，此可證中國史學中有經世思想，而其經世，着眼於人間的和平了。

中國政治，常偏重於中央的凝合，而不重於四圍的呑併，常偏於生民的康樂，而不重於國力的强大，已有的完整珍視之，希望中的獲得禁抑之，對外則曰昭文德以來之，對內則曰息兵以仁政化之，這是一種極偉大的和平精神。此種和平精神，受政治家的影響小，受史家的影響大。中國史家所講的春秋大一統之義，更引申一層言之，是所謂修身齊家治國平天下的治平之學，史家心目中的遠景，爲天下的治平，其選擇史料，與此遠景有關，其解釋史料，亦與此遠景有關，如秦始皇、漢武帝每被譴責，即以其窮兵黷武，敝中國以事四夷;漢文帝、漢景帝每蒙讚揚，則以其在政治上恭儉無爲，與民休息;大將軍中如魏靑，如霍去病，豈較納爾遜（Nelson）、威靈敦（Wellington）爲遜色？在中國史家筆下，他們是黯淡無光多了。近代中國史家每稱頌秦始皇、漢武帝的豐功偉績，那是由於受西方史學的影響。中國傳統史家，則絲毫不予以假借，如漢書武帝紀贊云:「漢承百王之弊，高祖撥亂反正，文景務在養民，至于稽古禮文之事，猶多闕焉。孝武初立，卓然罷黜百家，遂疇咨海內，舉其俊茂，與之立功，興太學，修郊祀，改正朔，定曆數，協音律，作詩樂，建封禪，禮百神，紹周後，號令文章，煥焉可述，後嗣得遵洪業，而有三代之風，如武帝之雄材大略，不改文景之恭儉，以濟斯民，雖詩書所稱，何有加焉。」是專贊武帝的文事，而武功則不置一詞。而實際上武帝之雄才大略，正在武功，其所闢疆土，視高、惠、文、景時，幾至一倍，且永爲中國四至，千萬年食其利。乃班固一概抹煞，並謂其不能法文景之恭儉，轉似以開疆闢土爲非計。蓋其窮兵黷武，敝中國以事四夷，當時實爲天下大害，故宣帝時議立廟樂，夏侯勝已有武帝多殺士卒，竭民財力，天下虛耗之語。至東漢之初，論者猶以爲戒。班固基於治平的觀點，所以作贊如此。其西域傳贊，亦謂光武閉玉門關，謝外國朝貢，雖大禹之敍西戎，文帝之却走馬，殆無以過。其持論猶是此意。論中國史學者，於此等處看，最能得其眞精神。

由上言之，可知中國史學中充滿和平精神，由此亦可窺出中國人對歷史的態度。魏吉瑞謂中國人對歷史的態度，是單簡的，靜寂的，但如果他知道在單簡靜寂後面，瀰漫着和平精神，他或許能對中國史學減少幾分輕視之意了。

第四節　中國史學瀰漫理性主義

西方史學中天道色彩極濃厚，歐洲歷史之父希羅多德，其解釋歷史變化，皆歸之於天道；希臘羅馬的史家，都僅知道一個命運（fate）哲學；基督教早期領袖奧古斯丁（St. Augustine, 354-430）在上帝之城（The City of God）一書中，謂歷史決定性的事件，是基督的生命，人類全部發展須由宗教思想來決定。以後中世紀宗教史家受其影響，虔誠的相信人類歷史操縱於上帝不可思議的手中；下逮近代，重語文考證的蘭克，心目中仍有一上帝存在，湯恩比解釋歷史到不能解釋時，便托出上帝來以作緩衝。西方科學史學的狂潮，不能澄清西方史學中的天道。即西方史家所談的歷史定律，似乎也是天道的另一面目。⑭

中國史學則不然，古代中國史家，言人事兼言天道，後來漸漸發展，史家天道觀念日趨淡薄，專以記人事爲職責，理性主義於是在中國史學中特別發達，西方史學中詭奇之說，驚人之論，如因果律，如進化論，如文化沒落論，在中國史學中，皆不見影踪。所以也無怪魏吉瑞認爲中國歷史很少論及歷史的性質與意義了。中國歷史，平靜發展，不若西洋歷史的動輒掀起軒然大波，這似是因素之一。

第五章　注釋:

❶見第二章註二六

❷參見 E. H. Carr, *What is History?* 1961, pp. 50-51

❸J. B. Bury, *The Science of History*, inaugural lecture of January 1903

❹R. G. Collingwood, *The Idea of History*, 1946

❺史記太史公自序

❻見漢書敍傳

❼見章學誠文史通義申鄭篇

❽參見趙翼廿二史劄記「後漢書編次訂正」「宋齊書帶敍法」「齊書類敍法最善」「明史」諸條。

❾意大利史家克羅齊（Benedetto Croce, 1866-1952）及英國史家柯林吾（R. G. Collingwood, 1889-1943）都如此主張。

❿西方歷史劃時代的進步，常在驚心動魄的震盪中產生，若以此意態來看中國史，則常如昏騰騰地沒有長進。中國史上，亦有大規模從社會下層掀起的鬬爭，不幸此等常爲紛亂犧牲，而非有意義的劃時代的進步。秦末劉項之亂，可謂例外。明祖崛起，掃除胡塵，光復故土，亦可謂一個上進的轉變。其他如漢末黃巾，乃至黃巢、張獻忠、李自成，全是混亂破壞，只見倒退，無上進。近人治史，頗推洪楊，夫洪楊固爲近世中國民族革命的光輝，然其十餘年擾亂，除予國家社會以莫大的創傷外，成就何在？建設何在？此中國史上大規模從社會下層掀起的鬬爭，常不爲民族文化進展之一好例也。然中國史非無進展，中國史之進展，乃常在和平形態下，以舒齊步驟得之。（說詳見錢穆國史大綱引論）

⓫見錢穆國史大綱引論及中國歷史研究法

⓬文史通義「浙東學術」篇

⓭詳見拙作「經世思想與中國史學」（載於中華學術與現代文化叢書第三册史學論集，民國六十六年四月）

⓮歐洲十八世紀的理性主義，係受中國思想的影響，Voltaire 有歐洲孔子之稱。

第六章　西方漢學家論中國史學

第一節　認識中國史學的初期

西方正統史家無學術上的寬容，所以不足與論中國史學；西方非正統史家有學術上的寬容，而無足够的基本知識，所以也不足與論中國史學；有學術上的寬容，而又略具基本知識，是西方研究中國歷史的漢學家，他們論中國史學，有時能有極珍貴的意見，值得重視與參攷。

漢學研究在西方，是一種專業，也歷盡艱辛的奮鬥。漢學家爲學術所表現出的熱情與勇氣，每令人欽羡嚮往不已！西方的社會環境，並不利於漢學的研究與發展，一般人心目中不怎麼珍視漢學。以英國而論，雖然博物館裡，貴族的豪華別墅中，賞心悅目的中國畫，古色古香的中國名物，琳瑯滿目，電影院裡，街頭巷尾的談論中，却充滿了諷刺嘲笑中國的聲浪。中國女人裹小脚，男人留長辮，做事顚三倒四，在他們的印象中最深。傾畢生精力去研究中國學問，他們認爲不値，如果有興趣的話，最好是把它當作民俗學去研究。這種論調，充滿於英國。❶所以在英國研究漢學，深受歧視，顯得冷清而落莫。可是不利的研究環境，並沒有影響英國漢學家們的研究精神，他們孜孜矻矻窮年不休的奮勉，令人感動，他們珍視中國學術的熱忱，使身為中國人的我們，自愧不如。英國人的偏執、武斷，使他們幾乎到了怒不可遏的程度，因此他們於「皓首窮經」的學者精神以外，每懷有一種學術上的憤憤不平之氣，挺身而出，維護天下學術之公，變成了他們的職責。充沛的戰鬥精神，毅然決然的殉道氣概，他們都有。如果有人感慨中西文化論戰為何迄今仍在國內有形、無形的進行，那麼這場戰爭早已擴展到英國去了！英國如此，整個西方可知。

中國史學是漢學中的一項，自亦受到環境的影響。西方漢學家與西方正統史家之間，對中國史學一直無法取得一致的論調，像浦立本與白特費爾德之爭，在西方史學界，似乎是必然的現象。晚近西方漢學家積極研究中國史學，似懷着深山尋寶的神秘心理，以期一旦有所發現，以震驚他們的學術界。

在較早的時期，西方漢學家對中國史學的認識與研究，是極為有限的。以下先作概略的介紹：

早在一八九五年法國大漢學家沙畹（Edward Chavannes, 1865-1918）在其所作司馬遷史記法文譯註六巨册中第一册卷首導論上的前言云：

> 「司馬遷史記，顧名思義，這是一部歷史著作；其次，這是中國人所寫的史書；復次，這是已經有兩千多年的古書。」❷

開宗明義即強調史記是一部歷史著作，為中國人所寫，寫成已歷時兩千多年，可見西方對中國史學認識的一斑。沙畹本人以其出衆的才華，及長期為史記作譯註，自然對中國史學的認識較深，其譯註導論的前言又云：

「歷史在古代西方，用我們今日眼光看來，不少是作者個人才華的表現，或者說，乃作者本人的聰明去對所得史料加以消化，而又隨着他的個人看法去加以調整，並照着他的凌空想像去加以解釋。

然而中國學人對於修史的觀念，則從來不是這樣的；歷史，照中國學人之見，是一種精巧的鑲嵌細工的作品，在裡面，前代篇章已經次第排列，只須由作者在其中去加以選擇取捨而再加以技巧的適當連繫。如果史家是第一個來開頭敍述某種史事，或者說，他必須加以他個人的印象去寫著時，則他對於這某種史事的層面上去參加添一些厚度；不過這一厚度之加，我們很容易去辨認出來，在原始資料與他的渲染之間。因爲這種層次好像結晶體的構造一樣，我們可以順着它的幾何式的壘積紋路去剖別出它的平列層片的而並不動亂它的構成的本質。這類史家的作品是相當客觀的，它對往蹟是以見證人的身份說話，它俾我們有機會去了解這是作者自己所親見而言，或者只是照抄今日已難再見的遺文。當其我們能够了解到這是中國史家着筆的結構方式時，我們便可以成立第二個假設去稱作者差不多都不願正式的說他在闡發他個人的主觀思想。

因是一册中國史作的每一章書並不是興到之時一氣呵成之作，而是常有其各種來源資料顯示出來，且在篇中，並不諱言其來源所自，不過它的方法是平等併列方式，而不是系統化的罷了。至於談到批判，則中國史家習於隨便捨棄其所自認爲是假的材料，而只敍述其所珍視的眞實事項；他很少去用反復推理的一種辨別方法來對於可疑之處加以細細審核；他好像是用羅篩在濾史料，只要細的，不要粗的。」❸

在十九世紀末葉，認識了中國史家作品的客觀性，是極爲難得的。但是認爲「中國史家習於隨便捨棄其所自認爲是假的材料」，「很少去用反復推理的一種辨別方法來對於可疑之處加以細細審核」，「好像是用羅篩在濾史料，只要細的，不要粗的」，則是極爲膚淺之論了。這也無怪他埋怨司馬遷在眞與假的辨認中，「過信其自己的正確見地」，「只是在證明他認爲好的正確的材料，而便抹煞了他前人還留得有其它的材料」❹了。

整個審察中國史學的，是一九三八年美國漢學家賈德納（C. S. Gardner, 1900- ）所寫的「中國傳統史學」（Chinese Traditional Historiography）一書。這是西方漢學界所公認的研究中國史學的開山之作。數十年來，西方漢學家討論中國史學的專文或專書，列舉參攷書目，皆以此書冠於其首；不少在此書所建立的基礎上，建立其壯觀❺；初學漢學的學生，也多讀此書，西方漢學界差不多以此書當成學生必讀的教本之一。此書的地位與重要如此，其內容的豐富正確與否，關係實極重大。一九六四年在英倫，借讀此書，深覺其內容簡單浮泛，與中國史學的博大精深，相去殆不可以道里計，讀後爲之怏怏者久之！十六年後（一九八〇年），自港大圖書館借此書重讀，而失望更深。大凡此書略有所見者，爲看清了中國考據學的悠久歷史，與認識了「沒有其他古代民族像中國人一樣，擁有整個過去的記錄，如此其浩瀚，如此其綿延不絕，如此其精審。」❻其他不是失之膚淺，即流於荒謬。如將中國所有史家的撰寫歷史，皆目之爲編纂（compilation），即似是而極非之論。一九六一年此書再版，無任何增刪，中國旅美學人楊聯陞教授有一短序，謂賈德納教授以健康關係，未作增刪。其實其書應徹底重寫，不是什麼增刪的問題了。❼

一九五八年美國漢學家霍森（Burton Watson, 1925- ）在沙畹的重大影響下，寫了「大史家司馬遷」(Ssu-ma Ch'ien: Grand Historian of China) 一書，其對司馬遷以及整個中國史學的認識，已較沙畹爲深，在討論到中西史學的異同時，頗能心平氣和，而不若賈德納之以輕蔑的眼光，對中國史學施以冷酷的攻擊。如云：

「司馬遷寫了一部世界史。他的歷史的大部分是中國史，此乃由於他認爲中國是世界的中心，人類進步與文明的最高峰，而且他也最知中國。但是他擴展其省察到各方面，包括了韓國、東南亞以及中國北部、西部等地區的敍述。換言之，他似乎盡其詳的愼重描繪中國邊疆以外的地方，祇要他有可靠的知識。例如，他未言及東方的日本與西方的歐洲，幾乎可斷言不是由於缺乏興趣，而是由於缺乏資料。」❽

「在中國文化發展的過程中，難以確言眞正的歷史意識 (a true historical consciousness) 出現於何時。……此一歷史意識，很自然地（雖然不是必然的）自周民族的人文主義滋長出來。他們一點一滴的改造古代的神話，去其粗糙的迷信及宗教的觀點，使其與理性主義及人文主義相吻合，理性主義及人文主義在中國思想中一直在猛烈增長之中。在同時，歷史寫作的觀念，以及歷史的觀念，逐漸發展。歷史的原始資料，史學的方法與目的 (the methods and objectives of historical literature)，皆由理性主義與人文主義的概念以形成。」❾

「中國（歷史）作品，其內容幾乎完全是戲劇性的插曲與情節，直接對話代替了敍事，史家不置評而人物的性格畢現。」❿

「歷史的誨訓功能……是中國歷史思想中的主要部分，從古迄今皆如此。」⓫

自然其中可議之處仍多，如認爲春秋一書中「往往寓有强烈的反歷史精神」⑫，即爲其一，强調「希羅多德之與希羅世界（the Greco-Roman world）的史學傳統，正如司馬遷之與中國、韓國及日本的史學傳統」⑬，亦有待商榷。

第二節　一九六一年「中日史家」(Historians of China and Japan) 一書的問世

一九五六年到一九五八年之間，英國倫敦大學亞非研究院（School of Oriental And African Studies, University of London）舉行了一連串關於亞洲民族史籍的討論會，南亞、東南亞、近東、中東及遠東，都包括在內。關於中國與日本的史籍，西方漢學家及日本問題專家提出近二十篇專題論文，以作討論的資料。一九六一年倫敦大學的畢斯利（W. G. Beasley）教授及劍橋大學的浦立本教授遂集合之以編成「中日史家」一書，在西方研究東方史學的一點上，這是劃時代的著作。雖然我們對它仍然不怎麼滿意，可是比起一九三八年賈德納所寫的「中國傳統史學」，已像是進步了幾個世紀。這應是中西史學合流的先聲。

1. 浦立本（E. G. Pulleyblank, 1922-　）

浦立本先生是加拿大漢學家，一九五五年至一九六六年，任英國劍橋大學漢學教授。一九六六年以後，返加拿大任教。浦氏治唐史，旁及語言學，對中國史學，尤有極濃厚的興趣。在西方漢學家中，他應是對中國史學認識最深的一位。⑭

浦氏極致慨於西方史家不知中國史學，與白特費爾德教授的爭辯，是不得已挺身而出的壯舉。在中國史家中，他對劉知幾、司馬光最有研究，而對王夫之、趙翼則極度推崇。推崇王夫之、趙翼，是由於他們二人的史學，與西方史學有暗合之處。探求中國史學之同於西方史學者，以爲中國史學辨，是西方漢學家研究中國史學的一種方法。

「中日史家」一書的敍論，中國部分，爲浦氏所寫，其中有云：

「稱之爲歷史的以往記錄，已獨立的發展成一主要的智慧活動，不超出三個時代。歐洲史學傳統，追溯到它的希臘羅馬淵源。伊斯蘭教發展其歷史，不像其哲學，顯然非受希臘典型的影響。最後，中國出產的歷史著作，有其特殊優點，亦有其特殊限制，且其出產量豐碩，記載悠久而又綿延不絕。如果一個人去正確地瞭解史學問題，以及史學在人類文化發展中所佔的地位，很明顯的他必須全顧到這三個傳統。可是，達到此一淵博境界，有難以克服的障礙。十九世紀西方史學經過變化之後，挾着西方文化的其他要素，向世界每一角落擴張，而即成爲『現代化』的一部分。……另一方面中國傳統有文化限制，它決不是死的，但是由於整個中國傳統文化，受西方入侵的吞沒及改變，西方史家很少有動機承認中國史學以往的成就，或重視其極不同的傳統，以與自己作比較。

必須承認，縱然動機存在，縱然西方史家希望去瞭解遠東史學，亦將困難重重。翻譯的作品太少，而且史學是傳統孔子文化的極密切的一支，受中國社會的支配，在能眞正瞭解之前，必須相當深入於其文化與社會之中。同時頗能採取兩種觀點的人，才能解釋中國史學。他們必須是精通中國學問的專家，同時深深曉得西方史家的興趣與先入之見，以便解釋時使其心目中的聽衆感覺到有意義。很少溝通此一鴻溝的嘗試，此一工作大部分要留待將來去做。本集中國史學論文的作者，不敢聲言已完成此工作，但是他們的意向是向此方向努力。」⑮

又云:

「對中國人來講，歷史大體上已代替了神話的地位，供給取之不盡的揷曲，以備說故事者、小說家以及戲劇家所取材。」⑯

他於「中國史學批評：劉知幾與司馬光」(Chinese Historical Criticism: Lin Chih-chi and Ssu-Ma Kuang) 一文中又云:

「中國擁有在近代以前未有其他國家可以與之相比的歷史載籍，最低限度在漢學家當中，這是公認的事實。然而說中國歷史寫作的方法與史學批評的標準永遠受到一致的崇高讚美，是不正確的。我們通常聽別人說，其方法僅爲一種機械的剪貼式的編纂(mechanical scissors-and-paste compilation)，材料的去取，祇經過原始的批評。但是，當此一評判適用於中國大多數官方及其他泛泛歷史著作有幾分眞理的時候，適用於中國大史家的學術智慧及史學思想，是難以公平的。

誠然，十九世紀末西洋方法的輸入，是中國史學研究的一巨大革命，就像在自然科學方面一樣。但是二十世紀中國史家能接近其自己的傳統同時擴大其觀念，接受外來影響的顯著情形，必使觀者觸目驚心。無疑地這部分是由於民族主義者的守舊性，且不經常是完全有益的，然而對中國傳統的富源來講，這也是一種貢獻。

同時，姑不論其延綿不絕的活力及其永恒的價值(那必爲將來所證明)，中國人對歷史的態度與對歷史的批評思想，很淸楚地爲瞭解世界民族中此一最富歷史觀念的民族既往的基本重要因素。」⑰

浦氏不將中國的史評、史論列入史學批評之內，他認爲此類作品大多係根據道德觀點，對歷史事件或歷史著作所下的泛論，是屬於政治的與倫理的歷史解釋 (political and ethical interpretations of history)。

對史通，他則盛爲推許：

「中文第一部實實在在談歷史寫作的論述（或者在任何語文中我所能發現的第一部），是劉知幾（661-721）的史通，完成於七一〇年。」⑱

又云：

「近代西方史家，對劉知幾着重中國官方史學的純然型式，或許感覺失望。然而其重要處，在以此可認出中國人對歷史的態度，與其他民族對歷史的態度顯著差異的一面。歷史對中國人來講，一是官方的，二是垂訓的。爲以往留一精審而確定的記載，是政府的任務，就像對死者與生者頒以官爵與榮譽是政府的任務一樣。同時此種記載，有其道德目的，展示出好與壞的例子，藉此可勸善而懲惡。」⑲

又云：

「徧於史通，强調省略不必要或不值得記載者，也强調措詞的簡明，這代表中國人對每一文學作品的最典型態度，但是影響在歷史作品上，其價值往往值得人懷疑。」⑳

又云：

「劉知幾在中國馳名，傳統上是由於他勇於發現前代史家的錯誤，甚至及於像春秋一類的經典。對我們來講，他的批評，像是頗爲浮淺。他仍遠未對孔子傳統作基本懷疑。」㉑

浦氏認爲中國的批評之學（critical scholarship），集中於孤立之點而不統觀全面（seeing things as connected wholes），是其普遍的缺點。

浦氏論通鑑則云：

「司馬光有限度地提供了事件的連環性，當然他遠不能將事件融於原因的關鎖上（binding events together in a causal nexus），以有關連的整體視之。在這方面中國傳統的史家永遠不能完全達到。」㉒

又云：

「司馬光實際上運用剪貼方法以編纂長編，當需要加入材料到長編去的時候，長卷便被剪斷，貼入要加入的部分。」㉓

又云：

「司馬光確是一位科學的史家，因爲他第一次嘗試建立眞理於客觀基礎之上。」㉔

從司馬光論到中國傳統史家的普遍缺陷則云：

「從我們的現代觀點來看，司馬光的方法最嚴重的缺陷之一，也是幾乎所有中國傳統史家的缺陷，是將注意力局於一個時代的一項孤立事件，約略敍其前後，以及綜論人的品德等等，可是不曾嘗試將每一事件與其他衆多事件編織成一錯綜的關係網。司馬光及其共同寫史諸公極度辛勤下所產生的，是一上乘的編年史，但僅是一編年史而已。以近代觀點視之，那不是歷史。

從技術的觀點來論，另一嚴重的缺陷，是疏於考察其本身材料的出處。這並非一絕對的疏忽，考異各處，可發現關於事實關係的論斷，以及論到原文來源的可靠性，不管是全部的或應用到特殊情況之下。但是通常的原文被視作最終極的材料，不去進一步分析其淵源或相互關係。原文B，部分基於原文A，而被認爲是獨立的，值得同樣考慮。這也不單獨是司馬光的缺陷，在大部分中國學術中，這是普遍的，雖然在十七、十八世紀是進步了。

無論如何，較深一步了解司馬光的方法，應當驅逐某些神話，比如富玄理的史學批評不能施之於剪貼編纂體的觀念，又如中國

史家沒有可能的概念而僅有確實的概念的說法。」㉕

論趙翼則云:

「趙翼雖受其學術限制，却或許是三人中（指趙氏與王鳴盛、錢大昕）最令人感興趣的，因為他在向着克服中國史學的傳統缺陷而進步。他的一生環境，給他相當少的機會去研究希奇的資料，他不得不欣然强調正史的重要，駁斥考據學家廣徵稗乘脞說。他反覆閱讀正史，不旁徵博引以作瑣碎的考訂，而僅將關於各書的一般評論或書中使他感興趣的事件，劄記下來。他討論各朝歷史如何編纂，根據些什麼資料，並與同時代的作品加以比較。……他的觀點，有些祇是標新立異，但是在很多情況下，他能觸及眞正使近代史家感興趣的問題，近代史家讀其作品，確實能得到益處。」㉖

2. 畢斯利（W. G. Beasley, 1919-　）

畢斯利曾任英國倫敦大學遠東史敎授（Professor of the History of the Far East, University of London)，他在「中日史家」一書的緒論中云:

「直到最近，用西文寫的中國與日本的專門書，才不是由曾經住在工作在遠東的人執筆。十六、十七、十八世紀，耶穌會傳敎士壟斷此業。十九世紀與二十世紀初期，繼耶穌會敎士而致力於此業者，為新敎傳敎士、外交家、新聞記者與去在中學或大學敎書的人。所有的這些人，有一點是相同，那就是他們的作品淵源於一種對該地區知識的興趣。此一事實，有重要的影響。比如，他們的作品不僅限於富學術性的歷史。有一些，歷史僅是全體的一部分，政治、法律、經濟、地理、文學、藝術也都包入其中。

其他部分，是起於對語言或哲學的原始興趣而產生的作品。事實上，研究的題目是一個國家或者其文化，不特殊或僅僅是其歷史。「漢學」(sinology) 一詞的概念，存在到今天，仍可在這方面作提示。

個人的經驗，也影響所研究題目的性質。除開當代或近於當代的記述，如中國的太平天國叛變，已寫的歷史，多以作者時代的社會，去說明歷史上的社會，或以其自己所經驗的知識以描寫事件的直接背景。同樣地，西方與該地區的關係史被加强，而此一主題誠然有時淹覆其他所有資料，縱然在公認的通史之中。另一方面，許多書以討論兩國遠古史的姿態出現。在中國，此種情形最低限度像是起於爲研究哲學提供歷史背景的動機。在日本，大致源於在語言或政治制度上的興趣。

在某些方面，西方作品更近於中日史學，而與西方史學本身，反有距離，尤其是在主題的解釋與選擇上。其原因能容易推想而出。因爲作者住在東方，他們想接受同時代的中國人與日本人同樣的影響，選擇同樣的題目研究：例如，重點放在古代史與近代史，而忽略了古代近代之間的時代，雙方都是相同的。另外的解釋是西方史家信賴他所研究的國家的學者，有時他與中國或日本助手共同工作。即使不是如此，語言的困難，經常使他們憑依中文或日文的近代作品，而不敢問津廣大的原始材料，結果，他常常有意無意地接受其觀點與其實際資料。」㉗

又云：

「這些評論並不意味着所有西方關於遠東史的作品都是沒有價值的。其中很多是有用，有一些確實極好；但是絕大部分，其價值是以其爲一將科目介紹給西方讀者的媒介，而不是以其對知識有

一新的貢獻。此外，西方作品並不能充作輸入中日歷史寫作新技術的孔道。」㉘

又云：

「當注意到二十世紀時，可能看清楚西方作品的性質在開始變，其變是由於中日與西方的政治關係起了變化。最早往遠東去的歐洲人，他們對在那裡所發現的，留有極深刻的印象。耶穌會敎士以極欣羡的筆調，記述中國的制度，這可以由很多根據其報告寫成的書反映出來。但是在十九世紀，西方列强的支配經濟政治勢力，以及中國與日本社會明顯的停頓，使態度改變了。這是一個口號的時代，像『不信上帝的中國人』(the beather Chinese) 及『中國的循環』(the cycle of Cathay)，都包含着藐視一個靜態的或衰落的文化的意味，最低限度不證明活潑有力的生長，而活潑有力的生長像是歐洲文化的特徵。由於此一判斷，遠東史遂成爲一門不值得認眞研究的科目，而留給到過那裡的人去研究。」㉙

又云：

「在趨向本世紀末葉之際，有兩項發展，預示了一條新路。第一是歐洲發現了中國與日本的藝術（或許是再發現），以此有動機與心願研究其藝術的歷史。第二是日本的崛起，迅速獲得國際地位。……遠東突然間重要起來了。大大不是靜態的了。結果，遠東漸漸爲西方國家所注意，也自然爲西方大學所注意。自一九三〇年以來，尤其是自一九四五年以來，在歐洲與美洲研究中國與日本學科的大學敎師，爲數急驟增加，其學科包括歷史在內。

此最近期間產生的作品，與以前的作品，在很多方面大相逕庭。作者不再住在工作在他們所寫的國家裡面，雖然他們爲了研究經常儘量設法去訪問。他們也比其前人更意識到『學術性』(being academic)，一種在客觀性質上的獲得爲人類經驗上的損失所平衡。所研究的時代，很少變化。仍然對晚今與遠古有普遍的偏好，雖然在晚今遠古之間作更詳盡研究的需要也已漸漸受到重視。仍然信賴中國與日本學術，然而是寧信賴團體，而不信賴個人——寧信賴一所大學而不信賴一位老師，寧信賴一個圖書館而不信賴一本書。這反映出所有變化中最顯明的變化，加重訓練、技術、研究與專業。代表性的書是專論：詳盡，富批評精神，並限之於專題上。事實上，第一次西方學者盡力克服語言困難，盡力接近材料，以研究西洋史的方式，同樣去研究中國史與日本史。這完全是有益的，但是尚含有某些危險。孤立的專論，數目必相當少，其確切的要旨與意義，僅能根據中國或日本的現有文獻而獲得完全瞭解，以致祇有專家，才能鑑賞。其術語與表現風格越技巧，這越眞實。因此，這類作品需要以更普通的研究去補充，在特殊時代或專題上頗詳盡的鑽研，足以彌補研究專題(research monograph)與通覽歷史(survey history)兩極端間的缺陷。」㉚

3. 房德龍(Van der Loon)

房德龍是荷蘭漢學家，現任英國牛津大學漢學教授，其於「中國古代編年史及其史學理想的成長」(The Ancient Chinese Chronicles and the Growth of Historical Ideas)一文中云:

「直到最近，最低限度在西方，相當於公元前一千年的中國上古史，遠比以後一千八百年受到密切注意。結果，中國史學多由大多數的古代載籍或較後的通史來衡量，少由較後的斷代史來品

評。」㉛

又云:

「周代現存的最豐富的歷史與民俗知識是左傳。……但是很難闡明其錯綜龐雜的文章及其書的傳播情形。」㉜

又云:

「整個的評判一下司馬遷的作品，雖然作者的意見偶然流露，雖然他有時表現十足的懷疑主義，可是通常地他僅將其資料以原來辭句再刋載一番而已，不曾嘗試深入研究資料。西漢亡後，踵司馬遷之例以寫史者，有漢書的作者，及其後所有的所謂正史。正史的三主要部分永遠是本紀、列傳及志，漸漸地其理想獲得了，嚴格地附屬於文字材料，且毋寧說是官方的文字材料。不可獲得證明的資料，如演說，被削除了，結果是一與人脫節的敍述（an inpersonal account），一本政府白皮書（a Government White Paper），用剪刀與漿糊編纂而成，不怎麼消化，幾乎沒有解釋。」㉝

又云:

「一切歸納中國史學所得的結論，大有值得懷疑的餘地。西方學者們或許太好以十九、二十世紀歐洲的歷史與之作比較，而不以較早時代的歷史與之相提並論。他們堅持的說中國史學沒有連接個別的事實，但是忘記不可勝數的散文與備忘錄已呈現了一幅史學景色（historical perspective）。此外，當批評一種或一組有目的的作品時，我們應當記得，其失經常地以其充滿材料而獲得補償，特別是將私家史學著作算入的話。」㉞

4. 何四維（A. F. P. Hulsewe'）

何四維也是荷蘭漢學家，他於「漢代史學註釋」(Notes on the Historiography of the Han Period) 一文中云:

「在新政治組織下的新中產階級社會（指漢初），產生了新的寫歷史方法，一種與較早以編年紀載重要事件的體裁在很多方面迥然不同的史學。」㉟

又云:

「中國方面，極注意漢代史。然而，歷代多數中國學者，主要致力於考證、訓詁、辨僞等問題，因之他們繼續了自第二世紀迄今註釋家們殫精於歷史原文的悠久傳統。此外的學者，如第一位思及史學一般問題的，即有名的劉知幾（六六一——七二一），在其史通一書中，已涉及更普通性質的問題。但是直到最近，更廣泛地寫漢代史上更一般更技術的問題的少數學者之一，是趙翼（一七二七——一八一四），其廿二史劄記的前三章即詳於此。」㊱

又云:

「史記與漢書的原文，其間有極密切的關係，但是這裡我們遇到一個迄未解決的困難，卽漢書像是大部分根據史記中漢的部分，現在兩者的原文大約完全一致。可是當漢書完成之後，及外界難以利用到史記的一個時期，史記在皇帝命令之下，遭受刪削，是衆所周知的事。因此不是不可能史記中漢的部分（或者最低限度其中片段），係後來根據漢書所重建。如果這被證明了，史記將相當喪失漢史獨立史源的價值。」㊲

5. 傅吾康 (Volfgang Franke, 1912-　　)

傅吾康是德國漢堡大學 (Hamburg University) 漢學教授，他深悉中國文化對世界的重大意義，於所撰「明代實錄」(The Veritable

Records of the Ming Dynasty）一文中論中國的史學與史官云:

「從最古到本世紀，史學在中國綿延發展，未嘗中斷。」㊳

「在中國，從古代到傳統政體結束，史官經常有一特殊重要的位置。」㊴

6. 福赫伯（Herbert Franke, 1914-　）

福赫伯是德國慕尼黑大學（University of Munich）漢學教授，他在「十三、十四世紀中國私家史學的幾面」(Some Aspects of Chinese Private Historiography in the Thirteenth and Fourteenth Centuries）一文中云:

「過去歐洲與中國史學最大區別之一，是官方史學支配了中國。各朝正史，集中於人事制度與行政方面，以致我們可以確切地說，它們大部分僅記錄了官樣文章。因此這種資料所繪出的過去，是片面的。僅偶然地我們能校正其精確程度，那經常是在中國有 multistate 制度的時代，或我們擁有與中國有外交（或交戰）關係的外國文件時。很多事件，例如各種農民叛變，我們僅從官方記載中獲知，幾乎沒有叛變文件留存下來，將他們的目的與觀念介紹給我們，即使此類文件曾經有的話。顯著的例外是太平軍叛變。由此環境產生的單面歷史（the onesidedness of historical outlook），如果我們作一比較，想到歐洲僅有中世紀帝王的功業以作歐洲中古史的主要資料，而沒有衆多補充檔案室文件的私人記載，我們當能予以充分的瞭解。

如果我們在中世紀的中國搜求類似的資源（similar sources），我們首先必須給私家史學下一個定義。或許合適的定義，是『私』的概念須以遠離宦途的程度來衡量，尤其是須超然於京師史局之上。準此定義，理想的私家史家（private historian），爲一永未參與公職的作者。但是卽使在這種情形之下，是否私家史學的基本概念，極區別於官方史學，是值得懷疑的。一些儒家思想成分，幾乎兩方面一定都具有。這是佛家編年史（Buddhist chronicles）値得特別注意的原因，因爲他們不但符合上述私家史學的定義，同時具有一個不同的思想背景。在很多情況之下，私家史學與官方史學之間，淸楚的劃出此疆彼界，是不可能的。」㊵

又論及胡三省注通鑑云：

「對於他，就像對幾乎所有的中國史家一樣，褒貶是史學的基本要素。歷史被認爲是政治倫理的鏡子，必須以儒家標準去評判。」㊶

又云：

「由各朝斷代史與司馬光通鑑所定的模型（pattern），像是太有聲勢了，而不容許獨立方法（independent）存在。」㊷

又云：

「以中國與中世紀歐洲相比，我們注意到中國頗缺乏個人表現（individual expression）。……歐洲的拉丁資料，遠較爲個人的，能反映個性，卽使是經過錯誤的文法或拼字法。在中國，歷史中的個人要素，不易獲得；我們祇能試着去找較官方報告能希望多得到一些消息的資料。換句話說，去找劄記，去找稗乘脞說，或者去找記個人親身經驗的少數作品。」㊸

7. 杜希德（D. C. Twitchett, 1925-　）

杜希德先生曾任英國倫敦大學及劍橋大學漢學敎授，他於「中國的傳記作品」（Chinese Biographical Writing）一文中評中國的傳記云：

「像在史學著作的每一領域，中國大量提供了傳記資料，僅正史便包括數以千計的列傳，方志中各類特殊傳記使其總數到達一龐大數字。如果我們將家庭中使用的哀悼或紀念作品計入，其數字能幾乎無限制的擴大。」㊹

又云：

「列傳典型的例子，像編年史一樣，枯燥而無人的氣息，近代讀者欲尋傳主人格的端倪，將發現極難形成每個人不同的寫照。」㊺

又云：

「總之，中國傳統史家，已爲我們提供了豐富的傳記資料。但是比較起來，時代不如其他歷史著作正確，同時不如其他歷史著作經過嚴密的批評。此外，嚴格說起來，傳記是出自家庭頌揚作品 (the eulogistic writing of family cults)，僅涉及傳主生平的一面。還有傳記幾乎僅寫與作者同一社會群體的人物。在這些自我限制 (self-imposed limitations) 之下，又憑作者嚴格受拘束的意向去觀察，成果完全稱得上豐碩，但是對近代學者來講，這些限制帶來一嚴重問題，大大說明了無個人的氣息，給初研究中國史的人一難以忍受的印象。」㊻

8. 戴密微 (P. Demiéville, 1894-1979)

戴密微是法國漢學家，去世不久，他於「章學誠及其史學」(Chang Hsüeh-Ch'eng and his Historiography) 一文中云：

「有清一代 (一六四四——一九一一)，中國文化到達另一高峰，在很多方面，即使是哲學，乾隆時代 (一七三六——九六) 可以說與我們的 Siécle des Lumieres 相當。」㊼

復極力推崇章學誠云：

「在考據學達到最高潮之際，對儒學傳統的將來，有摧毀性的影響，而此時中國出現一位第一流的史學天才，可與伊本凱爾東（Ibn Khaldun）㊽或與歐洲最偉大的史家並駕齊驅。」㊾

又云：

「如果中國官方夠聰明，將章氏在十八世紀末設立地方志科及重修方志的計劃實施，中國今天將在其近代史上使用無與倫比的文件，我們應不必以中央政府與皇家法庭的檔案室而滿足。」㊿

又云：

「總之，西方使中國注意了章學誠。面臨革新史學原理與方法的必要，中國必須在這方面宏揚科學所特有的客觀通則（objective generalization）的精神。憶及很久以前，十八世紀之末，此種精神已爲浙江一聲名甚晦的學者所預示，他的玄奧思想，不爲其時代所知，然爲近代思想却提供了有效的食糧（valid food）。」[51]

論及章學誠「六經皆史」之說則云：

「章學誠斷言儒家之經典卽歷史。仔細思考此一主張，倒轉來歷史也將構成經典，歷史將有經典的價值，一種有如規範的價值。那正是章學誠所相信的。聖經是歷史，因爲歷史是一聖經。我相信章學誠的目的，不是去褻瀆經典，而是將歷史經典化。」[52]

又將章氏與西方的維科（Giambattista Vico）相比：

「維科幾乎是與他同時代的人，維科一七四四年死於拿不勒斯（Naples），六年後他遠道的中國同伴生於黃海之濱。兩人都醉心於歷史，傾畢生精力，思索歷史的意義及其哲學基礎。他們都具有同樣的急燥的天性；同樣的獨立思想，同樣在事業上遭遇困難。……維科旣反對笛卡兒的理性主義與抽象論（Cartesian rationalism and abstraction），又反對其當代編纂者及聖經批評者的偏狹的博學。」[53]

又云:

「無疑的，就像維科在歐洲預示了諸多近代史學趨勢一樣，章學誠站在他時代的前端，在悠長的中國史學史上，預示了一個轉機。」[54]

9. 哥芮（J. Gray, 1926-　）

哥芮是英國倫敦大學遠東史講師，他在「二十世紀中國的史學著作：其背景及發展的註解」(Historical Writing in Twentieth-century China: Notes on its Background and Development) 一文中云:

「前面的論文（指討論會中所提出討論者），已將中國傳統史學所受政府的限制，社會的限制，及中國在世界所處地位的限制，說清楚了。因爲中國被信爲係惟一的文明國家，以致沒有外來標準的比較。因爲內部標準是傳奇式的黃金時代，所有以後建立的政權，皆大爲遜色，以致不可能有進化或發展的觀念。政權爲皇帝所任用的士大夫（scholar-officials）所獨佔，以致促使在史家之中不着眼與權勢主要來源相關的制度與群體，也導致了一個因果體系（a scheme of cause and effect），誇大官僚政治的作用，幾乎將所有其他因素剔除。在此一體系之中，官吏基本的道德訓練，導致過分強調歷史事件的道德原因。

傳統歷史著作的優點與缺點，出於同一來源。保存豐富而正確的事件與制度記載的習慣，編表的習慣，以及在政經機關工作的興趣，源於官僚的偏見（bureancratic bias），此一偏見，在其他方面，是一有限度的因素（a limiting factor)。公平判斷官吏、學者個人事業的需要，出產了無與倫比的傳記財富，這些財富，

迄今存留着，如果沒有這些財富的話，我們對於中國過去的所知，會更可憐些。」㊺

又云：

「民族傳統的限制是淸淸楚楚的，然而仍有相當貢獻。首先，在許多硏究領域中，最重要的是原文的處理與批評，這裡傳統的學者已經提供了作爲高深硏究基礎的技術與標準。第二，中國以往有自己的批評家。……第三，清代史學已相當進步，淸代學者不肯寫完全屬於歷史綜合的作品是其證明。」㊻

又云：

「在史學領域中，中國的先哲也爲近代化提供了基礎——更重要的是中國人所能接受的基礎。在梁啓超的中國歷史硏究法一書中，他不斷的徵引中國古代批評家之說，以駁斥傳統的史學觀念，他引劉知幾、鄭樵及章學誠以論斷代史、紀傳體以及官修歷史的缺陷，他又引劉知幾以議編年體之失。宋代學人楊萬里以紀事本末體能明因果，而服膺之，梁氏也徵引其說。」㊼

又云：

「雖然近代中國史家厭惡淸代史學作品，他們却不得不取法於淸代史學作品。西方能供給較深的史學目的與方法上的自覺，但是，即使是有機會精讀西方眞的歷史作品（異於空論性教科書的譯本）的中國史家，硏究中國史，惟一可能的實際訓練，是奠基於淸代作品上。西方能供給理想，淸代學術則供給日常硏究習慣（the day-to-day habits of research）。」㊽

又云：

「淸代史學遺產的價値與影響，或許已被低估了。中外有一趨勢，責備淸代傳統迂腐（pedantry）。」㊾

又云:

「乾隆學術中最出色的人物是多產的史家與經學家錢大昕。他的作品及其題目的選擇，顯示出他密切踵法顧炎武的理想與方法，雖然他沒有表明其理論觀點。他的最大特質，就像內滕虎次郎⑩所講的，是擁有『無與倫比的正確知識，研究一個問題時，可有效的當作歷史材料用』。其知識是經過了正確的通盤的批評。」⑪

又云:

「在中國，假設與求證的工作，很少合而爲一。」⑫

10. 白樂日 (E. Balazs, 1905–1963)

白樂日爲法國漢學家，他在「歷史爲從政的輔導」(History as a Guide to Bureaucratic Practice) ⑬一文中云:

「與西方史學比較起來，整個中國史學的顯著特徵安在？西方史家雖經審愼考慮，力摒成見，其所能提供的答案，將爲中國史學的刻板特性 (stereotype character) 而已。所謂『刻板』，意味着顯然相反的兩事。它意味着中國史學缺乏人的感觸 (personal touch)，也意味着缺乏到達綜合的抽象思維(abstract thinking); 因爲當涉及人物的時候，其人物非個人，而爲一群人物的代表，個人的特性溶於群體之中; 而當涉及事件的時候，僅載其詳細事實，雖相同事實，經常重複，而未能將其通觀 (generalization)。」⑭

又云:

「我認爲有三個主要因素，促使中國未能發展類似西方的史學: 將歷史斷代的習慣; 中國史家依靠政府薪俸的官方身份; 以及逐段引用原文的傳統藝術。」⑮

又云:

「一直沿用至今日的傳統引書藝術，爲逕自文獻徵引，而非概述其內容；且因徵引整個文獻，流於冗長，於是僅徵引其關鍵性的段落。如史家欲披露某一文獻的要點，他永遠不用自己的文字披露，而儘量自原文獻中節選。」㊅

又云:

「最壞的缺陷，既不是史官懾伏於當朝勢力之下，也不是史官缺乏客觀，而是史官不能擺脫朝代的架構（dynastic framework），這是由於他們職位性質的關係。必須設想歷史分代，而切斷事件的洪流爲明顯的片段，對中國史家的影響太壞了，迫使他們的觀念停留在不透風雨的密室中。還有，循環的原理與缺乏延續（continuity）的觀念，動搖了組合孤立事實的天秤，並且阻碍了在事實中發現系統關係或因果關係的企圖。」㊆

又云:

「面臨浩如煙海的中國歷史著作，首先要問的問題（所有文獻最重要的問題），是誰爲誰而寫？誰是作者及誰是讀者？答案是清清楚楚的：歷史係由官吏而寫，爲官吏而寫。直到近代，此爲一玉律，極少例外。即使是特立而獨行的作者（independent writers），也是官吏（致仕後悠遊林下），或寄望仕宦；整個歷史著作（包括歷史軼事、族譜、歷史小說、地方史及類書）寫給同一群衆，即受過教育的官吏及未來的官吏。因此作者與讀者之間，與趣不謀而合。」㊇

11. 瑞特（Arthur F. Wright, 1913-1978）

美國漢學家瑞特評「中日史家」一書云:

「二十世紀學術最偉大的工作之一，是將西方史學傳統與其他史學傳統，作一比較。當西方史家知道一些伊本凱爾東（Ibn Khaldun）的史學理論，知道一些東亞史家的動機與方法，他將發現西方人並沒有『發明』歷史。此種發現，會粉碎西方的褊狹氣量，而久之能產生一種西方史學傳統中所希有的健全觀念。」69

第三節　一九六三年以後

自「中日史家」一書問世後，西方漢學家對中國史學的研究，進入一新時代，繼之而作深入研究者，大有其人。以下就數家作說明，而以瑞特一九六三年發表之專文冠首。

1. 瑞　特

瑞特是西方維護中國史學最力的漢學家之一，他在一九六三年發表的專文「論研究中國歷史應用通則的方法」（On the Uses of Generalization in the Study of Chinese History）中云：

「人人盡知地球上沒有其他民族像中國人那樣擁有如此其浩瀚的過去記錄。正史所記兩千五百年的細節，其總和是難以計算的。翻譯二十五史，將需要四千五百萬英文字，而此僅代表全部記錄的極小部分而已。」70

又云：

「愼重的記錄，編纂再編纂的工作，以及注釋的工作，耗盡每一世紀無數學者的精力。我們可能問爲什麼過去的研究如此受重視，其價值安在？中國的思想家對此類問題提供了很多答案。……其中之一是以往的成敗，可爲後人的殷鑑。」71

又云:

「傳統史學提供了分類、排比與解釋中國過去浩繁史實的方法。現在這類方法的大部分，已被認爲不合時宜了。」72

瑞氏另在「中國史學」(Chinese Historiography) 一文中則云:

「中國史家所用的方法，分爲兩類，且彼此息息相關。一類是記錄當代事的方法，另一類是將上類記錄編纂成連貫敍事的方法。」73

又云:

「中國人尊重文字記載的態度，導致其處理過去文獻時，小心謹愼，不稍作改動。當一項事件兩種敍述衝突時，每取與所用其他資料較符合者，且整個揷入其著作中。」74

2. 浦 立 本

浦立本教授於一九六四年在道生 (Raymond Dawson) 所編的「中國文化之垂統」(The Legacy of China) 一書中，寫了一篇「史學的傳統」(The Historiographical Tradition)，其中有很精闢的論見，如云:

「司馬遷的著作最重要特色之一，成爲一個不變的原則的，可稱爲『客觀性』(objectivity)。這就是說，史家撰述，係纂輯而成，每自其資料刪節，不作更動，個人的論斷，與之劃分此疆彼界。史家的工作，是將一批文獻纂輯在一起，讓文獻自己講話，而不是將往事予以想像的重建 (imaginative reconstruction)。這並不意味着史家必然變成一個機械的編纂者，因爲材料的選擇、排比，都需要運用精密的判斷，而關於事件起因或歷史人物性格的結論，都要能於適當的地方分別表述的；但是這在平庸的史家那就很容易流於機械的編纂了。」⑮

又云:

「司馬遷著述的前面部分，必然採用了許多史實性可疑的材料。不過他的著述與他所根據的前人著述相比較，是較名符其實的歷史，因爲他是想從原有的證據中，寫成最可信的記錄。離他最近的時期，他大部分都利用第一手的政府檔案，因此其著述有其高度可靠性。而此後在中國歷史著述上成爲範例的，也就是這後一部分，政府檔案總是史料的重大來源。於是在評估歷史著述的史實性方面，任何人都會深感，自漢代起那就是政府官僚見地（the official bureaucratic outlook）的限制問題，而不是所採入材料的眞僞問題了。」⑯

又云:

「劉勰（四六五——五二二）的文心雕龍，爲當時最偉大的文學批評著述，有專篇討論歷史著作，批評迄至作者時代的主要史家，並概論記錄的銓配，信實、居正持平之不易。他强調史家扮演的道德家的角色及其所負秉筆直書、不畏强禦的重責。」⑰

又云:

「清朝學者在綜合的歷史著作（works of synthetic history）方面雖不出色，但對於過去作批評性的重估（critical reappraisal of the past），則建立很高的標準。今日研究中國歷史的嚴肅學者，仍然非依靠他們所奠立的基礎不可。如果我們沒有他們的那些作品，我們的工作就更要艱鉅異常了。」⑱

又云:

「與考據學家略爲有別的是廿二史劄記的作者趙翼（一七二七——一八一四）。考據學家藉其他材料，以補充、考訂正史，趙氏的劄記，則爲細心反復閱讀正史之所得。有時趙氏指出各卷中互有出入之處，但亦泛論各史的來源，而於綜論制度、社會結構以及世風方面，尤有莫大的興趣。他所創始許多觀念，已經播下了種子，在本世紀的現代史學方面，且已結起果實了。」⑲

又云：

「在十九世紀中，由於清朝國勢日衰，西方列強侵凌，中國陷於漫長而日益嚴重的危機。歷史研究這時趨於停頓。」⑳

又云：

「通西方史學非僅爲輸入新理想新方法以代替陳腐而了無生氣的傳統。將傳統中最精粹的部分予以發揚光大，庶乎得之。於是對於以往過分注重的編年體和剪刀漿糊方式，就有了更多不採用的自由和機會；考古方面發現了向所未有的新史料；但是今天的中國學者，在批評史料上，仍步他們十八世紀的先輩的後塵，而向西方學習者，微乎其微。外部世界的知識增廣，主要的促成了擺脫正統的羈絆，懷疑正統，在以往是不敢想像的，完全靠前此幾乎全無的外界觀點和資料來比較，始克臻此。

對西方而言，傳統的中國史學，有什麼重要性呢？或許與西方史學知識所貢獻於中國人對過去的概念者，並無不同。歐洲多種文明，在其文化傳統中，總有更多堪供比較的可能。儘管如此，中國的初步知識，像其他非歐洲文明的知識一樣，還是對十七、十八世紀的人類的思想，起了驚人的解放作用。甚至關於中國的錯誤的或過份粗淺的知識，也使人懷疑起神聖的偏見（hallowed prejudices），而被批評正統派者當作了武器。我們已經超過那個階段了，一個遠遠看起來的中國，不再能起一個虛無之國的作用了。但是在二十世紀的今天，當世界似乎注定要落入『西方的』

或『現代的』文明此一共同模式之中的時候，能發現中國獨立文化傳統的眞實知識，以作比較和批評，比以前越發重要了。爲了此一目的，中國的偉大而仍生氣蓬勃的史學傳統，能有很多貢獻。」81

3. 浦瑞查德（Earl H. Pritchard, 1907-　）

美國漢學家浦瑞查德於「傳統中國史學與方志」（Traditional Chinese Historiography and Local Histories）一文中云：

「中國人沒有問題的是所有民族最久最富歷史觀念的民族。通古爲儒學的基本之一，歷史知識對政府與社會正當功能的發揮，被認爲是必要的。」82

又云：

「傳統中國史學發展其自己的歷史概念（conceptions of history）、價値標準（canons of value）及方法上的技巧（methodological techniques），……寓有崇高的學術水準。正確、客觀與致力眞理被强調。考據學的藝術，高度發展。重視廣泛應用原始資料。爲保持客觀，而讓史實記錄說明自己，普遍的趨勢爲博引資料。此已引起很多近代史家斷言傳統中國史家是純編纂者，做一種剪貼工作。此固有其眞理，但大史家殊不止於此，他們在中國所留歷史作品的影像，與西方修西蒂笛斯（Thucydides）或吉朋（Gibbon）所留者，絕無二致。個人的判斷，經常見於論贊或敍論之中，自然亦滲入所引資料之中。當相反的資料無法取得協調時，一些作者兼引並用。」83

又云：

「所有的歷史著作，官修的或其他的，都經後起的學者，作了系統性的考據，一批補充、修正及審訂舊著的可觀文獻，應運而興。十七、十八世紀，大概看到傳統中國的批評史學發展至最精。雖然此一時期沒有出產能比美史記、漢書、新五代史、通鑑的鉅著，但是洋洋大觀的高等考據作品，却存留下來了。……此一時期最重要的作品，大概是考據學家所留下的較短的專論，題目限於一較小範圍內。」㉔

又云:

「以近代觀點來看，傳統中國史學有一些缺點。刻板的紀年與博引，而不以一家之言，作通貫性的敍事，阻礙了眞正的歷史綜合（real historical synthesis)。所有官修史著與大量私修史著，皆由官僚學者（scholar-bureaucrats）爲官僚學者的從政而寫，不可避免的影響了中國史學的性質，有些方面是好的影響，有些方面是不好的影響。文章風格的求簡與一些文學上的慣例，往往造成晦澀，而致省去有價值的詳細闡述。經濟、社會、甚至文學方面的消息，被認爲不重要，或不爲學者們興趣所在，致不被記錄下來，除了不經意的記錄，反而與帝王相涉的朝廷事件被强調了，連帶着有關地方的新聞被摒拒了。寫及與外族相關處，民族優越感經常是顯著的，但是中國歷史著作最大的缺點（縱然有其客觀的傳統），或許是歷史爲儒家道德主義下的產品，以褒貶衡量君主與官吏。」㉕

4. 杜希德

杜希德教授於一九七三年在其「銅器時代至滿清期間的中國政治與社會」(Chinese politics and society from the Bronze Age to the Manchus）一文中云:

「雖然中國是最古人類之一的『北京人』的家鄉，吾人所知的中國文明，並不特別古老。人類連續的佔據其地，以及不中斷的社會發展，其有確據可尋者，僅能溯及數千年前，吾人所確稱的中國型態的文化，其起源比起中東文明、印度文明或埃及文明，爲時要晚多了。

以中國記錄（Chinese record）與其他文明的記錄相比較，令人注意的，是其連續性有甚於其古老性。我們最早的文字記錄，上溯至公元前兩千年的末葉，從此我們有了一種歷史記錄（historical record），其連續性、準確性及其年代的可靠性，在其他文化中，找不出匹敵。」[86]

又云：

「如果將中國的歷史，從中國的傳統、中國的社會及其制度方面，加以分析，而不要動輒參攷歐洲不合用的標準，便可明白的看出，中國的確像任何國家一樣，是一個生氣蓬勃而又不斷進化的社會。

當考慮到中國歷史記錄的性質時，所有對中國安定及缺乏變化的印象，不難立刻清楚其原因。中國現代史家，比任何其他文化的史家，更依靠其複雜而高度發展的史學傳統。這個傳統，有很多特徵……首先，中國史是官方史（official history），設官修成。尤其中國史是『政治史』（political history），主要記載歷朝皇權的運用及其行政措施。中國史是訓誨史（didactic history），將正統的倫理與道德典範，應用到過去的事件上，目的在爲以後的帝王與官吏提供施政準則。中國史以朝廷爲中心，很少敍及京師以外各省的情況。中國史僅注重代表朝廷的統治階級，庶人很少出現，除非作爲國家政策的消極對象時，或被迫挺而走險時。

此類政治性的記錄，每根據按年代或朝廷年號編成的資料，且爲某一朝而寫。……純自政治觀點看歷史，將歷史按朝代斷限予以分割，視每一朝是獨立的，各有其政治發展的內在型態，而與任何歷史變遷的長遠概念，尠不相涉。令人遺憾的，傳統史學很少勇於捨朝代而另闢蹊徑。果爾，也易於從『正統』一類的政治觀點看長期的歷史變化。」87

杜氏在其一九七八年主編的「劍橋中國史」(The Cambridge History of China) 第十卷的「前言」(與 J. K. Fairbank 合寫) 裡則云:

「中國文化史比西方任何一國的文化史，都更爲淵博，僅略爲不如整個歐洲文化史枝葉扶疏而已。中國的歷史記錄，極爲詳贍浩繁，中國的歷史學術 (historical scholarship) 已高度發展無數世紀，且趨於成熟。」88

「最近西方學者已較全神傾注於中國及日本豐富的歷史學術傳統 (the rich tradition of historical scholarship)，不論在過去事件與制度的細密知識上，以及在傳統史學的批判性的瞭解上，都進步甚大。」89

第六章　註釋:

❶參見 E. G. Pulleyblank, *Chinese History and World History*, 1955, p. 4

❷Edward Chavannes: *Introduction aux Mémoires historiques de Se-Ma Tsien (traduits et annotés)*，其前言部分，由李璜教授譯成中文，今轉引之，見李著「法國漢學論集」，一九七五年香港珠海書院出版，頁二〇

❸同上，頁二〇至二一

❹同上，頁三〇（此見沙畹史記譯註的導論部分。）

❺Lien-Sheng Yang, *Foreword to the Second Printing of C. S. Gardner's Chinese Traditional Historiography*, 1961:

"When Charles Sidney Gardner's Chinese Traditional Historiography first appeared in 1938, American and European scholars in Asian studies welcomed it with enthusiasm.......

Now, after some twenty-three years, this pioneer work is still found to contain much information and insight that students in the field cannot afford to overlook, and from which more advanced scholars continue to profit. This is evidenced in a recent publication of Oxford University Press entitled Historians of China and Japan, edited by W. G. Beasley and E. G. Pulleyblank, containing articles by participants in a conference on Asian history held in London in 1956. A reading of the articles on China shows that several of the authors were building their contributions on the solid ground Gardner laid."

❻C. S. Gardner, *Chinese Traditional Historiography*, 1938, p. 105:

"No other ancient nation possesses records of its whole past so voluminous, so continuous, or so accurate."

❼朱士嘉曾寫「評賈德納著『中國舊史學』」一文，載於史學年報二卷五期（民

國二十七年十二月)，今刊於本書之後，作附錄之一。

❽Burton Watson, Ssu-ma Ch'ien: *Grand Historian of China*, 1958, pp. 3–4:

"Ssu-ma Ch'ien wrote a history of the world. Most of his space he devoted to the history of the area known to us as China, for the reason that this was, to him, the center of the world, the highest point of human advancement and culture, and the area about which he knew most. But he extended his examination in all directions, including in his book accounts of the area now known as Korea, the lands of south-east Asia, and those to the west and north of China. In other words, he seems to have taken care to describe, in as much as possible, all the lands outside the borders of China of which he had any reliable knowledge. The fact that he says nothing, for instance, of Japan in the east or Europe in the west, is almost certainly due not to a lack of interest but to a lack of information."

❾Ibid., pp. 135–136:

"It is impossible to say definitely when, in the course of the development of Chinese culture, a true historical consciousness appeared ......

This historical consciousness grew quite naturally (though not inevitably) from the humanism of the Chou people. Little by little they worked to remake their old myths, to refine their crude superstitions and religious ideas into conformity with rationalism and humanism that were grewing ever stronger in Chinese thought. At the same time that the idea of historical writing, and of history itself, was slowly developing, the raw materials of history, and the methods and objectives of historical literature, were being shaped by these concepts of rationalism and humanism."

❿Ibid., p. viii:

"The Chinese works often conist almost wholly of dramatic episodes and scenes in which direct speech replaces narrative and serves to reveal the character of the actors without comment from the historian."

⓫Ibid., p. 137:

"the didactic function of history,...... a concept that has been an essential part of Chinese historical thought from ancient times to the present."

⓬Ibid., p. 83

⓭Ibid., p. vii:

"What Herodotus was to the historical tradition of the Greco-Roman world, Ssu-ma Ch'ien has been to that of China, Korea, and Japan."

⓮維運在劍橋大學讀書期間，指導教授爲浦立本先生，因得親承教誨，悉其言論觀點。

⓯W. G. Beasley and E. G. Pulleyblank, *Historians of China and Japan*, pp. 1-2:

"The recording of the past which we call history has developed independently into a major intellectual activity not more than three times. The European historical tradition looks back to its Greek and Roman origins. Islam developed its history, unlike its philosophy, apparently uninfluenced by Greek models. And lastly, China produced an historical literature, peculiar both in its merits and in its limitations, but unique in the volume of its output and the length and continuity of its record. If one is to understand rightly the problems of historiography and the part that it has played in the development of human civilization, it is obvious that one must take into account all three traditions, but there are formidable barriers in the way of achieving such a comprehensive perspective. Western historiography, transformed during the nineteenth century, spreads with other elements of western civilization to every part of the world as a part of 'modernization'......The Chinese tradition on the other hand remains culture bound. It is by no means dead, but since traditional Chinese civilization as a whole is being engulfed and transformed by the impact of the West, there is comparatively little impulse among Wesetrn historians to recognize the past achievements of Chinese historiography or to consider the relevance of its very different tradition for comparison with their own.

It must be admitted that even if that impulse existed and western historians did wish to come to an understanding of Far Eastern historiography there would be great difficulties in the way. Little has been translated. Moreover, historiography is so intimately a part of traditional Confucian culture and so conditioned by the nature of Chinese society that one must penetrate rather deeply into that culture and society before one can really comprehend it. It requires to be interpreted by persons who are able to some extent to adopt two points of view at the same time. They must be specialists thoroughly versed in Chinese studies and at the same time sufficiently aware of the interests and preconceptions of western historians to interpret what they find in way that will be meaningful to their intended audience. There have been a few attempts to bridge this gap but the task largely remains to be done. The authors of the articles on Chinese historiography in this collection would not claim to have accomplished it but their intention has been to contribute towards this end."

⑯Ibid., p. 9:

"History largely took the place of mythology for the Chinese and provided an inexhaustible fund of episodes on which the story-teller, the novelist, and the dramatist could draw."

⑰Ibid., p. 135:

"It is truism, at least among sinologists, that China possesses a wealth of historical writing unequalled by any other country before modern times. It would not, however, be true to say that Chinese methods of history writing and canons of historical criticism would always receive correspondingly high praise. We are commonly told that the method was simply one of mechanical scissors-and-paste compilation with only a primitive exercise of criticism in the choice of rejection of material. Yet, while there in a measure of truth in this judgement as it applies to much run-of-the- mill official and other history writing in China, it hardly does justice to the quality of scholarly acumen and historical thought displayed by the great Chinese historians.

Certainly the introduction of western methods at the end of the nineteenth century meant a very great revolution in Chinese historical studies, as in the field of natural science, but it must strike an observer as remarkable the extent to which twentieth-century Chinese historians have been able to draw on their own tradition while enlarging their conceptions and introducing greater rigour through influences from outside. This has no doubt been partly due to nationalist conservatism and has not always been wholly beneficial but it is also a tribute to the resources available in Chinese tradition.

Moreover, quite apart from its continuing vigour and permanent value, which will have to be proved in years to come, the Chinese attitude to history and critical thought on the subject are clearly matters of fundamental importance for the understanding of the past of this most historically minded of all peoples."

⑱Ibid., p. 136:

"The first actual treatise on the writing of history in Chinese (or, as far as I can discover, in any language) was the Shih-t'ung (Generalities on History) of Liu Chih-chi (A. D. 661–721, also known as Liu Tzu-hsüan), completed in 710."

⑲Ibid., p. 143:

"The modern western historian is likely to feel disappointment at Liu Chih-Chi's emphasis on the purely formal aspects of official Chinese historiography. Nevertheless, it is important to recognize in this a salient aspect of the Chinese attitude to history which, in degree if in no absolute sense, distinguishes it from the attitudes of other peoples. History was to the Chinese (1) official and (2) normative. To make a just and definitive record of the past was a function of government just as it was a function of government to bestow titles and honours on the dead as well as on the living. Moreover, this record served an essential moral purpose by holding up good and bad examples through which virtues could be encouraged and vice deterred."

⑳Ibid., p. 146:

"Throughout the Shih-t'ung there is an emphasis on the omission of what is not essential or is unworthy of being recorded and on concision of expression, which represents a very typical Chinese attitude to literary composition of every kind but which one feels was often of rather dubious value in its effects on historical writings."

㉑Ibid., p. 147:

"Liu Chih-Chi's notoriety in China was traditionally due to his boldness in finding fault with previous historians, even with canonical works such as the Spring and Autumn Annals. To us his criticism, mostly confined as it is to ad noc objections to particular, often very minor, details, may seem rather superficial."

㉒Ibid., p. 152:

"Ssu-ma Kuang does to a limited extent provide connecting links, though he was far from binding events together in a causal nexus and treating them as connected wholes, something never fully achieved by traditional Chinese historians."

㉓Ibid., p. 155:

"Ssu-ma Kuang actually uses the expression 'scissors-and-paste' in describing the way in which the Long Draft was to be compiled. When it was necessary to insert material in the Draft, the long manuscript roll was cut with scissors and the inserted portion was pasted in."

㉔Ibid., pp. 157-158:

"Ssu-ma Kuang was certainly a scientific historian, since he first tried to establish the truth on objective grounds."

㉕Ibid., p. 158:

"From our modern point of view one of the most serious limitations of Ssu-ma Kuang's method—an often-mentioned limitation of almost all traditional Chinese historians—was the restriction of attention to one isolated event at a time, with a certain amount of backward and forward glancing, generalizing about a man's character, etc., but without the attempt to see each event interwoven into a complex mesh of interrelationships with other events. What resulted from the enormous labours of Ssu-ma Kuang and his team was a superb chronicle, but still a chronicle and not a history in our modern sense.

Another serious limitation from the technical standpoint was the failure to study sources as such. This was not an absolute failure —one dose find remarks here and there in the K'ao-i about the bearing of the facts about the authorship of a text on its reliability either as a whole or as applied to a particular case. Still, in general, texts were treated as ultimate data and no attempt was made to analyse further their origins or interrelationships. Text B. partially based on text A, was treated as if it were independent and worthy of equal consideration. This again was not a limitation peculiar to Ssu-ma Kuang alone but common to most Chinese scholarship though advances were made in seventeenth and eighteenth centuries.

At any rate, a better understanding of Ssu-ma Kuang's methods should dispel certain myths such as the idea that it was impossible to exercise sophisticated historical criticism within the framework of scissors-and-paste compilation or that Chinese historians had no conception of probability but only of certainty."

㉖Ibid., pp. 159–160:

"Chao I, though more restricted in his scholarship, is perhaps the most interesting of the three because of the advance he shows towards overcoming those traditional limitations of Chinese historiography mentioned above in connection with Ssu-ma Kuang. The circumstances of his life gave him comparatively few opportunities for studying rare and out-of-the-way sources. Making a virtue of necessity he emphasized the importance of the official histories as opposed to all the variety of subsidiary material drawn on by the K'ao-Cheng scholars. He read and re-read the Standard Histories but instead of drawing on vast erudition to comment on minute point of detail he noted down general remarks about the various books or the events they described that struck him as of interest. He discussed the way in which the various dynastic histories had been compiled and from what sources, and he compared those works which covered the same period.......Some of his points are mere curiosities but in many cases he has hit on problems which are of real interest to modern historians and his work can certainly be read with profit by them."

㉗Ibid., pp. 20–21:

"Until very recent times, most specialist books on China and Japan in Western languages were written by men who had lived and worked in the Far East. In the sixteenth, seventeenth, and eighteenth centuries, the period dealt with by Professor Boxer, the Jesuit missionaries dominate the field. In the nineteenth and early twentieth centuries the Jesuits were followed by others: protestant missionaries, diplomats, journalists, and those who went to teach in schools or universities. All these men had one thing in common, that their writing originated from an interest in and knowledge of the area. The fact had important consequences. It meant, for example, that their work was not exclusively history in the academic sense. For some, history was but part of a whole which embraced also government, law, economics, geography, literature, art. For others it arose as the product of an initial interest in language or philosophy. In fact, the subject of study was a country or its culture not specifically or solely its history. The concept of 'sinology' still exists as a reminder of this outlook.

Personal experience also had its effect in influencing the nature of the subjects studied. Apart from accounts of contemporary or near-contemporary events, like the Taiping Rebellion in China and the Satsuma Rebellion in Japan, much of the history written was designed to explain society as it existed in the writer's time or to describe the immediate background of events which had occurred within his own knowledge. Equally, there was a strong emphasis on the history of Western relations with the area. Indeed, such subject-matter occasionally swamped all other material even in books which were avowedly general histories. On the other hand, a number of books appeared dealing with the earliest history of the two countries. In the case of China, these seem to have been motivated, at least in part, by a desire to provide historical background for the study of philosophy. In Japan, they sprang largely from an interest in language or political institutions.

In some respects western writing has been more akin to the historiography of China and Japan than to that of the West itself, especially in interpretation and choice of subject-matter. The reasons for this can be readily conjectured. Writers, because they were living in the Far East, tended to be open to some of the same influences as their Chinese and Japanese contemporaries and to choose the same topics for study: the emphasis on early and on recent history, for example, with a consequent neglect of the periods that lie between, is common to both. A further explanation is to be found in the dependence of the Western historian on the findings of scholars in the country or countries which he studied. Sometimes he worked with Chinese or Japanese collaborators and assistants. Even where this was not so, language difficulties usually forced him to rely on modern works in Chinese or Japanese, rather than on a wide range of original source-materials, with the result that, consciously and unconsciously, he often accepted their viewpoint as well as their factual information."

㉘Ibid., p. 21:

"These remarks are not intended to imply that all Western writing on Far Eastern history has been worthless. Much of it has been useful, some of it very good indeed; but for the most part it has been valuable as a means of introducing the subject to the Western reader, rather than in the stricter sense of making 'a new contribution to knowledge'. Moreover, it has not served as a channel for the introduction of new techniques of historical writing into China and Japan."

㉙Ibid., p. 21:

"When one turns to the twentieth century, it is possible to identify the beginnings of a change in the nature of Western writing, stemming from changes in the political relationships between China, Japan, and the West. The earliest European visitors to the Far East had been much impressed by what they found there. The Jesuits, as Professor Boxer points out, wrote in terms of great admiration of Chinese institutions, in particular, and this was reflected in many of the books which were based on their reports. In the nineteenth century, however, the economic and political dominance of the Western Powers and the evidence of decay in Chinese and Japanese society led to different attitudes. This was the age of catchwords like 'the heathen Chinese' and 'the cycle of Cathay', with their implied contempt for a culture which was static, or decadent, or at least did not exemplify the viorous growth which seemed characteristic of that of Europe. By this estimate, Far Eastern history was not a subject worth serious study. It was left to the man who went there."

㉚Ibid., p. 22–23:

"Towards the end of the century there were two developments which heralded a new approach. First was Europe's discovery—rediscovery, perhaps—of Chinese and Japanese art, which gave an impetus and respectability to historical study of it. Second was the rapid emergence of Japan to a position of international importance and prestige.......The Far East was suddenly important—and far from static. As a consequence, it became increasingly a matter of concern in Western countries and, by natural extension, in Western universities. Since 1930, still more since 1945, there has been a rapid increase in the number of university teachers in Europe and the United States specializing in Chinese and Japanese subjects, including history.

The work produced in this latest period has differed in a number of ways from what went before. The authors no longer live and work in the countries about which they write, though they usually manage to visit them for purposes of study. They are also more conscious than their predecessors of being 'academic', a gain in the quality of detachment which may well be balanced by a loss in that of human experience. The periods studied have shown little change. There is still a general preoccupation with the most recent and the most remote, though there is also a growing appreciation of the need for more detailed investigation of what went between. The dependence on Chinese and Japanese scholarship also remains, but it is collective rather than individual—dependence on a university rather than a teach, on a library rather than a book. This reflects the most conspicuous change of all, the emphasis on training, technique, research, professional expertise. The characteristic book is the monography: detailed, critical, and limited in topic. In fact, for the first time Western scholars are subjecting the history of China and Japan, so far as difficulties of language and the accessibility of materials permit, to the same kind of study as has already been applied to that of their own countries. This is clearly to the good. Yet it involves certain dangers. Isolated monographs—and their number must remain comparatively small—the exact purpose and significance which can only be fully understood in the light of a knowledge of existing literature in Chinese or Japanese, can be appreciated only by the specialist. The more technical their terminology and manner of presentation, the more this is true. They need to be supplemented, therefore, by a range of more general studies, dealing at reasonable lenghth with particular periods or topics, which would serve to fill the gap between the research monography at one extreme and the survey history at the other."

㉛Ibid., p. 24:

"Until recently the period of Chinese history which corresponds to the first millenium B. C. has, at least in the West, received far closer attention than the eighteen hundred following years. As a result, Chinese historiography has been judged by the most ancient records or by later comprehensive histories rather than by those later works which deal with one dynasty or part of a dynasty."

㉜Ibid., p. 26:

"The richest mine of historical and folkloristic information on the Chou period that has been preserved is the so-called Tso Tradition (Tso Chuan). ......However, it is very difficult to unravel the complications of the composition and transmission of this book."

㉝Ibid., p. 30:

"Judging the work as a whole, although the author's opinion is occasionally brought out and he displays at times a healthy scepticism, as a rule he simply reproduces his sources in the original wording and dose not try to go behind them. After the fall of the Former Han Dynasty, Ssu-ma Ch'ien's example was followed by the author of the Han shu, or Han Document's (History of the Former Han Dynasty), and after him in all the so-called Standard Histories. The three main divisions are always annals, biographies, and treaties, but more and more the ideal is sought in strict adherence to written, preferably official, sources. Non-verifiable elements, such as speech, are dropped, and the result is an inpersonal account, a Government White Paper, compiled with scissors and paste but hardly digested or interpreted."

㉞Ibid., p. 30:

"All generalizations on Chinese historiography, including the ones in this paper, are open to grave doubt. Western scholars have perhaps tended too much to make comparisons with European histories written in the nineteenth and twentieth centuries instead of those of earlier times. They have insisted that Chinese historiography does not connect individual facts, but have forgotten the innumberable essays and memorials where a historical perspective is provided. Moreover, when criticizing the tendentious character of a particular work or group of works, we should remember that such loss is usually compensated by the fullness of the material, especially if private historical writing is taken into account."

㉟Ibid., p. 31:

"The new 'bourgeois' society under its new political organization engendered among many other things a new way of writing history, an historiography which was in many respects radically different from the earlier forms of chronicling important events."

㊱Ibid., p. 32:

"On the Chinese side an enormous amount of attention has been paid to the Han histories. However, the majority of the Chinese scholars through the ages have been primarily concerned with problems of textual criticism, philological explanation and antiquarian elucidation, so that they continue up to the present the long line of commentators who have devoted their energies to these texts since the second century of our era. Others, for example the first scholar who pondered the general problems of historiography, the famous Liu Chih-Chi (661–721) in his Generalities on History (Shih-t'ung), have touched on problems of a more general nature. But until recently one of the very few scholars to write more extensively on these more general and technical problems of the Han histories was Chao I (1727–1814), who did so in the first three chapters of his Notes on the Twenty-two Histories."

㊲Ibid., p. 34:

"Between the two first-mentioned texts the relationship is extremly close, but here we are confronted with a difficulty which has not yet been solved. It amounts to this: the Han shu seems to have been largely based on those parts of the Shih Chi which deal with the Han period and at present the two texts agree more or less perfectly. However, the Shih Chi is known to have been cut down by imperial order when the Had shu had been completed and at a period when it is hardly likely that it was available in many copies to the outside world. It is therefore not impossible that those sections of the Shih chi—or at least parts of these—which deal with the Han period were reconstructed from the Han shu text at a later date. If this could be proved, the Shih chi would lose considerably in value as an independent source of information for Han history."

㊳Ibid., p. 60:

"From the most ancient times down to our own century, historiography has been carried on in China carefully and without interruption."

㊴Ibid., p. 61:

"In China, from ancient times down to the end of the traditional political system, the historiographer always had a position of particular importance."

㊵Ibid., p. 115:

"One of the major differences between European and Chinese historiography in the past has been the predominance of official historiography in China. The standard dynastic histories concentrate on the institutional and administrative aspects of persons and events to such a degree that we may safely say they report for the most part only what was known to the metropolitan bureancracies. The picture of the past as given by these sources is, therefore, in a way one-sided. Only occasionally can we check their accuracy against independent sources, usually in periods when there was a multistate system in China or when we have documents from foreign states which had diplomatic (or belligerent) relations with China. Many events, for example the various rebellions of the peasantry, are known to us only from the official records, and almost no documents of the rebels, if they ever existed, have survived to present us their aims and ideology. A notable exception is the Taiping rebellion. The onesidedness of historical outlook which results from these circumstances can best be understood if we were to suppose, as a comparison, that we had only the res gestae of the medieval emperors in Europe to be our major source for European history in that period, that we did not have those numerous private chronicles and records which supplement the documents of the chanceries.

If we look for similar sources in medieval China we have to define first what is meant by private historiogrphy. Perhaps a suitable definition might be that the concept of 'private' should be measured according to the degree of independence from bureancracy, particularly from the historical offices in the capital. By this definition the ideal private historian would be a writer who never held any office. But even in this case it is doubtful whether the fundamental concepts of private historiography would be very different from those of official historiography. A certain element of Confucian ideology was almost invariably common to both. This is why the Budhist chronicles deserve special attention, because they not only correspond to the definition of private historiography given above, but also have a different ideological background. A clear distinction between private and official historiography is, in many cases, impossible."

㊶Ibid., p. 120:

"Praise and blame are for him, as for indeed almost all Chinese historians, essential elements of historiography. History is regarded as a mirror of political ethics, to be judged according to Confucian standards."

㊷Ibid., pp. 131–132:

"It seems that the pattern set by the dynastic histories and Ssu-ma Kuang's Comprehensive Mirror was too powerful to allow an independent method."

㊸Ibid., p. 133:

"We note a certain lack of individual expression, if we compare China with medieval Europe……European sources in Latin are much more individual and personal, and can reflect a personality, even if it be through faulty grammar or orthography. The 'individual element' in history is not easily accessible in China; we can only try to turn to such sources where we may reasonably hope to learn something more about a person or an event than we know from the official accounts, in other words to the pi-chi (notebooks) and similar works of a miscellaneous character, or to the few texts where somebody records his personal experiences."

㊹Ibid., p. 95:

"As in every field of historical writing, China is unusually well-supplied with biographical material. The Standard Histories alone contain thousands of biographical entries, while the collections of specialized biographies of various kinds and entries in Local Gazeteers bring the total to an enormous figure. If we take into account the works written for funerary or commemorative occasions, and for use in the family cults, the number can be almost indefinitely expanded."

㊺Ibid., p. 109:

"The typical example (of lieh-chuan) is as dry and impersonal as the Annals themselves, and the modern reader in search of some clue to the personality of the subject will find it very difficult to form any picture of the man as an individual."

㊻Ibid., pp. 113–114:

"In short, Chinese traditional historians have provided us with a wealth of biographical material. But this is less accurately dated and subjected to less scrupulous criticism than the other sections of historical works. It is, moreover, biography in a strictly limited sense, derived from the eulogistic writings of family cults, and concerned with only one aspect of the subject's life. Lastly, it is concerned almost exclusively with members of the same social group as its authors. Within these self-imposed limitations, and viewed from the strictly circumscribed intentions of the authors, the results are perfectly adequate, but for the modern scholar these limitations present a serious problem and account for much of the impersonal atmosphere which makes such a forcible impression on one beginning the study of Chinese history."

㊼Ibid., p. 167:

"During the Ching period (1644–1911) Chinese culture reached one of its apogees; in many ways, even in philosophy, the era of Ch'ien-lung (1736–96) may be said to hold its own with our Siècle des Lumières."

㊽Ibn Khaldun (1332–1406) 是阿拉伯大史家。

㊾W. G. Beasley and E. G. Pulleyblank, *Historians of China and Japan*,

p. 169:

"It was at the height of this remarkable tide of philological criticism, which was to have sweeping and devastating effects on the future of the Confucian tradition, that there appeared in China a historical genius of the first magnitude, ranking with Ibn Khaldun or with the greatest historiographers of Europe."

㊿Ibid., p. 176:

"If the Chinese authorities had been wise enough to carry into effect the project he worked out at the end of eighteenth century for the establishment of a methodical corpus of local archives and local gazeteers, China today would dispose of an incomparable ducumentation on her modern history and we should not have to be content with the archives of the central government and the imperial court."

51 Ibid., p. 177:

"It is, in short, the Western impact which made China turn her attention to Chang Hsüeh-ch'eng. Faced with the necessity of renovating the principles and procedures of her historiography, China had to vindicate in this field, as in others, the spirit of objective generalization which is proper to science. She then remembered that long ago, towards the end of the eighteenth century, such a spirit had been heralded by an obscure scholar of Chekiang whose whimsical ideas had been ignored in his own time, but provided valid food for modern thought."

52 Ibid., p. 178:

"Chang Hsüeh-ch'eng asserts that the Canon, the Confucian Bible, is history. Turn the proposition around, and inversely history will also constitute a Canon, history will have a canonical value, a value as a rule and norm. And that is precisely why Chang Hsüeh-ch'eng believed. The Bible is history, because history is a Bible. Chang Hsüeh-ch'eng's purpose, I believe, was not to profanize the Canon, but rather to canonize history, to sacralize it."

(53) Ibid., pp. 184–185:

"Giambattista Vico was almost his contemporary, since he died at Naples in 1744, six years after the birth of his Chinese colleague far away near the coast of Yellow Sea. Both were infatuated with history and spent their lives reflecting on its import and its philosophical foundations. They had the same ardent and impatient natures; the same independence of mind, the same difficulties in their material careers; ...... Vico battled both against Cartesian rationalism and abstraction and against the narrow erudition of the learned compilers and text-critics of his time."

(54) Ibid., p. 185:

"There is no doubt that, just as Vico foreboded many trends of modern historiography in Europe, Chang Hsüeh-ch'eng was in advance of his time and heralded a turning-point in the long history of Chinese historiography."

(55) Ibid., p. 186:

"The preceding papers have made it clear that the limitations of traditional Chinese historiography were related to the theory of government and society, and of the position of China in the world, which the theory involved. As China was believed to be the only civilized nation, there was no external standard of comparison. As the internal standard was a legendary golden age to which all succeeding regimes were by definition inferior, there could be no concept of progress or development. The monopoly of political authourity by the imperially appointed scholar-officials led to indifference among historians to institutions and groups which did not share this sole source of prestige and power, and led also to a scheme of cause and effect which magnified the role of the bureaucracy almost to the exclusion of other factors. Within this scheme, the essentially moral training of the bureaucracy led to an undue emphasis on moral causes of historical events.

The virtues as well as the vices of traditional historical writing sprang from the same sources. The habit of keeping full and accurate records of events and institutions and of compiling statistics, and the interest in the working of fiscal and political organs, sprang from that very bureaucratic bias which was a limiting factor in other respects. The need to do justice to the career of individual office-holders and scholars produced the unrivalled wealth of biography which survives, and without which, for all its faults, our knowledge of China's past would be considerably poorer."

㊺Ibid., p. 188:

"The limitations of the national tradition are clear. Nevertheless, it had a considerable contribution to make. In the first place, the first essential in many fields of research was the handling and criticism of texts, and here traditional scholars had provided techniques and standards which were a valuable basis for further advance. In the second place, China had had her own critics in the past.......In the third place, considerable advances had been made during the Ching dynasty in historiography, advances to which the reluctance of Ching scholars to write works of full historical synthesis should not blind us."

㊼Ibid., p. 191:

"In the field of history proper, Chinese precedents also offered a basis—and more important, an acceptable, because Chinese, rationale—for modernization. In his Methodology for the Study of Chinese

History, Liang Chi-ch'ao built up his case against traditional concepts of history by a series of quotations from China's own critics of the old ideas. He quotes Liu Chih-chi, Cheng Ch'iao and Chang Hsüeh-ch'eng on the limitations of dynastic history, of the composite annals-biography (chi-chuan) form, and of compilation by official committees in place of private individuals. He quotes Liu Chih-chi again on the inconvenience of the chronicle form. The Sung scholar Yang Wan-li is quoted on arrangement by topics (the chi-shih pen-mo form) and Liang's comments imply that Yang favoured it because it made possible a proper exposition of cause and effect."

㊳Ibid., p. 192:

"Although modern Chinese historians might affect to despise Ching historical writing, they were obliged to make use of it. The west could provide a deeper consciousness of historical ends and means, but even for those Chinese historians who had the opportunity to study thoroughly the actual historical writing of the west, as opposed to translations of theoretical textbooks of historiography, the only possible practical training in the study of Chinese history was based on Ching writing. The west might provide the ideals, but Ch'ing scholarship provided the day-to-day habits of research."

㊴Ibid., p. 192:

"The value as well as the influence of the heritage of Ch'ing dynasty historiography has perhaps been underestimated. There has been a tendency both in China and abroad to condemn the Ching tradition as one of pedantry."

㊵內藤虎次郞，日本近代史家，其英文譯名爲 Naitō Torajiro 以著「支那史學史」一書而馳名。

㊶W. G. Beasley and E. G. pulleyblank, *Historians of China and Japan*, p. 196:

"The most distinguished figure in Ch'ien Lung scholarship was the prolific historian and classicist, Ch'ien Ta-hsin. His work, and the choice of subjects for his many biographies, show his close adherence to the ideals and methods of Ku Yen-wu, although he did not express his theoretical views at length. His greatest quality was, as Naitō Torajiro puts it, "an unrivalled exact knowledge of what could usefully be used as historical material for a given subject, a knowledge which he applied in exacting and comprehensive critical studies."

㊷Ibid., 210:

"In China the complementary tasks of hypothecation and verification were too seldom brought together."

㊸白樂日在「中日史家」一書中用法文寫「歷史爲從政的輔導」(L'histoire Comme Guide de la Pratique Bureaucratique) 一文，一九六四年他出版「中國文明與官僚政治」(*Chinese Civilization and Bureaucracy*) 一書，其中「History as a Guide to Bureaucratic Practice」一章 (pp. 129–149)，與法文稿全同，今轉引之。

㊹E. Balazs, "*History as a Guide to Bureaucratic Practice*", in Balazs, Chinese Civilization and Bureaucracy, 1964, p. 129:

"What is the distinctive feature of Chinese historiography as a whole, when compared with that of the west? The answer a Western historian would give, even after thinking about the matter carefully and doing his best to rid himself of prejudice, would be: its stereotype character. And 'stereotype' would imply two apparently contradictory things. It would imply that chinese historiography lacks the personal touch, and that it also lacks the kind of abstract thinking required for reaching a synthesis; for when it deals with people, they appear not as individuals but as representative members of a group in which their individual characteristics are merged; and when it deals with events, it merely states detailed facts, and although the same facts may be constantly repeated, this does not amount to generalization about them."

⑮Ibid., p. 129:

"It seems to me that there are three main factors that have prevented the development of our kind of historiography: the habit of cutting history up into dynastic slices; the official status of Chinese historians, who were the salaried dependents of the state; and the traditional art of using quoted passages."

⑯Ibid., p. 130:

"The traditional art of quotation, still in use today, consists in quoting from documents instead of summarizing the contents; and since it would be tedious to quote the whole documents, only key passages are given. If a historian wants to convey the essential points of a document, he never does so in his own words, but tries to make a significant selection of extracts from the text."

⑰Ibid., pp. 132-133:

"The worst drawback of all, however, was not the fact that historian-officials were dependents of the reigning power, nor was it their lack of objectivity, but the fact that they were unable to escape from the dynastic framework because of the very nature of their office. The necessity for conceiving of history in dynastic terms, for cutting up the flow of events into clearly separated slices, was of poor service to Chinese historians, forcing them to keep their ideas in watertight compartments. Moreover, the cyclic principle and the lack of continuity swayed the balance in favor of amassing disconnected series of isolated facts, and discouraged attempts to find any system of relations or any sequence in these facts."

⑱Ibid., p. 135:

"Faced with the enormous mass of Chinese historical writing, the first question one must ask—the crucial question for all forms of literature—is this: who was writing for whom? Who is the author and who the readers? The answer here is a clear one: history was written by officials for officials. Right up until modern times, this is a rule with few exceptions. Even the independent writers were officials (in retirement), or men who wanted to make an official career; and the entire body of historical writings (including historical anecdotes, genealogies, historical novels, regional histories. and encyclopedias) was addressed to the same public, an educated public consisting of officials and future officials. Hence there was a community of interests between author and readers."

⑲ *American Historical Review*, Vol. LXVII, No. 4, July-1962:

"One of the great tasks of twentieth-century scholarship is to place Western historiographical traditions in a comparative context. As the Western historian comes to know something of the historical theories of Ibn Khaldun, and something about the motivations and methods of East Asian historians, he will discover that Western man did not 'invent' history. Such discoveries tend to break down western parochialism and produce, in their cumulative effects, a sounder sense of what is peculiar to the Western historical tradition."

⑳ Arthur F. Wright, "*On the Uses of Generalization in the Study of Chinese History*", in Generalization in the Writing of History, ed. by Louis Gottschalk, 1963, p. 37:

"It is well known that no people on earth possesses so voluminous a record of their past as the Chinese. The sum of recorded particulars for the two and a half millenniums of 'formal' history writing is incalculable. To translate the twenty-five standard histories would require forty-five million English words, and this would represent only a minute fraction of the total record."

⑪Ibid., p. 37:

"The careful record-keeping, the work of editing, re-editing, compilation, and annotation absorbed the energies of innumerable scholars in every generation. We may ask why the study of the past was so esteemed and what sorts of value were ascribed to it. Chinese thinkers offer many answers to these questions.......One is that the successes and failures of the past provide sure guidance for one's own time."

⑫Ibid., p. 45:

"Traditional historiography, for all its limitations, had provided methods of sorting, labeling, and interpreting the mass of particulars about China's past. Most of these methods came now to be regarded as anachronistic."

⑬Arthur F. Wright., "*Chinese Historiography*":

"The methods used by Chinese historians fall into two closely related groups. One consists of the methods of recording contemporary happenings, the other of the methods of compiling a coherent account from such records."

⑭Ibid., p. 5:

"The Chinese attitude of respect for the written word meant that he handled documents from the past with care and circumspection. He did not alter them lightly and when two accounts of an event were in conflict he generally chose the one that showed greater consistency with his other materials and inserted it integrally into his text."

⑮E. G. Pulleyblank, "*The Historiographical Tradition*", in The Legacy of China, ed. by Raymond Dawson, 1964, pp. 149–150:

"One of the most important features of Ssu-ma Ch'ien's work to become a constant principle may be called 'objectivity'. This means that the historian composed his narrative as a patchwork of excerpts, often abridged but otherwise unaltered, from his sources, with any personal comment or judgement kept clearly separate. The work of the historian was to compile a set of documents which would speak for themselves rather than to make an imaginative reconstruction of past events. This did not mean that an historian necessarily became a mere mechanical compiler, since the selection and arrangement of his material called for the exercise of critical judgement, and conclusions about the causes of events or the characters of historical persons could be expressed separately in the appropriate place; but it did easily lead to mechanical compilation in the case of inferior historians."

按 Raymond Dawson 之書，經張潤書先生譯成中文，名爲「中國文化之垂統」，民國六十一年出版（國立編譯館）。此處的中文翻譯，參用了張先生的譯文，但也作了一些修正，修正有的是關於文字方面的，有的是關於內容方面的。

⑯Ibid., p. 151:

"For the earlier part of his work Ssu-ma Ch'ien had necessarily to use a good deal of material which was of doubtful historicity. Nevertheless his work is history in a truer sense than the works which preceded him and on which he drew, since his intention was to establish the most probable account out of conflicting testimony. For the period closest to his own day he was for the most part using first-hand government archives and his work must be regarded as having a high degree of reliability. It is this later part of his work that has remained typical of history writing in China ever since, where archives have always provided the great bulk of the source material. From the Han period onward it is the limitations of the official bureaucratic outlook rather than inclusion of material of dubious authenticity that one must be most conscious of in assessing the historicity of historical works."

⑰Ibid., p. 153:

"The Wen-hsin tiao-lung of Liu Hsieh (A. D. 465–522), the greatest work of literary criticism of the period, devotes a section to historical writing, criticizing the major historians up to the author's time and making some general remarks about the difficulties in the way of a well-balanced, reliable, unprejudiced record. He stresses the role of the historian as moralist and his heavy responsibility to tell the truth without fear or favour."

⑱Ibid., p. 161:

"Though not remarkable for works of synthetic history, the Ch'ing scholars set high standards in critical reappraisal of the past. Every serious student of Chinese history at the present day must build on the foundations they laid and our task would be immensely greater if we did not have their works."

⑲Ibid., p. 162:

"Standing a little apart from these text critics is Chao I (1727–1814), author of the Nien-erh shih cha-chi (the 'Notes on the Twenty-two Histories'). Whereas they had sought to supplement and correct the standard histories by additional material, his notes arose out of careful reading and re-reading of the histories themselves. In some cases he is concerned to point out inconsistencies between different chapters but he also discusses in a general way the origins of the various histories and, most interesting of all, makes generalizations about institutions, social structure, and secular trends. Many of the ideas which he started have sown seed that has borne fruit in the modern historiography of this century."

⑳Ibid., p. 163:

"In the long-drawn-out, ever-worsening crisis which China underwent in the nineteenth century with the decline of the Ch'ing Dynasty and the imperialistic encroachments of the West, historical studies ceased to make progress."

㉑Ibid., pp. 163–164:

"Acquaintance with Western historiography has not meant simply the introduction of new ideals and techniques to replace an outworn and dead tradition. Rather it has meant the renovation and revival of the best parts of that tradition. There have been more freedom and opportunities to escape from the excessively annalistic and scissors-and-paste forms of the past, and archaeology has revealed wholly new types of source material; but in their critical handling of sources Chinese scholars of today are following in the footsteps of their eighteenthcentury predecessors and have little to learn from the West. Increased knowledge of the outside world has chiefly brought liberation from orthodoxies that it was previously inconceivable to question, simply by providing an external standpoint and material for comparison that was formerly almost wholly lacking.

What importance has traditional Chinese historiography for the West? Perhaps it is not different in kind from the contribution which knowledge of Western history has made to Chinese conceptions of the past. The plurality of European civilization has always meant that there was more possibility within its own cultural tradition for points of comparison. Even so, the first knowledge of China, as of other non-European civilizations, had a tremendous liberating effect on the thinking of men of the seventeenth and eighteenth centuries. Even erroneous or vastly oversimplified information about China called into question hallowed prejudices and was used as ammunition by critics of orthodoxy. We are past that stage, and a remotely seen China can no longer serve the function of a Land of Nowhere. But now in the twentieth century, when the world seems fated to be engulfed in acommon pattern of 'Western' or 'modern' civilization, it is more important that ever that we should be able to find in a real knowledge of China's independent cultural tradition a point of comparison and criticism. For this purpose China's great and still living historiographical tradition has much to offer."

㊽Earl H. Pritchard, "*Traditional Chinese Historiography and Local Histories*", inThe Uses of History,ed. by Hayden V. White, 1968, p. 198:

"The Chinese unquestionably have been the most historical minded of all people over the longest period of time. A profound knowledge of the past was a basic aspect of Confucianism, and historical information was considered essential to the proper functioning of government and society."

㊾Ibid., pp. 198-199:

"Traditional Chinese historiography developed its own conceptions of history, canons of value and methodological techniques. ...... They included high standards of scholarship. Accuracy, objectivity and devotion to truth were emphasized, and the art of textual criticism became highly developed. The wide use of source materials was emphasized, and in order to maintain objectivity and let the record of events or facts speak for itself, the universal tendency was to quote extensively from sources. This has led many modern historians to assert that traditional Chinese historians were mere compilers who did a scissors and paste job. While there is some truth in this charge, the great historians were vastly more than this, and they left an imprint on historical work in China equivalent to that of a Thucydides or a Gibbon in the West. Personal judgments were usually confined to concluding remarks or summaries of subjects discussed, although they, of course, entered into the selection of material quoted. When conflicting sources could not be harmonized, some writers quoted from both."

㉞Ibid., p. 199:

"All historical works, official and otherwise, were systematically criticized by later scholars, and a large literature supplementing, correcting and criticizing earlier works grew up. The seventeenth and eighteenth centuries probably saw traditional Chinese critical historical scholarship at its best. Although the period did not produce works that would rival the classics of Ssu-ma Ch'ien, Pan Ku, O-yang Hsiu, and Ssu-ma Kuang, it contributed a large body of high-class critical literature.......The most important works of the period, however, were probably the shorter monographs on more limited subjects by the critical scholars."

㉟Ibid., pp. 200–201:

"Judged by modern ideas, however, traditional Chinese historiography had certain weaknesses. The rather rigid chronological manner of presentation and the pratice of quoting extensively, rather than giving a unified account of events in one's own words, discouraged real historical synthesis. The fact that all official historical work and much of the private was done by scholar-bureaucrats for the use of scholar-bureaucrats in the conduct of government, inevitably affected the nature of Chinese historiography, in some respects favorably and in others unfavorably. Conciseness of style and certain literary conventions often created obscurities and caused the omission of valuable illustrative details. Certain types of economic, social and even literary information were considered unimportant or beneath the interest of scholars and hence were not recorded except inadvertently, while events at court and connected with the emperor were emphasized to the exclusion of information about developments in the provinces. Ethnocentrism was always evident in writings relating to foreign peopels, but perhaps the greatest weakness in Chinese historical writings, despite the tradition of objectivity, was to see in history the working out of certain Confucian moral principles which expressed itself in the form of praise or blame evaluation of rulers and officials."

⑯D. C. Twitchett, "*Chinese politics and society from the Bronze Age to the Manchus*," in Half the World, the History and Culture of China and Japan, ed. by Arnold Toynbee, 1973, p. 53:

"Although China was the home of one of the very earliest forms of man, Peking Man, Chinese civilization as we know it is not particularly ancient. Evidence of continuous human occupation, and of an unbroken chain of continuous social development goes back only a few thousand years, and the origins of what can confidently be called a 'Chinese' form of culture are quite late when compared with the great civilizations of the Middle East, with India or with Egypt. What is striking, in contrasting the Chinese record with that of the other ancient civilizations, is not so much its antiquity as its continuity. Our earliest written evidence dates back to the last part of the 2nd millennium BC. Since then we have a historical record which, for continuity, accuracy and reliable chronology, is unrivalled among other cultures."

⑰Ibid., pp. 53–54:

"If, however, one attempts an analysis of Chinese history in terms of the Chinese tradition, and of Chinese society and institutions, without constant reference to the inappropriate yardstick of Europe, it is clear that China was certainly as dynamic, changing a society as any other.

One reason for the overall impression of stability and lack of change immediately becomes clear when one considers the nature of the Chinese historical record. More than in the case of any other culture, the modern historian of China is dependent upon a complex highly developed native historiographical tradition. This tradition has a number of features.......Firstly, it is official history, written 'for the record' by servants of the state. Above all it is 'political history'. It is essentially a record of the exercise of dynastic power by successive royal houses, and of the conduct of their administration. It is didactic history, applying the models of orthodox ethic and morality to the events of the past, destined to provide models of political conduct, both good and bad, for future rulers and for the officials through whom they would in turn rule. It is court-centred, and tells us little of what went on in the vastly varied provinces of the empire beyond the imperial capital. It is concerned exclusively with the conduct of the ruling class, in their role as agents of dynastic power: the ordinary people rarely appear, save as the passive objects of state policy, or when they are driven by hardship to rebellion.

This political record was normally based on records compiled from year to year, or reign by reign, and written for one dynasty at a time.......It sees history in purely political terms. It breaks up history into short dynastic time spans which are considered as self-contained, each with its own internal pattern of political development, but with little connection with any long-term conception of historical change. Unfortunately traditional historiography rarely attempted to venture beyond the time span of a dynasty, and when it did, tended to view long-term change in such political terms a consideration of the 'legitimacy of succession' of one dynasty after another."

㊳J. K. Fairbank and D. C. Twitchett, *General Editors' Preface of The Cambridge History of China*, Volume 10, Late Ch'ing 1800–1911, part 1, 1978:

"The history of Chinese civilization is more extensive and complex than that of any single Western nation, and only slightly less ramified than the history of European civilization as a whole. The Chinese historical record is immensely detailed and extensive, and Chinese historical scholarship has been highly developed and sophisticated for many centuries."

㊴Ibid.:

"Recently Western scholars have drawn more fully upon the rich tradition of historical scholarship in China and also in Japan, and greatly advanced both our detailed knowledge of past events and institutions, and also our critical understanding of traditional historiography."

第七章　與西方漢學家論中國史學

第一節　西方漢學家的諍言珍論

從浦立本、瑞特等西方漢學家的言論，我們可以知道近年來西方漢學家已能比較深入而具體的研究中國史學，他們憤慨於西方史學界的偏狹，所以極富學術上的寬容，挺身而出，爲中國史學鳴不平；他們從另一角度，冷眼旁觀中國史學，所以每能別有所見，足發中國史學界的深省。他山之石，可以攻錯，稱之爲諍言，許之爲珍論，似非過分。謹分別詳言之：

1. 中國史學傳統受到尊重

像浦立本教授的論調，「中國不能被摒諸人類歷史的主流以外」，在西方漢學家中無疑問的是一致同意與强調的。尊重中國史學傳統，則是西方漢學界研究中國歷史已有頗久歷史以後所產生的學術寬容。中國有歷史，而不一定有史學，是西方學術界的先入之見；中國歷史寫作的方法，於是常常被批評爲一種機械的剪貼式的編纂，而未臻於一較高境界。浦立本教授能舉出中國史學傳統與歐洲史學傳統阿拉伯史學傳統並列，並認為正確地瞭解史學問題，以及史學在人類文化發展中所佔的地位，必須全顧到這三個傳統，是極卓越的見解，他已從西方的史學傳統裡面跳出來，高矚遠瞻的看世界所有的史學傳統。在觀念上，這是一大進步。於是再進一步就是認為中國史學傳統的「偉大而仍生氣蓬勃」了。瑞特教授認為「二十世紀學術最偉大的工作之一，是將西方史學傳統與其他史學傳統，作一比較」，則是石破天驚之論。他所謂「當西方史家知道一些伊本凱爾東的史學理論，知道一些東亞史家的動機與方法，他將發現西方人並沒有『發明』歷史。此種發現，會粉碎西方的褊狹氣量，而久之能產生一種西方史學傳統中所稀有的健全觀念」，是最耐人尋味的一段話。西方人認為他們自己「發明」了歷史，這足可說明西方人不承認西方以外復有所謂史學。西方漢學家知道尊重中國史學傳統，呼籲西方看看西方以外的史學理論，是漢學家觀念上的進步，也是西方史學界應有的健全觀念，有此健全觀念，西方史家才有可能認識中國史學。

2. 他們看中國史學的一般優點

中國最富歷史觀念，為當代西方漢學家所能一致承認，浦立本謂中國為世界民族中最富歷史觀念的民族，浦瑞查德謂中國人沒有問題的是所有民族最久最富歷史觀念的民族，是平情之論。

中國史籍出產量的豐碩，西方漢學家嘆為觀止。瑞特認為「人人盡知地球上沒有其他民族像中國人那樣擁有如此其浩瀚的過去記錄。正史所記兩千五百年的細節，其總和是難以計算的。翻譯二十五史，將需要四千五百萬英文字，而此僅代表全部記錄的極小部分而已。」杜希德在談到傳記資料時，帶點望洋興嘆的意味說：「像在史學著作的每一領域，中國大量提供了傳記資料。僅正史便包括數以千計的列傳，方志中各類特殊傳記使其總數到達一龐大數字，如果我們將家庭中使用的哀悼或記念作品計入，其數字幾乎無限制的擴大」，這就無怪他確言「中國的歷史記錄，極為詳贍浩繁」了。西方漢學家涉獵中國史籍，知其浩如烟海，故贊之復且嘆之。中國擁有在近代以前未有其他國家可以與之相比的歷史載籍，是西方漢學家公認的事實。

中國史學具有綿延不絕的活力，西方漢學家能够承認。傅吾康所謂「從最古到本世紀，史學在中國綿延不絕，未曾中斷」，是此意。浦立本所謂「記載悠久，而又綿延不絕」，也是此意。在西方歷史上，無此前例，所以他們能虛心的承認。

中國的歷史記錄，其連續性、準確性及其年代的可靠性，在其它文化中，找不出匹敵；中國的歷史學術，已高度發展無數世紀，且趨於成熟；中國史學發展其自己的歷史概念、價值標準及方法上的技巧，寓有崇高的學術水準，正確、客觀與致力眞理被强調。凡此，都是西方漢學家所鄭重承認的。

3. 他們看中國史學的一般缺點

中國史學缺乏整體性，徧中國史籍中，儘是孤立的事件，而事件與事件之間，不能交織成一個關係網，讓人看了有一完整的觀念。「從我們的現代觀點來看，司馬光的方法最嚴重的缺陷之一，也是幾乎所有中國傳統史家的缺陷，是將注意力局於一個時代的一項孤立事件，約略敍其前後，以及綜論人的品德等等，可是不曾嘗試將每一事件與其他衆多事件編織成一錯綜的關係網。」浦立本的評論，極為允當。中國史家很少能擺脫孤立歷史事件的傳統，清代的史家，雖然已稍為知道研究問題，歸納史實，但是他們僅局於小問題的研究，或訂一字，或校一譌，或正往史之失，或發前賢之覆，考據雖極精密，而支離破碎，不能產生有整體美的歷史作品，亦即不能將衆多事件編織成一錯綜的關係網。中國史學不容易爲西方史家所接受者在此，中國史學較西方史學最大的遜色亦在此。近代中國史家受西方史學的影響，亟思矯正此弊，而積重難返，完全擺脫傳統，尙有待於將來。

中國史學的刻板性，受到極大的抨擊。「與西方史學比較起來，整個中國史學的顯著特徵安在？西方史家雖經審愼考慮，力摒成見，其所能提供的答案，將爲中國史學的刻板特性而已。所謂『刻板』，意味着顯然相反的兩事。它意味着中國史學缺乏人的感觸，也意味着缺乏到達綜合的抽象思維；因爲當涉及人物的時候，其人物非個人，而爲一群人物的代表，個人的特性溶於群體之中；而當涉及事件的時候，僅載其詳細事實，雖相同事實，經常重複，而未能將其通觀。」「刻板的紀年與博引，而不以一家之言，作通貫性的敍事，阻礙了眞正的歷史綜合。」這類的批評，是極爲銳利的，也是有其部分眞理的。

中國歷史的政治性，中國將歷史斷代，以及中國官僚學者的寫歷史，西方漢學家予以極嚴厲的批評。「中國史是官方史，設官修成。尤其中國史是『政治史』，主要記載歷朝皇權的運用及其行政措施。」「所有官修史著與大量私修史著，皆由官僚學者爲官僚學者的從政而寫，不可避免的影響了中國史學的性質。」「此類政治性的記錄，每根據按年代或朝代年號編成的資料，且爲某一朝而寫。」「純自政治觀點看歷史，將歷史按朝代斷限予以分割，視每一朝是獨立的，各有其政治發展的內在型態，而與任何歷史變遷的長遠概念，杳不相涉。令人遺憾的，傳統史學很少勇於捨朝代而另闢蹊徑。」以致認爲中國未能發展類似西方的史學，是由於「將歷史斷代的習慣；中國史家依靠政府薪俸的官方身份，以及逐段引用原文的傳統藝術。」史官自然是他們攻擊的對象，他們認爲「最壞的缺陷，既不是史官懾伏於當朝勢力之下，也不是史官缺乏客觀，而是史官不能擺脫朝代的架構，這是由於他們職位性質的關係。必須設想歷史分代，而切斷事件的洪流爲明顯的片段，對中國史家的影響太壞了，迫使他們的觀念停留在不透風雨的密室中。」這類批評，不能說沒有灼見，但是中國史官及史家的獨立精神及其爲千古留信史的傳統，却被很輕易地抹殺了！

中國史學中的儒家道德觀念，西方漢學家施予最猛烈的攻擊。他們認爲中國史學太受儒家思想的影響，官方史學固然瀰漫儒家道德觀念，私家史學的基本概念，也富儒家道德觀念的色彩，歷史被認爲是政治倫理的鏡子，必須以儒家標準去評判，去褒貶。所以浦瑞查德認爲「中國歷史著作最大的缺點，或許是歷史爲儒家道德主義下的產品，以褒貶衡量君主與官吏。」所以福赫伯强調中國佛家編年史的重要性，因爲那是眞正的私家史學，具有一個不同的思想背景。浦立本不認爲中國的史評、史論是史學批評，也是由於中國史評、史論的一類作品，係根據儒家道德觀念，對歷史事件或歷史著作所下的泛論，是屬於政治的與倫理的歷史解釋，未達於史學批評的境界。誠然，中國兩千餘年來，由於儒家在思想界居於正統的地位，中國史家有意無意的將儒家思想成分，滲入了史學之中，中國今後的新史家，應當跳出儒家的圈子，去自由的獨立的論歷史的發展。不過，我們在這裡稍爲要辨護的，是中國的史學不像西方漢學家所想像的那麼受儒家思想的影響。以史記來言，司馬遷踵春秋之後，以作史記，應當是不折不扣的儒家思想了，而班彪評之云：「其論學術，則崇黃老而薄五經，序貨殖，則輕仁義而羞貧窮，道游俠，則賤守節而貴俗功。」❶班固亦本其父說而評之云：「是非頗繆於聖人，論大道，則先黃老而後六經，序游俠，則退處士而進姦雄，述貨殖，則崇勢利而羞賤貧。」❷揚雄也有「太史公記六國歷楚漢訖麟止不與聖人同，是非頗謬於聖人」❸的論調。以漢書來言，班固批評史遷是非頗繆於聖人，他應當完全符應聖人的思想了，而晉人傅玄評其書云：「論國體則飾主闕而折忠臣，敍世敎則貴取容而賤直節，述時務則謹辭章而略事實。」范曄亦評之云：「彪固譏遷，以爲是非頗謬於聖人，然其議論，常排死節，否正直，而不敍殺身成仁之爲美，則輕仁義，賤守節，愈矣。」❹中國史家不同於西方宗教史家，將其先入的成見，大量灌入歷史之中。西方漢學家用一般推理，以彼概此，而未深入探究，以致發生誤解，一若中國史學全受儒家思想支配，而不值一顧者。利用一般推理在學術上不易求得眞理，與「想當然」的臆測，有時犯有同樣的危險。而不幸西方史家常常利用此二者以論中國史學，此不可不辨。

中國史學中的傳記部分，枯燥而無人的氣息，傳主之間，沒有顯著的不同，傳主生平的全貌看不到，傳記史家也幾乎僅寫與自己同一社會群體的人物，資料取之於家庭頌揚作品，沒有經過嚴密的批評。杜希德如此評中國傳記，我們不認爲他評的過分。中國的傳記，資料固然極爲豐富，而與西方近代傳記學相較，似乎不容諱言的不能望其項背。西方近代傳記學，已充分應用心理學的知識，去分析探究所傳記的人的內在心理及精神，說明隱藏於其行動後面的動機。像路德威（Ludwig）、毛勞斯（Maurois）以及勃萊德福（Bradford）的作品，都曾充分利用過心理學。藉西方近代的傳記，可以淸楚過去人類生活的情形，可以瞭解過去時代心理的狀態，可以發掘人物的內在靈魂（inner soul）以及一般歷史所不容許細述的心理上的眞理（psychological truths）。英美的大傳記學家，像布斯威爾（Boswell）的約翰生（Johnson）傳，洛克哈特（Lockhart）的斯喀特（Scott）傳，福魯德（Froude）的卡萊耳（Carlyle）傳，毛利（Morley）的格蘭斯敦（Gladstone）傳，都是世界傳記學上第一流的作品，卷帙浩繁，動輒數十萬言，洛克哈特所寫斯喀特的傳記，至十本之巨，眞是洋洋灑灑，歎爲觀止！中國的傳記，兩千年來，沿襲司馬遷列傳的體例，不曾改變，沒有長篇鉅製，普通都是一千言左右；很少作心理上的分析；也絕少有人願傾數十年的精力，去爲一個人寫一篇詳細傳記。以致中國的傳記，流於大同小異，傳主的生平，永遠無法赤裸裸地表露無餘，傳主行動後面的心理狀態，後人無由而知。無怪乎杜希德認爲「無個人的氣息，給初研究中國史的人一難以忍受的印象」了。以清代史家全祖望的傳來講，碑傳集上他的傳，清史列傳上他的傳，以及清朝先正事略、清史稿上他的傳，大致差不了多少，都是浮泛粗略，不能將全氏一生心理上的隱痛及其在學術氣節上的發揚，充分表現出來。如果有人肯從全氏的鮚埼亭集上取材，就可以寫出他的學術氣節了，如果有人肯找尋他的交遊，研究他的時代，就可以將他活現在十八世紀了。中國有的是散於各個角落的傳記資料，只待有耐心有新史學技術的傳記學家去尋覓，去應用。

以上數者，是西方漢學家論中國史學的一般缺點，針砭之論，諍諫之言，我們應虛心的接納。至於有些方面，他們認爲是缺點，而我們却覺不以爲然，當於另節詳論，此不贅及。

4. 他們比較認識了中國的史學批評

中國的史學批評，自成體系，自劉知幾到章學誠，將比次之道，考證之法，著述之原則，以及經學史學文學三者之間的關係，剖析條陳，多能發凡起例，爲後世史學開山。雖中國史家，非若歐洲史家曾接受邏輯學的嚴格訓練，難期其於其理論體系，作有系統有組織的敍述，然其理論的博大，有如淵海，有如深山，令人有蒼茫之感，亦能令人無窮盡的取其寶藏。以章學誠而論，西方史學批評家，難有其人能如其博大，西方史家的理論每極精，體系極完密，而每就一重點層層發揮，不能如章氏理論的包羅萬象。一博大，一精深，此中西史學的最大不同處。

西方正統史家不能認識中國的史學批評，白特費爾德致函聽衆雜誌編者以答覆浦立本云:「他那篇文章標題中的另一人是劉知幾，我不知西方史學界人士將覺得此人如何？」白氏及西方史學界似乎對劉知幾完全陌生，那麼他們自不知劉知幾的史學批評了。

開始認識中國史學批評的是西方漢學家。浦立本推許史通爲他所能發現的世界最早的一部史學批評的書，並駁白特費爾德云:「說中國對證據不作科學的評價與分析，無較高境界的批評，可是我們可曾曉得中國懷疑理性主義的悠久傳統，燦然蔚成第七世紀與十八世紀的批評著作乎？由於中國經學的權威力量，關於經書的眞實、組成及遞變等重要問題，中國學者都一一予以探究。後期的史學接受此傳統，同樣地能重徹底的審察。」他不但重視中國第七世紀與十八世紀的史學批評著作，且知其由經學傳統發展而來，可證浦氏所知的已深了。戴密微則極推崇章學誠，認爲他是一位第一流的史學天才，可與阿拉伯史家伊本凱爾東或歐洲最偉大的史家並駕齊驅。西方漢學家能夠如此推崇中國史家，足使西方史學界震驚，亦可證中國史學能歷萬古而常新。章學誠在中國沉晦了一百年，而兩百年後，又揚名於外邦，這似乎不是天意，而是學術之公存乎人心。戴氏又將章氏細細地與十八世紀西方的大史家維科比較，認爲兩人都是醉心於歷史，傾畢生精力，思索歷史的意義及其哲學基礎，都具有同樣的急躁天性，同樣的獨立思想，同樣的在事業上遭遇困難，以致一在歐洲預示了諸多近代史學的趨勢，一在悠長的中國史學史上，展開了一個轉機。中國史家被西人如此重視，是極爲難得的事，也足可說明西方漢學家已比較認識了中國的史學批評。中國無史學的錯誤觀念，在西方漢學家中，似乎已不存在了。

5. 他們心目中的中國引書藝術與中國歷史著述的客觀性

早在一八九五年法國漢學家沙畹便說:「歷史，照中國學人之見，是一種精巧的鑲嵌細工的作品，在裡面，前代篇章已經次第排列，只須由作者在其中去加以選擇取捨而再加以技巧的適當連繫。」「這類史家的作品是相當客觀的，它對往蹟是以見證人的身份說話，它俾我們有機會去了解這是作者自己所親見而言，或者只是照抄今日已難再見的遺文。當其我們能够了解到這是中國史家着筆的結構方式時，我們便可以成立第二個假設去稱作者差不多都不願正式的說他在闡發他個人的主觀思想。」自此以後，西方漢學家論及中國的引書藝術與歷史著述性質時，大致皆沿沙畹之說。如白樂日云：「一直沿用至今日的傳統引書藝術，爲逕自文獻徵引，而非概述其內容；且因徵引整個文獻，流於冗長，於是僅徵引其關鍵性的段落。如史家欲披露某一文獻的要點，他永遠不用自己的文字披露，而儘量自原文獻中節選。」浦立本則云：「司馬遷的著作最重要特色之一，或爲一個不變的原則的，可稱爲『客觀性』。這就是說，史家撰述，係纂輯而成，每自其資料刪節，不作更動，個人的論斷，與之劃分此疆彼界。史家的工作，是將一批文獻纂輯在一起，讓文獻自己講話，而不是將往事予以想像的重建。這並不意味着史家必然變成一個機械的編纂者，因爲材料的選擇、排比，都需要運用精密的判斷，而關於事件起因或歷史人物性格的結論，都要能於適當的地方分別表述的；但是這在平庸的史家那就很容易流於機械的編纂了。」「司馬遷著述的前面部分，必然採用了許多史實性可疑的材料。不過他的著述與他所根據的前人著述相比較，是較名符其實的歷史，因爲他是想從矛盾的證據中，寫成最可信的記錄。離他最近的時期，他大部分都利用第一手的政府檔案，因此其著述有其高度可靠性。而此後在中國歷史著述上成爲範例的，也就是這後一部分，政府檔案總是史料的重大來源。於是在評估歷史著述的史實性方面，任何人都會深感自漢代起那就是政府官僚見地的限制問題，而不是所採入材料的眞僞問題了。」浦瑞查德亦謂中國史家「爲保持客觀，而讓史實記錄說明自己，普遍的趨勢爲博引資料。此已引起很多近代史家斷言傳統中國史家是純編纂者，做一種剪貼工作。此固有其眞理，但大史家殊不止於此，他們在中國所留歷史作品的影像，與西方修西蒂笛斯或吉朋所留者，絕無二致。個人的判斷，經常見於論贊或敍論之中，自然亦滲入所引資料之中。當相反的資料無法取得協調時，一些作者兼引並用。」認清了中國「傳統引書藝術，爲逕自文獻徵引，而非概述其內容」，而自此提出中國歷史著述的客觀性，是深有所見的。進一步破除西方流行的「傳統中國史家是純編纂者」的謬論，而躋中國大史家歷史著述於西方水準，尤其是眞知灼見。至於察覺到第一手的政府檔案總是中國史料的重大來源，也是極難能可貴的。

6. 他們給予清代史學的評價

任何學問皆有其演化歷程，換言之，亦即皆有其發展的歷史。一門學問，不經過相當時間的演化，突然燦爛輝煌，爲決不可能之事。牛頓（Sir Isaac Newton）的萬有引力定律，在物理學上爲絕大的發明。然牛頓之前，萬有引力已有一段頗長的發展歷史，牛頓循此歷史，繼續發展，直到那一枚赫赫有名的蘋果落地，而定律始出現。如牛頓之前，無人談及引力問題，則牛頓似不可能因睹蘋果的落地而驟然悟及萬有引力定律。智慧以漸啓而漸開，學問以日積月累而豐富，古今中外，未有例外者。

西方有演進觀念，以致西方學者論學能重演化歷程，亦因此往往有精當之論。如漢學家論清代史學便是一例：

中國晚近史家，往往認爲清代爲中國史學的衰微時期❺，諱言所承受的清代史學傳統，亦不承認其傳統的存在。這無疑是否定了史學的演化歷程。西方漢學家則不然，他們基於演進的觀念，對清代史學有極高的評價。浦立本認爲「清朝學者在綜合的歷史著作方面雖不出色，但對於過去作批評性的重估，則建立很高的標準。」浦瑞查德則認爲中國「所有的歷史著作，官修的或其他的，都經後起的學者，作了系統性的考據」，而「十七、十八世紀，大概看到傳統中國的批評史學發展至最精，雖然此一時期沒有出產能比美史記、漢書，新五代史、通鑑的鉅著，但是洋洋大觀的高等考據作品，却存留下來了。」哥芮更帶點感慨的說：「清代史學遺產的價值與影響，或許已被低估了。中外有一趨勢，責備清代傳統迂腐。」哥氏認爲在史學許多研究領域中最重要的原文處理與批評，清代學者已經提供了作爲高深研究基礎的技術與標準，他並認爲清代學者不肯寫完全屬於歷史綜合的作品，是清代史學已相當進步的證明。由此自然影響到近代中國史學，哥氏對此有一段極明快極透徹的評論：

「雖然近代中國史家厭惡清代史學作品，他們却不得不取法於清代史學作品。西方能供給較深的史學目的與方法上的自覺，但是即使是有機會精讀西方眞的歷史作品的中國史家，研究中國史，唯一可能的實際訓練，是奠基於清代作品上。西方能供給理想，清代學術則供給日常研究習慣。」

的確，中國晚近的史家，雖然極爲蔑視清代史學作品，但是其實際研究技術，受清代史學作品的影響最大。宋代富麗堂皇的史學作品，以代遠年湮，感應力已小；西方史學作品，則確乎僅能供給史學目的與方法上的自覺。歷史演進，綿綿延延，由宋不可能一躍而至今日，由西方亦不可能頃刻之間而史學盡飛來中國。迄今中國史學界，史家多集中精力研究史學上某一問題。或某一時期中某一部分史料，對於某一段時期的史事，作貫通的研究而撰述爲史著者則極少，仍係承乾嘉史學的餘習，最多加上一些蘭克學派的新方法罷了。

西方漢學家對清代史學的評價旣高，清代史家自是他們注意的對象。章學誠固然變成了熱門人物⑥，錢大昕也受到讚美，哥芮推許錢氏爲乾隆學術中最出色的史家，認爲他擁有無與倫比的正確知識。西方漢學家能如此認識錢大昕，似乎是已很難得了。

王夫之的讀通鑑論、宋論，受到了頌揚，趙翼的廿二史劄記，尤其獲得一致的好評。中國史學界重視趙翼，是從張之洞、梁啓超開始⑦。張梁之前，一般人不重視其書，其同時代的人，皆知其爲大詩人，而不甚知其爲史家，他的書與錢大昕的廿二史考異、王鳴盛的十七史商榷相比，論者皆最重錢書，王書次之，劄記陪末坐。一直到今天，史學界雖重其書，但仍然不肯認爲他是中國歷史上第一流的史家。西方漢學界則不然，他們對趙翼最感興趣，認爲他在向著克服中國史學的傳統缺陷而進步，認爲他創始許多觀念，已經播下了種子，在本世紀的現代史學方面，且已結起了果實。作者遊歐洲，在所邂逅的漢學家中，提到趙翼，無不致推崇之意。

中國史學，發展到清代，進入另一新紀元。清以前，中國的史學，最富創作精神，史家治史即爲寫史。清以後，中國的史學，由最富創作精神，演進到最富研究精神，史家不一定寫史，而將歷史視作一門值得深入研究的學問，殫畢生歲月於袪疑求信之間，這無疑是一大進步。沒有清代史學，中國史學將大爲減色，亦將難與西方近代新史學，一較短長。中國近代史學界不知之，而西方漢學家知之，這是西方漢學家論中國史學較中國史家遠爲精當之處，重演化歷程，其能發現眞理，往往如此。

總之，西方漢學家論中國史學，很多地方對中國史學界來講，是諍言，是珍論；施之於西方史學界，亦有發聾振聵之效。他們有西方史學的背景，而又入於中國史學之中，故其所見往往能出於二者之上，而值得珍視。

第二節　商榷於西方漢學家者

西方漢學家非無所蔽，其大者不能不辯:

1. 中國寫史方法不純是剪貼式的編纂

賈德納將中國所有史家的撰寫歷史，皆目之爲編纂；房德龍評判司馬遷的作品，及其他所有中國正史，像一本政府白皮書，「用剪刀與漿糊編纂而成，不怎麼消化，幾乎沒有解釋。」西方漢學界不少人斷言中國歷史寫作的方法純爲一種機械的剪貼式的編纂。像浦立本、浦瑞查德那樣，認淸中國大史家寫史，決非止於此，仍然是極爲少數的。

Scissors-and-paste historical method 卽所謂剪貼式的歷史方法，在西方最早由柯林吾（R. G. Collingwood, 1889-1943）以諷刺的口吻創此名詞，他在「歷史思想」（The Idea of History）一書中，攻擊此類歷史方法及由此類方法所產生的歷史作品，其言曰:

「有一類歷史，完全靠權威方面的證據（the testimony of authorities），我早已說過，此全然不眞是歷史，而苦於我們沒有其他名稱稱呼它。其方法是先確定我們希望知道些甚麼，然後去尋覓那方面的記載，口頭的或文字的，或由有關事件的當事人所提供，或由目擊者所描寫，或第三者重述當事人、目擊者所傾訴，或當事人、目擊者告訴報告者而由報告者再轉述過來。當發現一種記載與其目的有關連，史家就將它摘錄，編入於其歷史之中，必要時翻譯一番，改寫成他自己認爲合適的文體。通常地，在他有很多記載可引用之處，他將發現其中之一告訴他其他所不曾告訴他的，因此兩者或所有的將皆被編入。有時他將發現其中之一與其他相矛盾，則除非他能發現一種協調的方法，他必須決定捨棄其一；如果他憑良心，這將使他多少考慮相反權威方面的可信程度。有時其一甚或所有的一切告訴他一項他簡直無法相信的事蹟，或許是一項帶有作者時代或生活圈的迷信或偏見的事蹟，可是對於較開明的時代，它是不可靠的，因此予以略去。

以不同權威方面的證據予以摘錄、湊合，以組成的歷史，我稱之為剪貼式的歷史（scissors-and-paste history）。我重覆一遍說，那全然不眞是歷史，因為它不滿足科學的必要條件；但是，直到最近，祇有此類歷史存在，其絕大部分人們今天仍然在閱讀，甚至人們在撰寫中的多數仍屬於此一類型。結果知歷史甚少的人們將不耐煩的說：『為什麼你所謂的非歷史，正恰是歷史；剪貼正是所謂歷史；那正是歷史為什麼不是科學的原因，歷史是人人所知的事實，縱然職業史家們無理要求擴大他們的任務。』我因此應再敍說一些剪貼式歷史的變遷。

剪貼是較後的希羅世界（the later Greco-Roman world）或中古所知的唯一歷史方法。其方法極簡單，史家網羅證據，口頭的或文字的，用他自己的判斷以決定其可信與否，並將其集合到一塊出版：他所從事的工作，部分是文學的——其材料以一有關的同類的使人確信的敍述表現出來——，部分是修辭學的，如果我可以用其詞以指出大多數古代與中世紀史家目的在證明一項理論的事實。」❽

柯林吾將所有不用科學方法批評證據而僅將證據以私意摘錄入書的歷史，皆視之為剪貼式的歷史，其方法是剪貼式的方法。房德龍等西方漢學家沿用此詞，且將其限於更浮淺的一面，於是他們批評中國史學著作是「用剪刀與漿糊編纂而成，不怎麼消化，幾乎沒有解釋」，於是中國寫史方法，完全變成了一種剪貼式的編纂。

厚誣中國史學，似無過於此者。不能否認的中國有一部分史書，是在此方法下產生的，但是中國大史家的史學作品，決非剪刀與漿糊下的產物。司馬遷、司馬光寫史，固有其點竄古今文字的艱苦，其他數以千百計的中國史家，從蒐集史料到溶化史料，皆有其艱苦備嚐的歷程。

史記所根據的材料，是詩、尙書、春秋、左傳、國語、帝繫姓、世本、戰國策、秦紀、楚漢春秋以及漢代檔册，如果司馬遷應用剪刀與漿糊，那麼史記便不成其爲史記，而是詩、尙書、春秋等書的混合品了。世界史學之林，能如史記的陶鑄史料，以自成一家之言，且兼有信美之長，似不可多見。如果史記仍流於剪貼式歷史，那麼寰宇之內，不是剪貼式歷史的史學作品，怕寥如晨星了。房德龍說司馬遷通常地僅將其資料以原來辭句再刊載一番，不曾嘗試深入研究資料，並說司馬遷以後的中國正史，皆用剪刀與漿糊編纂而成，是最武斷的結論。史記爲一部極可信的中國上古史，由地下史料殷墟甲骨文，證實史記所記殷代史實的不虛，得到了最具體的說明。史記既足以徵信千古，則司馬遷未嘗不曾深入研究資料。至於司馬遷粹合古今，艱澀如尙書之文，予以明暢的譯述，不雅馴如百家之言，加以適當的修飾，千載而下，讀其文者，但覺昌茂爾雅，斐然自成一體，這更不能說他僅將其資料以原來辭句再刊載一番了。

通鑑所根據的材料，正史之外，雜史凡三百二十二種，其中絕大部分，我們今天都可以看到，如果拿通鑑與那些材料比較，便可以發現通鑑每一句話，甚至於每一個字，都有出處，而且都是費過一番心思考慮斟酌。作者曾將通鑑東漢部分的一字一句，在後漢書後漢紀等書裡面去尋找，幾乎完全可以尋找出來。溫公儘量沿用原句，必要時則加以删削潤色，往往數千字的奏疏詔議，經過溫公簡化爲數百字，仍絲毫不失其原意，且更明顯條暢；有時更易一二字，而較原來的字更能傳神，更能得其眞相，這是大史家的本領。所以通鑑是一部最傑出的史學名著，而不是東併西湊的斷爛朝報；通鑑的文章，自有其獨特的風格，而已絲毫不帶史記漢書後漢書等等他所取以爲資料的史籍的色彩。在剪貼式歷史方法下，能產生此類的作品嗎？洛陽有通鑑草稿盈兩屋，黃魯直曾閱數百卷，迄無一字草書❾。其稿卽長篇之稿，而細工如此，溫公寫通鑑，豈肯匆匆揮動剪刀，剪以貼之以了事？卽長編之修，亦非盡如浦立本教授所云運用剪貼方法，「當需要加入材料到長篇去的時候，長卷便被剪斷，貼入要加入的部分。」溫公與范內翰論修書帖，雖有云：「請從高祖初起兵修長編，至哀帝禪位而止。其起兵以前禪位以後事，於今來所看書中，見者亦請令書吏別用草紙錄出，每一事中間空一行許素紙，以備剪開粘綴故也。隋以前者與貢父，以後者與道原，令各修入長編中。」像是用了剪貼方法，而實際上則不然。溫公讓范祖禹修唐代長編之餘，將所見到的隋以前與唐哀帝禪位以後的史事，用草紙錄出，隋以前的交給劉攽（貢父），唐哀帝禪位以後的交給劉恕（道原），是爲了替劉攽劉恕蒐集修隋以前長編與五代長編的材料，蒐集材料自然有用剪貼方法的必要，且替劉攽劉恕抄錄不同時代的史事，又分別轉致之，史事必須區分，書吏亦自無區分能力，故每一事中間，空一行許素紙，以備區分時剪開粘綴。溫公固未嘗希望范祖禹以剪開粘綴之法修唐代的長編。觀其語范祖禹修長編之法云：

> 「其修長編時，請據事目下所記新書紀志傳及雜史小說文集，盡檢出一閱，其中事同文異者，則請擇一明白詳備者錄之；彼此互有詳略，則請左右采獲，錯綜銓次，自用文辭修正之，一如左傳敍事之體也，此並作大字寫；若彼此年月事迹有相違戾不同者，則請選一證據分明，情理近於得實者，修入正文，餘者注於其下，仍爲敍述所以取此捨彼之意。（先注所捨者，云某書云云，今按

某書證驗云云，或無證驗，則以事理推之云云，今從某書爲定。

若無以考其虛實是非者，則云今兩存之。其實錄正史未必皆可據，雜史小說未必皆無憑，在高鑒擇之。)」⑩

是長編之修，固已不止於材料的蒐集，而有選擇，有剪裁，有考證。事同文異者，擇明白詳備者錄之；彼此互有詳略，則左右采獲，錯綜銓次，自用文辭修正之；彼此年月事迹違戾不同，則選證據分明，情理近於得實者，修入正文，餘者注於其下，仍爲敍述所以取此捨彼之意，此豈僅憑剪刀漿糊二者所能畢其功者乎？修長編不苟如此，修通鑑費盡斟酌可知。

大抵通鑑一書，以前漢部分來講，無一語不出於史漢，而無一處全襲史漢。前漢部分如是，其他部分亦然。通鑑一書如是，其他中國史學名著亦然。這是中國史學的一大特色，儘量忠於原文，以求徵信，而又斟酌損益，運以別識心裁。西方史家不能知，故時時譏其一再重複敍述，譏其是剪貼式的編纂，這是一種錯覺與誤解。另以鄭樵的通志及清代史家治史的方法，可以作更好的說明：

鄭樵是中國的史學理論家，其通志一書，是其理論的實踐。「凡著書者，雖採前人之書，必自成一家言。」⑪是他寫史的最高原則。所以他於通志總序很自負的說：

「夫學術超詣，本乎心識，如人入海，一入一深。臣之二十略，皆臣自有所得，不用舊史之文。紀傳者，編年紀事之實蹟，自有成規，不爲智而增，不爲愚而減，故於紀傳，即其舊文，從而損益。」

章學誠亦盛推鄭氏云：

「鄭樵生千載而後，慨然有見於古人著述之源，而知作者之旨，不徒以詞采爲文，考據爲學也。於是遂欲匡正史遷，益以博雅；

貶損班固，譏其因襲，而獨取三千年來，遺文故册，運以別識心裁，蓋承通史家風，而自成經緯，成一家言者也。」⑫

我們今天看鄭氏的通志，其紀傳部分，固然極令人失望，因爲他幾乎全抄舊史，無所剪裁，做到了「卽其舊文」，不怎麼「從而損益」。可是其二十略能貫通各史書志，擴充文物範圍，如六書、七音、氏族、校讎、圖譜從未收入史部的，都包攬在史學範圍以內，其材料確經自己消化，所謂「皆自有所得，不用舊史之文」，不是鄭氏的好爲大言；所謂「獨取三千年來，遺文故册，運以別識心裁」，不是章氏的溢美之辭。以剪貼式歷史加之於鄭氏的通志二十略，鄭氏九泉下不能氣平。至於通志紀傳部分的卽其舊文，鄭氏亦有其理論基礎，「編年紀事之實蹟，自有成規，不爲智而增，不爲愚而減」，理由雖勉强，而中國史家對史料原文的態度，亦可看出一般了。

清代史家治史的方法，貌頗似剪貼式的史學方法，而細稽之，則亦殊爲不然。清代史家讀史必作劄記，心有所得，則條記於紙。梁啓超於「清代學術概論」一書中云：

「嗚呼！自吾之生，而乾嘉學者已零落略盡，然十三歲肄業於廣州之學海堂，堂則前總督阮元所創，以樸學敎於吾鄉者也。其規模矩矱，一循百年之舊。十六七歲遊京師，亦獲交當時耆宿數人，守先輩遺風不替者。中間涉覽諸大師著述，參以所聞見，蓋當時『學者社會』之狀況，可髣髴一二焉。

大抵當時好學之士，每人必置一『劄記册子』，每讀書有心得則記之。……推原劄記之性質，本非著書，不過儲著書之資料。」

此種劄記册子與宋李燾所用的資料木匣⑬頗類似，同是爲了蒐集材料，而劄記册子遠較木匣爲靈便，故廣泛被採用。清代的史學名著，很多都是劄記之書，如顧炎武的日知錄，錢大昕的十駕齋養新錄，盧文弨的鍾山札記、龍城札記，趙翼的陔餘叢考、廿二史劄記，兪正燮的癸巳類稿、癸巳存稿，不可殫擧。以資料性的劄記册子，寫成劄記之書，似乎是一種剪貼拼凑的工作了。而細考其過程，則相反的發現其極富科學的精神，合於西方近代新史家寫史的方法。以顧炎武的日知錄作例子，卽可予以說明。顧氏答友人問他日知錄又成幾卷云：

「嘗謂今人纂輯之書，正如今人之鑄錢。古人采銅於山，今人則買舊錢名之曰廢銅以充鑄而已。所鑄之錢，旣已麤惡，而又將古人傳世之寶，舂剉碎散，不存於後，豈不兩失之乎？承問日知錄又成幾卷，蓋期之以廢銅，而某自別來一載，早夜誦讀，反復尋究，僅得十餘條，然庶幾采山之銅也。」⑭

一年僅得區區十餘條，確可稱得上是采山之銅。其采的方法，是靠劄記，平時看到一條有意義的材料，便劄記下來，若干年後，陸續劄記了許多相類的材料，於是加以思想，組織成一條。所謂「早夜誦讀，反復尋究」，是組織成一條前的艱苦寫照。每每讀之愈久，劄記愈多，而愈待反復尋究，一條之出，往往基於數十條或千百條劄記，以致劄記做得愈綿密，愈能有創獲。一旦發現新材料，則更易或修正其說。如此一邊劄記，一邊撰寫，以舊的劄記，作撰寫的根據，以新的劄記，作補充的資源，交互爲用，相濟而成，時時立說，時時修正，成績的不够豐碩在意料中，又何怪顧氏一年僅能得十餘條之微？又豈能說顧氏作劄記之餘，用剪刀與漿糊成其日知錄一書？

無疑的顧氏由作劄記到寫成類似劄記之書，極富科學的精神，合於西方近代新史家寫史的方法。

以趙翼的陔餘叢考、廿二史劄記作例子，也可予以說明。趙氏自中歲退休，優遊林下者四十年，無日不以讀書著書爲事。其於陔餘叢考小引云：

「余自黔西乞養歸，閒視之暇，仍理故業，日夕惟手一編，有所得，輒劄記別紙，積久遂得四十餘卷，以其爲循陔時所輯，故名曰陔餘叢考。」

其於廿二史劄記小引云：

「閒居無事，翻書度日，而資性粗鈍，不能研究經學。惟歷代史書，事顯而義淺，便於流覽，爰取爲日課，有所得，輒劄記別紙，積久遂多。」

是陔餘叢考與廿二史劄記二書，都是劄記的結晶。細讀二書，我們知趙氏治史，深得春秋屬辭比事之旨，不執單詞孤事以論史，每每臚列諸多相類的史實，比而論之，以得一代的特徵。諸多相類的史實，是由數十年的悠長時間劄記而來。「古今風會之遞變，政事之變更，有關於治亂興衰之故者」⑮，他固然能自諸多相類的史實中作歸納說明，即是比較小的問題，像關張之勇，他能徧尋七部史籍，舉出十五個例子，以說明漢以後稱勇者必推關張⑯；像五代人多以彥爲名，他也能不憚其煩的舉出一百二十七個例子出來，以說明五代時人多以彥爲名的風尙⑰。如此歸納衆多史實以獲得結論的治史方法，極富科學的精神，合於西方近代新史家寫史的方法。也無怪西方漢學家對趙氏極度推崇了。

西方近代新史家寫史的方法如何？有加以比較說明的必要。

先廣泛的蒐集史料，再加以審愼的撰寫，是一般人所認爲的西方新史家寫史的方法。卡耳（E. H. Carr, 1892-）則有更精闢更深入的說明：

「局外人（指不曾受史學訓練的朋友或治其他學問的朋友）有時問我，史家寫歷史時如何進行工作。最普通的假定像是史家區分其工作爲兩個迥不相同的階段或時期。首先，他耗悠長的歲月，研讀資料，將史事寫入劄記册子（notebooks）上去。當此工作做完，他便丢開資料，拿出劄記册子來，從頭到尾的寫其大著。對我來講，這是一種不眞確的描述。以我自己爲例，當我已研讀我視爲主要資料（the capital sources）的一小部分時，寫的渴望極度增强，我於是開始去寫，不必要從開頭寫，而是從某些地方，任何地方。其後，讀與寫同時進行，我邊讀，邊將寫的稿子增加、刪減、修正、削除。讀以寫而得到指導，而收穫豐碩，我寫的越多，我越知道我正在找些什麼，我越瞭解我所發現的眞義。」⑱

蒐集史料與執筆撰寫，實在是難以完全分開的，也不應完全分開，完全分開了便有乖科學的精神。史學方法上所謂「再檢查」（re-examinatian），所謂「新解釋」（re-interpretation），都有賴於讀與寫的同時進行，以讀充實寫，以寫指導讀，以舊解釋作基礎，再去檢查新材料，以新材料作基礎，再去尋求新解釋。交流循環，生生不已。必如是才是近代寫史的新方法，必如是才不流於剪貼式的歷史。西方近代新史家所追求的理想如此，而中國淸代史家，早已在「早夜誦讀，反復尋究」了，早已在將「再檢查」與「新解釋」二者交互運用了。

尤須辨明者，古今中外引書的方法不同。中國古代史家引書，除經書之文以外，都是就原文擷取精華，刪節潤色，並非逐一照錄，不更一字。中國近代史家引書，則是奉原文爲經典，忠實引述，毫不變易，即使有所刪節，也以標點符號示出，這是由於受西方史家的影響。西方史家在從事大部頭著述的撰寫時，對史料原文的處理，較中國史家爲豪放，史料原文僅爲其註脚，他要在其上建立另一壯觀。可是在引到原文時，西方史家的態度極嚴肅，自己不妄動一字，也因此他們看中國史書引原文之多，認爲中國史家動一動剪刀，塗一塗漿糊，剪貼一番便可以了。殊不知這又是一種錯誤的推理。在中國史家引書自由刪節潤色的傳統下，他們似乎無法使用剪貼式的機械方法。

總之，中國史家寫史方法，不純是剪貼式的編纂，絕大部分史籍，不但不能限之於剪貼歷史的最浮淺一面，用剪刀剪斷，用漿糊貼入，也不能概之以柯林吾所謂的剪貼歷史，祇將證據以私意摘錄入書，而不用科學方法批評證據。

2. 中國歷史中非無個人要素

福赫伯說：「以中國與中世紀歐洲相比，我們注意到中國頗缺乏個人表現。……歐洲的拉丁資料，遠較爲個人的，能反映個性，即使是經過錯誤的文法或拼字法。在中國，歷史中的『個人要素』，不易獲得；我們祇能試着去找較官方報告能希望多得到一些消息的資料。換句話說，去找筆記，去找稗乘脞說，或者去找記個人親身經驗的少數作品。」在史學上，去找筆記，去找稗乘脞說，去找記個人親身經驗的作品，是不容爭議的；筆記等資料較官方報告富有個人要素，也似乎不容置疑。但是以中國與中世紀歐洲相比，我們不能苟同；中國歷史中的個人要素，也不是不易獲得，即使在官方報告之中。

中國與中世紀歐洲絕不相同，前文已討論過，此不再詳。中國歷史中的個人要素，則首先由中國人對歷史的基本看法，可以看到。中國人一向視歷史爲事與言的記錄，事與言的後面，站着的是人，所以中國歷史記載最主要的是在記人，中國人以人爲歷史的中心，屬於正史的廿五史，列傳佔絕大部分，可作最好的說明。研究中國歷史，首先要懂得人，不懂得人，便無法研究中國歷史。固然也有人脫離了人的中心而來研究中國歷史的，但其研究所得，將不會接觸到中國歷史的精髓。所以福赫伯認爲「在中國，歷史中的個人要素，不易獲得」，是片面之詞。他或許認爲由中國官方史學所提供的官方報告，僅記錄了官樣文章，如文稿，如檔案，無史家的個性，所以爲一種無個人要素的資料。可是他如果知道中國歷代史官所表現的個性，他就會知道中國歷史中最原始的官方報告有個人因素了；他如果再知道中國官修正史中史家所扮演的重要角色，他也會自動修正其錯誤與偏見了。

總之，中國的官修正史之學，西方漢學家似乎與西方正統史家一樣，永遠不能瞭解，他們認爲那是官樣文章，有其道德目的，集中於人事制度與行政方面，其所繪出的過去，是片面的，其所產生的歷史，是單面歷史。讓西方史學界淸楚中國官修正史之學的眞諦，似乎不是易事。

第三節　西方漢學家研究中國史學的途徑及其遠景

十六、十七、十八三個世紀，西方耶穌會敎士東來，他們住在與工作在中國，用西方文字寫有關中國方面的書，其寫書的動機，淵源於一種對中國知識的興趣。因此他們的作品，不僅限於富學術性的歷史，有一些，歷史僅是全體的一部分，政治、法律、經濟、地理、文學、藝術都包入其中；有一些，是起於對語言或哲學的原始興趣而產生的。事實上研究的題目是一個國家或者其文化，不特殊或僅僅是其歷史。

耶穌會敎士的作品在歐洲所發生的影響，是可以看得到的。一六八一年布斯德特（Bossuet, 1627-1704）寫世界史（Histoire Universelle）的時候，還不曾述及中國歷史。一世紀後，吉朋（Gibbon, 1737-1794）與伏爾泰（Voltaire, 1694-1778）皆敏銳的覺悟到其重要性。吉朋從其世界歷史知識的高峰，能淸楚的看出東方與西方如何互相影響，將看起來沒有關係的事件聯繫起來。伏爾泰的作品問世，中國在法國的地位，到達光榮的頂峰。伏爾泰大膽地主張中國信史的悠久，證明聖經的錯誤，這對耶穌會史家華路藍禝的辛勤，是一種諷刺，也是一種否定。⑲

十九世紀與二十世紀初期，繼耶穌會敎士而致力於用西文寫有關中國書的人，是新傳敎士，外交家，新聞記者，與來中國中學或大學敎書的人。他們的作品，到二十世紀時，很淸楚的開始在變，其變是由於中國與西方的政治關係起了變化。最早來中國的耶穌會敎士，以極欣羡的筆調，記述中國的一切。這可由很多根據他們的報告寫成的書反映出來。但是十九世紀，西方列强的支配經濟政治勢力，以及中國社會明顯的停頓，使來中國的人態度改變了，像「不信上帝的中國人」(the heathen Chinese) 及「中國的循環」(the cycle of Cathay)，都包含着藐視一個靜態的或衰落的文化的意味，最低限度不證明是活潑有力的生長，而活潑有力的生長像是歐洲文化的特徵。由於此一判斷，中國史遂成爲一門不値得認眞研究的科目，而留給來過中國的人去研究。

直到二十世紀初，來中國的歐洲人，其所寫關於中國的作品，價値是很有限度的，其中絕大部分，僅將科目介紹給西方讀者，而不能對知識有一新的貢獻，在史學方面，最大的缺陷，是其作品並不能將西方歷史寫作的新技術傳到中國來。他們的作品，更近於中國史學，而與西方史學本身，反有距離，尤其是在主題的解釋與選擇上。其原因能容易推想而出，因爲作者住在中國，他們想接受與同時代的中國人同樣的影響，選擇同樣的題目研究，例如重點放在古代史與近代史，而忽略了古代近代之間的時代，雙方都是相同的。另外的原因是西方史家信賴他們所研究的國家的學者，有時他們與中國助手共同工作，即使不是如此，語言的困難，經常使他們憑依中文的近代作品，而不大敢問津廣大的原始資料。結果，他們常常有意無意地接受其觀點與方法，西方歷史寫作的新技術，在他們的作品中，一點表現不出來，這無疑影響了中西史學的交流。

在趨向本世紀末葉之際，在西方有兩項發展，預示了一條新路。第一是西方發現了中國的藝術，以此有動機與心願研究中國藝術的歷史。第二是日本的崛起，迅速獲得國際地位。遠東突然間重要起來了，大大不是靜態的了，結果，遠東漸漸爲西方國家所注意，也自然爲西方大學所注意。自一九三〇年以來，尤其是自一九四五年以來，在歐洲與美洲研究中國與日本學科的大學教師，爲數急劇增加，其學科包括歷史在內。

此最近期間產生的作品，與以前的作品，在很多方面，大不相同。作者不再住在與工作在他們所寫的國家裡面，雖然他們爲了研究經常儘量設法去訪問。他們也比其前人更意識到學術性。所研究的時代，很少變化，仍然對晚今與遠古有普遍的偏好，雖然在晚今遠古之間作更詳盡研究的需要也已漸漸受到重視。仍然信賴中國學術，然而是寧信賴團體，而不信賴個人，寧信賴一所大學，而不信賴一位老師，寧信賴一個圖書館，而不信賴一本書。這反映出所有變化中最顯明的變化。代表性的書是專論，詳盡，富批評精神，並限之於一特殊題目上。事實上，第一次西方學者盡力克服語言困難，盡力接近材料，以研究西洋史的方式，同樣來研究中國史，這對西方史學的輸入中國，是很有貢獻的。⑳

近二十年來，西方漢學家又開闢了研究中國史學的新天地，他們感慨於西方史家很少有動機承認中國史學以往的成就，或重視其極不同的傳統，以與自己作比較，所以他們出來作嘗試研究。可是其間困難重重，中國史學作品翻譯到西方去的太少，像史記、漢書、通鑑等第一流史學名著，祇有部分的翻譯，沒有一部已全譯成英文的㉑。何況中國的社會與文化，產生中國的史學，在能眞正瞭解中國史學之前，必須相當深入於中國社會與文化之中，所以必須是精通中國學問的專家，祇憑透過翻譯作品，不能眞知中國史學。這眞是够不容易的了。又加上必須顧及到西方史學與西方史家，通達西方史學的精義，深深曉得西方史家的與趣與先入之見，以便論析中國史學時使其心目中的聽衆感覺到有意義。這是一溝通中西史學的艱鉅而又偉大的工作，西方漢學家近年來有勇氣去嘗試着做，似乎是世界史學界最值得興奮的事。

西方漢學家研究中國史學的途徑，約略有三：

一是以西方的一套史學，來衡量中國史學。他們仍然不能擺脫西方人的立場與觀點，來超然的客觀的看中國史學。中國史學傳統，與西方史學傳統，極不相同，他們不注意其不同者，最低限度不珍視其不同者，而僅由中國史學中所同於西方者，揭出之以質於西方史學界。有一同者，他們每欣然以喜，而昭告於西方說：「此非中國史學之同於西方者乎？此非中國史學之深值注意者乎？」西方史學界人士，初則將信將疑，繼則有可能感覺到有意義，這也是爲什麼西方漢學家研究中國史學必須深深曉得西方史家的與趣與先入之見了。有不同者，他們每施以攻擊與蔑視，如中國的官修正史之學，爲中國所獨有，而爲西方之所無，他們不去研究其特色，不去研究其起源、發展及影響，而一味視其爲官樣文章，不值一顧；如中國儒家思想影響到史學，他們很驚訝，但不去研究儒家思想究竟有多少滲入到中國史學裡面去，而僅囫圇地說中國史家全以儒家觀點去褒貶；趙翼受到特別重視與讚美，是因爲他的史學，能衝破中國史學傳統，而暗合於西方史學。不重其異，而重其同，不以新史學成分輸入西方，而僅錦上添花，以相比附，這無疑說明了西方漢學家潛意識中仍有天下史學盡於西方的觀念，以爲西方史學可以包羅一切，中國史學中有與之相同者，已是難能可貴，而應當值得注意了。不同的學術，作比較研究，重其同不如重其異。重其同而不重其異，不可能有新啓示與新發明。同者往往是偶合，卽使不是偶合，而有共同的客觀因素，所能說明者也少。異則異於是，異能有互相發明之功，異能有相反相成之效，所以由異能得到新啓示與新發明。西方漢學家不深求與重視中國史學所異於西方者，自難爲西方史學輸入新血輪，其能裨益於西方史學者無幾。且其胸中有一崇高的西方史學，自亦難完全瞭解中國史學。這似乎是西方漢學家研究中國史學最大的一個缺陷與障礙。

二是經由日文著作以通中國史學。中國學問，活潑空靈，入手極難，西方漢學家往往另闢蹊徑，先通日文，再由日文著作以通漢學。日人研究漢學，肯下功夫，肯作機械性的分析，利用他們研究的成績，進而研究漢學，每能收事半功倍之效。西方漢學家發現此一捷徑，所以極重日文，這是西人治漢學的方法之一。西方漢學家研究中國史學，乞靈於日文著作之處，尤其顯然。如日本史家內滕虎次郞的著作「章實齋年譜」與「中國史學史」，他們便常常資以爲用，章實齋的被認識，多少係受內滕虎次郞的啓示，錢大昕的被發現，情形更是如此，如哥芮評錢大昕云：「乾隆學術中最出色的人物是多產的史家與經學家錢大昕。他的作品及其題目的選擇，顯示出他密切踵法顧炎武的理想與方法，雖然他沒有表明其理論觀點。他的最大特質，就像內滕虎次郞所講的，是擁有『無與倫比的正確知識，研究一個問題時，可有效的當作歷史材料用』，其知識是經過了正確的通盤的批評。」這無疑是直取內滕之說了。就是趙翼的蜚聲西方漢學界，也與日文著作有關，日本史家寫中國史，取趙翼廿二史劄記之說最多，內滕虎次郞甚至全勒竊之㉒，趙翼對日本漢學界的影響如此，而西方漢學家幾皆通日文，自然趙氏在西方變爲風雲人物了。「取法乎上，僅得乎中」，西方漢學家經由日文著作以通中國史學，未免「取法乎中」，自難躋於上乘境界。這是西方漢學家論中國史學每有隔膜之感的關鍵之一。

三是憑依中文近代著作以瞭解中國史學。中國古書難讀，盡人而知之，西方漢學家自視爲畏途。加以中國傳統史家，每不明言其史學，僅將之寓於其著述之中，非精通其著述，爬梳而整理之，不能得其史學梗概。西方漢學家自難語於此。所以他們不敢問津於有關的廣大原始資料，而僅憑依中文近代論史學的著作，像梁啓超的中國歷史研究法（及補編），金毓黻的中國史學史，以及李宗侗的中國史學史，都變成他們研究中國史學主要的工具書，不少材料，取自其中，見解自然也有形無形的受其影響。如孔子在西方漢學家心目中，沒有任何史學上的地位，且備受攻擊，似乎是受梁啓超言論的影響。梁氏之言曰：「孔子修春秋，體裁似悉依魯史官之舊，吾儕得藉此以窺見古代所謂正史者，其內容爲何如。春秋第一年云：『元年，春王正月。三月，公及邾儀父盟于蔑。夏五月，鄭伯克段於鄢。秋七月，天王使宰咺來歸惠公仲子之賵。九月，及宋人盟于宿。多，十有二月，祭伯來。公子益師卒。』吾儕以今代的史眼讀之，不能不大詫異。第一，其文句簡短，達於極點，每條最長者不過四十餘字㉓，最短者乃僅一字㉔。第二，一條記一事，不相聯屬，絕類村店所用之流水帳簿，每年多則十數條，少則三四條，又絕無組織，任意斷自某年，皆成起訖。第三，所記僅各國宮廷事，或宮廷間相互之關係，而於社會情形一無所及。第四，天災地變等現象，本非歷史事項者，反一一注意詳記。吾儕因此可推知當時之史的觀念，及史的範圍，非惟與今日不同，即與秦漢後亦大有異。又可見當時之史，只能謂之簿錄，不能謂之著述。……而孔子所修，又藉以寄其微言大義，只能作經讀，不能作史讀。」㉕梁氏如此看孔子的春秋，西方漢學家自然有可能隨聲附和，不談孔子的史學了。如果他們眞正自己瞭解了孔子以後的史學，就不會否認孔子在中國史學上的地位及影響。司馬遷踵春秋之後，以寫史記，不容置疑的是沿着孔子的一線發展；「史之大原，本乎春秋，春秋之義，昭乎筆削」㉖，不談孔子，也似乎無法深論中國史學上的筆削。淸以前中國史家太將孔子神聖化。晚近以來，又太對孔子缺乏同情的諒解（sympathetic understanding）。西方漢學家憑依中文近代論史學的著作以論中國史學，所以他們輕視孔子，不討論其史學㉗，中國史學的淵源，於是語焉不詳，中國歷史上一位承前啓後的大史家，也被輕描淡寫的剔除㉘。這僅是西方漢學家憑依中文近代著作的流弊之一而已，其他殆難縷數。

嘗怪西方漢學家論中國史學，不談經學與史學的關係，不談學術思想對史學的影響，脫離群學，而專求之史籍。如戴密微論及章學誠「六經皆史」之說云：「章學誠斷言儒家之經典卽歷史。仔細思考此一主張，倒轉來歷史也將構成經典，歷史將有經典的價值，一種有如規範的價值。那正是章學誠所相信的。聖經是歷史，因爲歷史是一聖經。我相信章學誠的目的，不是去褻瀆經典，而是將歷史經典化。」這雖比中國近人所解釋的「六經皆史料」進了一步，但是仍有所蔽，其蔽在不知中國經學與史學的密切關係，而以西方的經典看中國的經學，將經學與史學看成兩門全不相干的學問。如果戴氏知道中國的經史非二學㉙，知道尙書春秋爲史家之權輿，知道官禮風詩爲掌故典要文徵諸選的淵源㉚，他就不會認爲章學誠有意將歷史經典化了。中國史學的遠源，也似乎可以看清楚了。不知經史的關係如此，其他學問與史學的關係，學術思想的影響史學，自亦不能了解，所以他們雖然想進入中國的社會與文化之中，雖然知道中國史學是傳統孔子文化極密切的一支，而不能作精密的討論。此無他，他們硏究中國史學的途徑，有待商榷。中西史學傳統不同，以西方史學來衡量中國史學，無法衡量；日本漢學家論中國史學，亦自難精闢周詳；而中國近代有關論史學的著作，也難找出一部理想的出來，梁氏的歷史硏究法，談自己的見解多，究能從其中看出多少中國史學，大是問題；金毓黻的史學史，是一種材料書，徧是書名與人名，開始卽於經史關係，毫無論述，漢魏以降，迄乎宋明，思想之影響史學者，亦概置不問。而西方漢學家卽以此類書作津梁，自然無怪不能深論中國的史學了。

不過，近二十年來西方漢學家研究中國史學，是有其蓽路藍褸之功的。他們於西方史學之外，另闢了一條史學大道；他們的呼聲，喚醒了部分西方史家的自我沉醉；他們小心翼翼的去研究，不在所知範圍以外，動則發表臆見；他們已不怎麼犯基本上的錯誤，如基本事實（basic facts)，都能予以正確而淸楚的考證，如引用原書，態度極嚴肅，以其譯文與原文相比較，令人驚歎其精確的程度。西方老一輩的漢學家衞利（Arthur Waley, 1889- ）的翻譯㉛，美麗動人，一向風靡西方學術界，今天則極爲西方漢學家所詬病，其原因即在於衞利的譯文雖美，而不甚忠於原文。引書是史學上最基本最重要的工作，西方漢學家引書，須經過翻譯，譯文一錯，一切便不能奢談，今天西方漢學家對翻譯能忠實，他們是可以與論中國的學術了。

在西方，研究中國史學，是一種新學術。新學方興，遠景美麗，西方漢學家不惟想藉此溝通相去甚遠的中西史學，同時很有野心用西方的一套方法，將中國歷史重新整理一番，就像整理希臘史羅馬史一樣。方法論大有助於治學，已爲不爭之論。國人治史，不重方法，西方漢學家用西方的一套方法，以重建中國歷史，藉西哲的精蘊，以發國史的幽光，應是令人興奮的事。惟中國學問，如天馬行空，飄忽無踪，單憑方法論，實不足以羈縻之。方法以外，靈活的運用，直覺的瞭解，詩意的體會，極爲重要。方法易學，直覺的瞭解，詩意的體會，却不是一蹴可幾的。不知中國的社會背景及民族習性，即不足以語此境界，西方漢學家的致命創傷在此，西方漢學家重建中國歷史的困難亦在此。何況中國史籍，浩如煙海，西方漢學家殫畢生精力，不足以窺其萬一。因之迄至今日，他們仍不能博覽群籍，作高瞻遠矚的研究，祇能埋首於歷史的個別問題中，以躋於專家之列。中國歷史的全貌，西方漢學家何日得以窺

見，殊成問題。其遠景何日得以出現於眼前，亦爲不可知之數。㉜

學術天下之公器，中國史學有那麼一群外邦人士，熱心硏究，國人聞之，自應興奮鼓舞。當然，中國數千年的史學，不能贏得西方多數人的注意，頗使人慨歎西方史學界的偏狹與倨傲。能有知之者愛之護之，我們也應當爲中國史學慶幸。國人慨然以中國史學的興亡自任，開展眼界，擴充知識領域，將中國史學放入世界史學中去硏究，似乎更是迫不及待的大事。

第七章　註釋

❶見後漢書班彪傳

❷見漢書司馬遷傳

❸見漢書揚雄傳

❹見後漢書班固傳

❺如陳寅恪於重刻西域人華化考序云:「有清一代, 經學號稱極盛, 而史學則遠不逮宋人。」

❻如美國漢學家 David S. Nivison 曾以頗長時間, 寫成「章學誠的生平與思想」(*The Life and Thought of Chang Hsüeh-Ch'eng* (1734–1801))一書。

❼張之洞於勸學篇云:「考史之書, 約之以讀趙翼廿二史劄記 (王氏商榷可節取, 錢氏考異精於考古, 略於致用, 可緩。)」梁啓超於清代學術概論云:「乾嘉以還, 考證學統一學界, 其洪波自不得不及於史, 則有趙翼之廿二史劄記, 王鳴盛之十七史商榷, 錢大昕之廿二史考異, 洪頤煊之諸史考異, 皆汲其流。四書體例略同, 其職志皆在考證史蹟, 訂譌正謬。惟趙書於每代之後, 常有多條臚列史中故實, 用歸納法比較研究, 以觀盛衰治亂之原, 此其特長也。」梁氏於中國歷史研究法、中國近三百年學術史二書中, 亦有類此之說。

❽R. G Collingwood, *The Idea oj History*, 1946, pp. 257–258

❾見文獻通考經籍考

❿司馬光「與范內翰論修書帖」附見於明萬曆刊本通鑑

⓫見通志總序

⓬見文史通義申鄭篇

⓭周密癸辛雜識云:「纂爲長編, 以木厨十枚, 每厨抽替匣二十枚, 每替以甲子誌之; 凡本年之事, 有所聞必歸此匣, 分日月先後次第之, 井然有條。」

⓮見亭林文集卷四與人書十

⓯見廿二史劄記小引

⓰見廿二史劄記卷七關張之勇條

⑰見廿二史劄記卷二二五代人多以彥爲名條

⑱E. H. Carr, *What is History?* 1961, pp. 22-23

⑲參見 W. G. Beasley, *Western historical writing on China and Japan,* in Historians of China and Japan, ed. by W. G. Beasley & E. G. Pulleyblank, 1961, pp. 19-23

⑳Ibid.

㉑法國漢學家沙畹 (E. Chavannes, 1865-1918) 曾以法文譯史記全書，氣魄之大，擧世無匹。在他以前，西方漢學家，僅以能譯史記之一傳爲滿足耳。

㉒西方漢學界甚懷疑內滕虎次郎勦竊趙翼之廿二史劄記，余曾以廿二史劄記與內滕之中國近世史相對照，其間完全相同之處甚多。李慈銘於桃花聖解庵日記卒集云:「趙翼之廿二史劄記，出於常州一老儒，武進、陽湖人多能言其姓氏。」如其爲事實，那眞是循環報應了。余曾草廿二史劄記之作者問題一文（載於大陸雜誌一九卷三期），辨明劄記仍爲趙氏之所自著，僅寶山李保泰參與修訂耳。

㉓梁氏自註云: 如定四年之「三月，公會劉子、晉侯、宋公、蔡侯、衞侯、陳子、鄭伯、許男、曹伯、莒子、邾子、頓子、胡子、滕子、薛伯、杞伯、小邾子、齊國夏於召陵，侵楚。」

㉔梁氏自註云: 如隱八年云:「螟」。

㉕見梁啓超中國歷史研究法頁一九——二一

㉖見文史通義答客問上

㉗西方漢學家鮮有承認孔子爲史家者，討論史學問題時，提到孔子，幾皆顯露不屑的顏色。一九五六年到一九五八年之間，倫敦大學亞非研究院擧行的亞洲民族史籍討論會，未曾有人提出孔子的史學來以作討論，是極自然的現象。孔子在他們心目中，是沒有史家地位的。

㉘孔子富有史家的考證與存疑精神，他說:「夏禮吾能言之，杞不足徵也；殷禮吾能言之，宋不足徵也，文獻不足故也。足則吾能徵之矣。」文獻不够他就不講，可見他對以往的史料是要加以審愼的考證的，證據不够就存疑。春秋二百四十二年間的史料，他似乎都能考其眞僞，明其因果關係，定其是非善惡，故其書絕不能視爲村店所用的流水帳簿，而是經過審查史料富有史學

觀點的史學著作。

㉙錢大昕於廿二史劄記序云:「經與史豈有二學哉？昔宣尼贊修六經，而尚書春秋，實爲史家之權輿。漢世劉向父子，校理秘文爲六略，而世本楚漢春秋太史公書漢著紀，列於春秋家，高祖傳孝文傳列於儒家，初無經史之別。厥後蘭臺東現，作者益繁，李充荀勗叙立四部，而經史始分，然不聞陋史而榮經也。」

㉚見文史通義方志立三書議

㉛Arthur Waley 是英國漢學界極出色的翻譯家，譯有詩經、論語、老子、九歌、玄奘法師傳、長春眞人西遊記、吳承恩西遊記、敦煌變文集、鴉片戰爭史料、中國詩選集數種，著有 *Three Ways of Thought in Ancient China, The Poetry and Career of Li Po, The Life and Times of Po Chö-I, Yuan Mei, The Secret History of the Mongols and other Pieces* 等書，文字無不美麗流暢。

㉜西方新起的漢學家，亦有其不可忽視的潛力。他們盡力學習中國的語言文字，儘量瞭解中國的社會文化，然後傾全副精神於專門問題的研究上，致成果頗有可觀。筆者遇到不少此類新起漢學家，如研究南明史學的司徒琳（Lynn A. Struve）小姐，卽爲其一，她能說流利的中國話，能直接閱讀文言文的中國史料，在南明史學的研究上，有不亞於國人者，筆者曾見其部分英文原稿，甚欽羨之，爲文評介，俟諸異日。

參考書目

甲、中文方面

一、專書

尙書		新興書局影印	岳珂相臺五經本
詩經		新興書局影印	岳珂相臺五經本
春秋		新興書局影印	岳珂相臺五經本
左傳		新興書局影印	岳珂相臺五經本
論語		中華書局	四部備要本
孟子		中華書局	四部備要本
呂氏春秋		中華書局	四部備要本
淮南子			盧文弨手校莊逵吉本
史記	司馬遷	藝文印書館	景印淸乾隆武英殿本
漢書	班　固	藝文印書館	景印長沙王氏刊本
後漢書	范　曄	藝文印書館	景印長沙王氏刊本
三國志	陳　壽	藝文印書館	
晉書	房玄齡	藝文印書館	
宋書	沈　約	藝文印書館	景印淸乾隆武英殿本
魏書	魏　收	藝文印書館	景印淸乾隆武英殿本
隋書	魏　徵	藝文印書館	景印淸乾隆武英殿本
舊唐書	劉　昫	藝文印書館	景印淸乾隆武英殿本
新唐書	歐陽修	藝文印書館	景印淸乾隆武英殿本
宋史	脫　脫	藝文印書館	景印淸乾隆武英殿本
金史	脫　脫	藝文印書館	景印淸乾隆武英殿本

元史	宋　濂	藝文印書館	景印清乾隆武英殿本
新元史	柯劭忞	藝文印書館	
明史	張廷玉	藝文印書館	景印清乾隆武英殿本
清史稿	趙爾巽	香港鑄版	據民國十六年刊本
清史列傳		中華書局	
通鑑	司馬光	中華書局	章鈺新校本
通典	杜　佑	新興書局	影印殿本
通志	鄭　樵	新興書局	影印殿本
文獻通考	馬端臨	新興書局	影印殿本
通鑑紀事本末	袁　樞	商務印書館	四部叢刊本
續資治通鑑長編	李　燾	世界書局	
唐會要	王　溥		廣州局重刻聚珍本
明實錄			中央研究院史語所校印
清實錄			
籌辦夷務始末	同治朝	寶鋆等修	光緒六年成書
湘報類纂			上海中華編譯印書館印
湘學新報		唐才常等編	華文書局影印
	光緒二十三年三月廿一日創刊，光緒二十四年八月停刊		
碑傳集	錢儀吉		四庫善本叢書初編
碑傳集補	閔爾昌		四庫善本叢書初編
論衡	王　充		漢魏叢書本
文心雕龍	劉　勰		四部叢刊本
史通	劉知幾		華世出版社本
新唐書糾謬	吳　縝		知不足齋本
五代史記纂誤	吳　縝		知不足齋本
癸辛雜識	周　密	見津逮秘書	
圭齋文集	歐陽玄	商務印書館	四部叢刊本

讀通鑑論	王夫之	中華書局	四部備要本
宋論	王夫之	中華書局	四部備要本
王船山詩文集	王夫之	中華書局	
日知錄	顧炎武	明倫出版社	原抄本
音學五書	顧炎武	福田書海	
顧亭林詩文集	顧炎武	中華書局	
蔣山傭殘稿	顧炎武	世界書局	景印本
南雷文約	黃宗羲	梨洲遺著彙刊	
南雷文案	黃宗羲	梨洲遺著彙刊	
南雷文定	黃宗羲	梨洲遺著彙刊	
南雷詩歷	黃宗羲	梨洲遺著彙刊	
初學集	錢謙益	商務印書館	四部叢刊本
有學集	錢謙益	商務印書館	影印原刊本
曝書亭集	朱彝尊	商務印書館	四部叢刊本
尙書古文疏證	閻若璩	藝文印書館	影印本
戴南山集	戴名世	上海大中書局	
群書疑辨	萬斯同	廣文書局	影印萬斯同刻本
春明夢餘錄	孫承澤	商務印書館	四庫全書珍本
鮚埼亭集	全祖望	商務印書館	四部叢刊本
鮚埼亭集外編	全祖望	商務印書館	四部叢刊本
四庫全書總目提要			萬有文庫本
文史通義	章學誠		國史研究室本
章氏遺書	章學誠	漢聲出版社	影印劉承幹嘉業堂本
戴震文集	戴　震	中華書局	
廿二史考異	錢大昕		潛研堂本
十駕齋養新錄	錢大昕		潛研堂本
潛研堂文集	錢大昕		潛研堂本

十七史商榷	王鳴盛		原刻本
廿二史劄記	趙　翼		湛貽堂原刻本
陔餘叢考	趙　翼		湛貽堂原刻本
考信錄	崔　述	世界書局	在崔東壁遺書內
讀書雜志	王念孫		原刻本
經義述聞	王引之		原刻本
漢學商兌	方東樹	廣文書局	影印浙江書局本
勸學篇	張之洞	兩湖書院印	光緒二十四年
書目答問	張之洞	范希曾補正	新興書局影印原本
經學歷史	皮錫瑞	藝文印書館	
嚴幾道文鈔	嚴　復	上海國華書局印	民國十一年
桃花聖解庵日記	李慈銘	商務印書館	據李氏新校手鈔本影印
中國歷史研究法	梁啓超	商務印書館	民國十一年
中國歷史研究法補編	梁啓超	商務印書館	民國二十二年
清代學術概論	梁啓超	商務印書館	民國十年
中國近三百年學術史	梁啓超	民智書局	民國十五年
章實齋先生年譜	胡　適	姚名達訂補	商務印書館民國二十年
國學概論	章炳麟		河洛出版社景印本
國學略說	章炳麟		河洛出版社景印本
通史新義	何炳松	商務印書館	民國十七年
治史緒論	劉咸炘	尙友書塾	民國十七年
四史知意	劉咸炘	鼎文書局	影印民國二十年原刊本
史諱學例	陳　垣	勵耘書屋	民國二十二年
國史大綱	錢　穆	商務印書館	民國二十九年
中國近三百年學術史	錢　穆	商務印書館	民國二十六年
中國歷史研究法	錢　穆	三民書局	民國五十八年
史學導言	錢　穆	中央日報社	民國五十九年

中國史學名著　錢　穆　三民書局　民國六十二年
中國史學史　金毓黻　商務印書館　民國三十年
中國史學通論　朱希祖　獨立出版社　民國三十二年
廿五史論綱　徐　浩　世界書局　民國三十六年
當代中國史學　顧頡剛　勝利出版社　民國三十六年
國史要義　柳詒徵　中華書局　民國三十七年
史學方法大綱　陸懋德　獨立出版社　民國三十四年
中國史學史　李宗侗　中華文化出版事業委員會　民國四十四年
史學概要　李宗侗　正中書局　民國五十七年
史學講話　張致遠　中華文化出版事業委員會　民國四十一年
歷史方法論　姚從吾　正中書局　民國六十年
史學與世變　沈剛伯　仙人掌出版社　民國五十九年
史學與史學方法　許冠三　環宇出版社　民國六十年
注史齋叢稿　牟潤孫　新亞研究所　民國四十八年
論魏晉以來之崇尚談辯及其影響　牟潤孫　香港中文大學　一九六六年
關於歷代正統問題之爭論　趙令揚　學津出版社　一九七六年
中國史學上之正統論　饒宗頤　龍門書店　一九七七年
歷史與思想　余英時　聯經出版公司　民國六十五年
論戴震與章學誠　余英時　龍門書店　一九七六年
史學方法　王爾敏　東華書局　民國六十六年
清乾嘉時代之史學與史家　杜維運　台大文史叢刊之一　民國五十一年
史學方法論　杜維運　華世出版社　民國六十八年

二、專　文

與范內翰論修書帖　司馬光　附見於明萬曆刊本通鑑
上明鑑綱目館總裁書　楊　椿
萬季野行狀　劉　坊

新史學　梁啓超　飲冰室文集第四册

治學的方法與材料　胡　適　胡適文存第三集

清代學者的治學方法　胡　適　胡適文存第一集

重刻元西域人華化考序　陳寅恪　陳寅恪先生全集上　九思出版公司

中國史綱自序　張蔭麟

評賈德納著『中國舊史學』　朱士嘉　史學年報二卷五期　民國二十七年十二月

西方史學輸入中國考　杜維運　台大歷史系學報第三期　民國六十五年五月

經世思想與中國史學　杜維運　中華學術與現代化叢書第三册史學論集　民國六十六年四月

「國可滅，史不可滅」　杜維運　時報雜誌第四期　民國六十八年十二月三十日至六十九年一月五日

世界各國漢學研究論文集　陶振譽等　國防研究院　民國五十六年

法國漢學論集　李　璜　珠海書院　一九七八年

史料與史學　包遵彭等編　中國近代史論叢第一輯正中書局　民國四十五年

史學通論　大陸雜誌社編　民國四十九年

史學　李宗侗編　見於二十世紀之科學第九輯正中書局　民國五十五年

中國史學史論文選集(一)(二)　杜維運、黃進興編　華世出版社　民國六十五年

中國史學史論文選集(三)　杜維運、陳錦忠編　華世出版社　民國六十九年

史學方法論文選集　杜維運、黃俊傑編　華世出版社　民國六十八年

乙、外文方面

一、專書

Thucydides, *History of the Peloponnesian War,* tran. by Rex Warner, Penguin Books

Leopold von Ranke, *Geschichte der Romanischen und Germanischen Völker von 1494 bis 1535*

Ernst Bernheim, *Lehrbuch der historichen Methode,* 1889

中譯本: 伯倫漢著 陳韜譯 史學方法論 商務印書館 大約初版於民國十五年至二十六年之間

Lord Acton, *A Lecture on the Study of History,* delivered at Cambridge, June, 1895, Macmillan, 1895

Ch. V. Langlois and Ch. Seignobos, *Introduction to the Study of History,* translated by G. G. Berry, Duckworth, 1898

中譯本: 朗格諾瓦、瑟諾博司合著 李思純譯 史學原論 商務印書館 民國十五年初版

Lord Acton, *Lectures on Modern History,* Macmillan, 1906

J. M. Vincent, *Historical Research,* Holt, 1911

J. H. Robinson, *The New History,* Macmillan, 1912

中譯本: 魯賓孫著 何炳松譯 新史學 商務印書館 民國十二年初版

G. P. Gooch, *History and Historians in the Nineteenth Century,* Longmans, 1913

G. M. Trevelyan, Clio, *A Muse and Other Essays,* Longmans, 1913

F. M. Fling, *The Writing of History: An Introduction to Historical Method,* Yale University Press, 1920

中譯本: 弗領著 薛澄清譯 歷史方法論 商務印書館 民國二十二年初版

Benedetto Croce, *History: Its Theory and Practice,* translated by D. Ainslee, Harcourt, Brace, 1921

J. B. Bury, *Selected Essays,* Cambridge University Press, 1930

Herbert Butterfield, *The Whig Interpretation of History,* Bell, 1931

Arnold Toynbee, *A Study of History,* Oxford University Press, 1934–61

C. S. Gardner, *Chinese Traditional Historiography,* Harvard University Press, 1938

Allan Nevins, *The Gateway to History,* 1938; Anchor Books, revised ed., 1962

J. W. Thompson, *A History of Historical Writing,* Macmillan, 1942

R. G. Collingwood, *The Idea of History,* Oxford University Press, 1946

T. W. Wallband and A. M. Taylor, *Civilization Past and Present,* Scott, Foresman and Company, 1949

G. J. Renier, *History: Its Purpose and Method,* Allen & Unwin, 1950

Herbert Butterfield, *History and Human Relations,* Collins, 1951

Marc Bloch, *The Historian's Craft,* translated by Peter Putnam, Alfred A. Knopf, 1954

Isaiah Berlin, *Historical Inevitability,* Oxford University Press, 1954

Denis Sinor, ed., *Orientalism and History,* Heffer, 1954

Geoffrey Barraclough, *History in a Changing World,* Blackwell, 1955

Herbert Butterfield, *Man on His Past: The Study of the History oj Historical Scholarship,* Cambridge University Press, 1955

Pieter Geyl, *Debates with Historians,* Collins, 1955

E. G. Pulleyblank, *Chinese History and World History,* Cambridge University Press, 1955

Fritz Stern, ed., *The Varieties oj History: From Voltaire to the Present,* Meridian Books, 1956

J. B. Bury, *The Science of History*, inaugural lecture of January 1903, in Fritz Stern, ed., The Varieties of History: From Voltaire to the Present

J. Barzun and H. F. Graff, *The Modern Researcher*, 1957; revised ed., Harourt, Brace & World, 1970

Burton Watson, *Ssu-ma Ch'ien: Grand Historian of China*, Columbia University Press, 1958

K. R. Popper, *The Poverty of Historicism*, Routledge & Kegan Paul, 1957

Patrick Gardiner, *Theories of History*, Allen & Unwin, 1959

Hans Meyerhoff, *The Philosophy of History in Our Time*, Anchor Books, 1959

E. H. Dance, *History the Betrayer:* A Study in Bias, Hutchinson, 1960

W. G. Beasley & E. G. Pulleyblank, ed., *Historians of China and Japan*, Oxford University Press, 1961

E. H. Carr, *What is History*? Macmillan, 1961

中譯本: 卡耳著 王任光譯 歷史論集 幼獅文化事業公司 民國六十七年初版

A. G. Widgery, *Interpretations of History:* From Confucius to Toynbee, Allen & Unwin, 1961

H. P. R. Finberg, ed., *Approaches to History*, Routledge, 1962

Louis Gottschalk, ed., *Generalization in the Writing of History*, The University of Chicago Press, 1963

Geoffrey Barraclough, *An Introduction to Contemporary History*, Watts, 1964

E. Balazs, *Chinese Civilization and Bureaucracy*, Yale University Press, 1964

Raymond Dawson, *The Legacy of China,* Oxford at the Clarendon Press, 1964

Alan Richardson, *History Sacred and Profance,* 1964

A. J. Toynbee, *Greek Historical Thought,* Mentor Books, 1965

A. D. Momigliano, *Studies in Historiography,* Weidenfeld & Nicolson, 1966

D. S. Nivison, *The Life and Thought of Chang Hsüeh-Ch'eng (1734–1800)*, Stanford University Press, 1966

K. Bourne & D. C. Watt, ed., *Studies in International History,* Longmans, 1967

G. R. Elton, *The Practice of History,* Cambridge University Press, 1967

A. G. Widgery, *The Meanings in History,* Allen & Unwin, 1967

John Lukacs, *Historical Conciousness, Harper,* 1968

H. V. White, ed., *The Uses of History:* Essays in Intellectual and Social History, Wayne State University Press, 1968

J. H. Plumb, *The Death of the Past,* Macmillan, 1969

Martin Ballard, ed., *New Movements in the Study and Teaching of History,* Temple Smith, 1970

Michael Grant, *The Ancient Historians,* Weidenfeld & Nicolson, 1970

Arthur Marwick, *The Nature of History,* Macmillan, 1970

E. H. Dance, *History for a United World,* Harrap, 1971

Sir H. Butterfield *Cho Yun Hsu & William H. McNeill on Chinese and World History,* The Chinese University of Hong Kong, 1971

W. H. McNeill, *A World History,* 1967; revised edition, Oxford University Press, 1971

Mark Elvin, *The Pattern of the Chinese Past,* 1973

Arnold Toynbee, ed., *Half the World, the History and Culture of China and Japan*, Thames & Hudson, 1973

Beryl Smalley, *Historians in the Middle Ages*, Thames & Hudson, 1974

Denis Twitchett & John K. Fairbank, ed., *The Cambridge History of China*, Volume 10, Late Ch'ing, 1800–1911, Part I, Cambridge University Press, 1978,

Dzo Ching-Chuan, *Sseu-ma T'sien et l'historiographie Chinoise*, Publications Orientalistes de France, 1978

內滕虎次郎　支那史學史　弘文堂　一九五三年

內滕虎次郎　章實齋年譜

內滕虎次郎　中國近世史

二、專　文

H. Butterfield's Preface to the Beacon Edition of Man on His Past, 1960

H. Butterfield, *History and Man's Attitude to the Past*, in the Listener, 21 September, 1961

E. G. Pulleyblank, *Letter to the Editor of the Listener*, in the Listener, 28 September, 1961

H. Butterfield, *Letter to the Editor of the Listener*, in the Listener, 5 October, 1961

Arthur Wright, *Historians of China and Japan*, in the American Historical Review, Vol. LXVII, No. 4, July, 1962

H. Butterfield, *The History of the East*, in History, Vol. XLVII No. 160, June, 1962

Wes Lawrence, *Review of W. H. McNeill's A World History in Cleveland Plain Dealer*

附錄一

西方史家心目中的中國史學　杜維運

(一)

歷史是人類智慧的淵藪，自有文字，人類便可能有歷史。歷史經過演變發展，記錄盈積，異同互見，於是有批評，有研討，而史學出現。世界的遼濶，人類的龐雜，是歷史發生成長的優良背景，而世界眞正歷史悠久的地區，不可多覯；史學是歷史的神髓，由悠久的歷史，蔚爲綿延不絕的史學，舉世求之，尤覺寥寥。中國自春秋以來，史學綿延發展，未嘗一日中絕，其餘力復開闢鄰近國家的史學，如日本、韓國、越南等國，其史學無一不深受中國史學的影響。而西方世界，自希臘時代起，經過羅馬、中世紀、文藝復興而至近代，史學發展成一門燦爛的學問，英、法、德、美等國的史學，都是屬於此一史學系統。舉世史學，値得稱道謳歌者，不出此兩大系統。所以雖說中國史學與西方史學是世界史學的總遺產，也未嘗不可。❶

世界兩大系統的中西史學，相去絕遠，各自獨立發展兩千餘年，不通聲息。以中國方面言之，十九世紀末葉以前，中國史學自闢蹊徑，不受西方史學任何激盪。雖然明清之際，西方學術一度急驟輸入中國，而當時中國朝野人士所欣賞的西學，乃天文、地理、水利、曆法等應用科學，西方史學不曾於此時影響中國。兩種文化接觸，到史學能够互相影響，發生交流作用，是極爲後期的。中國文化與西方文化，千餘年來，有過不少的接觸與相互影響，從中國科學技術的西傳，中國儒家思想的影響及於西方的啓蒙運動，到西方耶穌會敎士的東來，以及晚近西方學術、政治、軍事、經濟勢力的如怒潮湧至，無一不是中西文化交流史上的大事。但是在晚近以前，中國史學不曾流傳到西方去，西方史學也未曾輸入中土。作爲文化中樞的史學，極不易爲人類發現其價值。

西方史學大致在淸政權卽將結束的十餘年間，輸入中國。首先輸入的，應是歷史進化論，這是在光緒二十四年（一八九八）嚴復翻譯赫胥黎（T. H. Huxley, 1825-1895）的天演論（Evolution and Ethics）以後；輸入西方史學的第一功臣，應是晚淸民初言論界驕子梁啓超，他在光緒二十八年（一九〇二）發表的一篇題名叫做「新史學」的文章，係在西方史學的影響下而寫成，尤其深受歷史進化論的影響。自此以後，班漢穆（E. Bernheim, 1854-1937）、朗格諾瓦（Ch. V. Langlois, 1863-1929）、瑟諾博司（Ch. Seignobos, 1854-1942）的史學❷，輸入到中國來了；魯賓孫（J. H. Robinson, 1863-1936）的新史學❸，輸入到中國來了；蘭克（Leopold von Ranke, 1795-1886）的科學治史方法❹，輸入到中國來了；湯恩比（Arnold Toynbee, 1889-1975）的史學❺，也輸入到中國來了❻。兩千年以來中國史學所奠定的權威地位，大爲動搖。模倣西方史學體例，採用西方史學方法，以撰寫新的國史，變爲近代中國史學界的風氣。史家勇於拋棄紀傳、編年二體，而以西方的新紀事本末體作秉筆的極則，選題詳述，溯其淵源，明其發展，而窮其究極；歷史的背景、潮流、影響，皆不憚縷述；人物的傳記，由簡言直敍，而長篇鉅製，曲折舖陳；考訂史料，也不奢言乾嘉傳統，而以德國史家蘭克的語文考證爲準則。發展兩千餘年一向缺乏外來刺激的中國史學，滲入了新成分、新血輪；中國史學由獨立發展，開始與世界史學合流。這是中國史學界的可喜現象，也將大有裨益於世界史學。

史學交流，是雙方的事。中國史學西學，西方史學是否肯東學於中國，是極值懷疑的。中國的絲茶，中國的科學技術，中國的儒家思想，西傳於歐洲，而發生重大的影響；中國博大精深的史學，則西傳是極爲晚近的，且所傳去者有限，所發生的反響，令人沮喪。雖然治中國學問的西方漢學家，所知中國史學較多，但是他們係居於西方史學潮流之外；治亞洲史、非洲史或美洲史的西方史家，對中國史學富有同情的心理，而所知者無幾；執西方史學牛耳的治歐洲史及歐洲國別史的西方史家，對中國史學則採取藐視的態度，他們不認爲歐洲以外，復有所謂博大精深的史學。所以虛心的接受中國史學，對目前西方史學界而言，尙沒有這種意識型態出現。

人類的成見，有其形成的背景。雄據東亞數千年的中國，在歐風美雨尙未來襲之前，絕難承認有優於中國文化的文化存在，也極難想像中國史學之外復有所謂史學。一旦歐風美雨驟至，初則驚愕，繼則迷惘，終至接受或與固有者調和。所以在「全盤西化論」及「中西文化合璧論」出現以前，「西學源出中國論」的風靡一時，是必然的。「西學出於中國，本周秦諸子之遺。」❼「凡諸西學之急需，皆我中邦之素習。」❽此類學說，與「西學無提倡之必要」❾，「何必師事夷人」❿一類反抗西學的論調，在維護中國學術的立場上，是沒有什麼不同的。心目中的偶像，不易破除；知識的限制，形成胸襟的偏狹。

在中國如此，在西方亦然。發源於希臘的西方文化，有其宗教的傳統，有其科學的大原，西方人視之，浩浩乎，蕩蕩乎，舉世未有其比。其史學在其宗教的與科學的文化背景下，發展成一門燦爛輝煌的學問，西方人尤時時以其驕傲於世人。『惟有在西方文化中眞歷史始與起成長』

⑪。「有系統的研究人類過去與現在的事件，始自希臘」⑫。「我們的初祖希臘人與羅馬人，是屬於寫歷史的民族。基督教是一史家的宗教」⑬。「西方社會經常富有歷史觀念，擁有可觀的以往文獻。其性質與數量與任何其他已知文化所存留者不同。所以如此的原始力量，來自希臘的天才。其次的因素，是基督教的影響，基督教始終是寓有歷史意識的，不同於佛教與婆羅門教，或任何其他東方的宗教，不管是古代的或近代的。最後，在過去兩個世紀中，近代科學的進步與物質的發展，深深影響了西方世界的思想。」⑭「在古希臘時代，歷史的研究，興起於科學觀念及物質宇宙的研究開始出現之時。歷史與科學往往在其無數世紀的發展中，不尋常的連在一起。」⑮基督教、科學甚至於希臘人羅馬人，促使西方發展了極爲珍貴的史學，眞歷史自此興起成長，有系統的研究人類過去與現在的事件，自此開始。因此史學是西方文化的產物，西方以外的文化，不可能產生此類史學。有成見如此，中國史學在他們心目中，自然很難佔到重要地位，口頭上的肆意批評，想像中難以縷述，能形之於翰墨，不憚其煩的討論，已是對中國史學相當地注視與珍重了。

西方治歐洲史及歐洲國別史的史家，往往被稱爲正統史家（academic orthodox historians）⑯。在西方史學界，這是最能代表西方史學的一批史家，也是最有西方成見的一批史家。他們接受的西方史學訓練徹底，文字表達的能力高超，其史學著作往往震驚西方史學界，但是他們具有歐洲爲人類歷史重心的成見，歐洲以外的世界及其歷史，在他們的心目中，不佔重要地位。其論及中國史學，也就自然極盡蔑視嘲弄之能事，偶有稱頌，也鮮能觸及中國史學的精華。今謹就湯普森（J. W. Thompson, 1869-1941）、瑞查森（Alan Richardson, 1905-）、艾爾頓（G. R. Elton, 1921）、盧克斯（John Lukacs, 1923-）、浦朗穆（J.

H. Plumb, 1911-)、葛蘭特（Michael Grant, 1914-)、馬爾威克（Arthur Marwick, 1936-)、白特費爾德（Herbert Butterfield, 1900-）諸家所論及者，以見一斑。湯普森著有「中世紀後期歐洲經濟社會史」（Economic and Social History of Europe in the Later Middle Ages, 1300-1350, 1931)、「中世紀歐洲導論」(An Introduction to Medieval Europe, 300-1500, 1937)、「史籍史」(A History of Historical Writing, 1942）諸書；瑞查森著有「聖經研究序論」(Preface to Bible-study, 1950)、「宗教史與世俗史」(History Sacred and Profane, 1964）諸書；艾爾頓著有「一二〇〇年至一六四〇年的英國」(England, 1200-1640, 1969)、「都德王朝下的英國（England under the Tudors, 1974)、「改革與宗教改革：一五〇九年至一五五八年的英國」(Reform and Reformation: England, 1509-1558, 1977)、「歷史的訓練」(The Practice of History, 1967）諸書；盧克斯著有「最後的歐洲戰爭」（The Last European War: September 1939—December 1941)、「歷史意識」(Historical Consciousness, 1968）諸書；浦朗穆著有「十八世紀的英國」(England in the Eighteenth Century, 1950)、「華爾波爾爵士」(Sir Robert Walpole, 1956)、「一六七五至一七二五年間英國政治安定之發展」(The Growth of Political Stability in England, 1675-1725, 1967)、「過去的死亡」(The Death of the Past, 1960）諸書；葛蘭特著有「羅馬世界」(The World of Rome, 1960)、「歐洲文化」(The Civilization of Europe, 1965)、「古代史家」(The Ancient Historians, 1970)、「羅馬史」(History of Rome, 1973)、「羅馬帝國的衰落；一個新的審察」(The Fall of Roman Empire; a Reappraisal, 1976）諸書；馬爾威克著有「全面戰爭世紀的不列顛：一九〇〇年至一九六七年間的戰爭、和平與社會變遷」(Britain in the Century of

Total War: War, Peace, and Social Change, 1900-1967, 1968)、「歷史的性質」(The Nature of History, 1970)、「寫歷史的基本問題」(Basic Problems of Writing History, 1971)、「一九一四年至一九七〇年英國社會的爆炸」(The Explosion of British Society, 1914-1970, 1971) 諸書；白特費爾德著有「輝格黨的歷史解釋」(The Whig Interpretation of History, 1931)、「英國人及其歷史」(The Englishman and His History, 1944)、「近代科學的起源」(The Origins of Modern Science, 1949)、「基督教與歷史」(Christianity and History, 1949)、「歷史與人類的關係」(History and Human Relations, 1951)、「人類論過去」(Man on His Past, 1955)、「喬治三世與史家」(George III and the Historians, 1957) 諸書，皆可視爲西方正統史家。

(二)

認爲產生史學最基本的重視歷史的態度與觀念爲西方文化所獨有，而中國則極度缺乏，差不多是西方正統史家一致的論調。

瑞查森於「宗教史與世俗史」一書中云：

「事實上，亞洲與非洲正迅速歐化；其億萬人開始參與『歷史』。這種參與，不僅爲接受近代的科學與技術，也意味着近代歷史觀念 (modern historical mindedness) 的獲得，雖然後者較不顯著。在過去，亞洲文化很少歷史的意識 (sense of history)。」⑰

艾爾頓於「歷史的訓練」一書中云：

「在印度與中國的古典思潮裡，隱藏着顯著漠視歷史的態度。任何史學史有待注視希臘與猶太，一個主要學術大樹 (intellectual tree) 的根柢所在。沒有其他原始宗教作品，像舊約 (Old Testament) 那樣嚴格的編年，那樣富歷史性，明白記錄上帝爲後代的命運作安排；基督教的後裔在所有宗教中，爲惟一自歷史事件引出其典據（authority）者。在另一方面，有系統的研究人類過去與現在的事件，始自希臘。某類的歷史，已在各地研究、撰寫，從埃及與秘魯的編年史，至愛斯基摩人（Eskimos）與波里尼西亞人（Polynesians）的神話，皆是。但是祗有源自猶太與希臘的文化，歷史受到重視，歷史成爲將來的導師，歷史變作宗教的根據，歷史協助說明人類的生存與目的。」⓲

盧克斯於「歷史意識」一書中云:

「歷史思想（historical thinking）仍然是屬於『歐洲的』或『西方的』。」⓳

「我相信在過去三、四世紀，我們的文化最重要的發展，不僅爲科學方法的應用，同時爲歷史意識的增長。」⓴

白特費爾德於序其「人類論過去」一書云;

「雖然我們常常自我提醒，西方文化獨能發展自然科學，可是我們每每忽略西方文化同樣地以富有歷史觀念（historical-mindedness），而卓然與世不同。古代的中國，科學工藝甚發達，歷史著作極豐富，但是未臻於相當於西方十七世紀科學革命與十八世紀末十九世紀初史學運動（The Historical Movement of the late eighteenth and early nineteenth centuries）的境界（亦未有若何跡象將能臻此境界）。」㉑

於「歷史與人類對過去的態度」（History and Man's Attitude to the Past）一文㉒中則云:

「我相信沒有任何文化比西歐一四五〇年到一八五〇年間的文化更富歷史觀念。」㉓

種種論調，皆强調源自猶太與希臘的文化，也就是所謂西方文化，最重視歷史，最富有歷史觀念（或歷史意識，推其極致是歷史思想），其他文化則否，所謂「亞洲文化很少歷史的意識」，所謂「在印度與中國的古典思潮裡，隱藏着顯著漠視歷史的態度」，所謂中國「未臻於相當於西方十七世紀科學革命與十八世紀末十九世紀初史學運動的境界」，都說明在他們心目中，中國文化與其他任何文化，其重視歷史的態度與觀念，遠不能與西方文化相比擬。以致很自然的他們肯定」「有系統的研究人類過去與現在的事件，始自希臘」；「惟有在西方文化中，眞歷史（gennine history）始興起成長」㉔；「系統的研究歷史（the systematic study of history），視歷史爲一種學術（history as a discipline），是最近的事，爲歐洲與北美洲大學在十九世紀所創立。」㉕

不同的論調，發自馬爾威克與白特費爾德。馬爾威克於「歷史的性質」一書中云：

「我們的西方文化，從猶太基督教（Judaeo-Christianity）繼承了一種特別强烈的歷史意識（a particularly strong sense of history）。但是醉心歷史與依賴歷史，非僅西方爲然。回教的歷史學派，與偉大的中國歷史學派（the great Chinese school of history），皆爲其文化中的主要成分。」㉖

他承認了「偉大的中國歷史學派」，但是「系統的研究歷史，視歷史爲一種學術」，他仍認爲係西方文化的產品。（引文見上）

白特費爾德前後有不同的論調，當他在一九六〇年與一九六一年發表上述言論不久，一九六二年的六月，他又寫了一篇題名「東方的歷史」（The History of the East）的文章，大大修正了他的論調：

「與世界其他地區相比，中國與西歐都發展了富有科學特性與歷史觀念的文化。」㉗

不過他仍認爲：

「中國像是永未臻於相當於十七世紀的科學革命，亦永未現出向此一方向移動的跡象。直到直接受到西方影響之前，難以避免的結論，爲中國亦永未臻於相當於十八世紀末十九世紀初的史學革命——蘭克及其前哲的治史技術在此革命中確立。有兩事爲西方世界的特產，當西方與其遭遇的問題及經驗奮鬥時，不僅自過去吸取知識，而且根據過去，肆力研究。」㉘

一九七一年他到香港中文大學參加中國歷史與世界歷史的討論會，以「世界歷史與文化的比較研究」(Universal History and the Comparative Study of Civilization) 爲題，發表了進一步的意見:

「有些民族與文化，永無意於知其過去，他們或爲視發生於過去的事件若泡沫的哲學或宗教所支配——一切像在風中飛舞的枯葉，了無意義。有些民族，像是離說神話故事的階段不遠——不渴望更好，沒悟及可以幾於更好。兩個大的例外，一是巨大的中國文化，產生了可觀的歷史文獻，對世界有其永恆價值，一是我們所謂西方文化，溯源至古典的希臘，遠一點可追至古代的美索不達米亞與埃及。但是在自然科學的發展上，中國文化與西方文化是同樣重要的，同樣在各個時代爲世界的領導者。」㉙

白特費爾德論調的轉變，關鍵在於一九六一年至一九六二年之間，他看了浦立本 (E. G. Pulleyblank) 與畢斯利 (W. G. Beasley) 合編的「中日史家」(Historians of China and Japan) 一書，他的以研究中國科學技術史而馳名世界的老友李約瑟 (Joseph Needham)，也告訴了他一些有關中國歷史與科學的知識。由此看起來，西方正統史家對中國史學種種不良批評，種因於固有的成見上，也種因於知識的限制上。不眞知而又無闕疑精神，自然就鑿空立論了。

（三）

西方正統史家很肯定的認爲中國史學的發展，永遠沒有突破通往眞歷史的最後障礙——希望窺探往事的眞相，永遠沒有發展批判史學，永遠沒有意思視歷史爲客觀的瞭解。

在這方面，浦朗穆與白特費爾德發表的意見最多。浦朗穆於「過去的死亡」一書中云：

「自文藝復興以來，史家逐漸決定致力於瞭解曾經發生的往事，爲瞭解而瞭解，不是爲宗教，不是爲國運，不是爲道德，也不是爲神聖化的制度；……史家日趨於窺探往事的眞相，而希望自此建立有歷史根據的社會轉變的軌跡。這是一西方的發展，本人認爲如此。……中國史學的發展，永遠沒有突破通往眞歷史的最後障礙——希望窺探往事的眞相，不顧由此引發與利用過去的時賢衝突。中國人追逐博學，然永遠沒有發展批判史學（the critical historiography）。批判史學是過去兩百年西方史學的重要成就。至於中國人永遠沒有意思視歷史爲客觀的瞭解（objective understanding），則更不待細說了。」㉚

白特費爾德則云：

「我們今天很難對一種未能深入史家所用的原始資料且用複雜的設備以批評此類資料的史學，視之爲一種眞正的批判史學。……但是中國史家是否發現了以新原始證據考核其史學傳統的方式，或者追尋一種比傳統自我符合更進一步的方法，不够清楚。中國史學與歐洲一四五〇年至一七五〇年間史學，蓋在伯仲之間。近代西方用於原始資料的批判性的設備，一定會使中國的歷史寫作與研究，發生很大的變化。」㉛

他們持論如此，在於他們認爲中國有「一切確定」的觀念，相信凡屬歷史記載，皆完全客觀。浦朗穆云：

「歐洲知識份子，即使在第四、五世紀，亦有兩個過去在競爭。在啓蒙運動時代，他有三個。兩個其他的過去經常在隱秘接觸，或公開衝突，各深深自我陶醉，但在解釋方面不同，在應用資料方面也不同——猶太人的過去與回敎人的過去。因此歐洲人的過去，永未擁有一致（coherence）或統一（unity），若中國人的一切確定者然。這就是歐洲爲什麽能發展批判歷史（critical history）的關鍵所在了。歐洲眞的是應當發展出批判歷史的。」㉜

白特費爾德云：

「在中國史學後面，有一假想，即凡屬歷史記載（historical record），皆完全客觀。客觀被認爲僅僅將事實登錄上（registering the facts）即可獲得。……客觀事實（the objective facts）一旦被他們列入記載，即有其獨立性，所有未來史家所必須做的是重複旣已確定的敍述，或者或許是從旣已確定的敍述中去自己選取。」㉝

這就無怪以傑作如史記，在他們心目中，爲「令人百思不解之作」，非他們「所謂歷史」了！「其大部分爲編纂，司馬遷自其所能發現之古典資料中，逐一鈔錄，略作文字上的潤色，大部分則無條件接受，傳奇與眞理混而爲一。」㉞似是而非之論，讀後令人擲書三歎！

（四）

西方正統史家也屢屢强調：

中國的考據學沒有到達西方的境界，未能對證據作科學的評價與分析；中國歷史永遠沒有發展自我批評與發現的方法，無情的考驗通則，

有目的的蒐求文獻以證明假設;

中國史學未能到達西方「綜合」的境界，也沒有發展歷史解釋的藝術;

中國的修史，太官方化；中國歷史太有特徵被稱爲「資治歷史」。

白特費爾德云:

「從公元前第二世紀起，中國即有考據學（textual criticism）的產生。……惟此一考據學的發展，未能達到一較高境界，不配我們稱之爲批評。換言之，即爲未能對證據作科學的評價與分析。其中原因之一，爲中國的特殊修史制度，這是中國史學與世不同的主要原因之一，已曾有人作過重要的研究。

決定性的因素，在於中國的修史太爲一種官方事業了，太爲官僚化的組織了，歷史被視爲統治者的有效輔導，大體上歷史亦由官吏而寫，爲官吏而寫。中國歷史太有特徵被稱之爲資治歷史（civil service history）了。」㉟

「中國人能做龐大的分類工作，能編纂驚人的百科全書，並且能出產他們數不盡的瑣碎餖飣的地方史（local history），但是他們不能到達我們所謂的『綜合』(synthesis) 的境界，他們沒有發展歷史解釋的藝術 (the art of historical explanation)。不斷的襲用舊史原文，任憑私意的選用文獻而卽目之爲可信（取此而捨彼的原因不予以討論)，顯示出一牢不可破的歷史標準（a firm historical canon）已經確立，考據限於自我證明的工作上，而不科學地窺尋史學的眞相與看看史料與實際發生的事實符合的程度。所謂官方歷史（official history)，實際上祇含着一些歷史的意味，是由委員會產生的，這夠令人驚訝的了！中國豐富的史著，像是備官僚偶然的參攷，而不是較廣大群衆的普通讀物。我時常懷疑，當西方史學脫離蘭克（Ranke）的一些健全的指導時，是否不走此同一的路線？這裡或許是一個更進一步的原因，爲什麼西方學者應該審查東方。研究東方學問的人可能不原諒我，但是如果我說西方學者必須注意中國僅是爲了習知歷史學如何可能走錯路就好了，他們將會了解我。」㊱

浦朗穆云：

「歷史在中國所扮演的角色，與在西方所扮演的角色，其差別是顯而易見的。中國以朝代與朝代相接，而積有大量歷史檔案，其浩繁與西歐的歷史資料相埒，且所涉及時間之長過之。惟中國運用此類資料的方法，與綜合此類資料的方法，代代相因，無基本上的變化，二十世紀早期的中國學者運用歷史資料，其實際目的，無殊於唐朝或漢朝。在其傳統綜合的基本原則範圍內，他們偶而能瞥及超乎朝代更替的制度的發展，但是中國歷史永遠沒有發展自我批評與發現（self-criticism and discovery）的方法，無情的考驗通則（the relentless testing of generalization），有目的的蒐求文獻以證明假設，而此爲西方歷史的特徵。因此，當傳統中國史學在十九世紀末葉開始崩潰之時，其結果是混亂的。中國史家在西方學生的協助下，擷取西方的通則，以應用於中國材料，特別是馬克斯主義者的。但是這頗像高等化學的細密概念（the detailed concepts of advanced chemistry），被應用到大量新發現的生物資料上去一樣。西方歷史的通則，是經過窮年累月耐心的辨難而得出的精確產品，在其間通則與新資料不斷切磋。有意的應用此類通則到相關的中國資料上，殆不切實際。一旦舊的通則被取代了，中國歷史就碎屍萬斷了。自然朝代的敍事仍在，然其解釋則煙消霧失。」㊲

葛蘭特云:

「波力比阿斯 (Polybius) 的作品，與其他尚存的古代作品相比較，很顯然的是政治家的示例書 (a case-book)，頗像稍後一兩世紀出現而意在訓練文官的中國史一樣。(創自司馬遷，約公元前一世紀。)」㊳

盧克斯云:

「西方以外，史家學術 (historianship) 的不足，頗爲顯然，不僅由於方法的缺乏，也由於智力 (mentality) 的歧異；不僅由於『記錄』的殘闕，也由於文化的不同，其所追憶其過去者亦殊異。這是西方歷史所以在世界歷史中比較重要的原因之一。縱使在今天，西方的某人，可以忽視大部分的東方歷史，而對於歷史進展的瞭解，所失者甚少。相反則不然: 沒有東方智者 (intelligent oriental)，可以不知西方歷史，尤其是歐洲歷史。」㊴

關於考據學在中國所發展到的境界，白特費爾德的論調，也是前後不同的，「有證據可以證明中國史家雅欲批評其前代史家的敍事，甚或具有了懷疑所有過去作者的態度，考據學發展到一崇高境界，似昭然若揭，中國史家無疑問已臻於所謂智力的洗練 (intellectual refinement)」㊵，當白氏稍爲通曉中國史學時，他已不再堅持中國考據學的發展，沒有達到一較高的境界了。

(五)

西方正統史家也終於承認了中國史學精細，中國史學重視文獻，中國歷史資料浩繁。

浦朗穆既認爲「中國以朝代與朝代相接，而積有大量歷史檔案，其浩繁與西歐的歷史資料相埒，且所涉及時間之長過之」，復於「過去的

死亡」一書中云:

「竭盡能力閱讀翻譯作品，我已知曉中國史學的精細，知曉中國史學的重視文獻，知曉中國史學的發展其制度變遷的觀念，已大致能排除借歷史以衍出的天命觀念。中國唐代史家顯然遠優於恩哈德 (Einhard) 或奧圖 (Otto of Freising)，或任何中世紀早期編年家，就像中國聖人在技藝或行政方面的優越一樣。」㊶

白特費爾德既認爲中國「歷史著作極豐富」，「巨大的中國文化，產生了可觀的歷史文獻，對世界有其永恆價值」，也認爲「中國人能做龐大的分類工作，能編纂驚人的百科全書，並且能出產他們數不盡的瑣碎餖飣的地方史」，雖然後者含有相當大的貶抑成分。像一九四〇年代寫史籍史 (A History of Historical Writing) 的湯普森那樣，不清楚中國有所謂史書與史料者㊷，在今天的西方，似乎 (也應當) 已少有其人了。

(六)

中國史學與歐洲一四五〇年至一七五〇年間史學，蓋在伯仲之間，是西方正統史家最大的一個結論。他們承認中國史學超過了西方的中世紀 (中國唐代史家遠優於恩哈德或奧圖，或任何中世紀早期編年家)，但並不承認能與十八世紀末期以後的西方史學並駕齊驅。屢談中國史學的白特費爾德持論如此，竭力想窺中國史學之秘的浦朗穆，也以此作其最大的信念。所以整個看起來，西方正統史家對中國史學雖有稱譽的地方，基本上則是毀多於譽的。很明顯的他們不承認中國史學能與西方史學分庭抗禮，超過了中世紀，徘徊於歐洲一四五〇年至一七五〇年之間，但是西方史學的偉大時代——近兩百年，則未能企及。他們所肯定的中國史學的缺陷，促使中國史學落於西方史學之後。相信凡屬歷史記載，皆完全客觀，不希望窺探往事的眞相，不採取批評的態度，復缺乏重視歷史的觀念，中國史學怎能比美西方史學？綜合的境界不高，歷史解釋的藝術沒有發展，修史又是官方事業，中國雖歷史文獻浩繁，歷史著作豐富，其史學又豈能望及西方史學的項背？他們肯說「中國史學與歐洲一四五〇年至一七五〇年間史學，蓋在伯仲之間」，已是一種過分的恭維了！

（七）

他山之石，可以攻錯。西方史家以另一文化背景，品評中國史學，對中國史學而言，是極富啓發作用的。西方正統史家直指中國史學沒有到達西方綜合的境界，沒有發展歷史解釋的藝術，即是十分中肯之論，中國史家應拜受其言，而思所以創新。但是西方史家中的所謂正統史家一群，他們對中國史學的瞭解，是極爲間接的，僅憑閱讀翻譯作品及一般印象，又出於牢不可破的成見，其論斷往往荒謬離奇，盡失學術水準。所以當他們頌揚近代西方文化最富歷史觀念，而批評中國文化極度缺乏重視歷史的觀念與態度時，殊不知重視歷史的文化，中國已發展達數千年之久了（中國自商周時代起，存史的觀念，即已發達，宋元以後，「國可滅，史不可滅」的濃厚歷史觀念，極爲流行。）；當他們認爲文藝復興以後西方史學已突破通往眞歷史的最後障礙——希望窺探往事的眞相，已發展出批判史學時，殊不知中國的希望窺探往事眞相的史學意識，早在上古時代，即已形成，其批判史學的出現，也已有兩千年以上的歷史了（據事直書爲中國史學的一大傳統，形成於上古時代，對證據作科學評價與分析的考據學，也在兩千年前出現）；中國的修史，非盡如他們所謂純爲官方事業；中國史學的珍貴，也決非僅在史料的浩繁。至於整個比較中西史學，兩者實難分軒輊，論史學起源之早，成熟之速，綿延之久，範圍之濶，西方實遜於中國；若就晚近數世紀西方新與史學而言，其治史方法的爭奇鬥艷，其史學體例的五光十彩，其蒐集史料、批評史料的富有科學精神，其分析史實、解釋史實的獨擅精密系統，也似非中國所能望及。凡此，則有待以專文或專書詳論了。

❶中國史學與西方史學之外，世界上自有其他的史學，如阿拉伯史學即爲其一，但皆難與中西史學分庭抗禮。

❷有西方史學方法論鼻祖之稱的 Ernst Bernheim 於一八八九年出版「史學方法論」(*Lehrbuch der historichen Methode*)；法國史家 Charles Victor Langlois 及 Charles Seignobos 合著「史學原論」(*Introduction aux E'tudes Historiques*)，於一八九八年出版。兩者皆有中文譯本。

❸J. H. Robinson 的 *The New History* 出版於一九一二年，中國史家何炳松於一九二一年將其譯成中文。

❹Leopold von Ranke 的科學治史方法，甚風行中土。

❺Arnold Toynbee 的大著「歷史研究」(*A Study of History*) 極受國人注意，爲文介紹及節譯之者甚多。

❻有關西方史學輸入中國的詳情，參見拙文「西方史學輸入中國考」，載於台灣大學歷史學系學報第三期，民國六十五年五月。

❼皮錫瑞語，見湘報類纂乙集卷下頁三

❽江標變學論

❾曾廉語，見籌辦夷務始末，同治朝，卷四七，頁二四

❿倭仁語，見同上。

⓫John Lukacs, *Historical Consciousness*, 1968, p. 23

⓬G. R. Elton, *The Practice of History*, 1967, p. 12

⓭Marc Bloch, *The Historian's Craft*, 1954, p. 4

⓮J. W. Thompson, *Preface to a History of Historical Writing*, 1942, p. vii

⓯Herbert Butterfield, *Universal History and the Comparative Study of Civilization*, in Sir Herbert Butterfield Cho Yun Hsu & William H. McNeill on Chinese and World History, 1971, p. 20

⑯E. G. Pulleyblank, *Chinese History and World History*, 1955

⑰Alan Richardson, *History Sacred and Profane*, 1964, p. 268

⑱G. R. Elton, *The Practice of History*, 1967, pp. 11-12

⑲John Lukacs, *Historical Consciousness*, 1968, p. 2

⑳Ibid, p. 5

㉑Herbert Butterfield's Preface to the Beacon Edition of Man on His Past, 1960

㉒一九六一年白特費爾德在倫敦大學亞非研究院（School of Oriental and African Studies）講「歷史與人類對過去的態度」(History and Man's Attitude to the Past)，同年九月二十一日將講詞簡化，復在英國廣播公司廣播，聽衆（Listener）雜誌刊出其文。

㉓Herbert Butterfield, *History and Man's Attitude to the Past*, in Listener, 21 September, 1961

㉔John Lukacs, *Historical Consciousness*, p. 23

㉕Arthur Marwick, *The Nature of History*, 1970, p. 15

㉖Ibid., p. 13

㉗Herbert Butterfield, *The History of East*, in History, vol. XLVII No. 160, June, 1962, p. 162

㉘Ibid.

㉙Herbert Butterfield, *Universal History and the Comparative Study of Civilization*, in Sir Herbert Butterfield Cho Yun Hsu & William H. Mcneill on Chinese and World History, 1971, p. 20

㉚J. H. Plumb, *The Death of the Past*, 1969, pp. 12-13

㉛Herbert Butterfield, *The History of East, in History*, vol XLVII No. 160, June 1962, p. 165

㉜J. H. Plumb, *The Death of the Past*, pp. 89-90

㉝Herbert Butterfield, *History and Man's Attitude to the Past*, in Listener, 21 September, 1961

㉞J. H. Plumb, *The Death of the Past*, pp. 18-19

㉟Herbert Butterfield, *History and Man's Attitude to the Past*, in Listener, 21 September, 1961

㊱Ibid.

㊲J. H. Plumb, *The Death of the Past*, pp. 87-88

㊳Michael Grant, *The Ancient Historians*, 1970, p. 156

㊴John Lukacs, *Historical Consciousness*, p. 24

㊵Herbert Butterfield, *The History of East, in History*, vol. XLVII No. 160, June 1962, p. 165

㊶J. H. Plumb, *The Death of the Past*, p. 13

㊷湯普森 (J. W. Thompson, 1869-1941) 於「史籍史」(*A History of Historical Writing*) 一書裡面，談到中國史，使人感覺他似乎極不清楚中國史書出版的情況：

「唯一用蒙古文寫成的蒙古史，而存在於今日者，係出於 Sanang Setsen 之手，其人爲蒙古人，皈依佛教。該書原稿於一八二〇年在西藏發現，其寫成有賴於蒐輯中國編年史中的資料。在遠東方面，尤其在中國方面，蒙古史的知識，盡於此而已。」

("The sole history of the Mongols written in the Mongols language which has survived is that of Sanang Setsen, who was a Mongol convert to Buddhism. The original was discovered in Tibet in 1820. This book, supplemented by some information gleaned from Chinese annals, is the sum total of our knowledge of the history of the Mongols in Far Asia, especially in China." p. 354)

湯氏如不憚煩，略一翻檢所謂中國編年史及蒙古史，當知其誤謬的嚴重。誤謬的形成，由於湯氏不曾看過有關中國史的書，也不知中國史書的浩如煙海，所以便如此草率言之了。

附錄二

西方史學輸入中國考　杜維運

一、概說

起源於希臘的西方史學，與中國史學，是兩種不同文化的產物。以儒家學術思想爲主流的中國文化，產生了極富人文主義色彩的中國史學；而西方文化中的宗教與科學，促使西方史學從最富神學色彩，變至講求精確與客觀。綜合各自獨立發展兩千餘年的中西史學，取其精英，去其糟粕，將是人類史學上的盛事。

文化的接觸，到史學發生交流現象，是極爲後期的。中國文化與西方文化，千餘年來，有過不少的接觸與相互影響，從中國科學技術的西傳，中國儒家思想的影響及於西方的啓蒙運動，到西方耶穌會敎士的東來，以及晚近西方學術、政治、軍事、經濟勢力的如怒潮湧至，無一不是中西文化交流史上的大事。但是在晚近以前，中國史學不曾流傳到西方去，西方史學也未曾輸入中土。作爲文化中樞的史學，極不易爲人類發現其價值。

發現對方史學的價值，積極予以吸收，首先在中國而不在西方。一九四二年美國史學家湯姆森（J. W. Thompson）出版其大著史籍史（A History of Historical Writing）時，似乎不甚淸楚中國有史學著作；❶一九六一年英國史學家白特費爾德（Herbert Butterfield, 1900-）在倫敦大學亞非硏究院（School of Oriental and African Studies）講

「歷史與人類對過去之態度」(History and Man's Attitude to the Past) 則云:「我相信沒有任何文化比西歐一四五〇年到一八五〇年間的文化，更富歷史觀念。為窺尋此一期間西歐文化的淵源，我們必須注意到亞洲去；但是知道什麼因素促使我們文化的發展如此特殊，也同樣的有用。」「如果東方學者能從西方史學獲得啓示，那麼西方學者非到他瞭解了東方，將永不能領悟到重要問題的神奧處。一旦我們試着超越我們自己的思想界，等量齊觀地看中西兩大史學系統，主要的分歧，便暴露無遺。此兩文化對歷史與傳統皆有其可怕的成見；兩者歷史精神太不相同，兩者思想系統（太不相同的系統）太複雜。」❷一直到一九六九年浦朗穆（J. H. Plumb）仍然說:「自文藝復興以來，史學家逐漸決定致力於瞭解曾經發生的往事，為瞭解而瞭解，不是為宗教，不是為國運，不是為道德，也不是為神聖化的制度；……史學家日趨於窺探往事的眞相，而希望自此建立有歷史根據的社會轉變的軌跡。這是一西方的發展，本人認為如此。部分我所尊敬的史學家，將持異議，他們會感覺我過分誇大了中國與西方史學的區別。竭盡能力閱讀翻譯作品，我已知曉中國史學的精細，知曉中國史學的重視文獻，知曉中國史學的發展其制度變遷的觀念，已大致能排除借歷史以衍出的天命觀念。中國唐代史學家顯然遠優於恩哈德（Einhard），或奧圖（Otto of Freising），或任何中世紀早期編年家，就像中國聖人在技藝或行政方面的優越一樣。但是中國史學的發展，永遠沒有突破通往眞歷史的最後障礙——希望窺探往事的眞相，不顧由此引發與利用過去的時賢衝突。中國人追逐博學，然永遠沒有發展富批評性的史學（the critical historiography）。富批評性的史學，是過去兩百年西方史學的重要成就。至於中國人永遠沒有意思視歷史為客觀的瞭解（objective understanding），則更不待細說了。」❸西方史學家在西方逐漸失去軍事、政治、經濟方面的優勢時，仍然不肯輕易承認中國史學曾到達西方史學所到達的最高境界。虛心的接受中國史學，對目前西方史學界而言，尚沒有這種意識型態出現。

反觀中國則不然。兩千餘年唯我獨尊的中國史學，在西方軍事、政治、經濟的威勢下，其藩籬被衝破了，其所奠定的權威地位，開始動搖了，接受西方史學理論，採用西方史學方法，以從事於研究國史，變爲中國近代史學界的風氣。迄於今日，已極少有人否定西方史學的重要性，懷疑中國史學的價值與成就者，則大有其人。中國史學無疑問已面臨最嚴重的考驗階段，它能否歷久常新，與西方史學同放萬丈光采於世界史學之林，應是今後學術上極值注意的大事。

學術是天下的公器，綜合中西史學，以開創今後更進步更豐富的具世界性的新史學，應是人類學術史上的新猷，而首先承此重任者，必是以泱泱文化作背景的中國史學家。今謹略事爬梳資料，作西方史學輸入中國考，期以說明近代中國史學界接受西方史學的程度，進一步的綜合大業，則期之時賢。

二、西方史學輸入中國的初期——晚清

1. 晚清思想界與西方史學的輸入

西方史學輸入中國的確定時間，是一個頗難有明確答案的問題。十九世紀中葉以後，中國朝野人士，由於受西方的壓迫，紛言變法圖强，清廷也屢屢派遣留學生赴海外留學，然當時留學生在海外所攻習的科目，爲軍事、教育、經濟、政治等等，朝野人士所談的變法，也不出軍事、教育、經濟、政治等範圍以外，當時從未有談變史學以及在海外專門攻習西方史學者。所以在李鴻章等如火如荼推行洋務運動之際，西方史學似未曾輸入中國。

西方史學的輸入，大致在清政權卽將結束之十餘年間，此與晚淸思

想界有極密切的關係。

晚清是中國新舊思想互相激盪的一個時代，保守的人士，對於日漸向中國輸入的西學，持極力反抗的態度。如倭仁云：

「竊聞立國之道，尙禮義不尙權謀，根本之圖，在人心不在技藝。今求一藝之末，而又奉夷人爲師，無論夷人詭譎，未必傳其精巧，卽使敎者誠敎，學者誠學，所成就者不過術數之士。古今來未聞有恃術數而能起衰振弱者也。天下之大，不患無才，如以天文算學必須講習，博采旁求，必有精其術者，何必夷人？何必師事夷人？」❹

曾廉亦云：

「中人之學西學，不過爲通西人語言、文字諸藝術，借以刺取外國之國情，奪其利權而制之。」

「故必心術端愨而學問通達，學之始有用。無學之人學之，但知順夷意而變我民，使人相率入于夷狄；然苟其人爲學問通達，不一定能學外國語言文字，故西學實無提倡之必要。」❺

此種觀念，普及於一般讀書人的腦海中，對於接受西方史學，實爲莫大的障礙。於是稍有世界性眼光者，倡出西學源出中國之說，如江標云：

「凡諸西學之急需，皆我中邦之素習。蓋格致之學，本大學之所兆基，特機械之心，爲我儒所不尙耳。至於合中西爲一學，則異柯同本，異派同源，並非舍己而從人，背師而他學也。」❻

皮錫瑞則云：

「今之學者，有漢學，有宋學。講漢學者，有西漢今文之學，有東漢古文之學。講宋學者，有程朱之學，有陸王之學。近日又以專講中學者爲舊學，兼講西學者爲新學。學者黨同伐異，總以學自己是，人家不是。平心而論，漢學未嘗不講義理，宋學未嘗不講訓詁。同是師法孔子，何必入室操戈。西學出於中國，本周秦諸子之遺，莊列關尹諸書所載，是其明證。史記漢書皆云七國之亂，疇人子弟，分散海外。大約此時中國失傳，而外國得之。今仍傳入中國。仲尼問官於郯子曰，天子失官，學在四夷。據聖人之言，西學苟可采用，不必過分畛域。總之，無論何項學術，皆當自求心得，不當是己非人。意有不同，不妨周咨博訪，互相印證，以折衷於一是。卽學派宗旨，不可强合，儘可各尊所聞，各行所知，不妨有異同，不必爭門戶。」❼

西學與中學，本爲兩個世界的文化產物，絕不相同，其間雖有類似，祇是在「東海西海有聖人焉，此心同，此理同」的情況下，所自然形成的。一定說西學源出中國，實極盡牽强附會之能事。不過晚淸流行的西學源出中國說，另有其積極的意義，卽爲西學的輸入作護符。「合中西爲一學，則異柯同本，異派同源，並非舍己而從人，背師而他學。」「西學苟可采用，不必過分畛域。」此適可破保守派「何必師事夷人」、「西學實無提倡之必要」的主張。所以到眞正通西學的嚴復，便進一步說：

「夫西學之最爲切實，而執其例可以御蕃變者，名、數、質、力四者之學是已。而吾易則名數以爲經，質力以爲緯，而合而名之曰易。大宇之內，質力相推，非質無以見力，非力無以呈質。凡力皆乾也，凡質皆坤也。奈端（Sir Isaac Newton）動之例三：其一曰：靜者不自動，動者不自止。動路必直，速率必均。此所謂曠古之慮。自其例出，而後天學明人事利者也。而易則曰：乾其靜也專，其動也直。後二百年有斯賓塞爾（Herbert Spencer）者，以天演自然言化，著書造論，貫天地人而一理之，此亦晚近之絕作也。其為天演界說曰：翕以合質，闢以出力，始簡易而終雜糅。而易則曰：坤其靜也翕，其動也闢。至於全力不增減之說，則有自彊不息為之先。凡動必復之說，則有消息之義居其始。而易不可見，乾坤或幾乎息之旨，尤與熱力平均天地乃毀之言相發明也。此豈可悉謂之偶合也耶？雖然，由斯之說，必謂彼之所明，皆吾中土所前有，甚者或謂其學皆得於東來，則又不關事實，適用自蔽之說也。夫古人發其端，而後人莫能竟其緒，古人擬其大，而後人未能議其精，則猶之不學無術未化之民而已。祖父雖聖，何救子孫之童昏也哉！」⑧

承認中西之學相通，而不認為西方之所明，皆吾中土所前有，尤其否認其學皆得於東來，這已較西學源出中國之說，更進一步了。

晚清思想界既開放，西方史學遂有輸入的可能。當時有反中國傳統史學的理論出現，如嚴復云：

「生於民滿之日而遭亂者，號為暴君汚吏。生於民少之日獲安者，號為聖君賢相。二十四史之興亡治亂，以此劵矣。不然，有治而無亂，何所謂一治一亂哉！夫此羣中均身體弱智識昏之人，則其人愈多，為累愈甚，於是雖有善者，必為不善者所累而自促其生。積數十人或數百人以累一人，是不啻以勤儉自立之人，受役於游惰無業之人也。而有志者先死，因而劣者反傳，而優者反滅。然若優者盡死，則劣者亦必不能自存，滅種是矣。」⑨

此為反一治一亂的循環論。

黃尊憲云：

「自儒者以筆削說春秋，謂降杞為子，貶荆為人，所以示書法，是謬悠之譚也。自史臣以內辭尊本國，謂北稱索虜，南號島夷，所以崇國體，是狹陋之見也。夫史家紀述，務從實錄，無端取前古之人，他國之君，而易其名號，求之人情，奚當於理？」⑩

此爲反以天朝爲中心的歷史記載。

徐仁鑄云：

「西人之史，皆記國政及民間事，故讀者可考其世焉。中國正史，僅記一姓所以經營天下保守疆土之術，及其臣僕翼戴褒榮之陳述，而民間之事，悉置不記載。然則不過十七姓家譜耳，安得謂之史哉！故觀君史民史之異，而立國之公私判焉矣。今日欲考歷朝民俗，求之於正史反不可得，而別史雜史之類，時復記載之，亦學者所當厝意也。」⑪

此爲反以帝王爲中心的史學傳統。

唐才常云：

「司馬遷深於孔教者也。其文洞見本原，直刺時隱，進游俠，非好亂也，悼民權之衰也。稱貨殖，非逐末也，憫商學之失也。陳六家要指而評衡之，非等倫儒墨也，謂泥守弊生進于大同則有濟也。而目論之儒，誚其是非繆于聖人。嗚呼！孔教微，無公理；公理微，無信史。後世史家，言例、言法、言閏、言正、言道學儒林，其上能整齊故事，藉資參考；其下則魏收作色，棼如亂絲。無他，二千年來政學汶闇，微獨春秋文致太平之宏旨不可聞，卽司馬氏損益得失之微權不可復。讀史者，習見夫唐宋以降規規舊制，方謂老成；附會尊攘，方名忠義；務抑民氣，方尊朝權；禁談時務，方端士習；力遏新學，方正人心。於是事事求副于唐太宗、元世祖、明太祖網羅鉗束之私心，身衿纓而心圈苙，曰是固宜然。」⑫

此亦爲痛陳司馬遷以後中國史學的缺失。

以上種種反中國傳統史學的理論，未必然都極正確，但是不可否認地都有其時代性，西方的進化論輸入，自然要有人反對治亂循環的史觀了；萬國林立，國與國之間地位平等之義昌明，自然要有人反對內諸夏而外夷狄的史載了；民權思想高張，自然要有人斥正史爲帝王家譜，而嚮往西方注重民生社會之史了。

在這種情勢下，西方史學乃繼軍事、政治、經濟之後，向中國湧入。

2. 歷史進化論的輸入

西方史學首先輸入中國的，爲歷史進化論。

中國是一個留戀過去的民族，認爲愈是古代，愈是理想的時代，葛天氏之民，生活最美好，堯舜時則開創以天下相揖讓的局面，風俗亦由淳樸漸至澆譌。因此史學家是相信歷史退化的，歷史的發展，每況愈下。⑬歌頌古代，成爲史學家的自然心聲，治亂循環論也由此而產生。

光緒二十四年（一八九八）嚴復所譯赫胥黎（T. H. Huxley, 1825-1895）的天演論（Evolution and Ethics）問世，不啻中國思想界的晴天霹靂。赫胥黎是英國生物學家與實證主義哲學家，達爾文（C. R. Darwin, 1809-1882）的朋友，自達氏物種原始（Origin of Species）出版，他即是進化論的熱烈贊成者，他說「天演」云：

「天運變矣，而有不變者行乎其中；不變惟何？是名『天演』。以天演爲體，而其用有二：曰物競，曰天擇。此萬物莫不然，而於有生之類爲尤著。物競者，物爭自存也，以一物以與物物爭，或存或亡，而其效則歸於天擇。天擇者，物爭焉而獨存，則其存也，必有其所以存，必其所得於天之分，自致一己之能，與其所遭值之時與地，及凡周身以外之物力，有其相謀相劑者焉。夫而後獨免於亡，而足以自立也。而自其效觀之，若是物特爲天之所厚而擇焉以存也者，夫是之謂天擇。天擇者，擇於自然，雖擇而莫之擇，猶物競之無所爭，而實天下之至爭也。斯賓塞爾曰：天擇者，存其最宜者也；夫物既爭存矣，而天又從其爭之後而擇之，一爭一擇，而變化之事出矣。」⑭

這是赫氏天演論的主要觀念，嚴氏加以解釋說：

「復案：物競天擇二義，發於英人達爾文。達著物種由來一書，以考論世間動植物類所以繁殊之故。……知有生之物，始於同，終於異，造物立其一本，以大力運之，而萬類之所以底於如是者，咸其自己而已，無所謂創造者也。……自茲厥後，歐美二洲治生學者，大抵宗達氏。……故赫胥黎謂古者以大地爲靜居天中，而日月星辰，拱繞周流，以地爲主；自歌白尼出，乃知地本行星，系日而運，古者以人類爲首出庶物，肖天而生，與萬物絕異，自達爾文出，知人爲天演中一境，且演且進，來者方將，而宗教摶士之說，必不可信。蓋自有歌白尼而後天學明，亦自有達爾文而後生理確也。」⑮

可見赫氏天演的物競天擇之說，出於達爾文；達氏用科學的方法，考生物的發展，知道生物都由進化而來，其所以生存，源於競爭，優勝劣敗，適者生存。人是生物之一，所以不例外；人之能首出庶物，也是由於競爭，非得天獨厚。赫氏繼此說而其天演論出。

自從嚴復翻譯天演論以後，西方的進化思想，風靡於中國思想界，民鐸出進化論號二册⑯，內有陳兼善的進化之方法、進化論發達史、達爾文年譜；專書則有馬君武譯的達爾文物種原始，陳兼善的進化論綱要，張資平的人類進化論。胡適介紹達爾文的進化思想，尤其清楚：

「達爾文的主要觀念是：『物類起于自然的選擇，起於生存競爭裏最適宜的種族的保存。』他的幾部書都只是用無數的證據與事例來證明這一個大原則。……單只那書名——物類由來——把『類』和『由來』連在一塊，便是革命的表示。因爲自古以來，哲學家總以爲『類』是不變的，一成不變就沒有『由來』了。例如一粒橡子，漸漸生芽發根，不久滿一尺了，不久成小橡樹了，不久成大橡樹了。這雖是很大的變化，但變來變去，還只是一株橡樹，橡子不會成鴨脚樹，也不會變成枇杷樹，千年前如此，千年後也還如此。這個變而不變之中，好像有一條規定的路線，……這個法式的範圍，亞里士多德叫他做『哀多斯』(Eidos)，平常譯作『法』。……達爾文不但證明『類』是變的，而且指出『類』所以變的道理。……打破了有意志的天帝觀念。如果一切生物全靠着時時變異和淘汰不適於生存競爭的變異，方才能適應環境，那就用不着一個有意志的主宰來計劃規定了。況且生存的競爭是很慘酷的，若有一個有意志的主宰，何以生物界還有這種慘劇呢？」⑰

「物類由來出版以後，歐美的學術界都受了一個大震動。十二年的激烈爭論，漸漸的把上帝創造的物種由來論打倒了，故赫胥黎在一八七一年曾說：『在十二年中，物類由來在生物學上做到了一種完全的革命，就同牛敦的 Principia 在天文學上做到的革命一樣。』但當時的生物學者及一般學者雖然承認了物種的演化，還有許多人不肯承認人類也是由別的物類演化出來的。人類由來的主旨只是老實指出人類也是從猴類演化出來的。」⑱

進化思想輸入以後，自然直接影響國人對歷史的看法，而進化的史觀產生。自此以後，國人不再完全沉醉過去了；中國史學家不再以「古勝於今」作爲解釋歷史的最大標準了；中國史學自此進入一新世紀。

3. 梁啓超首倡「新史學」

從光緒二十年到宣統三年之間（一八九四——一九一一），是中國政治上的動盪時期，國人所醉心者，爲西方政治、軍事、經濟上的新說，以及中國前所未有而令人有驚心動魄感覺的學術思想。西方十九世紀初葉以來所發展的極富科學精神的史學，此時不曾廣泛引起國人的注意。由欣羡西方學術思想而及於史學，是一種額外的收穫。所以當對政治與學術思想極富興趣的梁啓超在光緒二十八年（一九〇二）發表了一篇題名叫做「新史學」的文章的時候，中國史學界即掀起了極大的波瀾。梁氏在這篇文章裏，對於西方史學，已有約略的認識:

「於今日泰西通行諸學科中，爲中國所固有者惟史學。史學者，學問之最博大而最切要者也，國民之明鏡也，愛國心之源泉也。今日歐洲民族主義所以發達，列國所以日進文明，史學之功居其半焉。」⑲

對於中國史學，梁氏則肆力攻擊:

「試一繙四庫之書，其汗牛充棟浩如煙海者，非史學書居十六七乎？上自太史公、班孟堅，下至畢秋帆、趙甌北，以史家名者不下數百。茲學之發達，二千年於茲矣。然而陳陳相因，一邱之貉，未聞有能爲史界闢一新天地，而令茲學之功德，普及於國民者。」⑳

進一步梁氏認爲中國史學「知有朝廷而不知有國家」，「知有個人而不知有羣體」，「知有陳迹而不知有今務」，「知有事實而不知有理想」，此即梁氏所謂四蔽。緣此四蔽，復生二病，「能鋪敍而不能別裁」，「能因襲而不能創作」:

「英儒斯賓塞曰:『或有告者曰，鄰家之猫，昨日產一子。以云事實，誠事實也。然誰不知爲無用之事實乎？何也？以其與他事毫無關涉，於吾人生活上之行爲，毫無影響也。然歷史上之事蹟，其類是者正多，能推此例以讀書觀萬物，則思過半矣。』此斯氏教人以作史讀史之方也。泰西舊史家，固不免之。而中國殆更甚焉。某日日食也，某日地震也，某日册封皇子也，某日某大臣死也，某日有某詔書也，滿紙塡塞，皆此等鄰猫生子之事實。往往有讀盡一卷，而無一語有入腦之價値者。就中如通鑑一書，屬稿十九年，別擇最稱精善，然今日以讀西史之眼讀之，覺其有用者，亦不過十之二三耳。其他更何論焉。」㉑

從以上可知梁氏已應用西方史學來批評中國史學作品了。所以在晚淸梁氏已有輸入西方史學的大功。雖然梁氏當時所瞭解的西方史學極爲有限，他沒有直接閱讀西文書籍的能力，僅能間接從日文書籍曉得一些西方史學，但是以他的言論在當時的影響力而言，其「新史學」一文，對於中國接受西方史學，實有開導的作用。至於梁氏瞭解較多的西方史學，則在歐遊以後，那已是民國時代了。

三、西方史學輸入中國的第二期——民國元年至民國二十六年（一九一二——一九三七）

從民國建立，到抗日戰爭發生，是西方史學輸入中國的最盛時期。此一時期所發生的五四運動，促使國人醉心於接受西方文化，史學界此時亦深深注意到西方異於中國的史學，而積極予以輸入。

1. 梁啓超所輸入的西方史學

此一時期梁啓超仍然是輸入西方史學的重要功臣之一。他曾遊歐洲，接觸到一部分西方史學。據李宗侗先生云：

「中國史學方法論第一部書是梁啓超的**中國歷史研究法**。梁先生到歐洲去的時候，我恰好住在巴黎，他請了很多留法學生給他講述各門的學問，恐怕史學方法論亦是其中之一。不過他另補充上很多中國的材料，但其原則仍不免受外國人的影響。」㉒

梁氏係於歐戰結束（一九一八年）後往遊歐洲，民國九年（一九二〇）返國。此時正值班漢穆（E. Bernheim）、朗格諾瓦（Ch. V. Langlois）與瑟諾博司（Ch. Seignobos）的史學方法最爲盛行的時候㉓，梁氏所請留法學生給他講述的各門學問，史學方法是其中的一項，應是不容置疑的。民國十年（一九二一）梁氏在南開大學講中國歷史研究法（翌年出書），所受西方史學方法的影響，極爲明顯。如梁氏云:

「近今史學之進步有兩特徵: 其一爲客觀的資料之整理——疇昔不認爲史蹟者，今則認之；疇昔認爲史蹟者，今或不認。舉從前棄置散佚之跡，鉤稽而比觀之，其夙所因襲者，則重加鑑別以估定其價值。如此則史學立於『眞』的基礎之上，而推論之功，乃不至枉施也。其二爲主觀的觀念之革新——以史爲人類活態之再現，而非其殭跡之展覽；爲全社會之業影，而非一人一家之譜錄。如此，然後歷史與吾儕生活相密接，讀之能親切有味；如此，然後能使讀者領會團體生活之意義以助成其爲一國民爲一世界人之資格也。歐美近百數十年之史學界，全向於此兩種方嚮以行。今雖僅見其進未見其止，顧所成就則既斐然矣。」㉔

梁氏所講中國歷史研究法，即以西方史學中客觀的資料之整理與主觀的觀念之革新兩特徵爲中心，尤其是前者。如說史料一章，將史料分爲在文字記錄以外者與在文字記錄以內者兩種，在文字記錄以外者，包括現存之實蹟、傳述之口碑、遺下之古物三類；在文字記錄以內者，包括舊史、關係史蹟之文件、史部以外之羣籍、類書與古逸書輯本、古逸書及古文件之再現、金石及其他鏤文諸類。此與班漢穆史源學的二體三元說，極爲接近。班氏所謂二體，是指文字的記載與古物的遺留；所謂三元是指口頭傳說、文字記載與事實自身之遺留。班氏以後，西方史學家作史料的分類，大致不出此範圍。梁氏去歐洲後，多少會受到啓示的。再如梁氏將史料分爲直接史料與間接史料，這也是班氏對史料的一種分類。

談到「史蹟之論次」，梁氏曾列擧一程序：

第一：當畫出一「史蹟集團」以爲研究範圍。

第二：集團分子之整理與集團實體之把捉。

第三：常注意集團外之關係。

第四：認取各該史蹟集團之「人格者」。

第五：精研一史蹟之心的基件。

第六：精研一史蹟之物的基件。

第七：量度心物兩方面可能性之極限。

第八：觀察所緣。㉕

這顯然已超出中國傳統史學的範圍，而係受西方史學的影響了。

2. 胡適輸入西方科學治史方法

梁啓超沒有直接閱讀英文、德文、法文等書籍的能力，他輸入西方史學，要輾轉經過第三者作媒介。因此他所輸入的，難免流於浮泛疏略。這也充分代表了梁氏在學術上的特殊性格。

梁氏在南開大學講授中國歷史研究法的同時，國內已有不少人更徹底地輸入西方治史方法，胡適已在北京大學講西方的科學方法，何炳松在北京大學史學系開歷史研究法一課，用美國史學家魯賓孫（J. H. Robinson, 1863-1936）的「新史學」（The New History, 1912）原本作課本，民國十年**新史學**譯本也已問世了。今先言胡氏所輸入的西方科學方法。

西方科學治史方法的輸入中國，自民國成立以後開始，而胡氏實居首功。顧頡剛在談到西方科學治史方法的輸入時曾云：

「過去的乾嘉漢學，誠然已具有科學精神，但是終不免爲經學觀念所範圍，同時其方法還嫌傳統，不能算是嚴格的科學方法。要到五四運動以後，西洋的科學的治史方法才眞正輸入，於是中國才有科學的史學可言。在這方面，表現得最明顯的，是考古學上的貢獻；甲骨文和金文經過科學的洗禮，再加上考古學上的其他發現，便使古代文化的眞相暴露了出來。此外如新的考據論文，多能揭發各時代歷史的眞相，而史料的整理，也比從前要有系統得多。這都是科學方法之賜。」㉖

又云：

「民國以來，西洋的治學方法和新史觀不斷的輸入，更予人們以莫大的啓示。胡適先生在北京大學講學，常根據他從西洋得來的治史方法，考證中國歷史上的問題，於是古代史的威信更爲動搖。頡剛等身逢其會，便開始提出古史上諸問題加以討論，『古史辨』便在這種情態之下出現了。」㉗

胡氏於五四運動以後，在北京大學講西方科學的治史方法，是當時極爲轟動的大事，其影響於史學界，也至深且鉅。胡氏自言其思想的來源，一是赫胥黎的存疑主義 (agnosticism)，一是杜威 (John Dewey, 1859-1952) 的實驗主義 (Pragmatism)：

「我的思想受兩個人的影響最大：一個是赫胥黎，一個是杜威先生。赫胥黎教我怎樣懷疑，敎我不信任一切沒有充分證據的東西。杜威先生敎我怎樣思想，敎我處處顧到當前的問題，敎我把一切學說理想都看作待證的假設，敎我處處顧到思想的結果。」㉘

「達爾文與赫胥黎在哲學方法上最重要的貢獻，在於他們的『存疑主義』(agnosticism)，存疑主義這個名詞，是赫胥黎造出來的，直譯爲『不知主義』。孔丘說：『知之爲知之，不知爲不知，是知也。』這話確是『存疑主義』的一個好解說。但近代的科學家還要進一步，他們要問，『怎樣的知，才可以算是無疑的知？』赫胥黎說：『只有那證據充分的知識，方才可以信仰。凡沒有充分證據的，只可存疑，不當信仰。』這是存疑主義的主腦。……嚴格的不信任一切沒有充分證據的東西——就是赫胥黎叫做『存疑主義』的。……到了達爾文出來，演進的宇宙觀首先和上帝創造的宇宙觀起了一個大衝突，於是三百年來不相侵犯的兩國就不能不宣戰了。達爾文的武器只是他三十年中搜集來的證據。三十年搜集的科學證據，打倒了二千年尊崇的宗教傳說。……赫胥黎是達爾文的作戰先鋒，從戰場上的經驗裏認清了科學的唯一武器是證據，所以大聲疾呼的把這個無敵的武器提出來，叫人們認為思想解放和思想革命的唯一工具。自從這個『拿證據來』的喊聲傳出以後，世界的哲學思想就不能不起一個根本的革命——哲學方法上的大革命。於是十九世紀前半的哲學的實證主義（Positivism）就一變而為十九世紀末年的實驗主義了。」㉙

介紹杜威的實驗主義，則特別注重其方法論：

「(1) 歷史的方法——『祖孫的方法』：他從來不把一個制度或學說看作一個孤立的東西，總把他看作一個中段：一頭是他所以發生的原因，一頭是他自己發生的效果；上頭有他的祖父，下面有他的子孫。捉住了這兩頭，他再也逃不出去了！……這種方法是一切帶有評判（Critical）精神的運動的一個重要武器。

(2) 實驗的方法：實驗的方法至少注重三件事：(一) 從具體的事實與境地下手；(二) 一切學說理想，一切知識，都只是待證的假設，並非天經地義；(三) 一切學說與理想都須用實行來試驗過；實驗是眞理的唯一試金石。……實驗主義只承認那一點

一滴做到的進步，才是眞進化。」㉚

胡氏以上面的思想作基礎，擴而及於治史，是尊重事實，尊重證據，大膽的假設，小心的求證：

「科學的方法，說來其實很簡單，只不過『尊重事實，尊重證據。』在應用上，科學的方法只不過『大膽的假設，小心的求證。』」㉛

紙上以外的材料，尤爲所注重：

「不但材料規定了學術的範圍，材料並且可以大大地影響方法的本身。文字的材料是死的，故考證學只能跟着材料走，雖然不能不搜求材料，却不能捏造材料。從文字的校勘以至歷史的考據，都只能尊重證據，却不能創造證據。

自然科學的材料便不限於搜求現成的材料，還可以創造新的證據。實驗的方法便是創造證據的方法。平常的水不會分解成氫氣氧氣；但我們用人工把水分解成氫氣和氧氣，以證實水是氫氣和氧氣合成的。這便是創造不常有的情境，這便是創造新證據。

紙上的材料只能產生考據的方法；考據的方法只是被動的運用材料。自然科學的材料却可以產生實驗的方法；實驗便不受現成材料的拘束，可以隨意創造平常不可得的情境，逼拶出新結果來。考據家若沒有證據，便無從做考據；史家若沒有史料，便沒有歷史。自然科學家便不然。肉眼看不見的，他可以用望遠鏡，可以用顯微鏡。生長在野外的，他可以叫他生長在花房裏，生長在夏天的，他可以叫他生在冬天。原來在人身上的，他可以移種在兎身上，狗身上。畢生難遇的，他可以叫他天天出現在眼前；太大了的，他可以縮小；整個的，他可以細細分析；複雜的，他可以化爲簡單；太少了的，他可以用人工培植增加。故材料的不同，可以使方法本身發生很重要的變化。實驗的方法也只是大膽的假設，小心的求證；然而因爲材料的性質，實驗的科學家便不用坐待證據的出現，也不僅僅尋求證據，他可以根據假設的理論，造出種種條件，把證據逼出來。故實驗的方法只是可以自由產生材料的考證方法。」㉜

胡氏所倡「大膽的假設，小心的求證」，變成了近人的口頭禪；他的注重紙上以外的材料，尤有極深遠的影響。中央研究院歷史語言研究所一派的史學（詳後），即是主要在他的影響之下形成的。

總之，胡氏所輸入的西方科學治史方法，風靡了中國近代史學界，此與這一套方法的新穎性有關，亦與胡氏的聲望地位有關。即如疑古學派的盛行，亦與之有相當的關係，如疑古學派大師顧頡剛云:

「適之先生帶了西洋的史學方法回來，把傳說中的古代制度和小說中的故事舉了幾個演變的例，使人讀了不但要去辨僞，要去研究僞史的背景，而且要去尋出它的漸漸演變的線索，就從演變的線索上去研究，這比了長素先生的方法又深進了一層了。」㉝

「聽了適之先生的課，知道研究歷史的方法在於尋求一件事情的前後左右的關係，不把它看作突然出現的。老實說，我的腦筋中印象最深的科學方法不過如此而已。我先把世界上的事物看成許多散亂的材料，再用了這些零碎的科學方法實施于各種散亂的材料上，就歡喜分析、分類、比較、試驗，尋求因果，更敢於作歸納，立假設，搜集證成假設的證據而發表新主張。」㉞

由此可以看出胡氏對疑古學派所發生的影響了。

3. 何炳松的譯述

何炳松於民國九年在北京大學史學系講授歷史研究法一課，以魯賓孫的**新史學**英文原本作課本，同時進行翻譯的工作，民國十年譯成問世。朱希祖曾述其始末云：

「民國九年的夏天，我擔任北京大學史學系的主任，那時我看了德國 Lamprecht 的近代歷史學，他的最要緊的話，就是：『近代的歷史學，是社會心理學的學問。現在歷史學新舊的論爭，就是研究歷史本於社會心的要素？還是本於個人心的要素？稍嚴密一點說起來，就是歷史進程的原動力在全體社會呢？還是在少數英雄？』Lamprecht 的意思，以爲歷史進程的原動力，自然在全體社會；研究歷史，應當本於社會心的要素。所以研究歷史，應當以社會科學爲基本科學。我那時就把北京大學史學系的課程，大加更改。本科第一二年級，先把社會科學學習，做一種基礎——如政治學、經濟學、法律學、社會學等——再輔之以生物學、人類學及人種學、古物學等。特別注意的，就推社會心理學。然後把全世界的史學綜合研究，希望我們中國也有史學的發展。那時史學系中又有歷史研究法一課，就請金華何炳松先生擔任。何先生用美國 Robinson 所著的**新史學**原本做課本，頗受學生歡迎。我那時就請何先生把**新史學**譯做中文，使吾國學界知道新史學的原理。不到一年，**新史學**一書果然譯成。」㉟

何氏自言**新史學**的翻譯云：

「Robinson 博士所說的話，雖然統是屬於歐洲史方面，但是很可以做我們中國研究歷史的人的䂨砭。我在北京大學同北京高師裏面，曾用這本書做講授西洋史學原理的教本。同學中習史學的人，統以這本書爲『得未曾有』。但是這本書的原本，用意既然深遠，造句又很複雜，所以同學中多『歎爲難讀』。今年春間，高師同學江君奐若願用他的求學餘閑，來幫我從事於這本書的翻

譯。我們兩人就從本年（民國十年）二月起着手進行，差不多經過六個月，才將這書譯完。」㊱

「我翻譯這本書的動機，實在發生在北京大學史學系主任朱逖先先生，同我的同學北京大學政治學教授張慰慈博士兩人的慫慂。譯成以後，他們兩人又代我校閱一遍，給我許多有價值的批評同改正。後來我的同學北京大學哲學教授胡適之博士，再代我細細的校閱一番。」㊲

「我譯完這本書的時候，在民國十年的夏天。後來我將譯本送給適之先生去看；他就發現了而且改正了好幾點錯誤。最後我再拿回來根據原本一字一字的校正，竭力希望我的譯本能够『一筆不苟』；——我雖然知道這是不容易完全做到的。十一年春間，適之先生又將這本書提出北京大學出版委員會，而且通過了爲北大叢書的一種。」㊳

可知新史學一書的譯成，當時北京大學史學系主任朱希祖與何氏的同學張慰慈有鼓舞的作用；參與翻譯的有何氏的弟子江奐若；參加意見的，有當時已享大名的胡適；翻譯的時間，約爲六個月（從民國十年二月開始）；使用的場合，爲北京大學與北京高師。

何氏所譯**新史學**，爲中國史學界所譯有關西方史學理論及方法的第一部書。在中西史學交流史上，這是值得大書特書的。此書出版後，對中國史學界有很大的影響。誠如朱希祖所云：「我國現在的史學界，實在是陳腐極了，沒有一番破壞，斷然不能建設。何先生譯了 Robinson 這部書，是很合我國史學界的程度，先把消極的方面多說些，把史學界陳腐不堪的地方摧陷擴淸了，然後慢慢的想到積極的建設方面去。所以何先生譯了這部書，是很有功於我國史學界的。」㊴在一九一二年魯賓孫的**新史學**在美國問世的時候，曾轟動美國史學界。然此書的譯本在中國所發生的影響，或不下於在美國所發生的影響。此皆非作者與譯者始料所能及。

中國史學界重視社會科學，係受何氏所譯新史學的影響。魯賓孫的新史學，與社會科學有不可須臾離的關係：

「『新史學』要脫去從前那種研究歷史的限制。新史學這樣東西，將來總可以應付我們日常的需要。他一定能够利用人類學家、經濟學家、心理學家、社會學家關於人類的種種發明——五十年來的種種發明，已經將我們對於人類的來源、進步同希望種種觀念革命了。五十年來沒有一種科學，無論是有機的或無機的，不受重大的變化，而且有許多新科學增加出來，他們的名字，在十九世紀中葉以前的歷史家亦都不知道。史學這種學問，當然免不了混入這革命潮流裏面去。不過我們不能不承認現在有許多歷史家，還不知道歷史有革命的必要。無怪現在普通人對於歷史的範圍同性質的觀念，還是陳腐的很。

這部書所以叫做新史學的緣故，就是特別要使大家知道歷史不是一種停頓不進步的學問，只要改良研究的方法，搜集、批評、融化新資料，他定能進步的；歷史的觀念同目的，應該跟着社會同社會科學同時變更的；而且歷史這種東西，將來一定能够在我們知識生活裏面，佔一個比從前還要重要的位置。」㊵

「歷史家始終是社會的批評者同指導者，他應該將社會科學的結果綜合起來，用過去人類的實在生活試驗他們一下。歷史家的事業，如此的有趣，如此的廣大，所以歷史家將來一定慢慢的能够專心致志的去研究歷史，將來總要脫離文學的關係。因爲歷史家將來的目的，比詩家或戲曲家還要高尙，還有希望，這種目的對於歷史家思想的要求同表示能力的要求，比對於文學家還要急

切。」㊶

「現在研究歷史的人，不但應該急起直追適合自己於一般智識狀況中的新分子，而且應該快快表明他們對於各種關於人類新科學的態度。各種新科學，因爲利用進化原理的緣故，所以進步得異常的快，而且能够改正一般歷史家所下的斷語，解除了許多歷史家的誤會。所謂關於人類的各種新科學，我以爲最重要的就是廣義的人類學、古物學、社會的和動物的心理學和比較宗教的研究。經濟學對於歷史已經很有影響，至於社會學，照我看來，不過是對於人類的一種很重要的觀擇點，並不是一種關於人類的新發明。各種新的社會科學各去研究人類的各方面，已經將我們許多歷史家慣用的歷史名詞的意義大大變更了——如種族、宗教、進步古人、文化、人類天性等。他們推翻了許多歷史家的舊說，解釋了許多歷史家所不能解釋的歷史上的現象。」㊷

「歷史家和地質學家、物理學家和生物學家一樣，即使沒有工夫去研究各種科學的原理，也不能不利用各種科學家有關係的學說。歷史家不一定要作人類學家或心理學家，才可以利用人類學和心理學的發明和學說。這種發明和學說，對於歷史家可以貢獻一種新眼光和新解釋，可以幫助歷史家矯正了許多謬見，消滅了許多貫澈歷史著作裏面舊的幻想。最要緊的，歷史學家應該絕對的懷有史心，利用進化的學說；而且要承認雖然以歷史家自居，以歷史家自負，自己的態度和方法，在所有研究人類的學者裏面，還是最不是歷史的。

有時他種科學的學說，固然未免言過其實一點，他們所貢獻的歷史解釋，也往往不能免歷史家的反對。社會學家、人類學家和經濟學家，往往走得太快，而且太不謹愼；所以有許多歷史家因此就不免有過度的保守，就絕對的不去想了。但是無論如何，想得太多還是冒險。假使把他種和歷史同盟的科學思想，好好的利用起來，很可以大大的增加歷史研究的力量和範圍，使研究歷史的結果，比自古以來還要有價值。」㊸

很明顯的魯氏希望史學能够經世，「可以應付我們日常的需要」；希望史學家能够利用人類學家、經濟學家、心理學家、社會學家關於人類的種種發明，以期將社會科學的結果綜合起來，用過去人類的實在生活試驗一下；希望史學與文學脫離關係，認爲史學家的目的，比詩家或戲曲家還要高尙，還有希望。這大致是魯氏的「新史學」，而希望史學家綜合社會科學的結果，是其重心。民國九年，在魯氏新史學理論基礎上，北京大學就將政治學、經濟學、法律學、社會學等社會科學，加到史學系課程裏面去了。自此中國史學界重視社會科學與史學的關係。李璜在一篇講稿中說：

「現在一個研究歷史的學生，特別是研究中國歷史的學生，要想不受古人之欺，而又能得個歷史事變的統整觀念，便該當注意歷史學與社會科學。這差不多已成了一般的定論，而無庸疑義了。因此大學歷史系的課程裏，都有社會科學，如經濟學、政治學、法律學、統計學、宗教學，以至社會學等等科目。」

「從前歷史學家研究的對象是人，而現今社會學家研究的對象也無非是人。不過從前歷史學家眼中的人都大半是『頂天立地的好漢子』，好像不受一切外物所左右的；所以從前歷史學家便多半目不斜視，專從這些所謂『歷史人物』身上用工夫。社會科學家眼中的人，他便處處都認爲受了環境的支配：他的生理，他的心理，他的日常生活和特別行爲，都被認爲與他的前後左右的社會有關係。於是社會科學家雖把人的能力看小了一些，却把人的研究擴大了許多。歷史學家也就不能不受這種影響，將他的研究範圍擴大起來。」

「社會科學和歷史科學彼此交互影響的關係，在近今是幾乎分不開的：社會科學每有所見，必定立刻要影響到歷史科學，而歷史科學每有所得，也必定要影響到社會科學。一種科學的成立，本來要（一）正確有據，（二）觀察有方，（三）歸納得例。現今社會科學與歷史科學如果要眞正進於科學之域，也必須辦到這三點。而在這三點上，一部份要靠歷史學家的用力（特別在正確有據上面）。這兩部份的力量可以說合則兩利，分則兩損。此所以社會科學自孔德而後，大半都主張歷史的研究和社會科學的研究打成一片，而近今歷史學家除了少數不改舊態以外，大半都願與社會科學家携手前進。」㊹

近代中國史學界大致接受了以社會科學的理論與方法治史的這一西方史學傳統，這是一種新史學，在中國史學傳統中所從未出現過的。雖然中國史學家實際以社會科學的理論與方法治史者仍然佔極少數，但是在大原則上是接受了。

繼新史學之後，何氏又譯古赤（G. P. Gooch, 1873-1968）的**十九世紀之史學與史家**（History and Historians in the Nineteenth Century, 1913），班茲（H. E. Barnes）的**史學史**㊺，紹特韋爾（J. R. Shotwell）的**西洋史學史**（An Introduction to the History of History, 1939，再版時，更名爲 The History of History, 1950）。古赤之書，譯本未克問世，其譯稿是否完成，亦未可知。班茲、紹特韋爾二氏之書，譯本皆由商務印書館出版。何氏對其所從事的翻譯事業，在自序其所譯紹氏的**西洋史學史**中曾云：

「譯者竊不自量，嘗思致力於中國史學史之編輯，以期於吾國之新史學界稍有貢獻。唯覺玆事體大，斷非獨力所能奏功。且此種研究爲吾國學術上之創舉，尤非先事介紹現在西洋新史學之名著不足以資借鏡。譯者近年來所以有編譯西洋史學叢書之計劃，其故蓋卽在此。

譯者抱此宏願業已數載於玆，終以謀生未遑，無從下手。四年之前，譯者曾一時掌敎於上海光華大學，無意中得一史學同志郭斌佳君其人。郭君本好學深思之士，自願於課餘之暇以全力臂助譯者從事於西洋史學之介紹。譯者聞之，不禁大喜過望，遂與之合譯此新出之名著，蓋已費時一載矣。

今春郭君應淸華大學之聘，擔任助敎，因得與北方羅志希朱逖先諸史學前輩游，學業益進，不日且將負笈北美以求深造。半年以來，彼仍輔助譯者翻譯古赤氏**十九世紀之史學與史家**一書，至今亦已譯成過半，不期年當可脫稿。吾人得此二書，則譯者計劃中之西洋史學叢書，可謂規模粗具矣。豈非平生一大快事哉！」

㊻

何氏擬致力於中國史學史的硏究，而先從事於西洋新史學名著的介紹，計劃編譯西洋史學叢書，其識見與氣魄，皆令人讚佩。其所譯紹特韋爾的史學史，在當時頗負盛名；其已進行翻譯而未出版的古赤之書，則迄至今日，尙爲談十九世紀史學的權威作品。

純粹翻譯以外，何氏尙以中國史學與西方史學相比論，其民國十六年所寫成的**歷史研究法**與民國十七年所寫成的**通史新義**，都是這方面代表性的作品。觀其於**歷史研究法**的序中說：

「吾國史籍，雖稱宏富，而硏究史法之著作，則寥若晨星。世之習西洋史者，或執此爲吾國史家病。殊不知專門名家之於其所學，或僅知其然而終不知其所以然，或先知其然而後推知其所以然。

此乃中西各國學術上之常事，初不獨吾國學者爲然也。西洋史家之着手研究史法也，不過二百年來事耳。然如法國之道諾（P. C. F. Daunou），德國之特羅伊生（J. G. Droysen），英國之夫里門（E.A. Freeman）輩，或高談哲理，或討論修詞，莫不以空談無補，見譏於後世。至今西洋研究史法之名著，僅有二書，一爲德國格來夫斯法爾特（Greifswald）大學教授朋漢姆（Ernst Bernheim）之**歷史研究法課本**（Lehrbuch der Historischen Methode），出版於一八八九年（清光緒十五年）。一爲法國索爾蓬（Sorbonne）大學教授朗格羅亞與塞諾波（Ch. V. Langlois and Ch. Seignobos）二人合著之**歷史研究法入門**（Introduction aux E'trudes Historiques），出版於一八九七年（清光緒二十三年）。兩書之出世，離今均不過三十餘年耳。

吾國專論史學之名著，在唐有劉知幾之**史通**（中宗景龍時作），離今已一千二百餘年。在清有章學誠之**文史通義**（乾隆時作），離今亦已達一百七八十年。其議論之宏通及其見解之精審，決不在西洋新史學家之下。唯吾國史學界中，自有特殊之情況。劉、章諸人之眼界及主張，當然不能不受固有環境之限制。若或因其間有不合西洋新說而少之，是猶譏西洋古人之不識中國情形，或譏吾輩先人之不識飛機與電話也，又豈持平之論哉？

德國朋漢姆著作之所以著名，因其能集先哲學說之大成也。法國郎格羅亞、塞諾波著作之所以著名，因其能採取最新學說之精華也。一重承先，一重啓後，然其有功於史法之研究也，則初無二致。吾國先哲討論史法之文學，亦何嘗不森然滿目？然今日之能以新法綜合而整齊之者，尙未有其人耳。」

「著者之作是書，意在介紹西洋之史法。故關於理論方面，完全本諸朋漢姆、郎格羅亞、塞諸波三人之著作。遇有與吾國史家不約而同之言論，則引用吾國固有之成文。書中所有實例亦如之。一以便吾國讀者之了解，一以明中西史家見解之大體相同。初不敢稗販西籍以欺國人，尤不敢牽附中文，以欺讀者。」

於**通史新義**自序則云：

「吾國近年來史學界頗受歐化潮流之激盪，是以努力於通史編纂者頗不乏人。其對於西洋史學原理之接受，正與一般政治學家、經濟學家、新文學家同，一時頓呈饑不擇食活剝生吞之現象。偏而不全似而非是之通史義例因之遂充斥於吾國現代之史著中。彼曾習統計學者，以為研究歷史應用統計法焉；彼曾習生物學者，以為研究歷史應用進化說焉；彼曾習自然科學者，以為研究歷史應用因果律焉；彼曾習經濟學者，以為研究歷史應用經濟史觀焉；彼曾習論理學者，以為研究歷史應用分類法焉。一時學說紛紜，莫衷一是，大有處士橫議百家爭鳴之概，誠不可謂非吾國史學界復興之朕兆也。」

「著者之作此書，唯一宗旨在於介紹西洋最新之通史義例，蓋因其依據各種最新人文科學研究而來，較吾國固有者為切實而適用，足備國內史家之採擇；初不敢因其來自西洋，遂奉之為金科玉律也。此外著者不揣固陋，並欲藉此書以與國人商榷三種管見焉：即史料與著作應分兩家而後通史之觀念方明；現代吾國流行之通史義例似而非是；及通史不宜獨尊是也。一得之愚，或未盡當，幸覽者有以糾正之。

本書凡分兩編。上編計分十章，專論社會史料研究法，凡史料考訂與事實編比之理論及應用，均加以系統之討論。下編計分十一章，專論社會史研究法，凡社會通史之著作及其與他種歷史之關係，均加以淺顯之說明，同時對於其他各種似而非是偏而不全之義例，亦復隨處加以相當之估值。……

至於本書所述之原理，十九採自法國名史塞諾波所著**應用於社會上之歷史研究法**（Ch. Seignobos: La Methode Historique applique aux Science Socials）一書。著者雖略有疏通證明之功，終未敢掩襲他山之美。」㊼

是何氏**歷史研究法**一書，完全本於班漢穆（即朋漢姆）、朗格諾瓦（即郎格羅亞）、瑟諾博司（即塞諾波）三人之說；**通史新義**一書，則十九採自瑟諾博司另外一部名著**應用於社會科學上之歷史研究法**。遇有與中國史學方法相通之處，則作比論，以互相發明。是何氏已頗能會通中西史學了。

4. 傅斯年與西方科學治史方法的輸入

新歷史考據學亦即科學的歷史學是民國以來中國史學的主要潮流，中央研究院歷史語言研究所是此一潮流的重心。治史不重寫史，而重考史；視史料爲史學的全部，擴充史料的範圍，增加批評史料的工具；上窮碧落，下及黃泉，目的在尋找史料；語言學、文字學、考古學、生物學等，也無一不被視爲批評史料解釋史料的工具學問。此一潮流，自然有乾嘉時代歷史考據學的傳統，也深受西方科學治史方法的影響。

中央研究院第一任院長蔡元培首先對史學下一新的定義：

「史學本是史料學，堅實的事實只能得之於最下層的史料中。」㊽

既視史學爲史料學，於是特別注重史料，尤其是直接的史料：

「歷史中直接的史料與間接的史料有很大的分別，以前治史者之濫用間接的材料，而忽略直接的材料，是一件很不幸的事，應該是以後治史學者所急當糾正的。例如**遼史**之成由於刪契丹列朝之實錄，刪實錄那能成信史？信史是要從檔案中考核出來的。這猶可說遼史成於胡元之朝，脫脫所領之局做不出學術上的大業。然試看馬班以後諸紀傳史家，那一位不是在那裏抄實錄，抄碑傳？那一位曾經充分利用過直接史料？我們展讀一部紀傳的史，每每感覺全是些人名官名，千人一面，千篇一腔，一事之內容不可知，一人之行品不易見，這豈不是刪削實錄碑傳的結果，只剩了架子，而把知人論世的菁華遺略嗎？即使那些做實錄做碑傳者，並沒有忌諱，沒有成見，沒有內外，已因和我們觀點之不同，他們所據直接材料以刪削者不正合於我們的要求，何況做實錄者本有所諱，做碑傳者本專務表揚，則有意的顚倒，乃至改換，是不可免的呢！史料愈間接愈不可靠，這道理本是極明顯的。假如民國初年修清史者知道史學的要求不能以刪削官書碑狀滿足之，則這些大庫檔案正該由他們調去整理的。然而他們不作，我們希望我們這次的整理檔案開些以後注重直接史料的風氣。」㊾

中央研究院歷史語言研究所（以下簡稱史語所）的輾轉收購明清內閣大庫檔案以及積極的加以整理刊印，可以說都是在院長蔡氏這種重視直接史料的觀念下所促成的。

繼蔡氏之後，胡適對中央研究院史語所的影響是很明顯的。他所輸入的西方科學治史的方法，史語所充分的予以應用。繼胡氏之後對史語所影響最大最直接的是傅斯年。從民國十七年（一九二八）十一月史語所成立，到三十九年（一九五〇）十二月傅氏逝世，他一直擔任所長的職務，史語所在史學上的成就，主要應歸功於他的領導。

傅氏在北京大學曾教授「史學方法導論」一課，其所擬之目爲:

第一講　論史學非求結論之學問

　　論史學在「敍述科學」中之位置

　　論歷史的知識與藝術的手段

第二講　中國及歐洲歷代史學觀念演變之綱領

第三講　統計方法與史學

第四講　史料論略

第五講　古代史與近代史

第六講　史學的邏輯

第七講　所謂「史觀」㊿

從以上的擬目，可以看出傅氏介紹了一部分西方的史學。惟七講中現存者僅爲第四講史料論略。「史學便是史料學」，「史學的工作是整理史料，不是作藝術的建設，不是做疏通的事業，不是去扶持或推倒這個運動，或那個主義，」是這一講裡很惹人注目的話，也是傅氏對史學的一貫看法。

史語所集刊第一本第一分刊載傅氏「歷史語言研究所工作之旨趣」一文，此文一出，決定了以後史語所所走的路線，迄至今日，還沒有什麼重大的修改。

傅氏首先認爲史學不是著史：

「歷史學不是著史，著史每多多少少帶點古世中世的意味，且每取倫理家的手段，作文章家的本事。近代的歷史學只是史料學，利用自然學供給我們的一切工具，整理一切可逢着的史料。所以近代史學所達到的範域，自地質學以至目下新聞紙，而史學外的達爾文論，正是歷史方法之大成。」(51)

歷史的研究，傅氏認爲應當遵守三個標準：(1) 直接研究材料，(2) 擴張研究的材料，(3) 擴充作研究時應用的工具。傅氏對以上三者都逐一加以發揮，並且很堅定的說：

「我們只是要把材料整理好，則事實自然顯明了。一分材料出一分貨，十分材料出十分貨，沒有材料便不出貨。」

「總而言之，我們不是讀書的人，我們只是上窮碧落下黃泉，動手動脚的找東西。」

民國以後，迄於抗日戰爭以前，史料上有幾項重要的發現，第一爲安陽的甲骨，第二爲敦煌千佛洞的手寫卷子，第三爲西北邊塞的漢簡，第四爲清代內閣大庫及軍機處的檔案。這四種新史料中，安陽甲骨是由史語所考古組李濟和董作賓領導下所發掘的結果。清內閣大庫的檔案係由史語所輾轉購得 52，**明清史料**四十册卽由其中輯出。敦煌卷子方面，史語所刊行的有陳垣的**敦煌刼餘錄**和劉復的**敦煌綴瑣**。漢簡方面，史語所刊行的有勞榦的**居延漢簡考證**。這些都是史語所的貢獻，也都是在傅氏領導下所進行的。

傅氏輸入西方科學治史方法，可以從李濟的一段話透露出來:

「以歷史硏究所爲大本營在中國建築『科學的東方學正統』，這一號召，是具有高度的鼓舞性的。擧起這面大旗領首向前進的第一人，是年富力强的傅斯年。那時他的年齡恰過三十不久，意氣豐盛，精神飽滿，渾身都是活力，不但具有雄厚的國學根柢，對於歐洲近代發展的歷史學、語言學、心理學、哲學以及科學史，都有澈底的認識。他是這一運動理想的領導人，他喚醒了中國學者最高的民族意識，在很短的時間內聚集了不少能運用現代學術工具的中年及少年學者。」53

5. 其他 54

此一時期班漢穆的 Lehrbuch der Historischen Methode 與朗格諾瓦、瑟諾博司合著的 Introduction aux E'tudes Historiques，皆經譯成中文。這比何炳松僅取其理論而以中國實例作疏通證明，已更徹底了一步。班氏的書，爲陳韜所譯，譯名爲**史學方法論**，出版的時間，約在民國十五年至二十六年之間。55 朗、瑟二氏之書，爲李思純所譯，譯名為「**史學原論**」，出版於民國十五年。被視為西方史學方法論鼻祖之作，一旦譯為中文，誠為西方史學輸入中國史上的大事。

陳韜翻譯班氏「**史學方法論**」的詳情，不可得而知。㊱李思純則於「**史學原論**」前冠以弁言云:

> 「史學原論一卷，著者朗格諾瓦、瑟諾博司二氏。朗氏法蘭西國家藏書樓主任，瑟氏巴黎大學歷史教授也。是書以一八九七年八月出版於巴黎，書雖稍舊，然遠西後出談歷史方法之書尚未有逾此者。
>
> 吾讀此書在一九二〇年之秋，於時瑟諾博司先生在巴黎大學文科講授近代史及歷史方法。吾自是年秋迄於一九二一年冬，凡閱時一年，朝夕挾書册親受先生講課。一九二二年三月，遊柏林，居康德街一小樓，日長多暇，乃以是書法文原本及英國 G. G. Berry 氏譯本參酌譯之，日成數章，二月而畢業。棄置篋底復年餘，今夏歸國居南京，乃取舊稿删訂潤色之。間於篇中徵引事實有不能明者，為附註於章後焉。
>
> 論歷史方法之專書，世不多見。英美所著者，有 Robinson 氏之 New History，有 Vincent 氏之 Historical Research，有 McMurry 氏之 Special Method in History，有 Woodbridge 氏之 The Purpose of History，有 Nordain 氏之 Interpretation of History，有 Seligman 氏之 Economic Interpretation of History，有 Gooch 氏之 History and Historians of 19th Century〔按應作 History and Historians in the Nineteenth Century〕，有 Barn 氏之 The Past and Future of History 等書。然以較此書體大思精，咸有遜色。法國史家 Fustel de Coulange 氏成書曰『歷史搜討之數問題』(Recherche des

Quelque Problems d' Histoire)，雖其書甚美，「然所論多具體事實而少抽象方法。本書著作者瑟諾博司先生於後此數年更成一書曰『應用於社會科學上之歷史方法』(Methode Historique Applique aux Science Socials)，其書亦佳，然特本書之撮要節本而已。故討論抽象史法而體大思精之作，本書應首屈一指也。

吾國舊史繁賾，史學之發達較他國爲美備，關於諮訪蒐輯校讐考證之事，與夫體例編次文辭名物之理，莫不審晰入微，措施合法。劉知幾氏『**史通**』，章學誠氏『**文史通義、校讐通義**』，其最著之作也。二氏所作，其間探討之道，辨晰之事，東西名哲，合軌符轍，無有異致。本書所陳，或符前哲舊言，或出遠西新諦。」

「斯譯參酌英法兩本，比較爲之，或有出入，其有與英譯辭語不盡符合者，則法文原本可覆按也。」

是李思純曾於巴黎大學親受瑟諾博司講授，又參酌英文法文兩種本子翻譯，此爲其翻譯的值得稱道處。

稍後董之學又譯班茲的 The New History and the Social Studies，譯名爲「**新史學與社會科學**」，民國二十三年四月出版。黎東方譯施亨利 (Henri S'ee) 的 Science et Philosophie d'e I'Histoire，譯名爲「**歷史之科學與哲學**」，民國十八年出版。

民國二十一年李璜曾出版「**歷史學與社會科學**」一書，中分歷史學與社會科學、歷史學方法概論、歐洲文化史導言、歷史教學法旨趣四篇，爲李氏民國十三年至十五年間在各大學的演講稿，主要介紹瑟諾博司之說。李氏在序中說：

「這本小書，原是我民十三至十五年在武昌大學、北京大學、北京師範大學擔任西洋史與社會學教授時，爲學生講演的幾篇講稿合成的。當時在青年學生中，革命的政治風氣雖然很盛，但是大學生的研究興趣同時也非常之高。每一系的學生都要組織學術研究會，請教授們爲他們作課外講演。當時我感到學生們這種努力是難得的。應該予以鼓勵的。因此我所擔任的正課鐘點雖已不少，但對這種課外的講演，也不願隨便應付，總希望能趁此機會，爲學生們的研究工作，指示出一些途徑與方法。——這本小書中的幾篇講稿，便是爲研究歷史學與社會學，說明下手研究所應注意的門徑所在而寫成的。」

四、西方史學輸入中國的第三期——民國二十七年至民國三十八年（一九三八年至一九四九年）

在此十二年中，爲西方史學輸入中國最緩慢的時期。八年的抗戰，四年的戡亂，促使學術的發展，受到最大的影響。西方史學的輸入不能與其他時期相比，自爲極自然的現象。

以寫中國史綱享盛名的張蔭麟，是此一時期輸入西方史學的功臣之一。

張氏曾負笈美國，習西洋哲學、社會學，而以史學爲歸宿。歸國後歷任清華大學、西南聯大、浙江大學教席。他先後發表過「論歷史學之過去與未來」㊼、「傳統歷史哲學之總結算」㊽、「評近人顧頡剛對於中國古史之討論」㊾等幾篇介紹西方史學的文章。在「論歷史學之過去與未來」一文中，介紹了不少西方觀察史料批評史料的方法。在「傳統歷史哲學之總結算」一文中，由談西方歷史哲學而涉及西方史學。「評近人顧頡剛對於中國古史之討論」一文則云：

「凡欲證明某時代無某某歷史觀念，貴能指出其時代中有與此歷史觀念相反之證據。若因某書或今存某時代之書無某史事之稱述，遂斷定某時代無此觀念，此種方法謂之『默證』(argument from silence)。默證之應用及其適用之限度，西方史家早有定論。吾觀顧氏之論證法幾盡用默證，而什九皆違反其適用之限度。茲于討論之前，請徵法史家色諾波（Ch. Seignobos）氏論默證之成說以代吾所欲言。其說曰：

吾儕于日常生活中，每謂『此事果眞，吾儕當已聞之。』默證卽根此感覺而生。其中實暗藏一普遍之論據曰：倘若一假定之事實，果眞有之，則必當有紀之之文籍存在。

欲使此推論不悖於理，必須所有事實均經見聞，均經記錄，而所有記錄均保完未失而後可。雖然，古事泰半失載，載矣而多湮滅，在大多數情形之下，默證不能有效，必根于其所涵之條件悉具時始可應用之。

現存之載籍無某事之稱述，此猶未足爲證也，更須從來未嘗有之。倘若載籍有湮滅，則無結論可得矣。故於載籍湮滅愈多之時代，默證愈當少用，其在古史中之用處，較之在十九世紀之歷史，不逮遠甚。（下略）

是以默證之應用，限於少數界限極淸楚之情形：（一）未稱述某事之載籍，其作者立意將此類之事實爲有系統之記述，而於所有此類事皆習知之。（例如塔克多 Tacitus 有意列舉日爾曼各民族 Notitia dignitatum，遍述國中所有行省，各有一民族一行省爲二者所未舉，則足以證明當時無之。）（二）某事蹟足以影響作者之想像甚力，而必當入于作者之觀念中。（例如倘法蘭克 Frankish 民族有定期集會，則 Gregory 之作法蘭克族諸王傳不致不道及之。）」（以上見 Ch. V. Langlois and Ch. Seignobos: Introduction to the Study of History, translated into English by G. G. Berry）

此爲張氏介紹西方史學中的默證方法。

以上張氏介紹西方史學的幾篇文章，都是在早年寫成的（民國十四年至二十六年之間）㊿。其成熟時期的作品，則爲民國三十年出版的**中國史綱**，這是在融會西方史學後所寫出來的一部中國新史。「(一）融會前人研究結果和作者玩索所得，以說故事的方式出之，不參入考證，不引用或採用前人敍述的成文，即原始文件的載錄亦力求節省；(二）選擇少數的節目爲主題，給每一所選的節目以相當透徹的敍述，這些節目以外的大事，只概略地涉及以爲背景；(三）社會的變遷，思想的貢獻，和若干重大人物的性格，兼顧並詳。」61 此顯然係得自西方的寫史方式。張氏又在自序中舉出了五種取材的標準以及四個組織材料的範疇，所謂新異性的標準（standard of novelty），實效的標準（standard of practical effect），文化價值標準（standard of cultural values），訓誨功用的標準（standard of didacticutility），現狀淵源的標準（standard of genetic relation with present situation），是五種取材的標準；所謂因果的範疇，定向發展的範疇，演化發展的範疇，矛盾發展的範疇，是四個組織材料的範疇。62 這五種標準，四個範疇，不容置疑的是張氏主要從西方史學中歸納出來的。

此一時期楊鴻烈的出版「**史學通論**」63、「**歷史研究法**」（民國三十三年出版），陸懋德的出版「**史學方法大綱**」（民國三十四年出版），都將部分西方史學輸入中國。楊著「**歷史研究法**」所引有關西方史學著作約有：

Eduard Meyer, Zur Theorie and Methodike der Geschichte

F. M. Fling, The Writing of History

E. Scott, History and Historical Problems

R. L. Marshall, The Historical Criticism of Documents

Daumon, Cours d'etudes Historique

Ch. V. Langlois and Ch. Seignobos, Introduction aux E'tudes Historiques

E. Bernheim, Einleitung in die Geschichtswissenschaft

J. M. Vincent, Historical Research

陸著所引則有:

B. Croce, Theory and Practice of History

K. Lamprecht. What is History?

J. H. Robinson, The New History

E. Scott, History and Historical Problems

F. Harrison, The Meaning of History

J. M. Vincent, Historical Research

H. E. Barnes, History and Prospect of Social Sciences

H. Taylor, History as a Science

F. M. Fling, The Writing of History

F. J. Teggart, Theory of History

S. A. Rice, Method in Social Sciences

A. Wolf, Essential of Scientific Method

Ch. Seignobos, La Methode Historique Applique aux Science Socials

E. Bernheim, Lehrbuch der Historischen Methode

A. Johnson, Historian and Historical Evidence

C. G. Crump, History and Historical Research

J. J. Jusserand, The Writing of History

Langlois and Seignobos, Introduction to the Study of History

R. A. Seligman, Economic Interpretation of History

H. E. Barnes, New History and Social Sciences

陸氏且於自序中說:

「近世歐美各邦人士，本其科學方法，以治史學，故其成績往往過於吾國。至於德人柏爾亥謨氏及法人塞音奴朴氏之言史法，其精密尤非吾國前人所及。此外英美學者亦多採取其說以著書，故西方專言史法之作，多能臚列條文，與人以便利。夫舉艱深之理，而示以坦易之途，此固科學之所尙，而爲吾人之所求者也。余昔年在北京清華大學、師範大學、輔仁大學，均曾主講史學方法，每於援引吾國舊說之外，多採取西人名著，以爲補助。蓋學問之道，無所謂中西，但取其長而求其是而已。及余避地西北，仍以是爲教。友人杜毅伯先生見而善之，因囑獨立社主人購其講稿，印行於世，此茲編之所以刊布也。余又聞法人塞音奴朴氏之言曰:『社會科學是用史學方法。』余謂史學雖與其他社會科學不同，而其研究之資料，固同爲根據個人之觀察，及根據他人之記載，故其所用之方法一也。方法不精，則根據失實，而所得之因果亦不可信，此固現代治史學及其他社會科學者之通病也。」⑭

此外周謙冲曾譯沙爾非米尼 (Gaetano Salvemimi) 的「史學家與科學家」(Historian and Scientist: An Essay on the Nature of History and the Social Sciences) 一書，約於民國三十二年出版。⑮周氏譯此書的目的，可於其「譯者敍言」中看出來:

「我在各大學授『歷史方法』有年，諸生極感參考書的缺乏。這本書可當『史學概論』和『社會科學概論』讀，也可作『史學方法』的參考書讀。」

五、近三十年來西方史學的輸入中國——民國三十九年迄於今日（一九五〇年至一九七六年）

自民國三十九年（一九五〇）大陸變色，政府播遷臺灣以來，到今日已將近三十年。在這將近三十年中，我政府所直接統轄的土地，雖只限於一隅，然而在政治上却極度安定，在經濟上有最迅速的發展，這是對史學發展極有利的一個環境。加以大陸上的慘變，國際政治上的風雲，史學所受外來的刺激，較任何一個時代爲深。在有安定環境與外來刺激的兩大因素下，史學有大發展的可能。就西方史學的輸入而言，已非前一時期所能比擬。

在臺灣大學歷史系講學的張致遠、姚從吾、沈剛伯、劉崇鋐諸教授，是此一時期輸入西方史學極重要的人物。

張致遠先生留學德國，深受十九世紀以來德國史學的影響。歸國後應中央大學之聘，講授西洋史、西洋史學史與西洋外交史。大陸淪陷，轉任臺灣大學歷史系教授，主講西洋史學史與西洋近世史，並以英國史學家費雪（H. A. L. Fisher）的「歐洲通史」（A History of Europe）爲藍本，編著「西洋通史」三册，頗流行於史學界。另著「史學講話」一書（民國四十一年九月初版），中分史學的涵義及其問題、史學的研究範圍、史學方法綱要、歷史與人文教育、陶恩培論文化的起源、西洋外交史研究六章，前三章主要介紹班漢穆的史學理論及方法。此外單獨發表的論文，如歌德與近代歷史思想的起源、最近幾十年的德國史學、蘭克的生平與著作、曼納克及其思想史的研究[66]等，均與輸入德國史學有關。

傾畢生歲月致力於輸入德國史學方法的，應首推姚從吾先生。姚先生於民國十一年留學德國，民國二十三年歸來，任北京大學歷史系教授，講授蒙古史及歷史方法論。以後在西南聯大，在河南大學校長任內，以及在臺灣大學的二十年，每年都開歷史方法論這門課，這將近延續了四十年。在課堂上，他以一半以上的時間，介紹德國從蘭克到班漢穆的史學方法。北大時代，曾將班氏「史學導論」譯成中文，用爲參考講義。在臺大，每年都印發一部分講義，其中涉及最多的是德國史學方法。如「近代歐洲歷史方法論的起源」、「略論直接史料中幾類最佳的史料」、「略論歷史學的補助科學」，多採用班氏之說，而濟以國史的例證。臨終前他曾將講義「近代歐洲歷史方法論的起源」改寫後發表在中國歷史學會史學集刊第二期上面，詳言德國尼博兒、蘭克的治史方法，這是他將歷史方法論講義改寫後發表出來的唯一的一篇。今其遺著**姚從吾先生全集**第一册**歷史方法論**，卽其講義的化身。[67]

沈剛伯先生早年負笈英倫，歸國後講授英國史、西洋上古史、西洋近代文化史近五十年，間取國史與西史相印證。如「古代中西史學的異同」一文，[68]卽將相去遙遠的希臘史學與中國春秋至西漢時代的史學，相與比論。臺灣大學歷史學系學報第一期「卷頭語」爲沈先生所執筆，專就西方近百餘年來史學風氣的轉變，申論中國今日治史應循的途徑，「建立一新而正當的史學以端人心而正風俗。」「講求『史義』以根絕一切史演之學，並培養『史識』以補考據之不足。」[69]均爲發人深省之語。

劉崇鋐先生留學美國，歸國後最有心輸入西方晚近新史學，於所習開的西洋通史、西洋近古史、西洋近世史、美國史等課外，每喜增開西洋史學名著一類新課。如於民國四十四年至四十五年間，卽增授「西洋史學名著選讀」，一九三八年奈芬司（Allan Nevins）出版的「史學入門」（The Gateway to History），被採作敎本之一，當時筆者是班上的學生，深覺獲益良多。一九六一年卡耳（E. H. Carr）出版其極爲風行的「**歷史論集**」（What is History?）一書後，翌年秋天起，劉先生卽爲臺大歷史系學生介紹其書。臺大歷史系學生較能接受西洋新史學知識，劉先生的熱心介紹，應是最主要的原因之一。

此一時期出版的史學理論與方法方面的論著，其頗能採納西方史學者，約有許冠三的「**史學與史學方法**」，許倬雲的「**歷史學研究**」，胡秋原的「**史學方法之要點**」，周培智的「**歷史學歷史思想與史學研究法述要**」。

此一時期從事翻譯西方史學理論與方法方面的論著者，約有王任光譯卡耳的「**歷史論集**」，華雪（W. H. Walsh）的「**歷史哲學**」（Philosophy of History）；黃超民譯柯林吾（R. G. Collingwood）的「**史意**」（The Idea of History）；淦克超譯米賽斯（Ludwig Von Mises）的「**理論與歷史**」（Theory and History）；廖中和譯羅斯（A. L. Rowse）的「**歷史的功用**」（The Use of History）；容繼業譯葛隆斯基（Donald V. Gawronski）的「**歷史意義與方法**」（History: Meaning and Method）；涂永清譯甘特（Cantor）和施奈德（Schneider）合著的「**史學導論**」（How to Study History）。

有世界大名的湯恩比（Arnold J. Toynbee），是此一時期國人所最注目的西方史學家之一。民國四十四年鍾建閎曾將其大著「**歷史之研究**」（A Study of History）的節本譯出。[70]寫專文以介紹其史學理論與方法者，則不可殫數。[71]

此一時期最樂於刊登有關介紹西方社會科學方法的論著與譯述的刊物，爲食貨月刊及思與言雙月刊。

六、結　論

1.

西方史學的輸入，有幾種途徑：一爲西方論史學的專書或專文的翻譯，二爲在大學講堂上的講述，三爲通西方史學的中國史家撰寫專書或專文的介紹，四爲西方學者來中國後的傳佈。就西方論史學的專書的翻譯而言，Bernheim, Langlois, Seignobos, Barnes, Collingwood, Carr 諸人之書，皆經國人譯成中文。惟譯文多晦澀難讀，使讀者難以直接獲得西方史學的眞諦，如陳韜所譯 Bernheim 的**史學方法論**，李思純所譯 Langlois 與 Seignobos 合著的**史學原論**，譯文都頗似天書。李思純曾於巴黎大學親受 Seignobos 講授，而譯文竟難讀如此。這是頗爲影響西方史學的輸入的。至於在量的方面，很感覺不够，西方晚近新出的論史學的專書，絕大多數未經譯出，殊爲憾事。

就西方論史學的專文的翻譯而言，前期極少，近三十年來已漸多，散見於各學術性刊物中。如能彙輯爲一編，將能發生較大的影響力量。

就在大學講堂上的講述而言，這是西方史學輸入中國極重要的一個途徑。從梁啓超、胡適、何炳松在各大學講授起，西方史學在談笑聲中輸入到中國來了。至於民國以來究竟有多少人在大學開有關介紹西方史學的課，則有文獻難徵之感。

就通西方史學的中國史家撰寫專書或專文的介紹而言，這是西方史學輸入中國後能否發榮滋長的關鍵。以西方史學理論與方法爲經，以中國例子爲緯，疏通證明，西方史學，將易被瞭解；如以中國史學與西方史學相印證，相切磋，則中西史學有融合的可能。惟此類作品不多見，精密者尤少。

就西方學者來中國後的傳佈而言，誠如西方一位學者所論述，二十世紀初，來中國的歐洲人，其所寫關於中國的作品，在史學方面，最大的缺陷，是其作品並不能將西方歷史寫作的新技術傳到中國來。他們的作品，更近於中國史學，而與西方史學本身，反有距離，尤其是在主題的解釋與選擇上。其原因能容易推想而出，因爲作者住在中國，他們想接受與同時代的中國人同樣的影響，選擇同樣的題目研究。另外的原因是西方史學家信賴他們所研究的國家的學者，有時與中國助手共同工作。卽使不是如此，語言的困難，經常使他們憑依中文的近代作品，而不大敢問津廣大的原始資料。結果，他們常常有意無意的接受其觀點與方法，西方歷史寫作的新技術，在他們的作品中，一點表現不出來。[72]

2.

翻譯爲學術文化交流的重要媒介。以印度佛學的輸入中國而言，佛經的翻譯，爲極令人注目的一項。根據唐代開元釋敎錄所述，自漢末迄唐代開元中葉，譯人一百七十六，所譯經典達二千二百七十八部，七千零四十六卷。以現存者而論，汰其僞託，刪其重複，亦有五千卷內外。佛學在中國的盛行及其後期的新創，與這一大批翻譯佛經的譯人，有最密切的關係。佛學如此，史學亦然。將與中國傳統極不相同的西方史學輸入中國，而爲國人所接受，要靠大量翻譯西方有關這一方面的著作。晚淸以及民國初年，亦卽嚴復翻譯天演論以後一段期間，中國的翻譯事業，頗爲盛行。晚近又趨沈寂，遊學歐美的學人雖與日增多，然皆醉心於專題研究工作，極少願以全力從事於譯述，以致西方近代大量出現的論史學之作，在中國甚少譯本，甚至不爲國人所知，這是極影響西方史學的輸入的。所以不談輸入西方史學則已，談輸入西方史學，則必須加强翻譯工作。而且於翻譯純粹論史學的著作以外，更重要的應積極翻譯 Gibbon, Mommsen, Macaulay, Trevelyan 等大史學家的歷史名著，[73]

以使國人瞭然於在西方史學傳統下，所寫出來的史著，與史記、通鑑有何不同。在這方面，目前國內史學界所做的，顯然極爲不够。市面所流行的幾部西洋史譯本，往往不是西方的歷史名著，而是西方的歷史教科書。

3.

中國近代的西化運動，其最初參與的份子，是一些不通西洋語言文字的人，西洋留學生殆全體未嘗參加，這是很特殊的一種現象。梁啓超曾於清代學術概論云：

「晚清西洋思想之運動，最大不幸者一事焉。蓋西洋留學生殆全體未曾參加於此運動；運動之原動力及其中堅，乃在不通西洋語言文字之人。坐此爲能力所限，而稗販，破碎，籠統，膚淺，錯誤諸弊皆不能免；故運動垂二十年，卒不能得一健實之基礎，旋起旋落，爲社會所輕。就此點論，則疇昔之西洋留學生，實有負於國家也。」

史學的西化也如此，最先將西方史學輸入中國的，不是留學生，而是不能直接閱讀西洋書籍的梁啓超。到民國以後，留學生才比較積極的輸入西方史學了。不過其中極少人專門研究西方史學，以致他們歸國後的介紹，不够深入徹底，影響力大受限制。晚近留學生又多赴歐美研究國史，歸國後始講授西洋史，自然也難將西方史學輸入。言及此，頗增人迷惘！

4.

在西方史學輸入中國史上，陳寅恪應佔極重要的一席：

「在大陸淪陷之前，我國學西洋史學的留學生，回國來多數是講西洋史，講中國史的殊不多見；即使有之，往往用西洋的格式，填充上中國材料。如果不是削足適履，這種方法自然很好；而多數作品，一望卽知其爲仿效。惟有寅恪先生能够眞正貫通中西，他有許多觀點誠然是受了西方影響，如論政治制度和社會習俗等等。他的著作中却一點不露模仿的痕迹，表現的很自然，使人感覺到是在討論中國本有的問題。他從來不像其他的人，由西方書中學來理論系統和問題名詞，在中國書中找材料，七拼八湊生吞活剝的講西方式的中國問題。那些著作，雖然有些地方還看得過去，可總覺得似是而非，彷彿走了樣，如同穿着錯脚鞋，走路有點彆扭。陳先生審查馮友蘭的**中國哲學史**報告書中說：『寅恪生平好爲不古不今之學，思想囿於同光之際，持論近乎湘鄉南皮。誠知舊酒味酸，姑注於新瓶之底，以待一嘗可乎？』眞的，他作到了用新瓶裝舊酒來，又會裝進新瓶去。旁人來買新瓶，多數只能裝新酒，想裝舊酒，往往不是沒釀好，就是裝錯了醋。」[74]

留學西洋，會通其史學理論與方法，歸而不露痕跡的硏究國史，撰寫國史，這是輸入西方史學的最高境界，因爲它已不是移植，而是加以融會貫通了。

本文之完成，得國家科學委員會之補助，謹此致謝。

（原載臺大歷史系學報第三期，民國六十五年五月）

❶參見拙著與西方史家論中國史學，頁六～七。

❷白氏演講後，復將講詞簡化，於同年九月二十一日在英國廣播公司廣播，Listener 雜誌刊其全文，今係自其中節引。

❸J.H. Plumb, The Death of the Past, 1969, pp. 12–13

❹籌辦夷務始末，同治朝，卷四七頁二四。

❺同上

❻江標變學論。

❼湘報類纂乙集卷下頁三。

❽嚴幾道詩文鈔卷四頁二～三。

❾同上卷二頁七。

❿黃遵憲日本國志，凡例。

⓫湘學新報第三十册。

⓬同上第五册。

⓭王夫之富有進化思想，似爲一特例。如他於讀通鑑論卷二〇云：「古之天下，人自爲君，君自爲國，百里而外，若異域焉。治異政，教異尙，刑異法，賦斂惟其輕重，人民惟其刑殺，好則相昵，惡則相攻，萬其國者萬其心，而生民之困極矣。堯舜禹湯弗能易也。至殷之末，殆窮則必變之時，而猶未可驟革於一朝。故周大封同姓，而益展其疆域，割天下之半，而歸之姬氏之子孫，則漸有合一之勢，而後世郡縣一王，亦緣此以漸統一於大同，然後風敎日趨於畫一，而生民之困，亦以少衰。故孟子之言治詳矣。未嘗一以上古萬國之制，欲行於周末，則亦灼見武王周公綏靖天下之大權，而知邱民之欲在此而不在彼。以一姓分天下之半，而天下之瓦合萍散者，漸就於合。故孟子曰：『定於一』。大封同姓者，未必卽一而漸之也。」

⓮嚴譯天演論頁二。

⓯同上頁四。

⓰民鐸卷三第三四號。

⓱胡適文存二集二卷頁二三四。

⓲同上頁二二一。

⓳飲冰室文集第四册頁一。

⑳同上頁二。

㉑同上頁五。

㉒見正中書局出版**二十世紀之科學**第九輯人文科學之部史學前言。

㉓一八八九年班漢穆出版其大著「**歷史方法論與歷史哲學**」(*Lehrbuch der Historischen Methode und der Geschichtsphilosophie*),一八九八年朗格諾瓦與瑟諾博司合著「**史學原論**」(*Introduction aux E'tudes Historiques*)。

㉔梁啓超**中國歷史研究法**自序。

㉕同上第六章。

㉖顧頡剛**當代中國史學**頁二~三。

㉗同上頁一二六。

㉘**胡適文選**「介紹我自己的思想」。

㉙同上「演化論與存疑主義」。

㉚同上「杜威先生與中國」。

㉛同上「治學的方法與材料」。

㉜同上。

㉝**古史辨**自序。

㉞同上。

㉟**新史學**朱序,此序作於民國十年八月十日。

㊱**新史學**譯者導言。

㊲同上。

㊳**新史學**譯者再誌。

㊴**新史學**朱序。

㊵**新史學**頁一四~一五。

㊶同上頁四三。

㊷同上頁五五。

㊸同上頁六四~六五。

㊹以上皆見李璜著**歷史學與社會科學**(民國五十年七月初版),頁一至二六。李氏於序中說:「這本小書,原是我民十三至十五年在武昌大學、北京大學、

北京師範大學擔任西洋史與社會學教授時，爲學生講演的幾篇講稿合成的」。

㊺何炳松未將原書之名列於書端（此爲何氏往往犯的毛病，譯書者寧有不當將原書名揭出者乎？），疑爲某百科全書中有關西洋史學史的一條。惟決非班茲所著 *A History of Historical Writing*（一九三九年初版時名爲 A History of American History，一九五四年更名。）

㊻西洋史學史譯者序，此序作於民國十八年八月七日。

㊼按何炳松作此序於民國十七年雙十節。

㊽明清史料序。

㊾同上。

㊿傅孟眞先生集中編丁。

51同上。

52詳見李宗侗史學概要第十七編第四章內閣檔案。

53見傅樂成著傅孟眞先生年譜。

54民國以來，西方唯物史觀的輸入，自爲史學的一件大事。惟此一在西方學術界極具勢力的史觀，東來中國後，完全喪失其學術性，變成政黨的工具，淪於蠻橫的教條，故本文不予介紹。

55陳韜所譯班漢穆的史學方法論，筆者所看到的本子，爲商務印書館「民國五十六年八月臺一版」本，初版於何時，有待確考。

56陳韜譯班氏之書，據姚從吾師生前相告云：「陳氏可能根據日譯本翻譯。」

57學衡第六十二期（民國十七年三月）。

58思想與時代第十九期。

59學衡第四十期（民國十四年四月）。

60張氏「傳統歷史哲學之總結算」一文寫成於何時，頗難確定。思想與時代係轉載之。

61張蔭麟上古史綱初版自序。

62參見中國史綱自序。

63楊鴻烈所著史學通論係於民國二十八年四月由長沙商務印書館印行，筆者於民國六十四年春間曾在英國倫敦大學亞非研究院（Scbool of Oriental and African Studies）圖書館見其書，國內圖書館似未收藏。

❻❹民國三十二年十二月二十日陸懋德於西北大學作此序。

❻❺筆者所見周譯史學家與科學家一書，爲商務印書館人人文庫本，未注初版年月，僅注民國五十六年六月臺一版。周氏作「譯者敍言」於民國三十二年，故略斷定其出版於是年，

❻❻以上諸文，均收入張致遠文集中。

❻❼詳見拙作德國史學的東漸（食貨月刊第一卷第二期，民國六十年五月）。

❻❽徵信新聞學藝周刊二期（民國五十三年十月十二日）。

❻❾臺灣大學歷史學系學報第一期（民國六十三年五月）卷頭語——從百餘年來史學風氣的轉變談到臺灣大學史學系的教學方針。

❼⓿由中華文化出版事業委員會出版，現代國民基本知識叢書第四輯。

❼❶如張致遠先生的史家的靈感——兼論陶恩培的治學經驗（自由中國第十五卷第十一期），陶恩培「歷史研究」的第十二本（新時代第一卷第九期），駱雪倫的湯恩比的「歷史研究」與歷史（思與言第二卷第四期），閻沁恆的湯恩比的史學方法及觀念（國立政治大學學報第二十二期），湯恩比與當代思潮（新時代第十五卷第十二期）。

❼❷參見 W. G. Beasley and E. G. Pulleyblank, Historians of China and Japan, 1961, pp. 21-22 Beasley 的論述。

❼❸梅寅生所譯 Gibbon 的羅馬帝國衰亡史（The History of the Decline and Fall of the Roman Emoire）爲節本，不足見其全。

❼❹牟潤孫「敬悼陳寅恪先生」，見談陳寅恪，傳記文學叢書之四五。

附 錄 三

梁著「中國歷史研究法」探原 杜維運

民國十一年（一九二二）一月梁啓超長及十萬言的「中國歷史研究法」問世，是近代中國史學界的一件大事。梁氏精通中國史學，又醉心西方史學， 他的這部書， 無疑是中西史學互相激盪下的產品。 數十年來， 中國史學界稱頌此書， 接受此書的影響， 但是此書中突破性的見解，究係梁氏的新創，抑係沿自西方，鮮有人道及。學術上的發現，是由涓滴成巨流。絕頂的天才，命世的學者， 無法頃刻創出嶄新的學說。從沿襲到新創，是新學說出現的一種自然過程。梁氏在此書中對史料的闡解， 對史料的分類， 對史蹟的論次， 都有突破性的見解， 都言數千年來中國史學家所未及言，其不能全出新創，而係接受了西方史學的影響，極爲明顯。所以梁氏此書的探原工作，有待試做。學術的清徹，是學術的價值所繫。

梁氏是晚清政治界極爲活躍的人物，人人能知。在學術界，他與嚴復同爲輸入西學最重要的人物。生值「『學問飢荒』之環境中」❶，「欲以構成一種『不中不西卽中卽西』之新學派」❷，所以他雖然沒有直接閱讀英文、法文、德文等西方書籍的能力，也毅然負起了輸入西學的大任務。史學是他最專門最酷嗜之學，西學中的史學，自爲他注視的焦點。從光緒二十八年（一九〇二）他所發表的一篇題名「新史學」的文章來看，他對西方史學，已有了約略的認識，他已用西方史學來批評中國史學，並提出了嶄新的寫史方法。民國七年（一九一八）十二月至民國九年（一九二〇）三月的歐遊，對他進一步瞭解西方史學，更富有關鍵性。民國十年（一九二一）他在南開大學演講中國歷史研究法，以及翌年的出書，不是出於偶然，而實是歐遊後應有的成果。

梁氏的歐遊，最大的目的之一，是「想自己求一點學問，而且看看這空前絕後的歷史劇怎樣收場，拓一拓眼界。」❸他的遊踪甚廣，英國、法國、德國、意大利、瑞士、荷蘭、比利時皆有足跡，而以停在法國的時間最久。在法國，他結交當時的名流，自謂「法國方面之名士，已見者殆十之七八，最多見者則政治家及哲學、文學家。」❹並且請了許多第一流學校教授，到他住的巴黎近郊的魯威寓廬，作專題演講，由蔣方震、張君勱、徐新六、丁文江把這些演講稿，從法文譯成中文，蔣方震發表的歐洲文藝復興史，就是其中演講稿之一❺。這些專題演講，除歐洲文藝復興史外，已難知其內容，其中似必有西方史學理論與方法一項。但是在梁氏的書札及歐遊心影錄中，全未提及。從表面上看，梁氏歐遊像是僅注意西方的政治、哲學、科學、文學等方面，而毫不關心史學❻。這是令人大惑不解的。他怎能不關心西方史學呢？他怎能不想深入認識西方史學理論與史學方法呢？

李宗侗師曾有這樣的一段記載：「中國史學方法論第一部書是梁啓超的中國歷史研究法。梁先生到歐洲去的時候，我恰好住在巴黎，他請了很多留法學生給他講述各門的學問，恐怕史學方法論亦是其中之一，不過他另補充上很多中國的材料，但其原則仍不免受外國人的影響。」❼這是極珍貴的同時人的記載。梁氏既聘請了法國第一流學校的教授，作專題演講，也極可能約請中國留法學生講述各門學問，而且當時正是西方史學方法論最爲盛行的時候，有「西方史學方法論鼻祖」之稱的班漢穆（Ernst Bernheim, 1854-1937）於一八八九年出版其大著「史學方法論與歷史哲學」(Lehrbuch der Historischen Methode und der Geschichtsphilosophie), 法國史學家朗格諾瓦(Charles V. Langlois, 1863-1929)與瑟諾博司(Charles Seignobos,1854-1942)繼其後於一八九七年合著「史學原論」(Introduction aux E'tudes Historiques), 翌年英譯本 Iutroduction to the Study of History(譯者爲 G. G. Berry)問世。自此法國變成史學方法論最重要的發源地之一。梁氏以中國史學家於一九一九年左右至其地, 著「史學原論」的朗、瑟二氏尙在, 他不可能絲毫不受朗、瑟二氏作品的影響。他請法國教授或中國留學生講述西方學問, 似必有朗、瑟二氏的「史學原論」在內。筆者撰寫「史學方法論」一書❽期間, 曾將梁氏的「中國歷史研究法」與朗、瑟二氏的「史學原論」細作比較, 深覺二者關係極爲密切, 梁氏突破性的見解, 其原大半出於朗、瑟二氏。下面是幾段的比較:

梁著「中國歷史研究法」頁六六:

「史料爲史之組織細胞, 史料不具或不確, 則無復史之可言。史料者何?過去人類思想行事所留之痕跡, 有證據傳留至今日者也。思想行事留痕者本已不多。所留之痕, 又未必皆有史料的價值。有價値而留痕者, 其喪失之也又極易。因必有證據然後史料之資格備, 證據一失, 則史料卽隨而湮沈。」

朗、瑟合著「史學原論」頁一七:

「史學家憑藉史料進行其工作。史料是以往人類思想與行爲所留下的痕跡。然而在這類思想與行爲之中, 極少留下清晰可見的痕跡, 且易遭遇意外而澌滅。舉凡未曾留下清晰痕跡的一切思想與行爲, 或其痕跡約已消失無踪了, 則歷史卽無從記載, 就像什麼都沒有發生一樣。人類過去重大時期的歷史, 由於史料缺乏, 永不可知曉。所以沒有史料, 就沒有歷史。」❾

以兩者作比較，前者原出後者，是極爲清楚的。認爲史料是「過去人類思想行事所留之痕跡」，梁氏簇新之說，顯係沿自朗、瑟二氏；確言「史料爲史之組織細胞，史料不具或不確，則無復史之可言」，與朗、瑟二氏所肯定的「沒有史料，就沒有歷史」，也沒有什麼不同。

梁著「中國歷史研究法」頁六七至六八：

「距今約七十年前，美國人有彭加羅夫 (H. H. Bancroft) 者，欲著一加里佛尼省志。竭畢生之力，傾其極富之家資，誓將一切有關係之史料蒐輯完備然後從事。凡一切文件，自官府公牘下至各公司各家庭之案卷帳簿，願售者不惜重價購之，不願售者展轉借鈔之。復分隊派員諏詢故老，搜其口碑傳說。其書中人物有尚生存者，彼用種種方法巧取其談話及其經歷。如是者若干年，所叢集之資料盈十室。彼乃隨時將其所得者爲科學分類，先製成『長編式』之史稿，最後乃進而從事於眞著述。若以嚴格的史學論，則採集史料之法，必如此方爲合理。雖然，欲作一舊邦之史，安能以新造之加里佛尼省爲比例？且此種『美國風』的搜集法，原亦非他方人所能學步。」

朗、瑟合著「史學原論」頁一九及二〇：

「當太平洋沿岸加利福尼亞史學家班可勞甫 (H. H. Bancroft) 決定由參與歷史事件的現存者身上採訪史料時，他動員了採訪大軍 (a whole army of reporters)，筆錄他們的口述。」

「班可勞甫……他富有，盡蒐市場所有的史料，不管是印刷的或手寫的；更商於經濟困窘的家庭與公司，購買其檔案資料，或邀其允許，雇人往鈔。當此一工作做完，即將所有蒐集到的史料，置於一專門爲儲藏此類史料而興建的大建築物中，並一一爲之分類。在理論上，這是蒐集史料最合理的方法。但是此等快速的美式方法（American method），僅能靠財富之力幾於成功。異時異地，難語於斯。沒有其他地方有此環境便利如此做的。」

梁氏所津津樂道的彭加羅夫搜集史料的方法，係承自朗、瑟二氏，似不必深辨。

梁著「中國歷史研究法」頁一三〇及二一五：

「凡史蹟之傳於今者，大率皆經過若干年若干人之口碑或筆述而識其概者也。各時代人心理不同，觀察點亦隨之而異，各種史蹟，每一度從某新時代之人之腦中濾過，則不知不覺間輒微變其質，如一長河之水，自發源以至入海中間所經之地所受之水，含有種種離異之礦質，則河水色味，隨之而變。故心理上的史蹟，脫化原始史蹟而喪失其本形者，往往而有。」

「凡史蹟皆人類心理所構成。」

朗、瑟合著「史學原論」頁六五：

「史料可分為兩種，有時過去的事件，留下實蹟（碑碣及製造品），有時，也是更常見的，事件所留下的痕跡，是心理的狀態（the psychological order）——一種文字上的描寫或敍述。」

以「史蹟皆人類心理所構成」，梁氏此等突破性的創見，與朗、瑟二氏所強調的「事件所留下的痕跡，是心理的狀態」之說，應有相當程度的關係。

梁著「中國歷史研究法」頁一四六至一四七：

「史料可分為直接的史料與間接的史料。直接的史料者，其史料當該史蹟發生時或其稍後時，即已成立。……此類直接史料如浪淘沙，滔滔代盡，勢不能以多存。……於是乎在史學界占最要之位置者，實為間接的史料。……譬諸紡績，直接史料則其原料之棉團，間接史料則其粗製品之紗線也。吾儕無論為讀史為作史，其所接觸者，多屬間接史料。」

朗、瑟合著「史學原論」頁六三及六四：

「凡事件能以驗知，僅有兩種方式：一爲直接的，當事件經過時，身在其間而得以直接觀察。一爲間接的，僅研究事件所留下的痕跡。」

「歷史知識基本上是間接知識。」

梁氏將史料分爲直接史料與間接史料，且承認間接史料的普遍，似乎不能說不是受了朗、瑟二氏的啓發與影響。

梁著「中國歷史研究法」頁一一九及一二一：

「某時代有某種現象，謂之積極的史料。某時代無某種現象，謂之消極的史料。」

「消極的史料…………其重要的程度，殊不讓積極史料。蓋後代極普通之事象，何故前此竟不能發生，前代極普通之事象，何故逾時乃忽然滅絕，其間往往含有歷史上極重大之意義，倘忽而不省，則史之眞態未可云備也。此等史料，正以無史蹟爲史蹟，恰如度曲者於無聲處寄音節，如作書畫者於不著筆墨處傳神。但以其須向無處求之，故能注意者鮮矣。」

朗、瑟合著「史學原論」頁二五三，二五四及二五六：

「運用推理之道有二，一爲消極的，一爲積極的。」

「消極的推理，亦可稱之爲『默證』(argument from silence)，係以一項事實缺乏存在的跡象作基礎。凡是一項事實爲任何史料所未提及，在此種情形下，可以推斷本無此項事實存在。……在日常生活中，每謂：『如其事果眞，吾人必曾聞之。』默證卽根據此種感覺而生。其中隱藏一普遍的定理：『倘若一假定的事件，眞正發生了，必當有一些提及此事件的史料存在。』

欲使此推理正確，必須所有事實均經目擊，均經記錄，而所有記錄均保全未失而後可。但是發生過的事件，大部分未經記錄，經記錄而成的史料，今天大部分散失，在大多數情形下，默證實不適用。」

「積極的推理，自史料中所已建立的事實開始，而推論出史料中未提及的其他事實。」

梁氏將消極的推理與積極的推理，一變而爲消極的史料與積極的史料，不啻化朽腐爲神奇。朗、瑟二氏詳論消極推理的缺陷（亦卽默證的缺陷），梁氏則以消極史料「正以無史蹟爲史蹟，恰如度曲者於無聲處寄音節，如作書畫者於不著筆墨處傳神」，突轉之下，也不無眞理。凡學說有由正以至反者，此爲其例。

梁著「中國歷史研究法」頁一八一：

「吾嘗言之矣：事實之偶發的孤立的斷滅的，皆非史的範圍。然則凡屬史的範圍，事實必其於橫的方面，最少亦與他事實有若干之聯帶關係；於縱的方面最少亦爲前事實一部分之果或爲後事實一部分之因。是故善治史者，不徒致力於各個之事實，而最要著眼於事實與事實之間。此則論次之功也。」

梁著頁二一二至二二一之間，舉出了史蹟論次的程序；

第一：當畫出「史蹟集團」以爲研究範圍

第二：集團分子之整理與集團實體之把捉

第三：常注意集團外之關係

第四：認取各該史蹟集團之「人格者」

第五：精研一史蹟之心的基件

第六：精研一史蹟之物的基件

第七：量度心物兩方面可能性之極限

第八：觀察所緣

突破中國孤立事實的史學傳統，而着眼於事實與事實之間的關係，畫出「史蹟集團」以為研究的範圍，這種治史的新方法，顯係受西方治史方法的影響。西方史學家喜將每一事實與其他衆多事實編織成一個錯綜的關係網，不類中國史學家僅將注意力局促於一個時代的一項孤立事實，約略敍其前後。所以到德國大史學家蘭克（Leopold von Ranke, 1795-1886）便倡出了「事件相關」（interconnectedness of events）之說。其後西方史學家在這方面的闡述甚多，梁氏多少會受到啓示，朗、瑟二氏對他的啓示，從下面幾段，可以隱約看出：

「研究同時發生的事實間的關係，須於一社會中所發生的各種事實搜得其相互間的聯絡。我們每有一種空泛概念，以為一切殊異事象，由抽象方法區分離立而置於殊異範疇之下者（藝術、宗教、政治制度），按其實際，俱非分裂離析，而皆具有共通特性，密切關連，若其一變，則其他隨之而變。」⑩

「吾人須將普遍事實（general facts）與獨特事實（事件）區分清楚。

普遍事實……吾人須確定其『性質所在』、『空間所被』與『時間所延』。

為了使普遍事實的性質公式化，我們將組成一項事實（習性、制度之類）的各種狀態，聯繫起來，使其與所有其他事實涇渭分明。我們將所有個別情況而彼此極相類似者，聯合在一起，受同一公式支配，而略去其相異者。」⑪

「為了確定一種習性確切空間所被，當探察其所呈現的最遠距點（於此獲知其所分布之幅員面積），及其最常被及的地區（中心區）。」⑫

「此項公式又須指其習性的時間所延，凡形式、主義、功利、制度、群體的最初出現與最後出現，皆須探察。但僅注意其兩孤立點，最初與最後，是不够的，須確定其實際活動的時間。」⑬

「在一個人的習慣中，需要確定其曾發生影響力的基本觀念，如他的人生觀，他的學識，他的特別嗜好，他的正常職業，他的行爲原則。凡此種種，變化無窮，而由此可形成此人的『人格』(character)，集此人格的各方面，即塑成此人的『肖像』(portrait)，用今日流行的辭彙，即是此人的『心理』。」⑭

梁氏在談及「史蹟之論及」，除着眼於事實與事實之間，畫出「史蹟集團」，並屬言「人格」、「心理」、及史蹟集團外的時間線、空間線，則其所受朗、瑟二氏的啓示，似乎是不應忽視的事實了。

從以上的比較，可以看出梁氏「中國歷史研究法」與朗、瑟二氏合著的「史學原論」的密切關係。雖然梁氏不可能祇受朗、瑟二氏的影響，但是我們可以有理由的假設，他在法國期間，必請了法國教授或中國留法學生爲他專門講解了朗、瑟二氏之書，而且作了相當詳盡的劄記。他自己的直接閱讀、怕是輔助性質的。研究梁氏最透徹的張朋園教授曾云:「任公在歐一年，他的求知慾似乎沒有滿足，因爲他不通西文。臨陣磨槍，從學英文做起，四十餘歲的人，除非有極大的耐心，不可能學好一種新的語文。他的知識，除了直覺的觀察，是間接得來的，頗爲有限，受隨員的影響甚大。」⑮ 梁氏的英文程度，確實很難毫無阻礙的直接閱讀有關史學方法的英文書⑯。他接受西方史學方法，大部分應是間接的。

丁文淵在丁文江編「梁任公先生年譜長編初稿」的前言云:

「二哥（按指丁文江）素性憨直、對人極具至性，有問必答，無所隱諱。與任公坐談之際，嘗謂任公個性仁厚，太重感情，很難做一個好的政治家。因爲在政治上，必須時時具有一個冷靜的頭腦，纔能不致誤事。又謂任公的分析能力極强，如果用科學方法研究歷史，必定能有不朽的著作，因此勸任公放棄政治活動，而從事學術研究，任公亦深以爲然。」

「二哥當時還曾設法協助任公如何學習英文，並且介紹了好幾部研究史學的英文書籍，任公根據此類新讀的材料，寫成『中國歷史研究法』一書。」

這兩段話，揭出了梁氏「中國歷史研究法」所受西方影響的眞相，但是梁氏是否完全由自己閱讀丁文江所介紹的幾部書，則有待存疑。

最値一提的，是梁氏綜合中西史學的卓越能力。他不是以西方理論配合中國事例以談史學方法，而是將中西史學方法作了極和諧的綜合。所以他不是稗販，不是籠統的將西方史學方法移植過來，朗、瑟二氏之說，有時正面的加以採用了，而細節處則加潤色；有時反轉過來採用，而更見奇縱；有時約略採用，而另建完密的系統，以致絲毫不着採摭的痕跡，渾若天成，圓而多神。至於文字的暢達優美，意興的恣縱英發，又其餘事了。

梁氏也決非祇接受朗、瑟二氏的影響。他將史料分爲在文字記錄以外者與在文字記錄以內者兩種，在文字記錄以外者，又區分爲現存之實蹟、傳述之口碑、遺下之古物三類，在文字記錄以內者，區分爲舊史，關係史蹟之文件，史部以外之群籍類書與古逸書輯本，古逸書及古文件之再現、金石及其他鏤文諸類⑰，顯與班漢穆的史料分類法有密切的關係，班氏提倡史源學的二體三元說，其所謂二體，是指文字的記載與古物的遺留，所謂三元，是指口頭傳說，文字記載與事實自身的遺留⑱。班氏以後，西方史學家沿其說者紛紛，如於一九一一年出版「歷史寫作：史學方法導論」(The Writing of History: An Introduction to

Historical Method）的弗領（F. M. Fling），卽極力呼應，並爲之說明理由。班氏的書，未有英譯本，梁氏不可能讀其德文原本，丁文江爲他介紹的幾部英文書，其中可能有弗氏之書，而梁氏矇矓讀之，受其影響，亦未可知。梁氏又精通日文，自日文書間接所知的西方史學，亦必可觀。「近今史學之進步有兩特徵。其一，爲客觀的資料之整理——疇者不認爲史蹟者，今則認之，疇者認爲史蹟者，今或不認。舉從前棄置散佚之跡，鉤稽而比觀之，其夙所因襲者，則重加鑑別以估定其價值。如此則史學立於『眞』的基礎之上，而推論之功，乃不至枉施也。其二，爲主觀的觀念之革新——以史爲人類活態之再現，而非其殭跡之展覽，爲全社會之業影，而非一人一家之譜錄。如此，然後歷史與吾儕生活相密接，讀之能親切有味；如此，然後能使讀者領會團體生活之意義以助成其爲一國民爲一世界人之資格也。歐美近百數十年之史學界，全面於此兩種方嚮以行。今雖僅見其進未見其止，顧所成就則旣斐然矣。」觀於梁氏在「中國歷史硏究法」自序中所言，當可瞭然他所受西方史學的影響，已非朗、瑟二氏所能範圍了。

❶梁啓超淸代學術概論（民國十年二月初版，商務），頁一六一。

❷同上。

❸梁任公近著第一輯（民國十一年十二月初版，商務），上卷，「歐行途中」，頁七三。

❹民國八年六月九日梁啓超與仲弟書，轉引自丁文江編梁任公先生年譜長編初稿（世界書局，民國四十七年），下册，頁五五八。

❺參見毛以亨著梁啓超（亞洲出版社，民國四十六年），頁一三二。

❻初看丁文江編梁任公先生年譜長編初稿，卽有此印象，再細稽梁啓超個人的作品，更感覺如此。

❼二十世紀之科學第九輯人文科學之部「史學」（正中書局，民國五十五年），

前言，頁一。

⑧民國六十八年二月初版，由華世出版社總經銷。

⑨本文根據「史學原論」的英文本翻譯。法文原本，非筆者所能譯，李思純中文譯本（民國十五年十月初版），僅作參攷，因其不妥處甚多。

⑩Charles V. Langlois and Charles Seignobos, *Introduction to the Study of History*, P. 284

⑪Ibid, p. 267

⑫Ibid, pp. 268-269

⑬Ibid, p. 269

⑭Ibid, p. 271

⑮張朋園著、梁啓超與民國政治（食貨出版社，民國六十七年），頁一五二。

⑯民國八年六月九日梁啓超致其弟梁啓勳函云：「此行若通歐語，所獲奚啻十倍？前此蹉跎，雖悔何裨，今惟汲汲作補牢計耳。」（丁編梁譜，頁五五九）又於仝年十一月五日致其女梁令嫻函云：「吾現在兩種功課，日間學英文，夜間寫遊記，英文已大略能讀書讀報了。……吾將來之英文，不能講，不能聽，不能寫，惟能讀耳。」（丁編梁譜，頁五六五）梁氏的英文如此，他似乎極難直接閱讀有關史學方法的英文書。卽閱之，亦必朦朦矓矓。

⑰見梁啓超中國歷史研究法頁六八至九九。

⑱參見班漢穆著陳韜譯史學方法論（商務），頁一九〇至一九三；並參用姚從吾師在臺大歷史系所開「歷史方法論」一課上的講述。

附 錄 四

中國舊史學 朱士嘉

CHINESE TRADITIONAL HISTORIOGRAPHY.

By Charles S. Gardner. Cambridge, U. S. A.; Harvard University Press, 1938, pp. 105.

中國舊史學一册，美國哈佛大學中國史教授賈德納先生著。全書分七章：第一章導言，略述十八世紀以來中國新史學之起源，及其發達之經過與影響，第二章作史動機，第三章校勘學，第四章史料批評，第五章史之組織，第六章史之體裁，第七章史部之分類。全書材料大都取自泰西學者之論文，搜羅尙屬詳盡，惜于中國典籍，徵引較少。顧中國典籍，浩如烟海，西洋學者難竭全力以事稽攷，然於其最重要之著作，似亦不應忽略。如劉知幾史通，於唐初以前史書之流別體例，評隲最詳，爲研究中國史學者所必讀，著者似未曾涉獵。其他如杭世駿之諸史然疑，章學誠之文史通義，張爾田（原名采田）之史微，劉咸炘之史學述林，亦討論中國史書最重要之著作，著者似亦未加注意，此其取材之可議者也。

至於中國史學之發展，則秦漢以前有編年史，有國別史，自漢至唐史籍甚富，其最著者厥惟紀傳體，創於司馬遷，其史記分紀、表、書、傳四類，其體相沿，至今不變。自史記至於三國志皆成於一人或一家之手，其內容與體例，甚多不同於後來官修之史。至宋而編年史盛行，其內容豐富而攷證精詳者，則有司馬光之資治通鑑，李燾之續資治通鑑長編，李心傳之建炎以來繫年要錄等書。此外袁樞又患編年之分，而合之以本末，朱子又患通鑑之難稽，而析之爲綱目，皆爲史學另闢途徑。明人以著野史勝，頗可補正史之缺。清代史學家輩出，其著述有長於攷證者，王鳴盛之十七史商榷，錢大昕之廿二史攷異是也；有長於注疏者，惠棟之後漢書補注，汪士鐸之南北史補注是也；有長於校勘者，盧文弨之魏書禮志校補，勞格之晋書校勘記是也；亦有長於補正史之未備者，萬斯同之歷代史表，洪亮吉之補三國疆域志是也。此不過擧其較爲重要者，其他類此之書，尙不可以數計，要皆可與正史相輔而行。至於崔述之考信錄發前人所未發，開後來疑古之風，又爲清代史學別樹一幟。此外若以派別言，則浙東史學，至有清一代，尤負盛名，其中如黃宗羲萬斯同全祖望章學誠等人皆各有其特殊之貢獻，此又究心中國舊史學者所應注意者也。撰是書者宜若何就各時代之重要史籍，溯其源流，辨其派別，而究其體例？乃作者此之不論，而僅就校勘學分類法等問題略加論列，似屬捨本逐末，隔靴搔癢！此其研究之對象可議者也。

以上猶僅就其大端言之，至於本書之內容與體例，則可議之點尤多，略擧一二如下：

（一）材料分配之失當。例如第三章校勘學多至四十六面，幾佔全書二分之一（全書一〇五面），尙不免於漏略（說詳後）。夫校勘學不過目錄學之一部，而目錄學又僅史學之一部，乃著者斤斤於此，反覆討論，此雖足以表示著者對此問題興趣之濃厚，無如其似未甚合於著書體例也。又第二章作史之動機，首論清代史學家，次及史遷，則先後失其次序，於例亦有所未安焉。

（二）事實之未妥。

（甲）錯誤之處

（1）中國史學史至今未有述作（頁三）。按討論中國史學史者如劉勰之文心雕龍史傳篇，劉知幾之史通，章學誠之文史通義等書，皆於中國史學源流，論述甚詳，不得謂至今尚無人注意及之。

(2) 孔夫子乃最高之官銜（頁十一注）。按「夫子」乃普通尊敬之稱，並非官名也。漢追封孔子爲褒成宣尼公，唐又追封爲文宣王，至元去王，稱「大成至聖文宣先師」，清順治朝又去「文宣」二字，改稱「至聖先師孔子」，此乃孔子之官名耳。

(3) 通鑑綱目乃朱熹所撰（頁十四）。按通鑑綱目非朱子所自撰，大抵出於其門人之手，特發凡起例，乃朱子所定，不得謂爲朱子所作也。

(4) 中國史學家對於檔册均認爲極可信之史料，而不加以審定與選擇，與西洋史學家之觀點不同（頁六四）。按中國舊日史學鉅著如通鑑攷異及明史考證攟逸等書，於史料辨別去取，極爲精密，不得謂舊史家對於檔册皆輕信不疑也。

(5) 官修書首列撰人姓氏，其中第一人往往無與纂修之役，讀者至不能辨其究屬何人所著（頁六六）。按此在有經驗之讀者觀，尙不若是困難。

(6) 中國史學家對於史事之可能性甚少加以精密之估計（頁六七至六八）。按此說全非，蓋修史者敍述一事，必臚舉若干種不同之材料，而加以比較，攷訂其曲直是非，而後筆之於書；卽達官顯宦之事蹟，亦必有所依據，非若著者所云，彰善隱惡，一唯人君之馬首是瞻也。

(7) 中國史學家於著作中不復標明材料之來源，亦無引用書目，以供讀者參攷（頁七五）。按此說亦不盡然，著者試檢邵晉涵所輯舊五代史（嘉業堂劉氏刊本）則知其所引徵之書，固猶歷歷在目。卽以方志而論，其出於名人之手者，亦無不各注所出（如錢大昕乾隆鄞縣志，洪亮吉嘉慶涇縣志）。且吾嘗讀舊日西洋史籍其不注出處者甚多，蓋時代不同，體例亦隨之而異也。

(8) 隋書經籍志有四部目錄之分（頁八六）。按四部目錄之分，始於魏鄭默之中經，荀勗因之復作中經（隋書經籍志卷二簿錄類作晋中經十四卷，此據隋志序），分甲、乙、丙、丁四部，而子猶先於史。李充爲著作郎，重分四部，而經、史、子、集之次始定，隋唐以來，志經籍藝文者，咸用其例（據錢大昕元史藝文志序）。著者於四部源流，未加論述，似屬失當。

(9) 西洋學者稱正史爲斷代史，其所載史事，大抵互相連續（頁八七）。按史記所載，始自上古，至於漢武，非以一代爲限，實爲通史；斷代史蓋自漢書始，厥後遞相撰述，代各有史，然而其間如南史北史新舊五代史所記皆非止一代。此外亦有重複者，如漢初之事，既見於史記，又見於漢書，漢末之事，既見於後漢書，又見於三國志。正史之中，此例甚多，亦不得謂各史皆互相銜接也。

(10) 皇史宬（頁九三），按「皇史宬」係「皇史宬」之誤，應改正。

(乙) 遺漏之處

(1) 崔東壁遺書有民國十三年重印本（頁四）。按此書初刊於嘉慶二年，自後屢有增訂本，多至八九種，詳洪師煨蓮崔東壁書板本表。惟其最稱完善者，爲民國二十五年上海亞東圖書館鉛印本，內有東壁書鈔、詩稿、荍田賸筆、與崔邁遺集四種，七卷，爲他本所無，著者似未注意及之。

(2) 墨翟論及周燕宋齊各國春秋（頁十一）。按墨子又謂「吾見百國春秋。」見隋書李德林傳，及史通正史篇，雖爲今本墨子所無，但亦應加徵引。

(3) 修養政治道德，乃修史之唯一動機（頁十三）。按關于中國舊日史家，作史之動機，史通書事篇言之頗詳：「昔荀悅有云，立典有五志焉，一曰達道義，二曰彰法式，三曰通古今，四曰著功勳，五曰表賢能。干寶之釋五志也，體國經野之事則書之，用兵征伐之權則書之，忠臣烈士孝子貞婦之節則書之，文誥專對之辭則書之，才力技藝殊異則書之。」又太史公自序亦云：「且余掌其官，廢明聖盛德不載，滅功臣世家賢大夫之業不述，墮先人所言，罪莫大焉。」固非限於政治道德也。

(4) 第三章論校勘學而不及清代。按中國校勘之學，至有清一代而極盛，其間如何焯盧文弨鮑廷博吳騫吳翌鳳陳鱣孫星衍顧廣圻臧庸錢儀吉錢泰吉勞格至竭其畢生精力，拾殘補闕，刊謬正誤，甚有功於史學家，今著者棄而不論，猶未足以窺中國是學之全豹也。又第四十二頁中國圖書館系統表亦有不少遺誤，例如澹生堂祁氏（承㸁）天一閣范氏（欽）書鈔閣蔣氏（鳳藻）萬卷樓馬氏（曰琯）均爲當時極著名之藏書家，而著者未加著錄；又如持靜齋丁氏（日昌）書大都得自藝海樓顧氏，（沅）詳藏書紀事詩（靈鶼閣叢書本卷六頁五四），作者亦宜叙及。

(5) 康有爲謂劉向竄改左傳，以媚王莽，著者據馬伯樂 Maspero 之說以正其誤（頁六四），固是，然而康氏之說，已爲錢穆先生所辨正，詳其所著劉向歆父子年譜。錢氏此文撰於一九三○年，曾在燕京學報第七期發表，較 Maspero 所發表者（在一九三二年）爲早，亦應詳加徵引。

(6) 葛洪西京雜記係僞書，見伯希和所撰論文（在一九三○年通報第二十七期，中國舊史頁八八至八九）。按此說已詳四庫提要，不始自伯君。

(7) 著者謂後世中國史多係官修，並舉明史爲例（頁九七）。按廿四史中官修之史，始於唐人撰晉書，此爲中國史學變遷之一大關鍵，著者宜詳加申論，似不得僅以明史爲例。

(8) 關於明史纂修委員會之組織，可參攷黃雲眉之明史編纂攷略（頁九七）按劉承幹之明史例案、李晉華之明史纂修考（民國二十二年鉛印本）視此書尤爲詳賅，亟宜參攷。又倫明著有清修明史攷稿（發表與否未詳），陳守實著有明史稿攷證（國學論叢第一卷第一號）見李君自序，及謝國楨跋。

中國舊史學範圍甚廣，恐非僅僅一小册所能容，竊以爲與其概括的敘述各時代之史學，不如區分爲數時期，依次撰述，或先擇其中之較重要者，加以探討，成功易而收獲鉅。雖然，著者以一人之力撰成此書，在東方學方興未艾之美國，又多一種新著作，其精神固自可欽。他日倘能更進而增補缺漏，訂正謬誤，俾成完善之書，則尤鄙人之所深望者也。

（原載史學年報二卷五期，民國二十七年十二月）

滄海叢刊書目

國學類

書名	作者
中國學術思想史論叢(一)～(八)	錢　穆　著
現代中國學術論衡	錢　穆　著
兩漢經學今古文平議	錢　穆　著
宋代理學三書隨劄	錢　穆　著
先秦諸子繫年	錢　穆　著
朱子學提綱	錢　穆　著
莊子纂箋	錢　穆　著
論語新解	錢　穆　著

哲學類

書名	作者
文化哲學講錄(一)～(五)	鄔昆如　著
哲學十大問題	鄔昆如　著
哲學的智慧與歷史的聰明	何秀煌　著
文化、哲學與方法	何秀煌　著
哲學與思想	王曉波　著
內心悅樂之源泉	吳經熊　著
知識、理性與生命	孫寶琛　著
語言哲學	劉福增　著
哲學演講錄	吳　怡　著
後設倫理學之基本問題	黃慧英　著
日本近代哲學思想史	江日新　譯
比較哲學與文化(一)(二)	吳　森　著
從西方哲學到禪佛教——哲學與宗教一集	傅偉勳　著
批判的繼承與創造的發展——哲學與宗教二集	傅偉勳　著
「文化中國」與中國文化——哲學與宗教三集	傅偉勳　著
從創造的詮釋學到大乘佛學——哲學與宗教四集	傅偉勳　著
中國哲學與懷德海	東海大學哲學研究所主編
人生十論	錢　穆　著
湖上閒思錄	錢　穆　著
晚學盲言(上)(下)	錢　穆　著
愛的哲學	蘇昌美　著
是與非	張身華　譯
邁向未來的哲學思考	項退結　著

現代藝術哲學	孫旗譯
現代美學及其他	趙天儀著
中國現代化的哲學省思	成中英著
不以規矩不能成方圓	劉君燦著
恕道與大同	張起鈞著
現代存在思想家	項退結著
中國思想通俗講話	錢穆著
中國哲學史話	吳怡、張起鈞著
中國百位哲學家	黎建球著
中國人的路	項退結著
中國哲學之路	項退結著
中國人性論	臺大哲學系主編
中國管理哲學	曾仕強著
孔子學說探微	林義正著
心學的現代詮釋	姜允明著
中庸誠的哲學	吳怡著
中庸形上思想	高柏園著
儒學的常與變	蔡仁厚著
智慧的老子	張起鈞著
老子的哲學	王邦雄著
逍遙的莊子	吳怡著
莊子新注（內篇）	陳冠學著
莊子的生命哲學	葉海煙著
墨家的哲學方法	鐘友聯著
韓非子析論	謝雲飛著
韓非子的哲學	王邦雄著
法家哲學	姚蒸民著
中國法家哲學	王讚源著
二程學管見	張永儁著
王陽明——中國十六世紀的唯心主義哲學家	張君勱原著、江日新中譯
王船山人性史哲學之研究	林安梧著
西洋百位哲學家	鄔昆如著
西洋哲學十二講	鄔昆如著
希臘哲學趣談	鄔昆如著
近代哲學趣談	鄔昆如著
現代哲學述評(一)	傅佩榮編譯

當代西方哲學與方法論　臺大哲學系主編
人性尊嚴的存在背景　項退結編著
理解的命運　殷鼎著
馬克斯・謝勒三論　阿弗德・休慈原著、江日新譯
懷海德哲學　楊士毅著
洛克悟性哲學　蔡信安著
伽利略・波柏・科學說明　林正弘著

宗教類

天人之際　李杏邨著
佛學研究　周中一著
佛學思想新論　楊惠南著
現代佛學原理　鄭金德著
絕對與圓融——佛教思想論集　霍韜晦著
佛學研究指南　關世謙譯
當代學人談佛教　楊惠南編著
從傳統到現代——佛教倫理與現代社會　傅偉勳主編
簡明佛學概論　于凌波著
圓滿生命的實現（布施波羅密）　陳柏達著
薝蔔林・外集　陳慧劍著
維摩詰經今譯　陳慧劍譯註
龍樹與中觀哲學　楊惠南著
公案禪語　吳怡著
禪學講話　芝峯法師譯
禪骨詩心集　巴壺天著
中國禪宗史　關世謙著
魏晉南北朝時期的道教　湯一介著

社會科學類

憲法論叢　鄭彥棻著
憲法論衡　荊知仁著
國家論　薩孟武譯
中國歷代政治得失　錢穆著
先秦政治思想史　梁啟超原著、賈馥茗標點
當代中國與民主　周陽山著
釣魚政治學　鄭赤琰著
政治與文化　吳俊才著
中國現代軍事史　劉馥著、梅寅生譯
世界局勢與中國文化　錢穆著

中華文化十二講　錢　穆　著
民族與文化　錢　穆　著
楚文化研究　文崇一　著
中國古文化　文崇一　著
社會、文化和知識分子　葉啟政　著
儒學傳統與文化創新　黃俊傑　著
歷史轉捩點上的反思　韋政通　著
中國人的價值觀　文崇一　著
紅樓夢與中國舊家庭　薩孟武　著
社會學與中國研究　蔡文輝　著
比較社會學　蔡文輝　著
我國社會的變遷與發展　朱岑樓主編
三十年來我國人文社會科學之回顧與展望　賴澤涵　編
社會學的滋味　蕭新煌　著
臺灣的社區權力結構　文崇一　著
臺灣居民的休閒生活　文崇一　著
臺灣的工業化與社會變遷　文崇一　著
臺灣社會的變遷與秩序(政治篇)(社會文化篇)　文崇一　著
臺灣的社會發展　席汝楫　著
透視大陸　政治大學新聞研究所主編
海峽兩岸社會之比較　蔡文輝　著
印度文化十八篇　糜文開　著
美國的公民教育　陳光輝　譯
美國社會與美國華僑　蔡文輝　著
文化與教育　錢　穆　著
開放社會的教育　葉學志　著
經營力的時代　青野豐作著、白龍芽　譯
大眾傳播的挑戰　石永貴　著
傳播研究補白　彭家發　著
「時代」的經驗　汪琪、彭家發　著
書法心理學　高尚仁　著

史地類

古史地理論叢　錢　穆　著
歷史與文化論叢　錢　穆　著
中國史學發微　錢　穆　著
中國歷史研究法　錢　穆　著
中國歷史精神　錢　穆　著

國史新論	錢　　穆　著
秦漢史	錢　　穆　著
秦漢史論稿	邢義田　著
與西方史家論中國史學	杜維運　著
中西古代史學比較	杜維運　著
中國人的故事	夏雨人　著
明朝酒文化	王春瑜　著
共產國際與中國革命	郭恒鈺　著
抗日戰史論集	劉鳳翰　著
盧溝橋事變	李雲漢　著
老臺灣	陳冠學　著
臺灣史與臺灣人	王曉波　著
變調的馬賽曲	蔡百銓　譯
黃帝	錢　　穆　著
孔子傳	錢　　穆　著
唐玄奘三藏傳史彙編	釋光中　編
一顆永不殞落的巨星	釋光中　著
當代佛門人物	陳慧劍編著
弘一大師傳	陳慧劍　著
杜魚庵學佛荒史	陳慧劍　著
蘇曼殊大師新傳	劉心皇　著
近代中國人物漫譚·續集	王覺源　著
魯迅這個人	劉心皇　著
三十年代作家論·續集	姜　　穆　著
沈從文傳	凌　　宇　著
當代臺灣作家論	何　　欣　著
師友風義	鄭彥棻　著
見賢集	鄭彥棻　著
懷聖集	鄭彥棻　著
我是依然苦鬥人	毛振翔　著
八十憶雙親、師友雜憶（合刊）	錢　　穆　著
新亞遺鐸	錢　　穆　著
困勉強狷八十年	陶百川　著
我的創造·倡建與服務	陳立夫　著
我生之旅	方　　治　著

語文類

中國文字學	潘重規　著

書名	作者
中國聲韻學	潘重規、陳紹棠　著
訓詁通論	吳孟復　著
翻譯新語	黃文範　著
詩經研讀指導	裴普賢　著
陶淵明評論	李辰冬　著
鍾嶸詩歌美學	羅立乾　著
杜甫作品繫年	李辰冬　著
杜詩品評	楊慧傑　著
詩中的李白	楊慧傑　著
司空圖新論	王潤華　著
詩情與幽境——唐代文人的園林生活	侯迺慧　著
唐宋詩詞選——詩選之部	巴壺天　編
唐宋詩詞選——詞選之部	巴壺天　編
四說論叢	羅盤　著
紅樓夢與中華文化	周汝昌　著
中國文學論叢	錢穆　著
品詩吟詩	邱燮友　著
談詩錄	方祖燊　著
情趣詩話	楊光治　著
歌鼓湘靈——楚詩詞藝術欣賞	李元洛　著
中國文學鑑賞舉隅	黃慶萱、許家鶯　著
中國文學縱橫論	黃維樑　著
蘇忍尼辛選集	劉安雲　譯
1984	GEORGE ORWELL原著、劉紹銘　譯
文學原理	趙滋蕃　著
文學欣賞的靈魂	劉述先　著
小說創作論	羅盤　著
借鏡與類比	何冠驥　著
鏡花水月	陳國球　著
文學因緣	鄭樹森　著
中西文學關係研究	王潤華　著
從比較神話到文學	古添洪、陳慧樺主編
神話卽文學	陳炳良等譯
現代散文新風貌	楊昌年　著
現代散文欣賞	鄭明娳　著
世界短篇文學名著欣賞	蕭傳文　著
細讀現代小說	張素貞　著

書名	作者
現代詩學	蕭　蕭　著
詩美學	李元洛　著
詩學析論	張春榮　著
橫看成嶺側成峯	文曉村　著
大陸文藝論衡	周玉山　著
大陸當代文學掃瞄	葉穉英　著
走出傷痕——大陸新時期小說探論	張子樟　著
兒童文學	葉詠琍　著
兒童成長與文學	葉詠琍　著
增訂江皋集	吳俊升　著
野草詞總集	韋瀚章　著
李韶歌詞集	李　韶　著
石頭的研究	戴　天　著
留不住的航渡	葉維廉　著
三十年詩	葉維廉　著
讀書與生活	琦　君　著
城市筆記	也　斯　著
歐羅巴的蘆笛	葉維廉　著
一個中國的海	葉維廉　著
尋索：藝術與人生	葉維廉　著
山外有山	李英豪　著
葫蘆・再見	鄭明娳　著
一縷新綠	柴　扉　著
吳煦斌小說集	吳煦斌　著
日本歷史之旅	李希聖　著
鼓瑟集	幼　柏　著
耕心散文集	耕　心　著
女兵自傳	謝冰瑩　著
抗戰日記	謝冰瑩　著
給青年朋友的信(上)(下)	謝冰瑩　著
冰瑩書柬	謝冰瑩　著
我在日本	謝冰瑩　著
人生小語㈠～㈣	何秀煌　著
記憶裏有一個小窗	何秀煌　著
文學之旅	蕭傳文　著
文學邊緣	周玉山　著
種子落地	葉海煙　著

書名	作者
向未來交卷	葉海煙 著
不拿耳朶當眼睛	王讚源 著
古厝懷思	張文貫 著
關心茶——中國哲學的心	吳　怡 著
放眼天下	陳新雄 著
生活健康	卜鍾元 著
美術類	
樂圃長春	黃友棣 著
樂苑春回	黃友棣 著
樂風泱泱	黃友棣 著
談音論樂	林聲翕 著
戲劇編寫法	方　寸 著
戲劇藝術之發展及其原理	趙如琳譯著
與當代藝術家的對話	葉維廉 著
藝術的興味	吳道文 著
根源之美	莊　申 著
中國扇史	莊　申 著
立體造型基本設計	張長傑 著
工藝材料	李鈞棫 著
裝飾工藝	張長傑 著
人體工學與安全	劉其偉 著
現代工藝概論	張長傑 著
色彩基礎	何耀宗 著
都市計畫概論	王紀鯤 著
建築基本畫	陳榮美、楊麗黛 著
建築鋼屋架結構設計	王萬雄 著
室內環境設計	李琬琬 著
雕塑技法	何恆雄 著
生命的倒影	侯淑姿 著
文物之美——與專業攝影技術	林傑人 著